UNTOLD FUTURES

UNTOLD FUTURES

TIME AND LITERARY
CULTURE
IN RENAISSANCE
ENGLAND

J. K. BARRET

CORNELL UNIVERSITY PRESS
Ithaca and London

Copyright © 2016 by Cornell University

All rights reserved. Except for brief quotations in a review, this book, or parts thereof, must not be reproduced in any form without permission in writing from the publisher. For information, address Cornell University Press, Sage House, 512 East State Street, Ithaca, New York 14850. Visit our website at cornellpress.cornell.edu.

First published 2016 by Cornell University Press
First paperback printing 2019

Library of Congress Cataloging-in-Publication Data
Names: Barret, J. K., 1977– author.
Title: Untold futures : time and literary culture in Renaissance England / J. K. Barret.
Description: Ithaca ; London : Cornell University Press, 2016. | Includes bibliographical references and index.
Identifiers: LCCN 2016012388 | ISBN 9781501702365 (cloth) |
  ISBN 978-1-5017-4680-2 (pbk.)
Subjects: LCSH: English literature—Early modern, 1500–1700—History and criticism. | Time in literature.
Classification: LCC PR421 .B37 2016 | DDC 820.9/003—dc23
LC record available at https://lccn.loc.gov/2016012388

For my parents

Contents

List of Illustrations   ix

Acknowledgments   xi

Introduction   1

1. Promising the Future:
   The Language of Obligation
   in Sidney's *Old Arcadia*   23

2. The History of the Future:
   Spenser's *The Faerie Queene*
   and the Directions of Time   62

3. The Fiction of the Future:
   Dangerous Reading
   in *Titus Andronicus*   104

4. Shakespeare's Second Future:
   Anticipatory Nostalgia in *Cymbeline*   147

5. Imminent Futures: Absent Art
   and Improvised Rhyme in
   Antony and Cleopatra and *Cymbeline*   177

   Afterword: Circles of the Future:
   Memory or Monument
   in *Paradise Lost*   209

Bibliography   225
Index   241

Illustrations

1. Edmund Spenser, *The Faerie Queene* (London, 1590)   70
2. Edmund Spenser, *The Faerie Queene* (London, 1590)   73
3. Edmund Spenser, *The Faerie Queene* (London, 1590)   76
4. Edmund Spenser, *The Faerie Queene* (London, 1609)   78
5. John Brinsley, *Ouids Metamorphosis Translated Grammatically, and also according to the propriety of our English tongue, so farre as Grammar and the verse will well beare* (London, 1618)   121

❧ Acknowledgments

This book has been a long time in the making. I have often looked forward to writing these thanks, which I gratefully offer to the many people who promised me that this future would come and helped to ensure that it did.

The future began because of extraordinary teachers and advisers; their confidence in this future has been the greatest antidote to its characteristic uncertainty. I cannot overstate the profound influence that Leonard Barkan has had on my intellectual life, and I am grateful for his eager and supportive anticipation of this book. From start to finish, I could not have faced the future without Oliver Arnold's wisdom, friendship, and humor. I hope the future will always include Jeff Dolven's insights, advocacy, and enthusiasm. I treasure the continued and unerring support of Susan Stewart and Nigel Smith. I cannot fathom how things would have turned out without the exceptional mentorship and friendship of Barbara Fuchs. Margreta de Grazia and David Kastan inspired and encouraged some of the earliest iterations of the ideas in this book, and have generously provided crucial advice ever since.

This book would not have been possible without the friendship, support, and incisive commentary provided by four inexhaustible readers: Colleen Rosenfeld, who makes every word she reads better and who reads every word; Dan Moss, who both lightens and enlightens, and who graciously stayed within a 200-mile radius; Cathy Nicholson, who blazes the trail, and who magically untangles even the knottiest ideas; Sarah Tindal Kareem, unselfish fount of hard-won perspective, who offers an uncanny blend of the forthright and the celebratory. They've read many drafts of many pieces, cheerfully and shrewdly and often at a moment's notice.

I owe special thanks to my colleagues at the University of Texas at Austin for their interest in the future that this project forecast; they have provided a thriving community in which to teach and write. Wayne Rebhorn has been a tireless champion; I am grateful for his sage advice and cheering mantras, and for making Philadelphia feel a little less distant. Frank Whigham has been an invaluable mentor and advocate. John Rumrich has been a vital interlocutor, and I am especially grateful for feedback that influenced and improved the afterword on Milton. I have benefited from conversation with all my Renaissance colleagues: Hannah Wojciehowski, James Loehlin, Eric Mallin, Elizabeth Richmond-Garza, Doug Bruster, and Doug Biow. I owe a particular debt to Liz Cullingford and Martin Kevorkian for many years of indispensable advice, encouragement, and guidance. The English department staff has offered untold support, and Andrea Golden and Cecilia Smith-Morris merit special mention. I have been fortunate to have such wonderful colleagues, and I thank especially Janine Barchas, Mia Carter, Matt Cohen, Alan Friedman, Jackie Henkel, Neville Hoad, Cole Hutchison, David Kornhaber, Donna Kornhaber, Allen MacDuffie, Gretchen Murphy, Domino Perez, Snehal Shingavi, Jennifer Wilks, and Jorie Woods. I thank also Loren Cressler and Kendall DeBoer for their research assistance. Participants in the vibrant Texas Humanities Institute Spring 2015 Fellows seminar led by Polly Strong, in which I had the great fortune to participate in the last stages of writing this book, also deserve my gratitude. I thank, too, the curious, attentive, and dedicated students who gave me many excuses to reread the texts treated in this book and regularly reminded me why and how they mattered to me in the first place. In addition to the Department of English, I appreciatively acknowledge the University of Texas at Austin especially for essential and generous support in the form of a College Research Fellowship in fall 2012, and a Book Subvention Grant funded by the Office of the President.

At a crucial time, the Institute for Research in the Humanities at the University of Wisconsin-Madison whisked me away to its magical clubhouse. I am beyond grateful for the Solmsen Fellowship, which offered me a restorative, lakeside year that was key to the development of this book; Teju Olaniyan, Ann Harris, and a vibrant cadre of fellows made that year perfect and unforgettable. For their intellectual companionship and acute understanding of winter, I thank especially Amanda Jo Goldstein, Jessica Keating, Elizabeth Bearden, Melissa Haynes, Karen Britland, Jordan Zweck, Monique Alleweart, Ellery Foutch, and Esther Eidinow. Thanks to the support and sponsorship of the Center for 17th- & 18th-Century Studies, I spent six blissful months as a Visiting Scholar at the University of California, Los Angeles. I am grateful also for short-term fellowship support from UCLA's Center for Medieval & Renaissance Studies and the William Andrews Clark Memorial Library. This project also benefited from rich conversation in a National Humanities Center Summer Institute in Literary Studies led by Marjorie Garber, and a

National Endowment for the Humanities Summer Seminar in New York led by Clare Carroll and Marc Caball.

For generous, keen commentary and crucial cheering on, I would also like to thank Chad Bennett, Aaron Kunin, and James Kuzner. For helpful feedback, advice, and abundant encouragement, I thank Stephanie Elsky, Heather James, Claire McEachern, Jerry Passannante, Rebecca Rainof, Stuart Sherman, and Julianne Werlin. This project also benefited from conversations with Jason Baskin, Harry Berger, Adrienne Brown, John Bugg, Michelle Coghlan, Eli Cohen, Hannah Crawforth, Nadia Ellis, Andrew Escobedo, Kasey Evans, Erin Forbes, Renee Fox, Rachel Galvin, Genelle Gertz, Ken Gross, Matthew Harrison, Abby Heald, Susannah Hollister, Bri Hopper, Anna Swartwood House, Michael House, Carrie Hyde, Patrick Jagoda, Meta DuEwa Jones, Larry Kim, Ben LaBreche, Jenna Lay, Julia Lee, Philippa Levine, Greg Londe, Julia Lupton, Marianne Montgomery, Cynthia Nazarian, Joe Ortiz, Natalia Perez, Anne Lake Prescott, Beth Quitslund, Philip Schwyzer, Jackie Shin, Dave Urban, Sam Pinto, Lindsay Reckson, Eileen Reeves, James Rutherford, Erwin Rosinberg, Sam Steinberg, Katie Unterman, Stefan Vander Elst, Sarah Van der Laan, Jen Waldron, Keri Walsh, Lina Wilder, Michael Wood, and Carolyn Yerkes.

I have benefited enormously from the opportunity to share portions of this project with smart and responsive audiences at Columbia University, Pomona College, Southern Methodist University, UCLA, and the University of Southern California. I also appreciate the feedback offered by audiences at talks I delivered at the 2014 MLA Annual Convention and several annual meetings of the Renaissance Society of America. I am grateful to *ELR* and Taylor & Francis for permission to reuse previously published material: a portion of chapter 1 appears as "'My Promise Sent Unto Myself': Futurity and the Language of Obligation in Sidney's *Old Arcadia*," in *The Uses of the Future in Early Modern Europe*, ed. Andrea Brady and Emily Butterworth (New York: Routledge, 2010): 54–72; an earlier version of chapter 3 appeared as "Chained Allusions, Patterned Futures, and the Dangers of Interpretation in *Titus Andronicus*," *English Literary Renaissance* 44, no. 3 (2014): 452–85.

At Cornell University Press, I thank Peter Potter, always kind and responsive, for his interest in and support of this project, and Mahinder Kingra for his thoughtful input as the finish line came into view. For shepherding this book into its final form with instructive, astute commentary, I am grateful to Jenny Mann and the anonymous readers. I thank also the generous, patient, and helpful Sara Ferguson and Bethany Wasik as well as all those involved in the preparation of the manuscript for publication.

This book was written during an unusually peripatetic interlude, and I offer these double thanks to Sarah Tindal Kareem, Allen MacDuffie, Vera Vine, Ellery Foutch, Jessica Keating, and Barbara Fuchs for generously lending me homes and offices in which to do this work.

To those friends and loved ones who have not directly impacted the life of this book, but have made all the difference to the life of its author, I offer you this sentence and more in the future. With boundless love for my parents, Earl and Barbara Barret, to whom this book is dedicated.

Introduction

On a typical day in Arcadia, a foreign prince disguised as an Amazon bemoans his unlucky love life. In a "sandy bank" with a "willow stick," Pyrocles-disguised-as-Cleophila tries to write a poem about the pain of impossible love. The verse that follows is notable for its repetitions, which its author claims "maintain" the "inward griefs" that "echo's force" puts on display. These "outward helps" enable the disguised visitor's determination to wallow in self-indulgent sadness—the poem's reference to Narcissus is not especially subtle—but by its close, the verse has gotten sidetracked; it has become a storehouse of future prediction: "Now in this sand I would discharge my mind, / And cast from me part of my burd'nous cares: / But in the sands my pains foretold I find" (104).[1] Pyrocles-disguised-as-Cleophila

---

1. All references are to Sir Philip Sidney, *The Countess of Pembroke's Arcadia (The Old Arcadia)*, ed. Katherine Duncan-Jones (1985; repr., Oxford: Oxford University Press, 1999). Cleophila's poem appears as follows:

> Over these brooks, trusting to ease mine eyes
> (Mine eyes ev'n great in labour with their tears),
> I laid my face (my face wherein there lies
> Clusters of clouds which no sun ever clears).
>   In wat'ry glass my watered eyes I see:
>   Sorrows ill eased, where sorrows painted be.
>
> My thoughts, imprisoned in my secret woes,
> With flamy breaths do issue oft in sound:

1

has stumbled into a prophetic sandstorm—the lines describe a ricochet of words that convert "cast" from a verb employed to throw the "cares" of the past away to one that invokes geomancy, the divination practice of casting points in the sand. Similarly, the recursive structure evidenced via repetition simultaneously informs the idea that the confessional verse might also be predictive. Cleophila's love interest, Philoclea, who happens to overhear the recitation, duplicates the future's forecasted recursiveness by suggesting that the poem anticipates her: she identifies so strongly with these sandy "pains foretold" that she thinks they "might with more cause have been spoken by her own mouth" (104). Poetic production might be an engine of foretelling, but when Cleophila reveals her true identity as Pyrocles, it is clear that Philoclea did not see it coming. Quite befuddled, Philoclea broadens the scene's future-oriented discourse by enumerating a string of possible futures: "Alas, what then shall I do? Shall I seek far-fetched inventions? Shall I seek to lay colours over my decayed thoughts?... Shall I say then I am sorry, or that my love must be turned to hate, since thou art turned to Pyrocles?" (106–7).

In his *Defence of Poesy*, Sir Philip Sidney claimed that the poet alone could "bring forth, quite anew, forms such as never were in nature"; in the *Old Arcadia*, he widens such purchase on the impossible by gesturing to a surprisingly elastic future.[2] Though brief, the bankside encounter highlights the future as both fragile and flexible: when the would-be lovers turn to yet another future-oriented linguistic structure to resolve their quandary—they "passed the promise of marriage" (107)—they also recast the poem's "pains foretold" as a prophetic misfire.[3] Notably, Philoclea's array of futures is

---

    The sound to this strange air no sooner goes
    But that it doth with echo's force rebound
        And make me hear the plaints I would refrain:
        Thus outward helps my inward griefs maintain.

    Now in this sand I would discharge my mind,
    And cast from me part of my burd'nous cares:
    But in the sands my pains foretold I find,
    And see therein how well the writer fares.
        Since stream, air, sand, mine eyes and ears conspire:
        What hope to quench where each thing blows the fire? (104)

2. Sir Philip Sidney, "The Defence of Poesy," in *Sir Philip Sidney*, ed. Katherine Duncan-Jones (Oxford: Oxford University Press, 1994), 105.

3. A qualifying clause in the revised *New Arcadia* clears up any ambiguity about what it means to "pass" a promise of marriage: "which fain Pyrocles would have sealed with the chief arms of his desire, but Philoclea commanded the contrary" (331). This episode appears mostly intact in the *New Arcadia*, though in that version the poem's ephemerality is foregrounded, perhaps an acknowledgement that the loveless future the verses presage will be brief: "she was ready with her foot to give the newborn letters both death and burial" (327). Sir Philip Sidney, *The Countess of Pembroke's Arcadia*, ed. Maurice Evans (New York: Penguin, 1977).

limited neither to the list she indicates with the word "shall," nor to a future union hinged upon a promissory structure. Before the pair light upon this latter, (supposedly) reliable future construct, Philoclea first laments her role in encouraging Cleophila's interest by proposing a curious binary. "[I]f I had continued as I ought," she tells Pyrocles, "you had either never been or ever been Cleophila" (106). Prone to self-blame, Philoclea is merely rehearsing ways in which she might be responsible. Had she not encouraged her suitor's attention, they would not be in this predicament. What is striking is that the terms of her lament offer two temporally distinct options for depriving her admirer of hope. Depending on the timing of that deprivation, either Pyrocles would never have been emboldened to don a disguise, or Cleophila never emboldened to remove it. Philoclea imagines these alternatives as though they were competing futures: what will not happen or what one can count on.

Though it might not surprise a reader to learn that the "promise of marriage" does not end up securing the future quite as neatly as the couple hopes, it is harder to account for some of the scene's other temporal embeddings, especially the binary that sketches two rather extreme possible outcomes, neither of which has come to pass. The numerous, self-conscious echoes throughout Cleophila's poem, for example, are mimicked in Philoclea's two options—"never been or ever been"—in a manner that draws attention to the resonance between these two radically different approaches to the future. More importantly, this is a scene about unrequited and forbidden love, about the passions and the joys of impending matrimony, not about the convoluted nature of time. Yet, the complexity and profusion of temporal perspectives that underwrite an exchange that leads Pyrocles and Philoclea to "the promise of marriage" belies easy paraphrase—though not its main subject, references to the future are part of the architecture that supports and constructs the amorous encounter. In both the poem and its prose aftermath, bursts of expectancy furnish a language of the future that slips to enable, or at least consider, any number of positions on a spectrum in between "never been" and "ever been."

As in the several distinct futures to which Sidney's characters give voice, the literature of sixteenth- and seventeenth-century England is loaded with considerations of the future that invite us to look beyond and between those outer poles, "never been or ever been." *Untold Futures* recovers from that literature assorted perspectives on past, present, and future by attending to an artistic generativity and experimentation particularly focused on uncertainty, flexibility, and possibility. Even in fictions that constantly and self-consciously foreground and reflect upon their own plot trajectories, the future rarely remains predictable. Imaginative literature regularly and notoriously manipulates linear time, but the articulations of time within it—and the many configurations of past, present, and future it embeds—also show that time is a key component of aesthetic capacity. I offer the scene above as but one example of how the language-level operations that underwrite the literature of sixteenth- and seventeenth-century England enable literary production to imagine, and render legible, futures predicated on their uncertain potential.

Philoclea's array of futures admits of more variety than is typically registered by critical studies of the literature of sixteenth- and seventeenth-century England. Whether it "never . . . or ever" comes to pass, the future is the *concern* of the present rather than its certain province. Our examinations of "the future" as a category have more often probed the limit points of "never been or ever been," either futures implicitly dismissed as impossible or aftertimes defined by inevitability and a single, fixed perspective. They have been hampered by our tendency to rely on a familiar set of stories: about poetic legacy and immortality; about apocalypse and last things; about scientific progress. The earthly future has never been a scholarly cornerstone for this period; it is regularly circumscribed because Judgment Day and apocalypse take precedence, or because it gets subsumed within soteriological debate.

This book's primary claim is that the literature of sixteenth- and seventeenth-century England offers an important and largely unexamined archive for understanding the history of the future. Rather than articulating one particular future, these artistic perspectives on and approaches to "aftertimes" register tremendous range. For example, imagining one's own lived future highlights the artistic, linguistic, and narratological resources called upon to conjure it. To put it another way, I am less interested in tracing Philoclea's "far-fetched inventions" or whatever "colours" she may "lay over [her] decayed thoughts," than I am in her repeated use of "shall" and in her capacity to generate and recognize various, even competing, potential futures.

I consider the future in works by Sidney, Edmund Spenser, William Shakespeare, and John Milton by looking closely at the rhetorical formulations, linguistic structures, and narrative strategies they employ. I argue that two crucial things emerge from this archive of articulations: first, that writing about the future in sixteenth- and seventeenth-century England didn't necessarily mean writing about the end of time, apocalypse, or even radical difference. Second, that considering the future in these literary texts allows us unique access to how these writers thought about their own present moment and their own place in time. In these texts, invoking the future often means looking forward to looking back, which, in turn, might shape action in the present moment. My analysis ranges from future-oriented language like the promise to more abstract concepts like the idea of future retrospection by locating and privileging those formulations that neither short-circuit the future by assuming apocalypse nor traffic as harbingers of scientific progress. What emerges in the course of my study is a broader picture that includes extraordinary variety, from modesty of ambition to a commitment to artistic experimentation, yet shares a sense of the uncertainty and boundlessness of artistic production. Whether in an extended passage, a recurring figure, or a casual remark, contemplating the future offered an active way of thinking about and understanding temporality evident through linguistic structures, rhetorical devices, grammar, a hyperawareness about the material text, and the management of the appropriation of classical models.

I

Just as Pyrocles and Philoclea turn to a linguistic structure ("the promise of marriage") that simulates a guarantee for a desired future acknowledged to be unstable, literature trades on that same uncertainty to call into question even the outcomes of familiar stories from the past. I aim to demonstrate that we can find a variety of futures in the imaginative writing even of poets who also explicitly consider the end of time.[4] In this regard, I do not exaggerate my claim in aligning sixteenth- and seventeenth-century writers with a pervasive conception of the future characterized by uncertainty and tentativeness. Rather, I do so in sympathy with a critical discourse that seeks to trouble or reconsider totalizing accounts of this period.[5] In the examples I collect, the privilege of having a story to tell and the practice of shaping art to tell that story result in the production of uncertainty. The conceptions of the future that enable such potential also advance perspectives so bound up in the imagined pleasure of relating a future story that even an aesthetic and ethical paradigm as old as Horace's dictum about the listener's edification might begin to slip from view. In isolating such future-oriented

---

4. For a variety of accounts tracing Milton's interest in the subject, see, for example, Juliet Cummins, ed., *Milton and the Ends of Time* (Cambridge: Cambridge University Press, 2003).

5. For a compelling critique of the "kinds of narrativizations that produce conventional literary history" (199), see Jonathan Goldberg's classic essay, "Dating Milton," in *Soliciting Interpretation: Literary Theory and Seventeenth-Century English Poetry*, ed. Elizabeth D. Harvey and Katharine Eisaman Maus (Chicago: University of Chicago Press, 1990), 199–220. John Milton has been a particular favorite for monolithic accounts; as John Rumrich has argued, in *Paradise Lost* the "theodicy must be seen as sincere because things *could* have worked out otherwise for Adam and Eve." Rumrich's study privileges the "theme of indeterminacy as a vital dimension of human experience and behavior" in arguing against and complicating a critically "invented Milton." See John Rumrich, *Milton Unbound: Controversy and Reinterpretation* (Cambridge: Cambridge University Press, 1996), 22.

details in fictional texts, *Untold Futures* recovers from them an evolving sixteenth- and seventeenth-century discourse of time. Imaginative literature enables and records ways of thinking about time and opens for us avenues for understanding approaches to the future not already bounded by our own categories and assumptions.

This book brings to light a conception of time that is not reflected in the available critical terms we use to discuss the period. "Renaissance" problematically anchors the period solely in reference to one particular past, while "early modern" problematically ties it to a future that was only one of many possible futures. Critical accounts that foreground temporal consciousness have traditionally privileged Renaissance England's artistic engagement with the past. In his magisterial and influential study *The Light in Troy* (1982), Thomas M. Greene detailed the melancholic context of "rupture" that determines "Renaissance"—that historical period defined by its awareness of an estrangement from the classical past—and predicates literary imitation on loss or alienation.[6] The term "early modern" initially emerged as a corrective to this label.[7] Though "early modern" sought to counteract the limitations of approaching the period from a vantage deemed too narrow and elite, in eschewing "Renaissance," the alternative terminology has itself introduced a different reduction—that is, early modern works in service of one particular outcome: modernity.

---

6. Thomas M. Greene, *The Light in Troy: Imitation and Discovery in Renaissance Poetry* (New Haven, CT: Yale University Press, 1982). His account extends the powerful argument offered by Erwin Panofsky in *Renaissance and Renascences in Western Art* (Stockholm: Almqvist and Wiksell, 1960), in which the Renaissance emerged because the "classical past was looked upon, for the first time, as a totality cut off from the present" (113). In "The Modern Divide: From Either Side," *Journal of Medieval and Early Modern Studies* 37, no. 3 (2007), Margreta de Grazia offers a provocative gloss on Panofksy's understanding of the "concept of an epoch": "When the present sees itself as discrete from what preceded it—when it in effect periodizes itself—modernity has arrived" (456).

7. For a lucid account of these terms and their histories, see Leah S. Marcus, "Renaissance/Early Modern Studies," in *Redrawing the Boundaries: The Transformation of English and American Literary Studies*, ed. Stephen Greenblatt and Giles Gunn (New York: Modern Language Association of America, 1992), 41–63. As Marcus writes, "To look at the Renaissance through a lens called early modern is to see the concerns of modernism and postmodernism in embryo—alienation, a disjunction from origins, profound skepticism about the possibility for objectivity (in literary studies or anywhere else), an emphasis on textual indeterminacy as opposed to textual closure and stability, and an interest in intertextuality instead of filiation" (43). For a discussion of the history and origins of periodization in continental Europe, see, for example, Reinhart Koselleck, *Futures Past: On the Semantics of Historical Time*, trans. Keith Tribe (New York: Columbia University Press, 2004), 225–28. In a useful account of Jacob Burckhardt's *The Civilization of the Renaissance in Italy*, de Grazia points out that though "along with Michelet, he is generally credited with introducing the term *Renaissance*," this attribution is never accompanied by "mention of his dissatisfaction with the term"; she notes that he repeatedly "refers to the period as the *early modern, beginning of the modern*, or the *start of the modern*" ("The Modern Divide," 459–60).

Our own terminology, then, obscures our understanding of temporal consciousness in the sixteenth and seventeenth centuries. On the one hand, many scholarly models predetermine approaches to time as always governed by a melancholic drive to commune with pastness. The future that follows on these terms often traces the period's seemingly inexhaustible supply of articulations about poetic immortality.[8] On the other hand, considerations of the future approached under the banner of early modernity tend to privilege ideas about scientific progress that pave the road to the Enlightenment. Such constraint has been exacerbated especially in twentieth-century discussions of modernity that investigate its status as a distinct historical epoch. The approaches to and conceptions of historical time that underpin this discourse depend upon a claim about the future. Reinhart Koselleck puts the issue in usefully bald terms: "It was only when Christian eschatology shed its constant expectation of the imminent arrival of doomsday that a temporality could be revealed that would be open for the new and without limit."[9] In other words, without apocalypse and the end of time as an organizing paradigm, the future changed: it became open-ended. To be sure, the implications for making secularization a precondition for modernity has been a matter of infamous debate.[10] Notably,

---

8. I mentioned earlier Greene's influential perspective of melancholic alienation and poetic imitation, but studies that approach the period on complementary terms often also engage other familiar mappings of a past-oriented perspective as either triumphalist humanism or as the burden of the past felt as the anxiety of influence. For examples of this tradition, see Hiram Haydn, *The Counter-Renaissance* (New York: Harcourt, Brace, and World, 1950); E. M. W. Tillyard, *The Elizabethan World Picture* (London: Chatto and Windus, 1943); Douglas Bush, *The Renaissance and English Humanism* (Toronto: University of Toronto Press, 1939); Harold Bloom, *The Anxiety of Influence: A Theory of Poetry* (New York: Oxford University Press, 1973). For a recent extension of Greene's perspective, see Brian Walsh, *Shakespeare, The Queen's Men, and the Elizabethan Performance of History* (Cambridge: Cambridge University Press, 2009). Walsh argues that efforts to stage the past in this period emphasize the fleeting quality of its resurrection. In making a case for this method of "intervening in Elizabeth historical consciousness," he also offers a perspective akin to Greene's, whereby playwrights "harnessed the potential of dramaturgy and dramatic poetry to respond to widespread feelings of historical loss with the power of aesthetic experience: an experience that revels in imaginative gestures toward a past that is always out of reach but that promises the possibility that such enjoyable experiences can be continually recreated through the collective will to have a past" (13).

9. Koselleck, *Futures Past*, 232.

10. In the realm of political theory in the twentieth century, debates over the concept of secularization offered heated challenges to assumptions about modernity's distinctive claim to progress. In *Political Theology: Four Chapters on the Concept of Sovereignty*, trans. George Schwab (Cambridge, MA: MIT Press, 1985), Carl Schmitt argues that "all significant concepts of the modern doctrine of the state are secularized theological concepts" (36). In *Meaning in History: The Theological Implications of the Philosophy of History* (Chicago: University of Chicago Press, 1949), Karl Löwith countered assumptions about modernity in an attempt to "show that philosophy of history originates with the Hebrew and Christian faith in a fulfillment and that it ends with the secularization of its eschatological pattern" (2). His challenge to views of secularization is, as Kathleen Davis puts it, "important for

however, religious paradigms are repeatedly reinforced as the most important component of the earlier period's future. As a result, the scholarship that reconstructs Reformation religious discourse about salvation and end-time sidesteps an interest in the earthly future, while those studies that view in the early modern period the precursor for secularization tacitly subscribe to modernity *as* the future.[11] The implications are twofold: first, a presumption that no one thought about the future except vis-à-vis Christian paradigms; second, an implicit association between a future characterized by open-endedness and modernity.

Though I use both terms—Renaissance and early modern—*Untold Futures* works to recuperate a set of ideas that falls in between these two descriptors. In isolating those moments in which English poets and playwrights imagine an earthly future shaped by the activity of human beings rather than classical precedent or divine providence, this book necessarily shares common ground with scholars concerned with secularity in this period, and charts a way that imaginative literature both enables and reflects the secularization of time and history. *Untold Futures* operates outside of, and in contradistinction to, sixteenth- and seventeenth-century conceptions of a future predicated on finality—apocalyptic prophecies that presage the end of days, or bids for poetic immortality that imagine an assured monumentality. Though I emphasize linguistic and poetic positions that operate outside of providential or theological points of view, that is not to suggest that those perspectives were not powerfully engaged, sometimes by the very same writers.[12] Nevertheless, I recover approaches to the future that ask us to

---

its insistence that conceptions of historical time must be understood as political strategy—and, in the case of periodized, progressive history, as a means of aggression" (Davis, "The Sense of an Epoch: Periodization, Sovereignty, and the Limits of Secularization," in *The Legitimacy of the Middle Ages: On the Unwritten History of Theory*, ed. Andrew Cole and D. Vance Smith [Durham, NC: Duke University Press, 2010], 45). In *The Legitimacy of the Modern Age*, trans. Robert M. Wallace (Cambridge, MA: MIT Press, 1983), Hans Blumenberg entered this debate to contest the "secularization theorem" and defend modernity's unique historical status; its progress builds on, but does not merely replicate, the theology it displaces. For his account, the new age, unlike the middle age, even in the earliest instances of secular reason operates freed of the burden of eschatology (181–203).

11. In *Mortal Thoughts: Religion, Secularity, & Identity in Shakespeare and Early Modern Culture* (Oxford: Oxford University Press, 2013), Brian Cummings offers a detailed account of shifts in the use of the words "secular" and "secularization," and the extent to which the debates over the link between modernity and secularization anachronistically cast the secular as "nothing less than the liberation of human ideas as well as institutions from a religious yoke" (3). For further discussion of the history of the term "secular" and the implications for its reappropriation, see Davis, "The Sense of an Epoch," 40; and Victoria Kahn's introduction to "Early Modern Secularism," special issue, *Representations* 105, no. 1 (2009): 1–11.

12. See Cummings for excellent recent work that investigates the "relation of problems of the self to problems of religion" in this period by shifting the prominence that has been afforded to the

imagine nondeterministic ends and boundless potential, but to do so while also decoupling open-endedness from modernity. By making modernity the implicit future (the "early modern"), we unnecessarily foreclose that future in ways that obscure perspectives available within sixteenth- and seventeenth-century literature. Instead of looking to this period in order to locate early versions of our own mirror image, I attend to the strategies that imaginative literature used for working out time, rather than using that literature to support a narrative about any one particular end point. By charting alternatives to the ends we know, *Untold Futures* calls attention to poems, plays, and prose fictions that expect and eagerly await future narratives, or, put more simply, that look forward to looking back. Rather than mapping a particular future, the writers treated in this study embrace a motivating uncertainty.

My central aim is not to prove the distinctiveness of these works or this period per se, but rather to uncover the extent to which literature shaped (and can shape) temporal consciousness. The centrality of that category to our construction of this period in particular, however, makes it a rewarding place to look to reconstruct a history of the future. The writers in this study lay bare considerations of the future through their extensive experimentation with literary techniques for capturing, pacing, arranging and reimagining linear time. Such experiments might be the province of the language arts beyond this period, but this period has been pivotal as a place to draw lines upon which our systems of periodization depend. This is the period charged with discovering the past as different; this is precisely that historical period that later readers have been eager to claim as containing modernity *in nuce*.[13] In recovering a perspective that is concerned neither with the rebirth of something old nor with planting the first seeds of something new, I argue that we gain access to an intriguing cross between past-consciousness and future-consciousness that proves fertile ground for writers experimenting

---

secular (*Mortal Thoughts*, 4). He argues that "the history of the self in the early modern period has been falsely constructed on an assumption of emerging secularism. We write as if an idea of the self could only come into being as a result of an emptying out of a religious framework," and challenges this assumption for a period in which "religion is in flux . . . but these fluxes are fundamental to concepts of the self, not a passing irrelevance" (15). Nonetheless, I leave aside the prospect that tracing time in early modern literature offers access to a given author's doctrinal allegiances; for work that contributes to this line of inquiry, see, for example, Theresa M. DiPasquale, "From Here to Aeviternity: Donne's Atemporal Clocks," *Modern Philology* 110, no. 2 (2012): 226–52.

13. Though it is useful to the argument that I am making to trace this history, it is imperative to note that in addition to obscuring intriguing aspects of the sixteenth and seventeenth century, these long-standing narratives have been constructed at the expense of the medieval period. For a powerful case for reclaiming that territory, see Davis, who points out the damaging extent to which "the 'Middle Ages' is a mobile category, applicable at any time to any society that has not 'yet' achieved modernity or, worse, has become retrograde" ("The Sense of an Epoch," 41).

with their conception of the present moment and considering the potential of its reach.

In turning away from historical recuperation as the most pressing ingredient of temporal consciousness on the one hand, and religion as a dominant mode of explanation for the future on the other, this book challenges the place that imaginative literature should hold in relation to the historical, and literary-historical, stories we tell. Critical studies have for too long understood "time" to mean history and historical pattern. Whether such inquiries privilege early modern conceptions of historical time as progressive, as charting an ever-degrading fall from perfection, as typological, or as fundamentally cyclical, they all uncover strategies for thinking about historical models on terms that presuppose and delimit ideas that literary texts, in turn, will dutifully reflect.[14] By contrast, the knowledge that literature produces need not be subordinated to any particular explanatory framework, whether historical, theological, or theoretical. If we want to account for the variety of futures to be found in these imaginative texts, agency must be restored to literature, not given away to history.

In recent years, any number of scholarly voices have emerged to express dissatisfaction with the current state of criticism, in which, as Andrew Hadfield has provocatively put it, "historicism has subsumed literary studies."[15] Rita Felski has recently argued that we "sorely need alternatives to seeing [artworks] as transcendentally timeless on the one hand, and imprisoned in their moment of origin on the other," lamenting a historicism whereby "the literary object remains trapped in the conditions that preside over the moment of its birth, its meaning determined in relation to texts and objects of the same moment."[16] We might productively shift this emphasis to say that literature is too often prized as a key to understanding history rather than as a resource for reconstructing, for example, philosophies of time or approaches to the future within that history. Though products of a culture well versed in attempts to presuppose the realm of what "will be," the fictions treated here investigate the certainty of future outcomes as narratological and linguistic problems.

This book seeks out and recovers uniquely literary means for projecting the future. For this reason, I trace the concepts of time that emerge from literary works rather than predetermining my readings by defining time through

---

14. See, for example, Achsah Guibbory, *The Map of Time: Seventeenth-Century English Literature and Ideas of Pattern in History* (Urbana: University of Illinois Press, 1986).

15. Andrew Hadfield, "Has Historicism Gone Too Far: Or, Should We Return to Form?," in *Rethinking Historicism from Shakespeare to Milton*, ed. Ann Baynes Coiro and Thomas Fulton (Cambridge: Cambridge University Press, 2012), 23.

16. Rita Felski, "'Context Stinks!,'" *New Literary History* 42, no. 4 (2011): 575, 577.

extraliterary sources. My study builds from a kind of close reading that aims to engage imaginative literature in its capacity to act like philosophy. The fictional works under investigation have theories of their own that we have a responsibility to tease out. This is not merely a matter of reconstructing and decoding the language in which concepts like subjectivity were articulated, but rather looking to choices within language that can guide us toward the resources used to build intellectual approaches. To put it another way, if we proceed from the centrality of literature, we can assess what was thinkable in sixteenth- and seventeenth-century England and gain purchase on the ideas produced in a poem or a play.[17] Yet, perhaps even this formulation cuts too close to replacing one context with another. Rather, I hope to engage what Simon Jarvis has eloquently termed "that extraordinarily intricate record of thinking through making."[18] In looking to literature's microstructures, we can work outward from the formal resources employed within a given text to investigate its conception of and experiments with larger philosophical and conceptual questions.

In isolating these subtle but pervasive glimpses of the future, we learn something about how thinking about time is a mechanism—in fact, a developing set of formal and narratological mechanisms—for artistic production. The philosophies of time that emerge complicate, rather than define, temporality. Though these texts resist any impulse we might have to produce an instrument—some new theory of time capable of explaining many examples—they do demonstrate the extent to which aesthetic capacity depends upon conceptions and articulations of time. Rather than being confined to the aesthetic, literary production furnishes imaginative frameworks for intellectual problems. The investigations of the future that pepper the literature of sixteenth- and seventeenth-century England require us to look beyond and between what has "never been or ever been." Because of their variety, they invite us, even, to recognize that linear time is most useful as an index to other configurations of past, present, and future.

Untold Futures recovers an archive of rhetorical formulations, linguistic structures, and narrative strategies that, despite their variety, share a striking feature and a central principle: they do not subordinate the possibilities of the future to deterministic conceptions. As a corollary, they approach without

---

17. I borrow the term "thinkable" in the sense in which David Scott Kastan proposes it in *Shakespeare after Theory* (New York: Routledge, 1999): "To a literary critic interested in the individuality of a particular work, that some idea is demonstrably thinkable is of consequence" (50).

18. Simon Jarvis, "For a Poetics of Verse," *PMLA* 125, no. 4 (2010): 934. Though I celebrate much of what Jarvis advocates in this inspiring essay, we part ways on several important issues. I do not exclude "thinking in prose" from my investigation. Like Jarvis, I see "language [as] one of the materials of verse," but I am less ready to abandon the idea that poetics is "a subset of linguistics" (934).

prejudice a future articulated or imagined independent of eschatology. Though sensitive to a number of relevant larger cultural frameworks that necessitate a historical dimension to this inquiry, I do not use the literary text to reinforce or explain the extraliterary. Instead, I privilege the artistic generativity that sparks would-be futures and renders them unknown and untold. My goal is to extract those contours of the future that illuminate the knowledge that imaginative literature produces, however uncertain or open-ended it may be.

Of course, the uncertainty of the future in linguistic terms is only reinforced for this period by the pervasive anxiety about the future both of England and of *English*. In a section of his published correspondence with Spenser concerned with artistic precepts and precedents, Gabriel Harvey foregrounds the perceived pressures facing both England and its vernacular:

> [T]o say troth, we Beginners haue the start, and aduauntage of our Followers, who are to frame and conforme both their Examples, and Precepts, according to that President which they haue of vs: as no doubt Homer or some other in *Greeke*, and Ennius, or I know not who else in *Latine*, did preiudice, and ouerrule those, that followed them, as well for the quantities of syllables, as number of feete, and the like: their onely Examples going for current payment, and standing in steade of Lawes, and Rules with the posteritie.[19]

Harvey imagines himself as a catalyst and guide shaping future literary production. Poised on the brink of an unsure future, he emphasizes the gravity of the responsibility inherent in "hau[ing] the start, and aduantage"—he and Spenser might be exemplars who set the course for England's poetic achievement.[20] In a series of letters filled with metrical verse experiments,

---

19. Gabriel Harvey and Edmund Spenser, *Three proper, and wittie, familiar Letters: lately passed betweene two Vniuersitie men: touching the Earthquake in Aprill last, and our English refourmed Versifying* (London, 1580), D4v–E1r.

20. The latter half of the sixteenth century, as has been extensively documented, obsessed over rhetoric and vernacular eloquence. In this same letter, Harvey dreams of standard orthography, which he desires in part because he believes that the technical features of the English language jeopardize its future: it is unable to offer the raw matter required for quantitative verse, and its written form offers little guarantee that future speakers will pronounce it properly. See, among others, Derek Attridge, *Peculiar Language: Literature as Difference from the Renaissance to James Joyce* (London: Methuen, 1988); Richard Foster Jones, *Triumph of the English Language: A Survey of Opinions Concerning the Vernacular from the Introduction of Printing to the Restoration* (Stanford, CA: Stanford University Press, 1953); Sean Keilen, *Vulgar Eloquence: On the Renaissance Invention of English Literature* (New Haven, CT: Yale University Press, 2006); Paula Blank, *Broken English: Dialects and the Politics of Language in Renaissance Writings* (New York: Routledge, 1996); Jenny C. Mann, *Outlaw Rhetoric: Figuring Vernacular Eloquence in Shakespeare's England* (Ithaca, NY: Cornell University Press, 2012); Carla Mazzio, *The Inarticulate Renaissance: Language Trouble in an Age of Eloquence* (Philadelphia: University of Pennsylvania Press,

his heightened awareness of his place in time helps to situate my claim that literary production intervened in and refashioned ways of thinking about the future. Like Cleophila's predictive verse, Harvey's letter offers access to another engagement with aftertimes—a future dictated by prosody, not apocalypse. Samuel Daniel's "ringing defense of English eloquence"[21] in *Musophilus* similarly voices great hopes for the vernacular:

> And who, in time, knows whither we may vent
> The treasure of our tongue, to what strange shores
> This gain of our best glory shall be sent
> T'enrich unknowing nations with our stores;
> What worlds in th'yet unformed Occident
> May come refined with th'accents that are ours?[22]

This ambitious account reproduces in even more optimistic terms Harvey's sense of poetic urgency in the face of linguistic uncertainty. Yet despite the novelty of Daniel's vision of linguistic expansion, there is no attention paid to what that future will hold—other than English. The singular notion of boundless temporal possibility made literary production a crucial vehicle for creating a memorable British future.[23]

Poetry regularly delights in claiming that its language is the most lasting substance of all (in the Renaissance this trope usually crops up by way of allusion to Horace's "aere perennius"). Still, England envies the quantity of ruins that Italy boasts. By contrast, the ephemerality of performance means that theater works contrary to the creation of artifacts, and this underwrites some of the effort in the literature that I treat to use antiquity's best treasures, but also get out from under its thumb.[24] Yet, my approach posits that if we trace

---

2009); Catherine Nicholson, *Uncommon Tongues: Eloquence and Eccentricity in the English Renaissance* (Philadelphia: University of Pennsylvania Press, 2014).

21. As Greenblatt notes, Daniel's poem "reverses the conventional image" whereby English is precious cargo outgoing rather than jewels being cargo incoming, an imagined situation in which "best glorie" is language, not faith, a "gift of inestimable value" rather than a "conquest." Stephen J. Greenblatt, *Learning to Curse: Essays in Early Modern Culture* (New York: Routledge, 1990), 16–17.

22. Samuel Daniel, "Musophilus: Containing a General Defence of Learning (1599)," in *Sidney's "The Defence of Poesy" and Selected Renaissance Literary Criticism*, ed. Gavin Alexander (London: Penguin, 2004), 279–80.

23. Such linguistic concerns were by no means limited to England. On the contrary, defenses and discussions of writing in the vernacular abounded on the Continent in this period. By the same token, an alternative version of this book that attended to authors like Ariosto, Machiavelli, Cervantes, and Quevedo would not want for explicit and interesting treatments of time.

24. For a discussion of theater as a "true opposite of artifactuality," see Aaron Kunin, "Poetry as Artifact," in *The Princeton Encyclopedia of Poetry and Poetics*, ed. Roland Greene, Stephen Cushman, Clare Cavanagh, Jahan Ramazani, and Paul Rouzer, 4th ed. (Princeton, NJ: Princeton University Press, 2012), 88–89.

out language's role in building and imagining the future, categories such as poetry and performance don't stay distinct in terms of their ephemerality or their longevity. Shakespeare, for example, takes as part of his raw material an inherent theatrical problem at the heart of Sidney's famous concern in his *Defence of Poesy* about the limits of visual representation on stage, and the need to use words to fill in the gaps.[25] In this period, language functions as the future's most powerful artifact.

Some of the period's most ambitious English writers foreground temporality in constructing complex narratives concerned with looking back only to show how that retrospection is surprisingly relevant to thinking about the future. The works they produce evince an interest not merely in having a past, but also in having the power to shape and recount that past, and to approach both past and present through active consideration of aftertimes. This book recovers an alternative, vibrant strand of imaginative literature's encounter with temporality in the sixteenth and seventeenth centuries; it turns to literary *techne* to unravel and understand a pervasive vantage, just one contour of which we find in the promise of marriage that Pyrocles and Philoclea "pass" in an attempt to bind future to present.

II

Memorable characters like Hamlet and Othello conclude their lives onstage by suggesting that they have a clear sense of the narratives their adventures should engender; they posit narrative as an antecedent that will persist long after they have expired: Hamlet implores Horatio to "report me and my cause aright . . . If thou didst ever hold me in thy heart . . . in this harsh world draw thy breath in pain / To tell my story" (5.2.293, 300–3); Othello asks that "[w]hen you shall these unlucky deeds relate, / Speak of me as I am; nothing extenuate, / Nor set down aught in malice" (5.2.339–41).[26] In isolating the engine of afterlife, they also endorse a single paradigm for the relationship between narrative and the future—they turn to art to solve the problem of future uncertainty. Jonathan Culler, revising Alice Fulton, has suggested that "if narrative is about what happens next, lyric is about what happens

---

25. "But if it be so in *Gorboduc*, how much more in all the rest, where you shall have Asia of the one side, and Afric of the other, and so many other under-kingdoms, that the player when he cometh in, must ever begin with telling where he is, or else the tale will not be conceived?" (Sidney, "The Defence of Poesy," 134).

26. William Shakespeare, *Hamlet*, ed. Ann Thompson and Neil Taylor, 3rd ser. (London: The Arden Shakespeare, 2006); and *Othello*, ed. E. A. J. Honigmann, 3rd ser. (London: The Arden Shakespeare, 1997).

now."[27] The protasis of Culler's statement—"narrative is about what happens next"—highlights the extent to which the future is *the* topic of narrative because it looks a step ahead. Othello and Hamlet privilege legacy—how they will be interpreted—in a manner that betrays a suspicion that future stories may evade control. In so doing, they acknowledge an unknowable and uncontrollable quality to storytelling. Narrative may look to what happens next, but cannot guarantee it.

Even as they voice self-conscious doubts about attempting to work in a language—English—hopefully imagined to be in its ascendancy, Renaissance writers highlight the power and flexibility of sequence, expectation, anticipation, and reflection by means of formal innovation. In chapters on Sidney's *Old Arcadia*, Spenser's *The Faerie Queene*, Shakespeare's *Titus Andronicus, Antony and Cleopatra,* and *Cymbeline*, and Milton's *Paradise Lost*, I trace articulations that foreground and explore expectant formal structures, including narrative, but that trouble the stability of future stories. We might think of this in terms of Shakespeare's Lady Macbeth: when she claims to "feel now / The future in the instant," she does so because she shuns the "ignorant present" (1.5.57–58).[28] Hers is at heart a providential fantasy: even if her violent impatience perverts its realization, her turn of phrase also describes an idea with more purchase beyond her reliance on such inevitability. The notion of a present moment wholly consumed by attention to an anticipated future—"in the instant"—applies to a host of characters who regularly contemplate and imagine their own, lived futures. Unlike Lady Macbeth, however, many characters betray a modesty of perspective when their present moment becomes dedicated to "feel[ing] now the future in the instant." Worrying about one's own lived future can scale *down* the ambition of legacy, and they prove alert to a process of mulling over the intricacies of time's passage.

Despite the topical allure of a phrase like "future in the instant," a hypersensitivity to time often operates in a manner that unsettles a fantasy about the certainty of narrative's "next." For this reason, I seek to expand a statement like Culler's to the extent that it presumes that genre furnishes literary study with macrostructures for thinking about time. In highlighting how stasis and telos are bound by genre, his distinction effaces some of the traffic between "next" and "now." I want to suggest that depending on macrostructures limits our options for identifying temporal techniques. All of the texts

---

27. Jonathan Culler, "Why Lyric?," *PMLA* 123, no. 1 (2008): 202.
28. William Shakespeare, *Macbeth*, ed. Kenneth Muir, 2nd ser. (London: The Arden Shakespeare, 1997).

I have assembled offer some new angle on categories of genre—romance is certainly a candidate for a common term that would most comfortably collect them. However, I do not approach the task of reclaiming literature's purchase on the category of "the future" as a means of systematically illuminating a single genre or literary mode. Rather than selecting texts that resemble each other in terms of genre (only poetry; only drama) or mounting an argument that rehearses the groundbreaking critical insights into the temporal features (dilation; delay) that make a category like romance distinctive, I proceed from microstructures that work across genres.

By microstructures, I mean isolable, identifiable forms such as a promise or a rhyme, to give but two examples. Not only do such microstructures operate on a small scale—at the level of the stanza or the sentence—but they also entail a temporal component or pattern. Promise and rhyme need not have much in common. Still, they share a future orientation because they both foreground anticipation and expectation. As individual forms, such microstructures might pull on time and inflect it differently depending on genre, but their temporality is not defined by genre. My purpose here is not to delimit those microstructures in order to offer a precise distinction between formal types. Instead I am proposing that it is the work of discovering the impact of such microstructures within a literary text—and identifying the relevant cultural contexts with which they are in dialogue—that enables us to understand the conceptual categories and intellectual parameters for thinking about the future in this period, and about time, more broadly, in our own. In unraveling the expectant patterns embedded in the language-level choices that literary artists make, we are called upon to rethink what we are looking for when we go to the archive.

Untold Futures differs, then, from recent studies that tend to privilege explicit confrontations with the mechanics of time, ranging from scientific advances in timekeeping devices to the legacies of material objects.[29] To reconstruct the future as it appears in sixteenth- and seventeenth-century English literature, I look not to things, nor to technological advances, but instead to the grammar and structures of language that struggle to distinguish

---

29. Chief among these is Jonathan Gil Harris's *Untimely Matter in the Time of Shakespeare* (Philadelphia: University of Pennsylvania Press, 2009), which consciously moves away from treating time as merely a force that acts upon the subject, and instead privileges "the time of the thing." Harris's interest in "polychronicity" leads him to generate a set of explanatory key terms aimed at taxonomizing the ways in which objects both exist in and carry with them a multitude of time. Harris helps to pinpoint why our understanding of time is and ought to be variable, and his is a valuable attempt to develop a more precise vocabulary for accommodating time's complexity, though I do not share his sense that what he describes is "untimely."

between time schemes. I tease out and recuperate interchanges between time schemes not only to reconstruct broader period dialogues about futurity and temporality, but also to offer new insights into influential literary texts. In the archive I assemble, literary texts do not passively reflect temporality or chronometric innovation. Rather, they actively develop art through experiments with the raw materials of poetic craft, especially those elements that foreground time, sequence, and expectation: syntax, grammar, narrative, rhyme, meter.[30]

I also turn to a range of co-texts to show how these language-level approaches operate alongside larger cultural frameworks, such as legal debates over the adjudication of debt, emerging historiographical practices that prompt interest in the poet's prerogative to tell history, and critiques of long-standing hermeneutic practices. The chapters in this study simultaneously make a historical argument about approaches to the future in this period and a formal argument about imaginative literature's textual techniques for conceptualizing and accessing possible futures. To this end, I position the literary text at the center of each chapter as an interlocutor in an ongoing conversation about strategies for defining and understanding the place of the present moment. I endeavor to identify the mechanics by which narrative seeks to encode time's passage, and I propose that unlocking the temporal components of formal techniques, linguistic structures, and narrative strategies reveals not only a broader conception of the future, but also new insights into how sixteenth- and seventeenth-century writers understood art's capacity to hold open possibility and potential by redefining and reconfiguring time.

III

My core focus on six texts penned by English writers concerned with the future means that the examples collected here are not exhaustive. Even within England, consideration of virtually any poet or playwright from the period would quickly yield more examples of complex literary temporalities: Thomas Wyatt's "newfangleness," Andrew Marvell's "winged chariot," Christopher Marlowe's extraordinary compression of time at the end of *Doctor Faustus*, the strikingly unremarkable and short-lived prophetic powers

---

30. In doing so, I am indebted to a study such as Jeffrey J. Cohen's, which, though extremely different from my own, powerfully articulates what is lost in assuming that time does not provide a serious engine of thought because it is so rarely granted the benefits of defamiliarization (as he puts it, because it "seems so obvious"). See Cohen, *Medieval Identity Machines* (Minneapolis: University of Minnesota Press, 2003), 2.

granted in George Chapman's *The Gentleman Usher*, Ben Jonson's horrified fascination with the temporalities of the market in *Bartholomew Fair*—the list could be endlessly extended. Another version of this book might have focused on examples that aggressively foreground strange or disruptive temporalities, or even texts that thematize time.[31] Instead, I draw out the subtle, often elusive, constructions and depictions of possible futures that don't slot neatly into preexisting explanatory grids. As with the exploratory series of futures that Philoclea signals with the word "shall," I focus on the complex and abundant temporal perspectives that furnish scaffolding in the works of four major poets. The conceptualizations of the future that emerge resist overarching narratives, those grand schemes developed to define a set of perspectives they have instead obscured. I chart perspectives that evade detection when approached on the grounds of theme or disruption, those that neither coordinate a singular approach to the future nor invite a unifying critical terminology. I focus on poems, plays, and prose narratives that share in a practice of experimentation, and whose agency builds from the internal resources of imaginative making. The texts treated in this study share and revisit a number of overlapping concerns: they are examples of or in dialogue with the genre of romance; they foreground the material text only to undermine it; they form part of a series (or, especially in Sidney's case, undergo a conspicuous revision); they reveal a future particularly concerned with the present moment; they privilege the ancient past as a point of reference, and show that characters' backward glances and appropriations of classical culture transformed the way they looked ahead, and often enabled them to imagine what kind of past the present would become. Not every text fits squarely into every category, but they interlock with each other such that each individual case study contributes to and advances elements of the broader inquiry.

For these writers, to imagine what kind of past the present will become is also to grasp how thinking about the future is always an effort to understand the present. In this regard, the text at the heart of each chapter of *Untold Futures* produces a distinct interaction between looking forward and looking back. These relationships are structured by forms of thought and feeling such as expectation, ambition, and obligation: looking forward might

---

31. For studies concerned with time as a thematic, see, for example, Inga-Stina Ewbank, "The Triumph of Time," in *The Winter's Tale: A Casebook*, ed. Kenneth Muir (London: Macmillan, 1968), 98–115; Ricardo J. Quinones, *The Renaissance Discovery of Time* (Cambridge, MA: Harvard University Press, 1972); Frederick Turner, *Shakespeare and the Nature of Time: Moral and Philosophical Themes in Some Plays and Poems by William Shakespeare* (Oxford: Oxford University Press, 1971); and G. F. Waller, *The Strong Necessity of Time: The Philosophy of Time in Shakespeare and Elizabethan Literature* (The Hague: Mouton, 1976).

enable a look back; looking back might pose a threat to moving forward; looking forward to looking back might supply an emotional reward. These texts build toward positive articulations of provisional and alternative futures. Though they do not reflect a systematic attempt to use "the future" as an index of sociological categories, each chapter highlights a specific cultural context—from law and historiographical debate to grammar and classical allusion—that claims to shape temporal consciousness. Beginning with the promise in Sidney's *Old Arcadia*, I establish how forward-looking linguistic structures enabled literary artists to rethink their place in time.

In chapter 1, "Promising the Future: The Language of Obligation in Sidney's *Old Arcadia*," I argue that the romance undermines devices intended to cast and secure particular futures, such as promises and prophecies, to foreground the generative potential of the flux of experience. Sidney repeatedly employs the vocabulary and context of retrospection and judgment in scenes that investigate the fixity afforded to art. His use of legal language invites comparison to the disputes over debt, exchange, and contractual responsibility that became paramount in the English common law courts in the sixteenth century. However, rather than striving to establish mechanisms by which language can ensure outcomes, Sidney highlights the failure of forms that depend upon intention and obligation to reveal that individual identity is no more binding than artistic representation.

In chapter 2, "The History of the Future: Spenser's *The Faerie Queene* and the Directions of Time," I argue that Spenser's poetry unsettles the credibility of both historical account and consequence, serving as a hinge between an inaccessible past and an unknown future. The poem's presentation of history and prophecy emphasizes the unstable aspects of both while the present gives shape to gaps and missing links. Through his treatment of time, Spenser foregrounds England's simultaneous awareness of a lack of access to its own past and its overwhelming desire to aggrandize its origins. The poet manipulates familiar devices like prophecy and providential patterning to emphasize contingency over inevitability, thus illustrating that he does not merely report the past, but also plays a significant role in creating it.

In chapter 3, "The Fiction of the Future: Dangerous Reading in *Titus Andronicus*," I argue that in Shakespeare's play the literature of antiquity prescribes—and forecloses—the future. Shakespeare links the misuse of ancient literary models to the millennium-long tradition of moralization that had sought to correct Ovid's *Metamorphoses* because the pagan text posed a danger to Christian readers. The playwright critiques this practice by inverting its terms: his pagan characters model action on Ovid's text by employing the hermeneutics that undergird *moralizatio*. The onstage ramifications are brutal: repetitions of the literary past result in the dismemberment of characters' bodies, and the play's ending denies its own rhetorical promises of a brighter future. Shakespeare brings classical literature onstage both to suggest the consequences of bad reading and to show the danger antiquity poses to a Renaissance literary culture too focused on the works of the past.

If our conception of Renaissance culture presupposes a reanimation of antiquity, my account of literary allusion, retelling, and reenactment in these texts also unearths the importance of the present moment in poetic creation. The first two chapters introduce the inquiry into the future by attending to writers who influenced artistic production within the period (in both fictional and theoretical works); the second and third chapters show how the present can be shaped by harnessing and exploiting the literature of the past. The third chapter also provides a bridge to the second half of this study because Shakespeare (and especially Shakespeare's vantage on classical antiquity) furnishes a body of work through which to trace a set of ideas. Beginning with his most overtly classically allusive play, Shakespeare conceives of a present molded by the consideration of its own afterlife, which also casts futurity in terms of subjective experience. The next chapters focus on two proleptic structures—the grammatical "second future" and improvised rhyme—to examine characters that imagine the stories they eventually will tell about the present. In chapter 4, "Shakespeare's Second Future: Anticipatory Nostalgia in *Cymbeline*," I draw on vocabulary and concepts from early modern grammatical treatises to chart characters' competing approaches to time through statements that invoke (or deny) alternative outcomes. My inquiry builds toward a scene in which Arviragus and Guiderius, two disgruntled rustic youths, worry that their present moment is so boring that they will have no stories to tell when they reach old age. I argue that their anxiety about their own future narrative functions as anticipatory nostalgia. Their perspective has the potential to shape action, however they yearn not for a particular activity in the present moment, but rather for the memories it will furnish in an undistinguished future.

In chapter 5, "Imminent Futures: Absent Art and Improvised Rhyme in *Antony and Cleopatra* and *Cymbeline*," I argue that Shakespeare strategically turns time into a stage resource across and between his plays. I begin with the repeated descriptions of impending triumph in *Antony and Cleopatra* to trace a version of the future characterized by immediacy rather than immortality. Cleopatra's fears about a future in which she will witness herself performed "extemporally" highlight the play's persistent interest in improvised artistic forms like rhyme—at once spontaneous and dependent on predictive formal structures—even in the face of well-known legacies already afforded by antiquity. Cleopatra's suicide follows from a denial of anticipatory nostalgia, and that novel temporal signature informs her reappearance on an imagined tapestry in *Cymbeline*. Her return signals the overlap between Shakespeare's use of classical models and his efforts to frame English history. The playwright gestures toward England's future by imagining himself not only as the originator of the drama and poetry of Renaissance England, but also as the sole mediator of the past.

In the works considered in the chapters of *Untold Futures*, Sidney, Spenser, and Shakespeare resist teleological conceptions of time by using literary techniques that open up indeterminate futures. Milton's writing provides a unique opportunity to track the legacy of that innovation. In the afterword, "Circles of the Future: Memory or Monument in *Paradise Lost*," I argue that Milton's epic proves literature capable of unsettling the inevitability of the future. As Adam lingers in paradise in the precious moments between fall and expulsion, he imagines memories he would have shared with his sons. Yet, these are not projected, proleptic memories. Rather, postlapsarian Eden is thwarted by a revised, insufficient version of anticipatory nostalgia: Adam fills the imagined future with the same past-oriented mourning that already haunts his present. Instead of providing an anticipation that motivates present action, Adam's rhetorical visions prove destructive; they threaten to turn the Edenic landscape into a memorial site filled with ruins. Whereas the poem denies this anticipatory nostalgia because it is too dependent on the past, the present it offers beyond the garden becomes a boundless space of imagination. Milton's conception of the future, both within and without his poetry, registers a fellowship that renders the earlier Renaissance poets treated in this book a potent presence. Along with them, or perhaps in spite of them, he privileges the importance and potential of literature to shape, advocate, and establish England's national and poetic fortitude.

Just as Cleophila's poetic self-projections allowed "pains foretold" to be recursive, predictive, and even almost instantly outdated, searching out an eclectic archive of formulations and literary strategies highlights those conceptualizations that elude explanation according to some familiar master category or catchall framework. In the case of the complicated temporal fancy I term "anticipatory nostalgia," for example, I anachronistically employ the word nostalgia in its contemporary sense—as wistful longing.[32] What does it

---

32. For a comprehensive account of the history of the term "nostalgia" as well as its more contemporary usage, see Kevis Goodman, "Romantic Poetry and the Science of Thought," in *The Cambridge Companion to British Romantic Poetry*, ed. James Chandler and Maureen N. McLane (Cambridge: Cambridge University Press, 2008), 195–216.

mean to discuss a feeling, an emotional attitude, at a historical moment that lacked our vocabulary to describe it? Such a label attempts to make recognizable to us an affective state or feeling that seems strikingly misplaced, but purposefully foregrounds its alienating effect. Though they are key concepts for this book, neither anticipatory nostalgia nor the relationship between looking forward and looking back furnishes a formula for approaching literary texts. In working to tease intellectual categories out of textual moments, I uncover an archive of rhetorical formulations employed in plays, poems, and prose fictions that record variegated approaches to the future: a speech act such as a promise; a grammatical construction such as the "second future"; references to improvised rhyme. Rather than resolving the questions raised by these artistic experiments, *Untold Futures* foregrounds the expectant patterns embedded in these microstructures and examines them alongside competing models of and resources for certainty in order to call attention to a range of futures, from the modest, familiar, rehearsed, discarded, and unrealized to the desired, dreamed, unprecedented, dreaded, and unscripted. In attempting to recover those perspectives that are scattered along the continuum between "never been" and "ever been," or to recuperate those ideas that have gotten lost in between "Renaissance" and "early modern," the present moment in which these texts were written (and which they imagine) becomes visible not only as a point of intersection between past consciousness and future consciousness, but also as an access point to the future in the sense that it unlocks conceptions of lived possibility. Artistic production enables and builds the expectant structures through which we might catch sight of those futures. In looking to moments that foreground temporality, the readings in individual chapters of *Untold Futures* argue in favor of an emerging literary culture not only keenly alert to conceptions of time, but also routinely engaged with possibility and contingency in place of inevitable outcomes. The writers treated in this book generate literary experiments in terms of those futures, both countless and unaccounted for, that inspire the unexpected.

CHAPTER 1

Promising the Future
The Language of Obligation in Sidney's Old Arcadia

What does the future hold? Sir Philip Sidney's prose romance, *The Old Arcadia*, announces an interest in this question in its sixth sentence when Basilius, the Duke of Arcadia, visits the oracle at Delphos,

> stirred . . . with the vanity which possesseth many who, making a perpetual mansion of this poor baiting place of man's life, are desirous to know the certainty of things to come, wherein there is nothing so certain as our continual uncertainty. (4–5)[1]

Despite the narrator's moralizing disclaimer, the prophetic verses that follow initiate a narrative that eventually endorses them. True to oracular literary precedent, Basilius seeks the future as a "certainty," but once he has heard it foretold, he attempts to alter the fated course. By making Basilius follow in footsteps that lead back as far as Oedipus, Sidney launches his plot by signaling an ending that already lies in wait.[2] That the fiction's future will occasion a look back is underscored by the trial that concludes it—the *Old Arcadia* begins with an account of where the plot will end up and ends by

---

1. All references are to Sir Philip Sidney, *The Countess of Pembroke's Arcadia (The Old Arcadia)*, ed. Katherine Duncan-Jones (1985; repr., Oxford: Oxford University Press, 1999).

2. Studies of narrative have long claimed that even fictions not aided by oracular insight are structured by the reader's awareness that the end has already been scripted. See, for example, Peter Brooks, *Reading for the Plot: Design and Intention in Narrative* (New York: Knopf, 1984).

recounting and assessing where it has been. In this regard, however, the trial only redoubles the retrospective structure established by the prophecy. Hindsight, it would seem, matters more to this text than foresight.

Sidney may open with a familiar setup that trades on the "certainty of things to come," but curiously the romance does not much linger on the providential structure the prophecy implies. The gesture to a bounded plot belies the romance's investment in what the narrator calls "our continual uncertainty." Throughout the fiction, Sidney experiments with linguistic, narrative, and poetic structures that attempt to guarantee outcomes, but he proves far more interested in the ways that both individuals and texts fail to secure both the future and the past. He repeatedly employs the vocabulary and context of promises and judgment in scenes in which characters appeal to artistic representations of reality as though they were binding. In so doing, he teasingly signals the unwritten rules that govern the crafting and consumption of poetic fictions, while pretending that the flux of experience lacks the fixity afforded to art.

In this regard, the *Old Arcadia* invites an intriguing analogy. The decades that preceded Sidney's romance witnessed the development of complex social networks that enabled economic connections. Craig Muldrew has demonstrated how this "culture of credit" and "currency of reputation" also prompted changes in the established system of legal recourse in matters of dispute.[3] Sidney's investigations of the mechanisms by which language might ensure a particular future overlap intellectually with an emerging early modern legal theory of contract. Contracts attempt to confirm the future in the face of two different species of uncertainty: the unpredictability of "things to come" and the true intentions of the other party in an agreement or exchange. I do not suggest that the connection between the legal context and Sidney's romance is causal. On the contrary, the final judgment for the landmark contract case of the period—Slade's case—came some fifteen years after Sidney's death. Nonetheless, this chapter considers Sidney's experiments in light of the broader context of debates over contract, debt, and obligation that were a source of dispute in and beyond Sidney's lifetime in the common law courts. Indeed, the questions about intention and interiority that shaped legal debate were also vital to poetic inquiry into how (and if)

---

3. Craig Muldrew, *The Economy of Obligation: The Culture of Credit and Social Relations in Early Modern England* (New York: St. Martin's Press, 1998), 2–3. Muldrew's excellent study, of course, focuses on neither poetry nor law, but rather on the early modern culture of credit. What he details in terms of law, exchange, and social systems, however, provides a set of useful concepts for thinking about the connections between Sidney's *Old Arcadia* and sixteenth-century culture more broadly.

writing commits its author to the future. Sidney's explicit engagement with legal language and procedures highlights his interest in a variety of future-oriented instruments that his imaginative enterprise routinely undermines.

The *Old Arcadia*'s opening gambit makes overt the predetermination of its end. Yet, despite this apparent neat enclosure, the romance stages explicit confrontations with a future that has turned out differently than imagined. Sidney's narrative manipulates distinctions between past, present, and future, and holds in suspension a clear separation between these temporal categories. On the one hand, the prophetic structure claims that it is possible to know the future ahead of schedule, which also means that "the future must already exist in the present."[4] On the other hand, the promise holds out the possibility of using language "to make certain future actions predictable, so that [people] might be able to depend on them."[5] Sidney exposes the extent to which promises seek to mimic the logic underlying prophecy—they signal a desire to put an end to possibility. In offering verse promises—made, but also broken—as an index to the instability of experience, Sidney sketches out and expands art's imaginative power.[6] He adjusts patterns of expectation and retrospection in order to investigate "continual uncertainty" as a crucial feature of the future—his approach privileges that uncertainty as a building block of possibility. In disclosing the limitations of our linguistic, narrative, and imaginative resources for securing the future, Sidney instead makes prominent the open-endedness of artistic production. Not only is the *Old Arcadia* unabashedly concerned with justice, but it also employs legal language throughout to establish a present moment always aware of its eventual revisitation, always tied to a future that will be retrospective. Sidney employs a variety of strategies—from compromising

---

4. Michael Wood, *The Road to Delphi: The Life and Afterlife of Oracles* (New York: Farrar, Straus and Giroux, 2003), 35. Leslie K. Arnovick has pointed out that the "validity of statements about the past can be evaluated. They are 'either true or false at the time of their utterance' and therefore the speaker's belief in their truth can indeed be unqualified and objective. On the other hand, because it is phenomenologically impossible (unless he is omniscient) for the speaker to know the truth value of his future proposition at the time of his assertion, references to future time are subjective and qualified to some extent" (Arnovick, *The Development of Future Constructions in English: The Pragmatics of Modal and Temporal* Will *and* Shall *in Middle English* [New York: Peter Lang Publishing, 1990], 93).

5. Muldrew, *Economy of Obligation*, 5.

6. It is, of course, important to this argument that Sidney pursues these maneuvers in a fiction that both dangles and denies providence. We need look no further than the critical history of considering theology in *Paradise Lost* to find articulations that seek to discipline moments in literary texts that subvert easy handles on the period. See, for example, Kingsley Widmer's classic essay that recuperates the final books of Milton's epic by claiming that the poet repudiates the "flux . . . of worldly activity" that detracts from providence (Widmer, "The Iconography of Renunciation: The Miltonic Simile," *ELH* 25, no. 4 [1958]: 264).

promises to temporarily withholding details about the action that he narrates—to encourage his readers to privilege a perspective beyond a single present moment. In a recent study of oaths and vows in early modern England, John Kerrigan makes the appealing suggestion that "we are not quite ourselves when we asseverate or promise. We are trying to manifest a truth, or lean into the future self that will deliver on the vow."[7] However, Sidney's fiction comes at the implications of such linguistic future-casting from a different direction: the *Old Arcadia* probes speech acts that furnish the hope that we might commit ourselves (and often more than ourselves) to an unknown future only to show that imaginative literature delivers instead unbounded access to "continual uncertainty."

Though he does not fully understand the prophecy, Basilius takes it to mean that his daughters are in danger of being seduced, and that he is in danger of losing his throne:

> Thy elder care shall from thy careful face
> By princely mean be stolen and yet not lost;
> Thy younger shall with nature's bliss embrace
> An uncouth love, which nature hateth most.
> Thou with thy wife adult'ry shalt commit,
> And in thy throne a foreign state shall sit.
> All this on thee this fatal year shall hit. (5)

It is the prediction that a "foreign state" will usurp his "throne" that most concerns Basilius. He responds by removing his family to a solitary, deserted location, and putting his daughters, Pamela, the "elder care," and Philoclea, the "younger," under watch. Yet, rather than endorsing "the certainty of things to come," Sidney's fiction routinely slackens the security of any particular future as well as the inevitability of any particular plot. In this chapter, I pay particular attention to Sidney's use of the promise in order to demonstrate his interest in a future predicated on challenging and defining the capacity of language and linguistic structures to secure or verify a future outcome. The scrambled temporalities heightened in this romance reinforce the extent to which Sidney undermines future certainty in favor of indeterminacy by repeatedly pretending to establish a future and then discarding or troubling those viewpoints. In a text that uses a number of familiar devices—prophecy, trial, promise—to foreground the future's relation to retrospective judgment

---

7. John Kerrigan, "Shakespeare, Oaths and Vows," *Proceedings of the British Academy* 167 (2010): 78.

and evaluative frameworks, the pressure that Sidney's romance puts on form, intention, and obligation also generates an unknown future, one that privileges the role poetics plays in producing possibility.

I

In the *Old Arcadia*, artistic creations such as paintings and poems regularly lay claim both to accessing interiority and anticipating a future that presumes retrospection. Sidney repeatedly draws a connection between the future and retrospection and establishes it using legal language, especially the language of judgment. In so doing, he highlights the importance of the perspective of the present moment, which is imagined to hold a privileged place in any future. That is, the certainty of the future depends on how it will be evaluated by the light of present perspective. In Sidney's text, legal language enables this vantage whereby the future is beholden to the present, but the romance also calls such eventual retrospection into question.

With the Duke and his family removed to the pastoral because of the prophecy, the itinerant princes Pyrocles and Musidorus arrive at an empty court. Pyrocles instantly falls in love with a painting that depicts Philoclea with her parents:

> she drawn as well as it was possible art should counterfeit so perfect a workmanship of nature. For therein, besides the show of her beauties, a man might judge even the nature of her countenance, full of bashfulness, love, and reverence—and all by the cast of her eye—, mixed with a sweet grief to find her virtue suspected. This moved Pyrocles to fall into questions of her. (11)

The painting piques Pyrocles's interest in terms that participate in the familiar contest between art and nature. In the case of the portrait, nature is perfection, art mere imitation. Though an "excellent artificer," the painter has only done "as well as it was possible" (10–11). Nonetheless, the comparison is a testament both to the skill of the artist (as evidenced by Pyrocles's interest) and the beauty of the figure represented. However, instead of describing "her beauties" in words, the ekphrasis that follows probes beyond external "show," allowing a glimpse "therein" to a realm of interiority—her "bashfulness, love, and reverence." The emphatic interjection "and all by the cast of her eye" remarks on the elusive ability of the painting to convey a narrative of cause and effect stemming from a realm of subjectivity. These words emphasize the incredible power of expression of the visual image, an ekphrasis that heralds the deep capabilities of artistic representation.

The portrait painter has managed to render the *cause* of her grief—the burden of suspicion, presumably inspired by the prophecy—and this small revelation should give us pause because all of these remarkably communicated inner qualities are shrouded in the language of judgment: "a man might judge" Philoclea. By itself, the word "judge" might suggest a relatively benign register of meaning—"to form an opinion or conclusion about," to "appraise"[8]—or signal the prolepsis inherent in the act of prejudgment or bias. However, the word takes on a more legalistic cast when paired with the description of "virtue suspected."[9] The context reframes Pyrocles's role as judging viewer in a harsher light, emphasizing a different meaning of the verb—"to consider the case of (a person) in a court of law"; "to sit in judgment upon"; "to pronounce sentence upon."[10] When joined with the unexpected word "judge," the notion of suspicion suggests that both Philoclea and her image are on trial. But of what is Philoclea suspected? And by whom? The narrative's prophetic framework—"Thy younger shall with nature's bliss embrace / An uncouth love, which nature hateth most"—suggests that the voluntary exile of Basilius and his family was necessitated, in part, by Philoclea's assailable virtue. Does her portrait pose convey all this, or does she merely cast a grieving eye as she predicts herself the uncomfortable subject of such future voyeuristic gawking? Despite the depth of the visual reproduction, the description admits a fair amount of doubt, and the flicker of the young woman on trial is reinforced by Pyrocles's juridical recourse to "fall into questions of her."

In keeping with the climate of adjudication, Pyrocles is "desirous to see herself, to be judge, forsooth, of the painter's cunning" (11). An aesthetic judgment of the painter shades into a moral judgment of the subject and back again, making spectatorship into a juridical activity. Falling in love and falling into questions become mutually entailed, and both states inspire Pyrocles's plans for future action—he will go in search of his new love. The sentence that announces this plan, however, is constructed via reversal: we might expect Pyrocles to want to see Philoclea because he has fallen in love at first (painted) sight, but instead, the narrator suggests that finding her will allow

---

8. *Oxford English Dictionary* (hereafter *OED*), s.v. "judge, *v.*," def. 1a.

9. For a discussion of suspicion in this period more generally, see Lorna Hutson, *The Invention of Suspicion: Law and Mimesis in Shakespeare and Renaissance Drama* (Oxford: Oxford University Press, 2007).

10. See *OED*, s.v. "judge, *v.*," def. 7a.

him to "judge" the painting. Pyrocles's viewing of this painting spurs a great deal of narrative activity: he falls in love and infiltrates the Arcadian camp disguised as an Amazon with a not-so-stealthy pseudonym, Cleophila. The painting pushes the plot forward toward the fulfillment of the prophecy, but Sidney's wording—"desirous to see herself, to be judge, forsooth, of the painter's cunning"—suggests that all this movement forward actually happens in the service of looking back.

In reinforcing the context of judgment that will organize a retrospective future, Pyrocles also raises a question about an unexpectedly vulnerable component of subjectivity that complicates the painter's cunning: is a self consistent over time? In the ekphrasis, Philoclea's exalted "nature" only stays pure for a few words before it is "mixed" with "grief." By dubbing that grief "sweet," the description admits the possibility that the mixing muddies the waters of Philoclea's virtue. Presumably it is her inner goodness that makes even her sadness lovely, but the description also flashes the more sinister suggestion that she takes pleasure in painful scrutiny. If her "bashfulness, love, and reverence" can be undone by the "cast of her eye," then the ekphrasis calls into question whether the inner "beauties" captured on canvas are actually *just* "show." Though the painting is never mentioned again, Pyrocles's view of it highlights both the unsettling nature of interiority and the possibility that art boasts unique access to that interiority. In linking an anticipated future (Pyrocles finding Philoclea) to an evaluative look back ("to be judge, forsooth, of the painter's cunning"), Sidney adds to the prophecy's concern a question about the relationship between subjectivity and temporality. At the same time, his characters struggle to reconcile the volatile passion they confront with the heroic constancy they crave, and they turn to art in search of that same stasis.

The convention of the oracle, and its inevitable misinterpretation, set the reader's expectations for the future of the narrative.[11] However circuitous the road to the prophecy's reconciliation might be, because of it, the romance begins with a tacit narrative promise: the story will follow the trajectory of a (murky) future foretold, thus removing the indeterminacy of future action at a basic level. Likewise, the painting of Philoclea implicitly promises a real Philoclea sufficiently stunning to twist Cupid's arrow even deeper into

---

11. See Michael McCanles, "Oracular Prediction and the Fore-Conceit of Sidney's *Arcadia*," *ELH* 50, no. 2 (1983): 240 for a discussion of the "mutual implication between constraint and freedom" inherent in the paradoxical "double status of the oracular text as both a priori fore-conceit and generator of actions within the plot." I would add to this that Sidney counts on the expectation—the prophecy demands its own fulfillment, but the ancient topos of the misleading (albeit true) oracle means that the future will include some unforeseen twists, just as it did in *Oedipus Rex*.

Pyrocles's heart.[12] Once Cleophila infiltrates Arcadia, however, the romance turns to trade in explicit promises. In the second book of the *Old Arcadia*, the narrator abruptly returns his attention to Philoclea: "But alas, sweet Philoclea, how hath my pen forgotten thee, since to thy memory principally all this long matter is intended" (95). Though the narrator exaggerates his neglect of Philoclea in suddenly claiming her to be the center of his story, he also blames the fallibility of his forgetful pen at a moment when she seems most attuned to the memory of her *own* pen. Up until Cleophila's arrival, we learn, Philoclea had lived a life entirely of virtue; she was a heroine "whose eyes and senses had received nothing but according as the natural course of each thing required, whose tender youth had obediently lived under her parents' behests without the framing (out of her own will) the forechoosing of anything" (95). She is so pure, in fact, that even when her desire is stirred by Cleophila, she remains "ignorant of her own disease, although (full well) she found herself diseased" (95). She comes to find these first pangs of love distressing, and the narrator recounts her visit to the "fair white marble stone" on which she wrote a set of verses "a few days before Cleophila's coming" (96). Philoclea sneaks out into the night:

> [G]oing with uncertain paces to a little wood, where many times before she had delighted to walk, her rolling eye lighted upon a tuft of trees, so closely set together as with the shade the moon gave through it, it bred a fearful devotion to look upon it. But well did she remember the place, for there had she often defended her face from the sun's rage, there had she enjoyed herself often while she was mistress of herself and had no other thoughts but such as might arise out of quiet senses. But the principal cause that made her remember it was a fair white marble stone that should seem had been dedicated in ancient time to the sylvan gods; which she finding there a few days before Cleophila's coming, had written these words upon it as a testimony of her mind against the suspicion she thought she lived in. The writing was this: (96)

---

12. When Cleophila finally encounters Philoclea, she more than exceeds the beauty promised by the painting. In fact this "ornament of the earth" so astonishes Cleophila that the narrator compares the faux Amazon to a piece of sculpture: "[S]he stood like a well wrought image, with show of life, but without all exercise of life, so forcibly had love transferred all her spirits into the present contemplation of the lovely Philoclea" (34). Curiously, Musidorus was similarly dumbstruck upon first seeing Pyrocles in his disguise: "[A]mazedly looking upon him (even as Apollo is painted when he saw Daphne suddenly turned to a laurel)" (16). Musidorus's reaction bears resemblance not just to the myth of Daphne and Apollo, but to a painted version of it. Cleophila elicits no such mediation—she is transformed without recourse to Ovid, much less to a painting of a scene out of Ovid, even though she mimics a metamorphosis into a work of art upon encountering the subject of painting in real life.

At this moonlit moment in the narrative, the reader hears of Philoclea's verses for the first time, and the narrator brings their occasion and purpose into view before reproducing the actual lines. Sidney withholds information from his reader in order to take full advantage of the scene's temporal complexity. He ensures that the verses are fully absorbed and contemplated before he reveals that, because of the interference of natural conditions, the marble stone is a palimpsest and Philoclea's verses have been destroyed.

Sidney's description of Philoclea's tentative visit sets up careful parallels between the exterior scene and Philoclea's internal struggles: night has replaced day such that a "walk" previously associated with "delight" now occasions "uncertain paces." The repetition of the word "remember" couches the visit to the inscription as a visit to the past; indeed, the verses provide a snapshot of an earlier moment—they were crafted *before* she fell in love. Yet even these past daytime visits, halcyon days of peaceful musings occasioned by "quiet senses," hinted at a violent prosecution, as when Philoclea "defended her face from the sun's rage." That she would write poetry as a "testimony of her mind against the suspicion she thought she lived in" suggests the appropriateness of legal analogy. In writing, she reveals her belief that her poetry can provide a defense and antidote to unjust judgment. The reference to the "suspicion she thought she lived in" echoes the earlier description of her portrait in which Pyrocles saw her "sweet grief to find her virtue suspected." Once again, it is in the context of artistic production that Philoclea confronts this perceived sleight. She intends her words to codify the contents of her mind, suggesting that poetry can do what the painting did—provide an outward show of interiority, and one that will provide written evidence or proof. Philoclea's verses, like her portrait, aspire to a poetics of stasis and constancy that Sidney's romance does not support.

Both the testimony and the suspicion of judgment, like the defense from the sun, usher in a vocabulary that seems better suited to a courtroom than to sylvan *poiesis*. Philoclea's verse is imbued with purpose because it aims to provide proof and to safeguard her from unjust suspicion. The word that the narrator uses to introduce her verses—"testimony"—suggests a poetics of advocacy and protest as she moves beyond "sweet grief" to a more active self-defense. Yet this diction is not terribly precise, since it seems simultaneously to invoke a range of valences—evidence, proof, written certification, confession, protestation;[13] it is a word that will, in fact, be turned against her

---

13. See *OED*, s.v. "testimony, *n.*," defs. 1a, 1b, 2, 5a, 5b. Perhaps ironically in this case, the word "testimony" can also refer to "the Mosaic law or decalogue as inscribed on the two tables of stone" (def. 4a).

on the very next page. Does this imprecision, this potential for multiplicity of meaning, stem from a misalignment of poetic and legal discourse? Even if the term is not entirely clear, it is evident that in writing this "testimony," Philoclea's secluded verses attempt a more public defense—she creates a display outside herself that will change external perception; the "testimony of her mind" aims to codify her innocence.

Notably, the "suspicion she thought she lived in" and Philoclea's counteracting "testimony" seem temporally out of sync with one another. Testimony is the province of the present moment—a way of accounting for a present or past misjudgment. In this context, however, suspicion is decidedly future-oriented—the scrutiny that Philoclea protests does not betray misgivings about some undiscovered past transgression, but rather assumes that her character will lead her to future sin. As a result, the narrator's introduction to the poem asks not how to defend poetry, a familiar Sidneian construct, but rather if poetry can provide a defense:

> Ye living powers enclosed in stately shrine
> Of growing trees, ye rural gods that wield
> Your sceptres here, if to your ears divine
> A voice may come which troubled soul doth yield,
>   This vow receive, this vow O gods maintain:
>   My virgin life no spotted thought shall stain.
>
> Thou purest stone, whose pureness doth present
> My purest mind; whose temper hard doth show
> My tempered heart; by thee my promise sent
> Unto myself let after-livers know.
>   No fancy mine, nor others' wrong suspect
>   Make me, O virtuous Shame, thy laws neglect.
>
> O Chastity, the chief of heav'nly lights,
> Which makes us most immortal shape to wear,
> Hold thou my heart, establish thou my sprites;
> To only thee my constant course I bear.
>   Till spotless soul unto thy bosom fly,
>   Such life to lead, such death I vow to die. (96)

In the poem, structured in three apostrophic stanzas—to the gods, to the marble stone, and to chastity respectively—what Philoclea offers looks not so much like testimony as it does a promise. In the course of eighteen lines, the word "vow" appears three times, and the word "promise" once, so Philoclea's poem brings her in line with the future-oriented nature of the "suspicion" she hopes to address. If the prophecy sets up an expectation that Philoclea will act badly, will "embrace / An uncouth love," then her "testimony" works not to establish her virtuous record, but rather to rewrite the future. Through a poetic promise, she vows not to transgress; she will ignore "fancy" and suspicion in order to uphold shame's "laws."

Sidney emphasizes the future-oriented structures at work in the narrative, and the promise provides a particular grammatical construct for establishing "the certainty of things to come." It aims to secure the future. Unlike a "prediction," which "expresses a belief about the possibility of a future event," a promise "or related declaration of volition . . . expresses [the speaker's] will for the realization of a future event."[14] A promise relies on the belief that present words can mandate future action; it constructs a reciprocal relationship between present and future as it negotiates the present's ability to control the future, and the future's obligation to take seriously the intentions and commitments of the present.[15] In a letter printed in 1592, Gabriel Harvey employs a proverb well known in Sidney's time—"Promise is debt: and I hadd rather perfourme, then promise any thinge"[16]—highlighting the obligation built into an assumed epistemic modality. The proverb—"Promise is debt"—encapsulates the accountability that the speech act both demands and offers.[17] In addition to introducing a legal framework by alluding to

---

14. Arnovick, *The Development of Future Constructions*, 91. Arnovick goes on to describe this distinction in terms of modality. For an argument that considers modality in Sidney's "theory of aesthetics" both as "a verbal construction and as the way of thinking about necessity and contingency that such a construction facilitates," see Julianne Werlin, "Providence and Perspective in Philip Sidney's *Old Arcadia*," *Studies in English Literature* 54, no. 1 (2014): 29. For a discussion of the historical distinction between an oath as something "sworn *by* God or one of his creatures" and a vow as something sworn "not *by* God but *to* God, or . . . to another person," see Kerrigan, "Shakespeare, Oaths and Vows," 69.

15. For the classic account of the distinction between the "illocutionary" and "perlocutionary" aspects of a speech act, see J. L. Austin, *How to Do Things with Words* (Oxford: Clarendon Press), 1962.

16. Gabriel Harvey, *Fovre Letters, and Certain Sonnets* (London, 1592), B4v. The letter is written to Christopher Bird.

17. Morris Palmer Tilley, *A Dictionary of the Proverbs in England in the Sixteenth and Seventeenth Centuries* (Ann Arbor: University of Michigan Press, 1950), 557. William Kerrigan points out a set of proverbs that reveal suspicion about promises, such as "All is not paid that is promised" (*Shakespeare's Promises* [Baltimore: Johns Hopkins University Press, 1999] 10). Still, the proverb Harvey uses also finds its way into a variety of Renaissance literature. For example, the second part of George Whetstone's *Promos and Cassandra* (London, 1578) opens with Polina saying: "Promise is debt, and I my

external judgment, Philoclea's poem communicates the proverbial seriousness of promising; she combines the modal, and even social, force of the promise with the sanctity of codification.

Philoclea's poetry suggests that the written word—inscribed on the stone's hard "temper"—leaves an enduring mark by which her actions can later be judged. The second stanza, addressed to the stone itself, works to collapse the distance between inner and outer, moral and physical, poetic content and its display. It reiterates the earlier parallels between the natural world and Philoclea's inner struggles—the daytime filled with carefree walking, and nighttime of uncertain paces. Yet the thought conveyed—"Thou purest stone, whose pureness doth present / My purest mind"—simultaneously draws two metaphors, both of which hinge on the verb "present." Despite the insistence on purity, the registers of the metaphor seem crisscrossed. On the one hand, the physical stone "presents" or displays her poem, yet the phrasing necessitates the collapse of her poem and her "purest mind." The poem, she implies, is synecdochal, a part that seamlessly stands for its creator. On the other hand, the elision of mind, thoughts, and poetry is extended because of a concomitant elision between presenting and representing. The stone is not relied on merely to display written words; that pure white surface is also already a physical representation of her "purest mind" even without any words. Philoclea draws a parallel between the unadulterated marble and her own inner purity only to write a poem on that marble that she claims is the unadulterated outpouring of her thoughts.

The word "temper" is even more slippery, and it stutters in the near-sonic doubling between "temper hard" and "tempered heart." The word carried a dizzying array of meanings in Sidney's time—a proportionate mixture of qualities or elements, fit condition, a middle course, a compromise, equanimity, character, quality, the particular degree of hardness and elasticity or resiliency imparted to steel by tempering.[18] Given the context, Philoclea presumably means that the hard, resilient easel—the stone—displays her poem.

---

vowe have past, / Andrugios Tombe, to wash with daylie teares" (G3r). George Gascoigne uses the phrase in the dedication to Eduardo Donati of his *Certain Notes of Instruction* (1575): "since promise is debt, and you (by the law of friendship) do burden me with a promise." George Gascoigne, "Certain Notes of Instruction (1575)," in *Sidney's "The Defence of Poesy" and Selected Renaissance Literary Criticism*, ed. Gavin Alexander (London: Penguin, 2004), 237. Henry Petowe's *Philochasander and Elanira* (London, 1599) takes up the phrase as a license for love: "Promise is debt and debt shalbe repayde, / Receaue thy dewe to kisse be not affrayde" (G1r). And in Richard Brathwaite's more serious poetic moment in *Love's Labyrinth*, Thisbe tells Pyramus that "[t]o that same treasure thou hast promis'd me, / promise is debt, it must be kept by thee" (in *A Strappado for the Diuell* [London, 1615], V1v).

18. See *OED*, s.v. "temper, *n.*," defs. 1, 2, 3, 4b, 5.

Yet her phrasing admits ambiguities that undermine her purpose. Though Philoclea conflates her inner life (represented this time by a vital organ) with her artistic production, the phrase "hard doth show" simultaneously communicates a secondary meaning: the difficulty of that display. Because it hosts her verse, the stone also shows something besides the poem she has inscribed upon it. Ironically, the complexities of these two metaphors of exchange between surface and substance introduce the part of the stanza that should be absolutely unambiguous—her promise to uphold shame's laws. The convoluted collapse of physical and emotional substance, and the purity of ideas they ought to communicate, jar with the straightforward mechanism of promising. Philoclea's verses, forged in the language of metaphor, representation, and ambiguity, call into question the effectiveness of poetic obligation: can poetry be promissory? And if it can, can it be so only by taking up the implication of Philoclea's repetition—that is, through the hardening of her heart?

In the first stanza, she begs the gods to "receive" and "maintain" her vow that her "virgin life no spotted thought shall stain." Though we later learn that she unequivocally means that even a "spotted thought" will compromise her sworn purity, the language of the commitment admits a slight duality. Her syntax allows for the suggestion that her "virgin life" will remain intact no matter what the content of her fantasies. The emphasis in either case is on the maintenance of her current state, one that makes the present and future uninterrupted and effectively indistinguishable. I argued earlier that the poem's promissory language afforded it a future orientation befitting the timing of suspicion. However, it is also the case that there are a number of temporalities operative in the poem. This is a poetics of maintenance—Philoclea makes a promise not because she wants a hold on the future per se, but rather because she wants the constancy of a perpetual present moment.[19] The second stanza, which also introduces explicitly promissory language, similarly emphasizes the continuity of present and future. Her promise stresses the equivalence of present and future, but the promise does not aim to fix a radically different future. Rather, it works to ensure that the future will look exactly like the present. This desired parity is underscored in the stargazing imagery of the third stanza. In the poem's final lines, Chastity is her guiding star, and it will hold her

---

19. Though in *Sir Philip Sidney: Rebellion in Arcadia* (New Brunswick, NJ: Rutgers University Press, 1979), Richard C. McCoy points out that rebellions and political plot points in the *Arcadia* lack "ideological clarity," he identifies constancy as the fiction's "principal virtue" and flags the "tension between constancy and change" as "one source of the work's extraordinary complexity" (40–42).

"constant course" even as she moves forward temporally. This stanza, which ostensibly discusses her life and death ("Such life to lead, such death I vow to die"), also participates in maintaining the status quo. That is, her vow does not suggest consequences—she will not die if she breaks her promise; rather, she vows to live *as is* until her clock runs out.

Thus, because of their ambiguity, Philoclea's verses undo the precision of the legal analogy they invoke. Likewise, the promissory structures that signal a grammatical interest in controlling the future do so in the hopes of maintaining a present moment, of entering into a kind of timelessness. As a result, the most jarring aspect of this poem is not its content or form, but its context. These lines appear in the narrative when Philoclea visits them because she has broken her promise, or, put another way, because the poetic present inscribed on the marble has encountered a radically different future. The narrative doubles this breached promise: though the verses are reproduced and offset in the prose narrative in the copy of the *Old Arcadia* that *we* read, it is only after we have read them that the narrator reveals that the ink has smudged (and the verses have been rendered illegible) within the world of the fiction. Philoclea's intended collapse of present and future in poetry fails at this point in the narrative. She revisits the verse knowing that her vows have already been broken, thus she does so as a very different kind of "after-liver" from the one she poetically imagined.

II

On the one hand, as I have just argued, Philoclea's poem toys with an ambiguity that complicates its supposedly straightforward content. On the other hand, against the backdrop of a legalistic vocabulary of "testimony" and "laws," Philoclea's employment of the words "promise" and "vow" lends her poem a contractual charge. The terms of such a contract prove somewhat tricky to untangle, since each stanza is a separate apostrophe, but taken as a whole her verses at least suggest a rhetoric of exchange. On her account, chastity will hold her heart, and the gods will "receive" and "maintain" her vow. The "purest stone" functions as both addressee and poetic receptacle, the physical manifestation of her inner feelings. In addition, the stone becomes the instrument of contract and exchange: "by thee my promise sent / Unto myself let after-livers know." Philoclea initiates a curious boomerang: she not only makes a promise, but also nominates herself as its recipient. She invokes the traditional components of contract—offer and acceptance—by specifying two parties to the transaction, yet she simultaneously collapses the categories by having one person play both roles; that is, she enters into a contract with herself.[20] As in the first stanza, she is keen to have her promise received, but why should the stone serve as middleman to the exchange? Why must a poetic promise to herself be codified at all? The end of the line offers some explanation, and also works to bring her verses even further in line with the temporal requirements of "others' wrong suspect." In promising, she employs the future-oriented language of obligation, and relies on the stone both to communicate her commitment and to bolster it with physical permanence. These future-oriented gestures are reinforced by her mention of a future audience of "after-livers." The poem's promissory language furnishes a formalism that indicates a contractual act. The combination of proleptic language and a readership in perpetuity rolls the "after-livers" familiar to the topos of poetic immortality into the construct of contract.

Philoclea's appeals to both promise and contract resonate with a set of legal questions that surrounded the act of promising in Sidney's lifetime. While "Promise is debt" may have been a popular proverb, in the years leading up to and following the composition of the *Old Arcadia*, the common law courts in England were sorting out the reverse proposition: did debt necessarily signal an implied promise? In one well-documented case, a man named John Slade sued

---

20. The notion of a self-reflexive contract seems particularly apt given that it is Philoclea's inviolate body—her virginity—under consideration. Along these lines, her choice of wording bears comparison to novitiate vows, though the first post-Reformation English convent is not established until 1598. In her headnote "Sister Joan Seller, English Nun's Oath of Obedience (1631)," in *Reading Early Modern Women: An Anthology of Texts in Manuscript and Print, 1550–1700*, ed. Helen Ostovich and Elizabeth Sauer (New York: Routledge, 2004), 145–47, Caroline Bowden reproduces one example: an oath of obedience signed by Sister Joan Seller in 1631 upon joining an English Benedictine convent in Flanders. Bowden points out the force of this "solemn profession," which "defines the parameters of her life for the next fifty years," and the oath stands out for its overwhelming proportion of bureaucracy to promissory content. The oath itself, simple if not pro forma in style, comprises less than two of the eight lines: "I Sister Joan Seller . . . Promise before God and his Saints, Povertie, Chastitie and Obedience, and Conversion of my maners, according to the Rule of our most holie Father Saint Bennett" (145–47). Additional contemporary examples exist in both Latin and in the nun's own hand, but in Seller's case, Bowden suggests that the "choice of English for the language of her profession was a deliberate attempt to involve her in the words of the promise" (145), and ascribes the oath's most personal quality not to its content but to its vernacularity. Lawrence Anderton's *The English Nunne* (1642), despite deeming "*Mariage to be honourable*, but . . . Virginity to be *more honourable*" (A2v), does not seem much impressed by Philoclea's poem. Anderton appeals to his imagined female reader by means of the "greedines" with which they would read his book if it "were a second *Syr Philip Sidneys Arcadia*, treating of amourous Conceyts" (A6r). According to Anderton, both books treat love, but Sidney's concerns "sensuall and *vayne Loue*, attended on with sinne, and Repentance," while his figures "chast, and *holy Loue*, whereby a *Soule* by solemne vow espouseth herselfe to *Christ* her Bridegroome" (A6v).

Humphrey Morley over the sale of "wheat and rye": Morley had agreed to pay Slade for his crop by a particular date in 1595. When Morley did not produce the money, Slade sued him not for the debt itself, but rather for damages, claiming that a promise had been breached.[21] With Edward Coke arguing for the plaintiff and Francis Bacon representing the defense, *Slade's Case* (1595–1602) was for many years considered "the watershed of English contract law."[22]

Though Sidney did devote some time to the study of law,[23] I consider the legal climate leading up to *Slade's Case* not to suggest that Sidney directly engaged with emerging contract theory or judicial debate in his fiction, but rather to highlight questions and tensions over the adjudication of debt and the conditions of contract that had been brewing for over half a century. They bespeak the complexity of structures of future-oriented obligation and the attention with which promises were discussed and emphasized at the time of the *Old Arcadia*'s composition. In the common law courts, three important concerns interlocked: the status of a promise when making a bargain; the timing involved in such promises; and the legal mechanisms, still developing, that might lay the "secret sanctuary of the [individual] conscience" open to "public tests."[24] In recent years, literary critics have shown interest in *Slade's Case*, but they have done so almost exclusively in the service of analyzing early modern drama. Yet the debates and common law court politics that culminated in *Slade's Case* draw attention to questions that were also crucial to poetic representation. A promissory poem such as Philoclea's combines issues of intentionality, temporality, and future fixity intrinsic to the commissive speech act with the lyric preoccupation with poetic expression and the challenges inherent in publishing thought.[25]

---

21. See David Harris Sacks, "The Promise and the Contract in Early Modern England: Slade's Case in Perspective," in *Rhetoric and Law in Early Modern Europe*, ed. Victoria Kahn and Lorna Hutson (New Haven, CT: Yale University Press, 2001), 31.

22. David Ibbetson, "Sixteenth Century Contract Law: *Slade's Case* in Context," *Oxford Journal of Legal Studies* 4, no. 3 (1984): 295. For Coke's account, see *English Reports*, vol. 76 (Edinburgh: William Green and Sons, 1907), 4 *Reports* 91a–95b. In the past fifty years, some legal historians have begun to question how pathbreaking the case actually was; see Ibbetson, 295. J. H. Baker initiated further scrutiny of the case in "New Light on *Slade's Case*: Part I—The Manuscript Review," *Cambridge Law Journal* 29, no. 1 (1971): 51–67. He particularly urges the "detailed analysis and study" of an "enormous mass of unpublished material" (51). See also Luke Wilson, *Theaters of Intention: Drama and the Law in Early Modern England* (Stanford, CA: Stanford University Press, 2000), 70–71 and 81–82.

23. See Brian C. Lockey, *Law and Empire in English Renaissance Literature* (Cambridge: Cambridge University Press, 2006); and Alan Stewart, *Philip Sidney: A Double Life* (London: Chatto & Windus, 2000).

24. Sacks, "The Promise and the Contract," 41.

25. For a discussion about promises and commissive speech acts, see John R. Searle, *Speech Acts: An Essay in the Philosophy of Language* (Cambridge: Cambridge University Press, 1969).

Sidney famously outlined such difficulties of acts of creation by fallen humans in his *Defence of Poesy*:

> Neither let it be deemed too saucy a comparison to balance the highest point of man's wit with the efficacy of nature; but rather give right honour to the heavenly Maker of that maker, who having made man to His own likeness, set him beyond and over all the works of that second nature: which in nothing he showeth so much as in poetry, when with the force of a divine breath he bringeth things forth surpassing her doings—with no small arguments to the incredulous of that first accursed fall of Adam, since our erected wit maketh us know what perfection is, and yet our infected will keepeth us from reaching unto it.[26]

The distance between the "erected wit" and "infected will" emblematizes the difficulty between knowledge and its representation. By combining this challenge, often raised in terms of poetics, with the problematic of promising, Philoclea's poem takes up the same concerns at stake in the adjudication of credit disputes in the early modern marketplace: intention, obligation, permanence, and exchange.

As Muldrew argues, the rapid expansion of market transactions meant that early modern society relied on elaborate social and economic credit networks.[27] In a climate of increased market activity, routine sales and exchanges could not reasonably function through formalized, codified contracts because the acquisition of a sealed bond was both time-consuming and expensive. Instead, contracts could be made more informally through oral, or "parol," agreements, which had the advantage of simplicity and immediacy, but the disadvantage of insecurity in instances of dispute. It was difficult to prove not only the circumstances of execution or default, but also the existence of the original bargain. Muldrew records that between 1550 and 1580, "disputes caused levels of litigation initiated over unfulfilled obligations to rise to hundreds of thousands of suits per annum."[28] In actions of debt, the common law courts allowed defendants to "wage their law"; this practice, more formally known as the doctrine of compurgation, automatically ruled for the defendant if he brought witnesses to swear on his behalf.[29]

---

26. Sir Philip Sidney, "The Defence of Poesy," in *Sir Philip Sidney*, ed. Katherine Duncan-Jones (Oxford: Oxford University Press, 1994), 106.
27. Muldrew, *Economy of Obligation*, passim.
28. Ibid., 3. Yet despite these staggering numbers, Muldrew also points out that the expense of litigation was a deterrent to many (202).
29. J. H. Baker, "New Light on *Slade's Case*: Part II," *Cambridge Law Journal* 29, no. 2 (1971): 219; and Ibbetson, "Sixteenth-Century Contract Law," 311.

Since "most actions on simple contracts were brought for comparatively small sums" and concerned "debts which had probably been contracted by word of mouth," they faced "genuine difficulties of proof."[30] As a result, a dispute occasioned by a private bargain by two parties could be settled by calling forth "compurgators" to attest not to the relevant details, but rather to the general character of the defendant. The preeminence of reputation over proof grew out of the assumption both that honest character was a vital component to social standing in economic transactions, and that witnesses would not perjure themselves. Yet because bringing witnesses to a centralized court was both inconvenient and impractical, "professional wagermen" were often hired instead.[31]

Despite the potential for "abuse by false testimony from paid strangers," decisions from at least the 1530s emphasized the importance of the promise and the sacrosanct nature of promissory, contractual obligation.[32] Moreover, since approximately 1540, if a debtor had promised to pay a debt subsequent to the making of his original bargain, the courts would grant the action of *assumpsit*, since a contract had been broken.[33] *Assumpsit*, meaning "he undertook; he promised," refers to a

> promise or engagement by which one person assumes or undertakes to do some act or pay something to another.... A common law form of action which lies for the recovery of damages for the non-performance of a parol or simple contract; or a contract that is neither of record nor under seal.[34]

In the 1560s and following, cases involving "broken credit arrangements" were increasingly being brought to court as *assumpsit*, or as officially entered into the records, as "trespass on the case."[35] In other words, creditors increasingly opted not to file suit to recover debt, but rather sought damages for breach of contract. Legal historians have long attributed the rise in instances of suits of *assumpsit* over actions of debt to the plaintiffs' desire to avoid wager of law.[36]

The response to actions of *assumpsit* in matters of debt remained unsettled in the common law courts for some sixty years, because the two central

---

30. Baker, "Part II," 229.
31. Baker, "Part II," 228–30; Muldrew, *Economy of Obligation*, 206.
32. Muldrew, 206. Muldrew quotes legal arguments about promises, such as a "Serjeant" before Common Pleas who states that "the strongest thing which is against justice is to break a covenant which is a faithful promise" (*Economy of Obligation*, 209).
33. Muldrew, *Economy of Obligation*, 207; Wilson, *Theaters of Intention*, 76.
34. Henry Campbell Black, *Black's Law Dictionary*, 6th ed. (St. Paul: West Publishing, 1990), 122.
35. Muldrew, *Economy of Obligation*, 207.
36. See Baker, "Part II," 228.

courts that heard such cases at Westminster, King's Bench, and Common Pleas faced the problem that an unfulfilled debt might occasion two different forms of legal action.[37] If the action of debt was available and applicable, could a plaintiff pursue *assumpsit* instead?[38] The courts held that if a debtor had promised to pay his debt subsequent to making the bargain, then the courts could justify an action of *assumpsit,* since a contract had been broken.[39] However, from the 1560s, the approaches at King's Bench and Common Pleas differed: Common Pleas required proof of a subsequent promise, whereas King's Bench maintained that because the debt arose from a transaction, the promise was implied.[40] Luke Wilson has described the difference at issue between Common Pleas and King's Bench in terms of timing: "If you have a promise you have an interval [between promise and performance]; if you have an interval it becomes relevant to ask if there has been a promise."[41] The question of a promise and its timing remained central throughout the latter half of the sixteenth century. As Bacon argued in *Slade's Case*, an action of debt, not *assumpsit*, was appropriate because a bargain was *executed* as soon as it was made. In other words, making a bargain enacted an exchange, leaving only the logistical matter of delivering goods or monies to their new, rightful owner. To argue for *assumpsit*, on the other hand, implied that the bargain was *executory*—a promise that still needed to be performed—whereby the debt itself signaled a breach of promise.[42] In differing in their requirements

---

37. For a discussion about "objection[s] to overlapping remedies," see A. W. B. Simpson, *A History of the Common Law of Contract: The Rise of the Action of Assumpsit* (Oxford: Clarendon Press, 1975), 283–86. For a history of the differences between the two courts, including their power struggles and respective worries about revenue, as well as the legal maneuvering by which King's Bench was able to hear cases of debt in the first place, see J. H. Baker, *An Introduction to English Legal History*, 4th ed. (London: Reed Elsevier, 2002), 37–47.

38. See Ibbetson, "Sixteenth Century Contract Law," 303.

39. Muldrew, *Economy of Obligation*, 207; Wilson, *Theaters of Intention*, 76, Ibbetson, "Sixteenth Century Contract Law," 296.

40. This was not a matter of semantics: as Coke asked in 1597, "Would you have every plain man use the proper words 'I assume' and 'I take upon myself'? It is not necessary. If he says 'I promise' or 'I agree' it is as much as and all one," as qtd. in Baker, "Part I," 56n27. Legal historians make the same point: see Ibbetson, "Sixteenth Century Contract Law," 308; and Baker, "Part II," 227. In other words, it was not necessary to utter a particular phrase to indicate that a promise had been made. The difference between the two courts actually rested on jury instructions, that is, on whether or not the jury would need to be persuaded that a promise had been proved (Ibbetson, "Sixteenth Century Contract Law," 299). Moreover, the jury was faced with the task of assigning damages in cases of *assumpsit*, and some legal experts even worried that juries might assign damages of lesser value than the debt underlying the breached contract (Ibbetson, 309n83).

41. Wilson, *Theaters of Intention*, 80. See also Baker, "Part II," 214, in which he describes it as a matter of "tense."

42. As Bacon reportedly argued in 1602, "[A] contract is not a ground for action on the case. For action on the case must be grounded on deceit or breach of promise, but in debt on a contract

for proof of a subsequent promise to sue in *assumpsit*, the courts highlighted the question of timing by effectively asking whether or not the promise in any such transaction was implied.[43]

Although the eventual decision, in favor of Slade and the suit of *assumpsit*, is often cited as the foundation of modern contract law, the climate over this course of decades indicates that perspectives on the timing and force of a promise were in flux and a source of lively debate. Indeed, such discussions were operative beyond the courtroom: Wilson notes that "contract-related terms like assumpsit and consideration appear with striking frequency in the nontechnical literature of the period."[44] More significantly, the extension of *assumpsit* to cases concerning debt signaled a larger shift that resulted in a situation whereby "promissory liability" might be extended "into areas previously outside the scope of the common law."[45] Ultimately, through judgments on *Slade's Case*, the justices "agreed first that the making of a simple contract was simultaneously the making of a promise," and understood executory agreements as "agreements requiring the future performance of their terms."[46] The decades of legal dispute over both subsequent and express promises as well as matters of tense and timing help to illuminate the link between poetry and accountability that Sidney draws when he introduces and reproduces Philoclea's poem only to reveal that her contract has been broken.[47]

---

there is no deceit or breach of promise supposed. For a bargain is in any manner a thing executed and not executory as an *assumpsit* is. For a bargain changes the property of each part, and therefore in action of debt it is alleged that the defendant detains the money or thing demanded as if it were his before; to wit, that the plaintiff had the property of it by the contract" (as qtd. in Baker, "Part I," 60.)

43. Wilson, *Theaters of Intention*, 81. See also Ibbetson, "Sixteenth Century Contract Law," 297, 315; and Wilson, *Theaters of Intention*, 78–81

44. Wilson, *Theaters of Intention*, 71. In *Spenser's Legal Language: Law and Poetry in Early Modern England* (Cambridge: D. S. Brewer, 2007), Andrew Zurcher provides a tally of selected legal terms in a handful of poetic texts. His comparison of Edmund Spenser's *The Faerie Queene*, Geoffrey Chaucer's *Works*, Sidney's *Arcadia*, John Harington's translation of *Orlando Furioso*, and Edward Fairfax's translation of *Godfrey of Bulloigne* reveals that Sidney's romance "provides the closest match for Spenser's technical diction," yet he contends that "Sidney does not demonstrate the same multi-level use of legal diction . . . as Spenser" (79). Spenser might well have employed more technical terms than Sidney, but my analysis proceeds contra Zurcher's claim that this indicates a relative lack of interest "in legal process and theory" on Sidney's part, even if he "resort[s] to legal diction fairly superficially in explicitly legal narrative" (79). See esp. Zurcher, 77–80.

45. Simpson, *A History of the Common Law of Contract*, 316.

46. Sacks, "The Promise and the Contract," 33.

47. Philoclea's emphasis on contractual obligation in matters of chastity and virtue proves prescient—in the seventeenth century, disputes over contract often focused on arrangements for betrothal and marriage. Henry Swinburne, for example, writes about the difference between *de futuro* and *de praesenti* marriage contracts at the beginning of the seventeenth century. Swinburne favored the *de praesenti* contract, preferring a present engagement to a future one, a distinction that generated

III

At the end of Philoclea's poem, which the narrator introduced without qualification ("the writing was this:"), we learn that our heroine actually has not yet arrived at the stone, the first in a series of narratorial dissimulations in the episode. Philoclea approaches the verses only *after* her poem has been reproduced in our text. The single sentence that intervenes between the narrator's reproduction of the verses and Philoclea's arrival at them warrants particular attention:

> But now that her memory served as an accuser of her change, and that her own hand-writing was there to bear testimony of her fall, she went in among the few trees, so closed in the top together as they seemed a little chapel; and there might she by the moonlight perceive the goodly stone which served as an altar in that woody devotion. (96–97)

Sidney's sentence employs a legal language that emphasizes the disjunction between the inscribed poetic promise, now broken, and Philoclea's current state of mind. Practically speaking, Philoclea has little need to reread the verses; the fact that her memory can play prosecutor renders her journey to the marble stone redundant, since she already knows she has breached her poetic contract.[48] The initial notion that poetry might provide a defense—the "testimony of her mind against the suspicion she thought she lived in"—has given way, as reflected in the new tenor of the word "testimony": "her own hand-writing" serves to "bear testimony of her fall." As I argued earlier, the poem itself effected a collapse between interiority and its seamless poetic display, enacted through the parallel that Philoclea drew between her mind and heart and the substance of her poetic tablet. These pressure points remain active as the narrator suggests that the force of the indictment stems from her codified words, precipitating a judgment of increased severity—memory merely accuses "change," while the inscribed words "bear testimony" of a "fall," suggesting that the physical manifestation of the verses is even more damning than the memory or recitation of their content.

---

legal opinion, engendered by temporal concerns, divided about how to establish a hierarchy between the contracting of actual and intended action. See Victoria Kahn, "Margaret Cavendish and the Romance of Contract," *Renaissance Quarterly* 50, no. 2 (1997): 534n17.

48. The sympathetic reader might be inclined to see Philoclea's "change" as a minor infraction, the normal course of love and desire. But Philoclea's reaction to her verses shows definitively that her interpretation allows no room for ambiguity: the "constant course" her verses pledged specified that her "virgin life no spotted thought shall stain," so even daydreams driven by love and desire occasion indictment.

Philoclea's poem pairs the difficulty of poetic representation with the burden of eventual performance inherent in the vow and promise. Yet the verses, filled as they were with utterances of proleptic force, unexpectedly communicated a desire for stasis, for a future moment that would be indistinguishable from the present. It is precisely the destruction of this fantasy of timelessness—the rupture that has occurred between present and future—that occasions Philoclea's return. In this reckoning, contrary to the vision of temporality imagined in her poetry, Philoclea revisits her verses as the representative of an unexpected future. Though only a few days have passed, she is now one of the "after-livers" that her poem anticipated. This future, actually the present moment from the reader's perspective, is characterized by review and judgment, and despite her employment of vows and promises, her writing turns out to be devoid of predictive or contracting force. As a result, a poem that struggled to define selfhood by linking the heart and mind to their poetic representation now prompts a return that exposes selfhood as a temporal concern.

The prominence of the link between temporality and selfhood inheres in the contractual aspect of her poetic promise. The lines "by thee my promise sent / Unto myself" cast Philoclea as both promisor and promisee, engaging herself on both sides of a contractual exchange as she provides both offer and acceptance. Her revisitation, however, raises a crucial question: did she send that promise to a present self, to a future self, or to both? According to the logic of her rhetoric of stasis and timelessness, the distinction ought to be irrelevant. However, despite her intentions, she breaks the contract as the result of "change." Her poem implies she sent the promise to her present self, since she names "after-livers" separately, suggesting two distinct parties. At the same time, this distinction compromises the promissory force of the bargain even as it is being made: despite her promissory language, rigid legal framework, and gesture to "after-livers," she fails to foresee the consequences that promising has for a future self precisely because she does not acknowledge that a future self might be predicated on difference. Even given her atemporal fantasy, the act of promising aims to control a future self. In other words, she does not distinguish between present and future within her own lifetime.

Within the narrative, the appearance of the poem necessarily signifies crisis—the contract has already been breached. And as much as Philoclea's poem tries to nail down the relationship between thought and its outward, testimonial expression, her assumption that these are equal, despite the poem's hiccups, mirrors a temporal collapse between a transaction *executed* and *executory*. The things that she took for granted in her poem return to work against her when she faces the reckoning of time, which makes manifest how alien her own handwriting looks from the vantage of her current perspective. Through Philoclea, Sidney works out a change of heart—the difference between temporal registers—based on a confrontation with promissory poetry. In so doing, he sets side by side two competing versions of permanence. The familiar problem of poetic representation—inner and outer—combines with the implicit temporal rigidity of promises to highlight a distinction between thought and its manifestation in words. The trouble arises when the permanence of words, as enduring emblems of self-incrimination, clashes with the impermanent feelings they represent. If poetry struggles to make interiority manifest, what does it mean if that interiority is subject to change? If Philoclea's own signature can "bear testimony" against her, then words, even promissory ones, do little to ensure permanence against the ravages of time.

The promise proves a particularly apt emblem for the challenges of poetic representation. Philoclea's "uncertain paces" may have been prompted by the memory of her verses or the knowledge of a broken contract, but the emphasis that the verses themselves and the language surrounding their revisitation puts on the difficulty of certain expression invokes a culture of insecurity and suspicion. As a result, both the promissory and the poetic undermine the proverbial simplicity of the moral imperative to keep one's word. Indeed, in the sixteenth century, justifications for promise breaking abounded even if such breaches were routinely said to endanger one's very soul. Casuistic discourse, to name but one poignant example, stressed the "quality of the intention" of a promise as "something visible to God alone."[49] Though a performative speech act, the promise could not guarantee delivery of its terms, and, even more disconcerting, could not even reliably guarantee intention. In other words, a promise did not necessarily indicate anything about interiority. The threat of deceit and the inscrutability of conscience shaped concerns and developments in the common law, as evidenced by one of Coke's myriad arguments in favor of *assumpsit*, which championed the eradication of wager of law in an effort to save the souls of would-be perjurers.[50] Christopher St. German, author of one of the most influential source texts for early modern common law, writes that

> no accyon can lye ... vpon suche promyses for yt ys secrete in hys owne conscyence whether he entendyd for to be bounde or naye. And of the entent inwarde in the herte: mannes lawe can not Juge and that ys one of the causes why the lawe of god ys necessary (that is to saye) to Juge inwarde thynges.[51]

---

49. Katharine Eisaman Maus, *Inwardness and Theater in the English Renaissance* (Chicago: University of Chicago Press, 1995), 21.

50. See Baker, "Part II," 228. As Wilson puts it, "the period in question is clearly one during which ways of thinking about time, intention, and the person, both in the law and in the culture at large, were undergoing a relatively rapid transformation" (*Theaters of Intention*, 82).

51. Christopher St. German, *Doctor and Student*, ed. T. F. T. Plucknett and J. L. Barton, Publications of the Selden Society 91 (London: Selden Society, 1974), 230.

Indeed, the inability to make conscience manifest influenced the debates over the adjudication of debt and contract. If a bargain of exchange is considered an *executory* agreement, then the law acknowledges that the contract governs an *intention* to act. In establishing a future commitment, whether implied or express, the law was also deciding if a defendant was guilty of deceit.[52]

English legal history suggests that the philosophical ground between the unreachable interiority of promissory intention and conscience and an action that accused a defendant of deceit informed the development of the doctrine of consideration, which

> for a promise meant the factors which the promisor considered when he promised, and which moved or motivated his promising. . . . The essence of the doctrine of consideration, then, is the adoption by the common law of the idea that the legal effect of a promise should depend upon the factor or factors which motivated the promise.[53]

Although consideration eventually becomes a sine qua non for contracts, in Sidney's day it was still a nascent doctrine.[54] David Harris Sacks argues that consideration functioned to negotiate between the private interiority of intention and conscience, and the public act of contracting:

> Consideration made the forming of a contract simultaneously the yielding of a promise to meet the obligations it entailed. It mediated between the will to do a thing and the actions by which that will was accomplished, moving parol agreements from the inner world of the parties' intentions, where conscience alone bound them, to the outward world of enforceable obligations.[55]

Thus while a promise uttered did not guarantee its speaker's motives, consideration attempted to codify the obligation to fulfill a contract. It functioned

---

52. See Simpson, *A History of the Common Law of Contract*, 222–25, 409 for a discussion of nonfeasance and misfeasance.

53. Simpson, *A History of the Common Law of Contract*, 321.

54. See, for example, *OED*, s.v. "consideration, *n*.," def. 6. In his period handbook of legal terms, John Cowell describes consideration as "the materiall cause of a contract, without the which no contract bindeth. This consideration is either expressed, as if a man bargain to giue 20.shillings for a horse:or els implyed, as when the law it selfe inforceth a consideration; as if a man come into a common Inne, and there staying sometime, taketh both meat and lodging, or either for himselfe and his horse:the lawe presumeth, that he intendeth to pay for both, though nothing be farder couenanted betweene him and his host:and therefore if he discharge not the house, the host may stay his horse." John Cowell, *The Interpreter* (Cambridge, 1607), R4v.

55. Sacks, "The Promise and the Contract," 41. See also J. L. Barton, "The Early History of Consideration," *Law Quarterly Review* 85 (1969): 373 and 377, who discusses the extent to which consideration arose because of questions of deceit.

as an establishment of quid pro quo, and, in so doing, distinguished a contract as a two-party exchange, rather than a one-sided "nude contract," or legally unenforceable promise.[56]

In the *Old Arcadia*, though Philoclea breaks her promise, it is the narrator who seems guilty of deceit. For even as Philoclea's poem might make us wonder how the doctrine of consideration touches a change in the factors that originally motivated a promise, the narrator's next sentence reveals that the verses have been rendered illegible. Philoclea finally reaches the stone only to find that

> neither the light was enough to read the words, and the ink was already foreworn and in many places blotted; which as she perceived, 'Alas,' said she, 'fair marble, which never receivedst spot but by my writing, well do these blots become a blotted writer; but pardon her which did not dissemble then, although she have changed since. Enjoy, and spare not, the glory of thy nature which can so constantly bear the marks of my inconstancy!' (97)

After so much concern about outward show, we learn that the bold statement that "[t]he writing was this" was sleight of hand. In fact, the lines we have just read exist *only* in the *Old Arcadia*, that is, *only* in the text we are reading. Whereas at the beginning of the episode it was the narrator's "pen" that had "forgotten" Philoclea by failing to give her the immortalizing attention she deserved, now actual writing seems ephemeral except in memory. After all this buildup, and an unqualified recreation of the poem, the narrator introduces a set of verses only to take them away. Sidney wants to have it both ways—the general category of permanence is heightened because the poem has disappeared. Thus all the questions about obligation and codification must be reexamined in the absence of material proof.[57] Sidney reveals that the physical verses have been damaged only after he has insisted that the physical verses codify an undisputed intent that has since changed. Thus the uncertainty about interiority and conscience in promising gives way to an examination of temporality, revision, and change. The emphasis on the

---

56. See Muldrew, *Economy of Obligation*, 207; and Barton, "The Early History of Consideration," 372–73. In *Slade's Case*, Morley's plea was based on his claim that he had not made a "separate promise," but rather a "'simple contract' with Slade" (Sacks, "The Promise and the Contract," 31).

57. Holmes discusses the use of the wax seal as a means of indisputable authentication in real estate transactions in the early modern period. Whereas medieval law held that "an instrument ceased to be operative as a sealed instrument if the seal fell off or was eaten by mice," this was no longer the case by the late sixteenth century. He cites a 1588 case in which "debt on an obligation" holds despite the mischievous murine activity. This is perhaps evidence of a change in thought about commitment and its physical form. See Eric Mills Holmes, "Stature and Status of a Promise under Seal as a Legal Formality," *Willamette Law Review* 29, no. 4 (1993): 630n45.

ephemerality of the written word is heightened by the perfect, offset reproduction of the verses in Sidney's own text.

At the same time, the physical trouble seems to stem from a natural intervention: it is too dark to read the verses; they are "foreworn" and "blotted," suggesting either an erasure due to rain or perhaps a marble incapable of holding ink on its surface. Whatever the reason, the natural world seems to exonerate Philoclea by removing the physical remains of a promise no longer appropriate to its circumstances.[58] In fact, nature's attempt to erase the obligations on Philoclea's slate takes consideration in an unexpected direction: do the motivating factors of a promise withstand the test of time? Even in the absence of physical evidence, however, Philoclea does not read the compromised verses as a release from her contract. Rather, she ascribes to the palimpsest a communicative force equal to the poem itself: she maintains her stance that the stone provides a physical reflection of her inner state—"these blots become a blotted writer"—and claims that writing both reflects her soul and sullies the stone.

Philoclea's initial vision of the future was predicated on the hope that the present and the future would be indistinguishable, and her promise and vows sought to ensure that. With the promise broken, Philoclea holds herself accountable, but also asks for leniency, hoping the stone will "pardon her which did not dissemble then, although she have changed since." Sidney carefully insists that the conflict stems not from faulty original intentions, but rather from a future that has turned out differently than supposed: her language reiterates the veracity of her original, true promise—she "did not dissemble then." Philoclea's forward-looking poetry arrives at a future that needs to account for and deal with the effects of possibility and change. As expected, the future is characterized by revision and review, and she requires "pardon" precisely because the human world in time functions differently than her linguistic constructs, undergirded though they are with a diction that holds out a false hope of permanence and fixity. The idea that a marble stone might "constantly bear" legible marks of character seems even more naive and unlikely by the dim light in which the future is reached and reassessed as a present moment. Though both Philoclea and the narrator insist she made her promise in good faith, her dilemma still circles around the problem of intent: she questions whether or not she remains accountable to her initial feelings even though her circumstances have changed.[59]

---

58. Sidney suggests precisely this kind of natural equivalence earlier in the text through the language of decorum in his initial, rather ungenerous, description of Miso: "Neither inwardly nor outwardly was there anything good in her but that she observed decorum, having in a wretched body a froward mind" (27).

59. The narrative makes possible the notion that the verses disappear *because* she has broken her promise, a kind of sympathetic magic that upholds her intended action. However, Philoclea treats physical erasure as both an impediment and an opportunity to demonstrate the steadfastness of her inner conscience.

IV

As Sidney slowly reveals information about poetry's physical condition in Arcadia, he also places characters' memories and his own codex manuscript in apposition.[60] Despite the crisis of the illegibility and ephemerality of writing, Philoclea's distressed instinct is to compose more verses. Sidney's description tags the creative impulse as both organic and unstoppable: "And herewith hiding her eyes awhile with her soft hands, there came into her head certain verses which, if the light had suffered, she would fain presently have adjoined as a retractation to the other" (97). In keeping with her previous choice of medium, Philoclea's crisis produces poetry, which in turn reveals an unerring trust in a fixity inherent to the act of writing:

The verses were to this effect:

My words, in hope to blaze my steadfast mind,
This marble chose, as of like temper known:
But lo, my words defaced, my fancies blind,
Blots to the stone, shame to myself I find;
    And witness am, how ill agree in one,
    A woman's hand with constant marble stone.

My words full weak, the marble full of might;
My words in store, the marble all alone;
My words black ink, the marble kindly white;
My words unseen, the marble still in sight,
    May witness bear, how ill agree in one,
    A woman's hand with constant marble stone. (97)

Philoclea's desire to add these new lines to the original set of smudges suggests that poetry has a unique communicative capacity, a belief that Sidney can hardly wait to subvert. The narrator introduces these twelve lines slightly

---

60. In her article "Sidney's Didactic Method in the *Old Arcadia*," *Studies in English Literature* 24, no. 1 (1984): 44, Ann W. Astell suggests that it is precisely this emphasis on "remembering and reexamination" that allows Sidney's text to serve its didactic function. She claims that through memory, the reader "comes to the *gnosis* Sidney intends," and locates her belief in Sidney's *Defence of Poesy*, in which Sidney claims that "reading be foolish without remembering, memory being the only treasurer of knowledge."

more honestly than he did the first set. His initial, unqualified phrase, "[t]he writing was this," floundered upon the revelation that the verse he faithfully recorded has not survived in the world of the fiction. Now, however, he overcorrects: in writing that "[t]he verses were to this effect," he emphasizes that these words will not be codified even as his words suggest that his very report might not be accurate. *Our* version of the poem is codified, so the narrator upgrades his credibility at the same moment that he undermines the verses that follow.

The new verses mimic the uncertainties of their introduction: in these twelve lines, "marble" appears most frequently, with "words" running a close second. But these "words," even in their repetition, are difficult to pin down: do they refer to the original poem or to the current act of *poiesis*? The first stanza may accurately report the situation at hand, but the second seems to vacillate: "words in store" and "words unseen" indicate her imagined verse, yet the "words black ink" invoke the original poem. Similarly, in dubbing her words "weak," does Philoclea lean on their ephemerality or the illuminative barrier to inscribing them? Or are they weak because they do not guarantee anything no matter what they say? The phrase "words unseen" is capable of double duty—it could reasonably describe the illegibility of her original verses. Her refrain also repeats the word "witness," the retraction's synonym for "testimony"; these new lines attempt the same collapse between self and writing that the first poem effected. For though "witness" can replace "testimony," it can also refer to the person supplying the statement.[61] Thus Philoclea's retraction adds agency that connects herself ("And witness am") to her words ("May witness bear"). But the poem resists this move by means of Philoclea's repeated lament "how ill agree in one, / A woman's hand with constant marble stone." In the fantasy of written verse, the retraction ironically codifies its own intellectual destruction—how can she portray a woman's hand as unerringly inconstant only to rely on that same hand to be constant enough to codify its own inconstancy? This conundrum, reminiscent of the narrator's opening certain uncertainty, means that despite the repetitions, these new lines do not provide much stable meaning. Instead, they reiterate the overriding sense that no matter what the grammar suggests, a promise does not guarantee fixity. Sidney mocks the notion of testimony and the idea of permanence even as his own codex supplies Philoclea's missing words. He playfully highlights her irrational self-punishment by preventing her from inscribing a retraction that undercuts its own meaning, and by

---

61. *OED*, s.v. "witness, *n.*," defs. 2a, 4a, 5a, 6a.

asking us to doubt whether his report faithfully records her verses, or if they are merely "to this effect."

For Philoclea, the return to poetry occasions a temporal reckoning that complicates the notion that the present moment might control the future. Yet, even though her trip to the woods is filled with broken promises and palimpsest, the desire for a future characterized by stasis persists; in the aftermath of poetic confrontation, she renews the language of judgment: "O ye stars, judge rightly of me; and if I have willingly made myself a prey to fancy, or if by any idle lusts I framed my heart fit for such an impression, then let this plague daily increase in me till my name be made odious to womankind" (97–98). The stars may not answer her prayer, but her formulation envisions a future indebted to a familiar literary past: on her account, "fancy" or "idle lusts" should provoke an extreme that will make her legible as the latest entry in the register of classical female figures immortalized with respect to their virtue—becoming "odious to womankind" conjures the negative exemplarity of a Helen of Troy. In other words, Philoclea wants a judgment that will trigger undeniable evaluation, a fixed story that can admit no ambiguity; she wants to put an end to possibility. Not only does she echo the synthesis of present and future imagined in her poetry, but the parallels of her logic also deepen the legal analogy. She might set the terms of her own, enduring sentence, but she leaves the act of judgment to the stars. However, this time her conditional language—"if I have willingly" and "if by any idle lusts"—signals that she no longer considers herself capable of accounting for her own intentionality. Although her poetic contract failed to guarantee the permanence of self and signature, she holds fast to her model of futurity; she prays to embody a wrong so unequivocally that her very name will be inseparable from her sin. On the other hand, when Philoclea later refers back to this episode, her perspective seems to have softened. A markedly temporary poem that Cleophila scratches into a "sandy bank" prompts the Amazon to reveal herself as Pyrocles to Philoclea (104).[62] Philoclea's moonlit verses might offer new purchase on the series of future-oriented considerations she generates in response to Pyrocles's revelation: "Alas, what then shall I do? Shall I seek far-fetched inventions? Shall I seek to lay colours over my decayed thoughts?" (106). She concludes, "Or rather, though the pureness of my virgin mind be stained, let me keep the true simplicity of my word" (106). Cleophila's fleeting verses replay a

---

62. I discuss this exchange at greater length in the introduction.

startling number of the dynamics on display on Philoclea's marble stone. It is not surprising, then, that Philoclea easily identifies with them. Yet, she changes course rather starkly: not only does she think she can still keep her original promise, but once Pyrocles reveals his true identity to her, she trades it in for the "promise of marriage" (107).[63]

Though Philoclea implicitly abandons her fantasy of unequivocal exemplarity only to double down on promising, Sidney transfers that concern, predicated as it is on external judgment, to the trial in the *Arcadia*. The final two books focus on the act of judging, the concept of justice, and the force and purpose of law. Sidney initially explored a futurity characterized by a lack of change by filling poetry with legal language; in the trial, he investigates law and promise by taking up exemplarity as an emblem for justice. The swerving plot of the romance leads Duke Basilius to drink a cupful of love potion, which, rather than quenching his thirst or igniting an amorous flame, kills him (or so the narrative purports). Basilius's trusted counselor, Philanax, charges Gynecia with the Duke's murder, and names Pyrocles and Musidorus as coconspirators and adulterers. After a long speech enumerating the charges leveled against the princes, Philanax turns the floor over to Euarchus: "Therefore I will transfer my care upon you, and attend, to my learning and comfort, the eternal example you will leave to all mankind of disguisers, falsifiers, adulterers, ravishers, murderers, and traitors" (346). The iterations of exemplarity that follow seem almost uncontainable: Euarchus will prove an exemplary judge, issuing an "eternal example" that will have an impact upon a host of future criminals. Philanax's statement could just as easily be addressed to either prince: once judged and sentenced, they will become "eternal example[s]" of actions that ought to be avoided.

Thus Sidney posits the act of judgment, ostensibly an evaluation of the events of the past, as most forceful for its role in shaping future actions. Euarchus takes up precisely this principle and even pushes it a step farther when he suggests that laws are most relevant for their effect on futurity: "But herein we must consider that the laws look how to prevent by due examples that such things be not done, and not how to salve such things when they are done" (352). If, as Euarchus suggests, law ought to have a guiding, if not predictive, force akin to the relationship between present and future established by a promise, then finding guilt and issuing a punitive sentence mark

---

63. As John Kerrigan points out in "Coriolanus Fidiussed," *Essays in Criticism* 62, no. 4 (2012), Renaissance culture supports a long-standing "paradox, familiar to antiquity, that it can be right *not* to keep a promise" (323). See Werlin for a useful discussion of this dynamic in Sidney's romance, when "Musidorus cannot resist a 'promise-breaking attempt'" ("Providence and Perspective," 30).

a failure. Not only is judgment unable to "salve such things when they are done," but the notion of exemplarity in law assumes its power lies in controlling the future rather than reviewing and adjudicating the past. The *Old Arcadia* has struggled variously with the commitments guaranteed by future constructions like the promise, yet the trial occurs just as Sidney's text fulfills the past-oriented emphases of the plot's opening: we have reached the future, and its primary vantage is retrospective.[64] Even so, in this text the logistics of the trial seem redundant—readers are well aware of the preceding events. However, the plot review is not merely expositional: Sidney's dalliance with a law that proclaims its own future reach coincides with testimonies that offer accounts of the past in direct conflict with the original narrative. Both Pyrocles and Gynecia offer false confessions that endorse the long, conspiracy-laden charges that Philanax invents. Even when Pyrocles, now using the pseudonym Timopyrus, offers a lucid and straightforward summary of most of the *Old Arcadia*, he alters a significant detail about Gynecia's plans for adultery.[65] In other words, impermanence is not a challenge faced solely by the future. The constant misrepresentation of preceding events reveals that in this text the engagement with the past is no surer than the attempts to codify and fix the future.[66]

Sidney softens the devastating suggestion that the past is impermanent and that the law might fail to impact the future by reviving female exemplarity as one of the *Old Arcadia*'s closing gestures. Gynecia's legacy parodies exemplarity while also allowing it to take effect. In the eleventh hour of the romance,

---

64. A situation that certainly calls to mind Sidney's own circumstances in writing the *Old Arcadia*, a text he would later attempt to revise. For example, Elizabeth Dipple cites Sidney's prefatory address to the Countess of Pembroke, which she claims was "published indiscriminately with the *New Arcadia*." Dipple believes that the address refers to the "composition, especially of the *Old Arcadia*." In this address, Sidney refers to the composition of the romance "being done in loose sheets of paper, most of it in your presence, the rest, by sheetes, sent unto you, as fast as they were done." Though Dipple might be overly dramatic as she imagines Sidney handing "each completed sheet, the ink still wet, to his sister," even a milder version of this arrangement would have required an exceptional reliance on memory for Sidney to keep the plot clear if he was giving away his work during the composition process (Dipple, "'Unjust Justice' in the *Old Arcadia*," *Studies in English Literature* 10, no. 1 [1970]: 85).

65. "I bare no more love to the chaste Philoclea than Basilius, deceived in my sex, showed to me, insomuch that by his importunacy I could have no time to assail the constant rock of the pure Philoclea's mind, till this policy I found: taking (under colour of some devotions) my lodging to draw Basilius thither with hope to enjoy me, which likewise I revealed to the duchess, that she might keep my place, and so make her husband see his error" (340).

66. In this regard, Sidney heightens a dynamic familiar to narrative. Brooks, for example, has written that the awareness of a scripted ending encourages a certainly readerly flexibility; the audience can "read in a spirit of confidence, and also a state of dependence, that what remains to be read will restructure the provisional meanings of the already read" (*Reading for the Plot*, 23).

Basilius wakes up and issues a joyful round of pardons, exonerating Gynecia, who, like her husband, intended and even attempted to commit adultery:

> And so kissing her, left her to receive the most honourable fame of any princess throughout the world, all men thinking (saving only Pyrocles and Philoclea who never bewrayed her) that she was the perfect mirror of all wifely love. Which though in that point undeserved, she did in the remnant of her life duly purchase with observing all duty and faith, to the example and glory of Greece—so uncertain are mortal judgements, the same person most infamous and most famous, and neither justly. (360)[67]

Whereas the law tries, and often fails, to shape society by means of example, Gynecia proves a more perfect exemplar, even though her status is initially "undeserved." Ironically, it is the falseness of the reputation she enjoys that determines her future actions, shaping them so that those actions might match her fame. The narrator holds this curious causality up as an example in and of itself—"so uncertain are mortal judgements"—boiling the instance down to a pithy lesson. Jeff Dolven has persuasively argued that Sidney's fiction satirizes the system of education that teaches aphoristic reading and interpretive practices.[68] To be sure, Sidney uses such lessons to ask his readers to "think twice about what they learned and how they learned it,"[69] and in the remainder of this chapter I will propose that Sidney extends such critical thinking to questions of future and expectation by presenting arbitration between a series of hierarchies in both law and contract. In so doing, the substance of the lesson about Gynecia's exemplarity, pitched as it is in the language of uncertainty with which the fiction began, also admits the power of possibility. It privileges a kind of boundlessness as a hallmark of futurity that trumps the many attempts to guarantee thought, action, and even endings.

V

In the final two books, Sidney draws together the strands of criminal and common law justice, and extends the legal framework to narrative itself. To begin with, each of the central players tells a version of the events that lead up to Basilius's untimely demise. Critics have long noted that the trial

---

67. For a discussion of irony and judgment in this passage, see Stephen J. Greenblatt, "Sidney's *Arcadia* and the Mixed Mode," *Studies in Philology* 70, no. 3 (1973): 278.
68. Jeff Dolven, *Scenes of Instruction in Renaissance Romance* (Chicago: University of Chicago Press, 2007), 132–33.
69. Ibid., 133.

requires the reader to participate in the act of reviewing and judging; there is particular emphasis on comparing testimony to the preceding text of the *Old Arcadia*, which also requires a moral review, forcing readers to evaluate the extent to which they have been complicit in the wrongs committed by Pyrocles and Musidorus over the course of the narrative.[70] Indeed, the trial makes explicit the context of review and evaluation that has been present from the text's opening, and ties it particularly to the experience of reading and evaluating text. As I argued above, Sidney indicates a double temporal problem—the law is unable to control the future, and the past is equally unstable.

In the midst of conflicting and inventive testimony, Sidney revisits questions of permanence—linguistic and physical—and memory well-worn at Philoclea's marble stone. Denied voice in the proceedings, Pamela and Philoclea write heartfelt letters to Euarchus. The missives, which only Sidney's readers see in their entirety, attempt to acquit the princesses' respective lovers. The fear and urgency that the content conveys are echoed by the compromised sheets: "Many blots had the tears of these sweet ladies made in their letters, which many times they had altered, many times torn, and written anew, ever thinking something either wanted or were too much, or would offend, or (which was worst) would breed denial" (344). The narrator describes writing as a painful procedure of editing, emendation, and doubt. Whereas the final product encodes this palimpsest blotted by tears, within the fiction, the reproduced text reaches us intact. Philanax intercepts the letters,

> which he suddenly opened, and seeing to what they tended by the first words, was so far from publishing them (whereby he feared, in Euarchus's just mind, either the princesses might be endangered or the prisoners preserved, of which choice he knew not which to think the worst) that he would not himself read them over, doubting his own heart might be mollified, so bent upon revenge. Therefore utterly suppressing them, he lent a spiteful ear to Pyrocles. (344)

One of the few models for reading in the text, Philanax proves as destructive as any physical force—without even reading, he draws conclusions regarding the letters and "to what they tended"—that is, the content of the ideas. He stops short both because he assumes the first few words sketch the remainder of the message, and because in the palliative register of the

---

70. See, for example, McCoy, *Sir Philip Sidney*, 124.

word "tend," the letters might actually prove *too* effective; Philanax has no interest in quashing his hunger for vengeance. He censors his own potential response by "utterly suppressing" the letters. The stifled dispatches highlight the act of reading through both a refusal to read, and the act of denying Euarchus access to the text. At the same time, Sidney provides his own readers privileged access, underscoring that the *Old Arcadia* trial stages judgment based on an incomplete set of facts. The letters, unblotted in Sidney's text, are never admitted into evidence, nor do they enjoy unadulterated form within the fiction, but they do enable Sidney to keep pressure on questions of futurity that pair the legal context with writing, reading, and the physical text.[71]

Sidney offers his readers privileged access to evidence that requires us to sift through the various, often distorted, versions of the plot. By reviewing and remembering, we can assess what we have read in light of the judgment Euarchus pronounces. This call for comparative deliberation and choice finds its echo in the repeated act of ordering at the trial—the proper hierarchy of rules and bonds is sorted out as a prerequisite for "right" judgment. Such ordering in the trial recalls the pivotal events that have taken place in Philoclea's bedroom. At the end of book 3, Philoclea consummates her love outside of wedlock with the no-longer-disguised Pyrocles. Their tryst is discovered, and Pyrocles presciently fears "the cruelty of the Arcadian laws which, without exception, did condemn all to death who were found in act of marriage without solemnity of marriage" (251). That is, he worries over the consequences of the letter of a very harsh law. Philoclea, by contrast, remains unconcerned. All reference to her earlier, contractual commitment to lead a "virgin life" has vanished, and in its place we find her confident that her actions and emotions are in harmony—she proceeds "with an innocent guiltlessness, not knowing why she should fear to deliver her unstained soul to God" (255). In other words, she subordinates the letter of the law to natural law. Her attitude proves naively ineffectual in the context of a complicated trial, a vengeful prosecutor, and a strict-constructionist judge. Nonetheless, despite abandoning her reliance on promissory structures, her unqualified trust in the

---

71. Of course, one might argue that rather than being implicit "jurors," readers are simply engaged in the "process of judgment" that McCoy suggests. On the other hand, it seems that invoking a process of judgment has natural implications in a text that both conducts a trial and ponders the ability of people to fill their judicial roles. In the same way that "Euarchus is judged as judge by the justice of his verdict" (Astell, "Sidney's Didactic Method," 44), readers may take on not only processes inherent to the trial process, but the roles implicit in them as well.

preeminence of natural law anticipates the hierarchical negotiations that surround judgment at the trial.

Indeed, a call for proper jurisdictional hierarchies forms the basis of the princes' first objections to the trial: "[T]hey demanded to know by what authority they could judge of them, since they were not only foreigners, and so not born under their laws, but absolute princes, and therefore not to be touched by laws" (333). Their two-pronged attempt to avoid judgment is answered piecemeal in a measured enumeration of the process and rationale of criminal evaluation. The visitor's defense is instantly refuted: "Arcadia laws were to have their force upon any were found in Arcadia, since strangers have scope to know the customs of a country before they put themselves in it" (333). Similarly, Euarchus, firmly installed in his role as guest judge, provides a thoughtful answer to their claim that princes need not stand trial: "[S]o is not a prince a prince but to his own subjects" (349). Since they are not at home, nor traveling as anything other than "private" persons, they can indeed be judged. Such competing rules are swiftly slotted into place, but the situation becomes decidedly more complicated when Euarchus issues his capital sentence, because Sidney immediately pits the bonds of citizen and state against the bonds of family.[72] Notably, this is the same moment that the rule of law begins to jar with the narrative's generic cues. First, Euarchus sacrifices family bonds to the cause of justice, holding fast to his sentence even after the identities of the defendants—his son and nephew—have been revealed: "If rightly I have judged, then rightly have I judged mine own children, unless the name of a child should have force to change the never-changing justice. No, no, Pyrocles and Musidorus, I prefer you much before my life, but I prefer justice as far before you" (356).[73] The harsh sentence, routinely accused of preferring an unflinching justice to the more laudable quality of mercy, forces readers to reflect on their threshold for vice as evidenced by their outraged sympathy. The injustice of the sentence, however, seems all the more pronounced because it comes at the expense of the fulfillment of generic expectation. Sidney opposes fair criminal judgment to narrative contract. As Fredric Jameson argues, "Genres are essentially contracts between a writer and his readers," and this type of "literary *institution*" has held steady in the reader's mind ever since the opening prophecy gestured toward its resolution

---

72. Euarchus sentences Philoclea to life in a convent, Gynecia to a "living burial," Pyrocles to be pitched off a high tower, and Musidorus to be beheaded.

73. Euarchus's interest in the "never-changing" quality of justice echoes Philoclea's earlier idealization of stasis. For a discussion of the difficulty the text presents in sending down a sentence that, though "absent clemency or equity," is just and technically unobjectionable, see Dolven, *Scenes of Instruction*, 125.

at the story's end.[74] Whereas the narrative contract between Sidney and his reader does not depend on the romance's concern with justice, in the *Old Arcadia*, the context of the contract is undoubtedly heightened by putting narrative expectation in parallel with the conclusion of the trial. Euarchus's judgment is a particularly bitter pill to swallow because, as Margaret E. Dana notes, readers "expect resolution through the literary convention of the recognition scene."[75] Indeed, Sidney spends a full two pages building up to that recognition. The princes' would-be saviors rush in and "brake the press with astonishing every man with their cries" (355). Dramatically, Kalodoulus falls at Euarchus's feet, "telling him those he had judged were his own son and nephew, the one the comfort of Macedon, the other the only stay of Thessalia" (355). This generic intervention makes Euarchus's unwavering response shocking—he privileges law over family bond, a decision that simultaneously breaks Sidney's narrative contract.

In his reading of what he calls the *Arcadia*'s "mixed mode," Stephen Greenblatt borrows Giambattista Guarini's description of tragicomedy, emphasizing the idea that a work of fiction is capable of being "tragic in possibility but not in fact."[76] The substitution of the "conventions of a different genre" allows for fiction's capacity to include and invoke other genres even if they are not "fully realized" in a given text.[77] Sidney's fiction repeatedly dramatizes the fragility and ephemerality of physical text, and the generic break pitches such uncertainties in a more metaphorical key. Yet given the trial's insistence on the tragic component of the "mixed mode," the ineffectual recognition scene points to an *Old Arcadia* that might not be particularly mixed. Comedy and romance may prove mere whispers if tragedy, now aligned with judgment, becomes "fully realized." Greenblatt argues that Sidney's "mixed mode" exposes the "instability and uncertainty of human judgment," and I would add that this is true both within the fiction and for the reader.[78] In other words, just as tragedy and comedy jockey for the last word in this fiction, so do political, legal, and textual structures. Philoclea's calm sense of her innocent adherence to the dictates of natural law is refuted by a trial faithful to the letter of the law. Meanwhile, the easy distinctions of a jurisdictional pecking order reached within the trial provoke the troubling generic shift.

---

74. Fredric Jameson, "Magical Narratives: Romance as Genre," *New Literary History* 7, no. 1 (1975): 135.

75. Margaret E. Dana, "The Providential Plot of the *Old Arcadia*," *Studies in English Literature* 17, no. 1 (1977): 57.

76. Greenblatt, "Mixed Mode," 272, quoting Guarini, 522.

77. Ibid., 272.

78. Ibid., 274.

As a result, Euarchus's commitment to his sentence may reveal that genre and generic possibility are up for grabs, as Greenblatt suggests, but Sidney simultaneously reveals that the future might be up for grabs, too. From the start, the future in the *Old Arcadia* has been couched in terms of eventual judgment: looking forward, then, has been inseparable from an interest in looking back. Sidney's text, brimming though it is with ruined and ignored textual artifacts, is put most palpably in peril by the failure of the recognition scene to alter Euarchus's sentence. Of course, generic signals, along with the bulk of pages that remain to be read, might encourage the reader's expectations that a deus ex machina will enable resolution, which is precisely what Sidney ultimately provides. Nonetheless, the deferral of resolution precipitated by the failed generic signal of the much-anticipated recognition scene, as well as the emphasis on a preeminent juridical schema, unsettles, if only briefly, the promise made at the beginning of the fiction. Even as Euarchus announces that his ruling will establish an exemplarity capable of controlling future action, we arrive at the future only to discover that it is different from what was promised at the beginning of the text. Through the practice of law, the narrative contract is broken, upending genre in a manner that illuminates the interplay between past, present, and future. The generic break both removes and provides possibility—tragedy, that genre "present in possibility," when taken up in fact, changes the future upon which the romance had relied.

However, Euarchus is both an agent of future possibility and an emblem for the kind of immutability that the text resists: if the *Old Arcadia* insists upon thinking of temporal relations by keeping us in touch with prospective judgment and review, reaching the future, in the trial, shows the instability of the past. The testimonies at the trial, in all their inventive multiplicity, literalized the idea of an uncertain past through the profusions of retrospection, even if the majority of those retrospective versions were false or distorted.[79] At the same time, Euarchus's merciless sentence also loosens the shackles of the prophecy, ushering in an unexpected future that is all the more dramatic for its overthrow of generic expectation. It encourages us to consider how constricting the initial prophecy really was.[80] In the brief space when it really

---

79. Those distortions are only heightened when Sidney turns to revise the romance. In the trial, Musidorus uses his past actions as defense: "Were not we the men that killed the wild beasts which otherwise had killed the princesses if we had not succoured them?" (346–47). In the *New Arcadia*, we learn that those "wild beasts" were released by Cecropia precisely for the purpose of doing harm. See Sir Philip Sidney, *The Countess of Pembroke's Arcadia*, ed. Maurice Evans (1977; repr., London: Penguin, 1987).

80. My study of the *Old Arcadia*, then, resists some of the constructions of literary time proposed in Frank Kermode's influential *The Sense of an Ending*. Here the weighty knowledge invoked by prophecy actually points to possibility, and yokes providence and prophecy together in a Protestant universe.

does look like the *Old Arcadia* might end in tragedy, Sidney uses the future to show how many versions of the past there might be, and forces us to consider how prophecy and expectation might limit or liberate the future. But the hierarchy of law over narrative contract does not have much staying power in the *Old Arcadia*. The recognition scene may have failed, but it is quickly followed by a deus ex machina that rights the course of the romance—Basilius is not really dead. Gynecia's love potion, we learn, was actually a sleeping potion. Basilius wakes up, and while he regains his senses, he is treated to an update on the Arcadian antics that took place during his slumber. As soon as he can speak, he invokes the prophecy, which he finally understands: "At length, remembering the oracle, which now indeed was accomplished (not as before he had imagined), considering all had fallen out by the highest providence" (360). Basilius jettisons Euarchus's sentences and pardons everyone. Romance is restored at the expense of legal judgment, but a path that unfolded as neither we nor Basilius had imagined preserves the emphasis on future possibility despite the mention of "highest providence."

Long before any criminal trial introduced the problems of justice and equity into Arcadia, an innocent virgin walked alone in the woods wondering about the nature of obligation, using poetry to puzzle out the links between contract, memory, and intention. Notably, Philoclea ends up playing the part of both author and reader in her secluded grove. She views the poetry she has written (mired in legal language) as a contract, and one that the reading of the text reactivates. At the close of the *Old Arcadia*, Sidney hopes that his many narrative strands "may awake some other spirit to exercise his pen in that wherewith mine is already dulled" (361). His proposition is complicated by our future vantage point, since we already know that Sidney himself picked up that same pen to rewrite and expand the narrative, and that his early death resulted in a complicated editorial future for the unfinished *New Arcadia*.[81] Those revisions exceed the length of the original, and the incomplete manuscript leaves the project in a state that makes it resemble the ephemeral, blotted writing so abundant within the fiction. The *New Arcadia* breaks off midsentence in the middle of a combat scene: "Whereat ashamed, (as hauing neuer done so much before in his life)."[82] In the *Old Arcadia*, the

---

81. For a lucid overview of the publication history of both versions of the *Arcadia*, see Sidney, *The Countess of Pembroke's Arcadia*, ed. Evans, 12–13.

82. As reproduced in Jenny C. Mann's illuminating account of the function of parenthesis in Sidney's work, and the powerful way that rhetorical forms can structure larger patterns and ideas more broadly. See Mann, *Outlaw Rhetoric: Figuring Vernacular Eloquence in Shakespeare's England* (Ithaca, NY: Cornell University Press, 2012), 89–91.

very mention of it belies the notion of a "dulled" pen, an assertion that allows Sidney to demonstrate his authorial control of both this story and the errant nature of romance. Thus at the final moment when the resolution of the story finally fixes the genre (romance, not tragedy), his conclusion unsettles it as he exits the romance. In this work that belies the precision of the language of future structures, the future does have faith and interest in forward potential and the viewpoints it affords. In Sidney's closing words, the future retains an open-endedness that replaces the fixity and precision implied by grammatical and legal constructs. Once reached, the future can always provide an opportunity for judgment and review of preceding events, but the "spirit to exercise [one's] pen," once awakened, suggests that the future enjoys a certain freedom that the present moment can neither control nor dull. By choosing the moment at which to exit an infamously errant genre, Sidney demonstrates a mastery and control that undercuts the notion of the "dulled" pen. In the end, of course, the *Arcadia* escaped Sidney's own careful plotting. Even if Sidney could not foresee or forechoose the eventual career of his text, his romance equips us with a vantage on how we might embrace such continual uncertainty. The gesture to the artistic future at the end of the *Old Arcadia* replaces an ending with a sense of boundless possibility.

Chapter 2

The History of the Future
Spenser's The Faerie Queene *and the Directions of Time*

In the previous chapter, I argued that Sidney undermined devices intended to cast and secure particular futures, such as prophecies and promises, and instead privileged "continual uncertainty." As time passed in his narrative, characters encountered futures that failed to deliver on their anticipations and commitments. The *Old Arcadia* dislodged a stable narrative reference time by toggling between a present that looks ahead to a future that will be retrospective, and the revisitation of anticipated futures *as* present moments. In *The Faerie Queene*, Edmund Spenser similarly approaches the future in terms of a past that is subject to constant revision. Like Sidney, Spenser uses the structure of his poem's narrative as a resource for reshaping and unsettling the future, but the lost pasts and potential futures he invokes do not fade away as quietly as words wiped from a marble stone. Instead, a twisted perspective pervades Faerieland. Characters traverse the poem uncomfortably attuned to what lies behind them:

Tho as she backward cast her busie eye (3.11.50.1)	Britomart
But when againe he backeward cast his eye (3.10.14.4)	Malbecco
Still as he fledd, his eye was backward cast (1.9.21.5)	Trevisan
Still as she fledd, her eye she backward threw (3.1.16.1)	Florimell
Still fled he forward, looking backward still (3.10.56.1)	Malbecco

Carried her forward with her first intent: And though oft looking backward, well she vewde (3.4.50.5–6)	Florimell
For as he forward mooud his footing old, So backward still was turnd his wrincled face (1.8.31.3–4)	Ignaro
And euermore when with regardfull sight She looking backe, espies that griesly wight Approching nigh, she gins to mend her pace, And makes her feare a spur to hast her flight (4.7.22.4–7)	Amoret
So as I entred, I did backeward looke (4.10.20.1)	Scudamour
His name was *Doubt*, that had a double face, Th'one forward looking, th'other backeward bent (4.10.12.3–4)	Porter, Temple of Venus
And euer as she rode, her eye was backeward bent (5.8.4.9)	Samient[1]

Why might Spenser infect his allegorical world with so much backward-headedness? Both widespread and exaggerated, the image of a character moving forward while looking back operates beyond the implications it carries for any one episode. This chapter considers forward-moving backward glances writ large to show how Spenser's poetic treatment of national history discovers and invents a future enabled by a retrospective, even backward-headed, process and prospect.

In *The Faerie Queene*, when a character moves in one direction while looking in the other, the description communicates not merely a spatial orientation, but a temporal orientation as well. Upon first appearance, for example, Florimell rushes by a group of astonished onlookers: "Still as she fledd, her eye she backward threw." In desperate motion, Florimell's "[l]oosely disperst" hair initiates a simile that compares the embattled maiden to a comet. Unlike the shocking and portentous "blazing starre" that "importunes death and dolefull dreryhedd" to which she is compared, however, Florimell's posture belies any straightforward status as a sign of future doom: her ride forward is perpetually ("still") oriented backward (3.1.16). She sustains this dual orientation when she resurfaces three cantos later—the "griesly foster" that pursued her has vanished and "fayrest fortune" and "chaunce" have finally allowed Arthur

---

1. All references are to Edmund Spenser, *The Faerie Queene*, ed. A. C. Hamilton, 2nd ed. (New York: Longman, 2001).

CHAPTER TWO

to gain on her (3.1.17.2; 3.4.47.6–7). As in her earlier sprint, here her "former feare of being fowly shent, / Carried her forward with her first intent" (3.4.50.4–5). Not only does the past ("former feare"; "first intent") "carry" her into the future, but she keeps it squarely in view by "oft looking backward" (3.4.50.6). Though casting an eye behind her shows her that Arthur has replaced the earlier threat, it is her orientation to that past that keeps her rushing headlong into a future to which she does not look forward.

The image of moving forward while looking back recurs enough times throughout the poem that it is notable for both its consistency and its universality: Spenser applies the description to female knights, chaste maidens, jealous jilted husbands, near suicides, and even the figure of Ignorance. The posture sounds painful. Had Spenser used the image once, it might have suggested a pointed emblem. Yet, though it cannot be reduced, say, to a clear image of wrong-headedness, the poem doesn't particularly endorse the impulse.[2] Rather than allegorical shorthand for a dangerous obsession with or longing for the past, the pose offers a means for understanding a bolder narrative operation: that looking to the status of the past can affect the promised (or threatened) futures it predicts.

In those two vignettes, Florimell is the physical site of the collapse of opposing motions, and her consistency in repetition figures both an approach to time and a method of traversing the poem by connecting distinct episodes. In placing a variety of characters in this position, Spenser renders literal a fantasy of simultaneity and privileges a perspective that views in tandem events widely dispersed across the poem. The twists and contortions of those characters' bodies are uncomfortable in a way that underscores the effort required to put such perspectives together. The simultaneous orientations—looking backward while moving forward—offer an image of a present moment actively engaged in a capacious construction of narrative.

For Spenser, looking to the past unlocks the future. The poet's own backward glances open up opportunities that rattle what lies ahead. The embodiment of a multidirectional time scheme expressed through the trope of moving forward while looking back—those coterminous, contradictory movements in and across physical space—finds its reflection in the disjunctive scattering of episodes of British history across the poem. Spenser illustrates in *The Faerie Queene* that he does not merely report the past, but also plays a significant role in creating it. In this chapter, I argue that Spenser investigates the enterprise, and even the very possibility, of writing history by making poetic narrative central to the production of the historical imagination, placing the impending past forever in the hands of the poetic future.

---

2. Florimell, of course, has a point in assuming all those who ride after her pose a threat. However, in Arthur's case, the poem does not linger on this implication for long.

Spenser offers a comprehensive account of British history in three central episodes; he treats England's history from the founding of the island all the way to Elizabeth, though not always in chronological order. That history is fractured into pieces, and, what is more, despite the consistent features of the Spenserian stanza, the poem imagines it in three radically different forms: first, as the chronicle histories—*Briton moniments* and *Antiquitee of Faery lond*—that Arthur and Guyon discover and read in Eumnestes's library (2.9–10); second, as the repetitive prophecy that Merlin offers Britomart (3.3); third, as the table talk that Britomart, eager to hear the Brutus legend of the founding of Troynovant, coaxes out of Paridell over dinner at Malbecco's castle (3.9). This chapter works through chronicle, prophecy, and sociable chatter in sequence to detail how Spenser invites readers to build links between the three episodes. The poet draws attention to their shared components, including prosody, punctuation, syntax, an emerging lexicon of affective response built from rhetorical figures of repetition, and the very status of his poem as a printed, material object. In innovating these elements across the three episodes, he establishes the poet's privilege to tell history and make claims on the future by unsettling both. These recurring details furnish techniques for linking these historical episodes that do not rely upon linear time. Whereas complex, even impossible, temporalities might garner notice in discussions of the poem's status as a romance, they are generally absent from critical accounts of the episodes devoted to British history in the poem, which ostensibly trade in a more straightforward chronology. Spenser exacerbates gaps in his nation's history, but his innovations in bridging the history he fractures do not rest, as he coyly pretends, on the discovery of lost documents. Rather, the poem's interlaced historical episodes reclaim the future by troubling the "streight course of heuenly destiny" on which Merlin's prophecy will claim one can rely (3.3.24.3).

Far from clearing up a notoriously contested national story, Spenser's version of it establishes his control over the telling of history and ties it to the way readers might approach the poem by capitalizing on the questions it raises. The poem places an emphasis on the process of moving back and forth between textual moments without establishing a privileged destination. Those figures with their heads on backward might have their eyes trained on and "bent" toward the past, but Spenser shows how attending to the past can unsettle origins and end points. His poem illustrates that any story might be different than what we have been told, or even that it awaits its own revision. Because revisiting the past has unexpected and continued consequences, moving forward while looking back has the power to destabilize the past in order to trouble assumptions about any narrative's next step. Spenser radically extends the commonplace, asserted in the writings of his own literary models, that historical figures rely on poets for their reputation: he shows that poets make the future possible.³ By using the past to revise future expectations, Spenser reevaluates and revalues approaches to history in favor of *poiesis*. *The Faerie Queene* negotiates between the challenges of an inaccessible past and an unknown future, serving as a hinge or pivot point between them. But Spenser is equally interested in engaging the present as a tool for giving shape to gaps and missing links. His fiction turns to the past to orient his imaginative inventions, putting pressure on how the poet makes history, rather than how he tells it. Spenser reveals the potential for his stories that implies a future not yet settled, one that highlights contingency over inevitability: he demonstrates that poetic narrative is a critical component of the historical imagination.

I

At the end of book 2, canto 9, in Alma's castle, the book's hero, Guyon, and Prince Arthur encounter Eumnestes, an "old oldman" who is at once a figure of the past and an allegory of the brain's memory chamber (2.9.55–58). In his library, each knight finds a book relating to his own national history. The question of the future comes immediately into view because in Eumnestes's chamber Spenser places side by side two texts that exist in different temporal registers. Though Guyon and Arthur read simultaneously, and both texts seem to record history up to the present, *Briton moniments* ends with the reign of Uther Pendragon, Arthur's own father, while *Antiquitee of Faery lond* reaches Spenser's 1590s. The chaotic relation between time and narrative timing only escalates when in book 3 the history begun in *Briton moniments* is extended via prophetic vision.

The scene of historical reading in book 2 stands out not only because it lacks a direct precedent from classical epic or Italian romance, but also because it is so rare to find a genealogical moment in this poem born of anything other than one character asking another to give an account of his or her own history. Indeed, the introduction of written history provides a reminder that Arthur is ignorant of his roots, as he admits in book 1 when Una requests that he tell "his name and nation" (1.9.2.7):

> Faire virgin (said the Prince) yee me require
> A thing without the compas of my witt:
> For both the lignage and the certein Sire,
> From which I sprong, from mee are hidden yitt. (1.9.3.1–4)

---

3. For the former, see, for example, Ludovico Ariosto's *Orlando Furioso* 35.24–29.

The terms in which Arthur betrays his ignorance about his own identity play on temporal registers—it is Arthur's own lineage, his own past, that is hidden from him. But not knowing doesn't mean the past is lost or unknowable. Rather the word "yitt" suggests that Arthur expects to learn this "hidden" information about himself later. The contorted syntax in these two lines mimics Arthur's relationship to his own identity—just as he is denied access to his genealogy until more time has passed, Spenser withholds "yitt" until the close of the line and the end of the sentence. Arthur never actually discovers his "lignage"; rather, in books 2 and 3, Spenser goes out of his way to furnish a comprehensive, though fractured, history of Britain that narrates everything but Arthur's place in it.

Arthur's remark offers in miniature a larger concern that gets played out in the poem: putting the past in the hands of the future is at once obvious and inevitable, but it also destabilizes the relationship between history and fiction. His small window onto temporal slippage also speaks to the poem's habit of putting pressure on when we know, from something as simple as withholding the name of a character for several stanzas to something as complex as the status of the present moment of the narrative itself. Fortunately, Eumnestes's tools—"immortall scrine" and "infinite remembraunce" (2.9.56)—ought to enable a journey to these historical and genealogical outer reaches. Yet his library contains volumes that have fallen victim to the physical destructions of time. Rather than filling in the proverbial blanks, the damaged material items in memory's chamber acutely depict the barriers to reconstructing a coherent, favorable, and credible national history—a pressing source of anxiety for many of Spenser's contemporaries. Of particular concern was the status of the Brutus legend, which linked English origins to Troy by claiming that the island had been founded by Brute, Aeneas's great-grandson. Polydore Vergil famously called Geoffrey of Monmouth's *Historia Regum Brittaniae* (ca. 1135), a key source for the legend, into question with the publication of his *Anglica historia* in 1534. His allegations precipitated a period of intense change and debate surrounding the category of what we would now call history.[4] In the decades that followed, many writers began to concede that

---

4. McKisack points out that Polydore Vergil was not alone in his skepticism about the Brutus legend, but identifies his as the "first general history of England to be written in a judicious and critical spirit and in a deliberately literary style." Vergil's accusations, while incredibly damaging to a coherent British history, drew stern critique from English writers concerned with national history, such as John Leland and Sir Henry Savile. See May McKisack, *Medieval History in the Tudor Age* (Oxford: Clarendon Press, 1971), 103. Woolf attributes the "firm distinction" that evolved between narrative accounts of the people of the past and antiquarian interest in "things rather

these genealogies were merely potent national fictions, but others fiercely defended them as an accurate lineage. The writings of William Camden, John Dee, John Leland, John Stow, Raphael Holinshed, and John Selden, to name but a few, staged not only disagreements over facts, but also over methodology: what were the best means and modes of finding, establishing, and conveying the Matter of Britain?[5]

The sixty some stanzas of *Briton moniments* in book 2, canto 10, are heavily indebted to Geoffrey of Monmouth's history of Britain, so it might be tempting to conclude that Spenser reveals his historiographical stance by simply repeating, and thus implicitly validating, this contested chronicle fare. However, as Arthur and Guyon prepare to open their respective books, Spenser describes them by means of a curious inversion: his two knights are "burning both with feruent fire, / Their countreys auncestry to vnderstond" (2.9.60.6–7). Books and fires are hardly strange bedfellows, as Paolo and Francesca can attest, but it is usually reading that ignites the sparks of passionate flames. Don Quijote's books are condemned to their fiery fate only *after* reading has done its damage, even if the charring might also benefit future would-be readers. Moreover, the usual association of reading with fire centers on the dangers of reading romance. Arthur and Guyon, however, "[c]rau'd leaue" of their hosts Alma and Eumnestes in order to settle into *Briton moniments* and *Antiquitee of Faery lond*.[6] The flickering signal of romance that introduces the two tomes ostensibly filled with national history echoes the criticisms of the dying medieval chronicle tradition, miti-

---

than men" to "the sharp increase in the publication of antiquarian and topographical treatises which began in the 1570s and continued through the last two decades of the century." See D. R. Woolf, "Erudition and the Idea of History in Renaissance England," *Renaissance Quarterly* 40, no. 1 (1987): 21–23.

5. Though I do not deal with historiographical debates directly in this chapter, the works of antiquarians and their opponents provide a useful backdrop to Spenser's project in the historical episodes of the poem. The Matter of Britain, and historiography more generally, have been treated at length in F. Smith Fussner, *The Historical Revolution: English Historical Writing and Thought, 1580–1640* (New York: Columbia University Press, 1962); F. J. Levy, *Tudor Historical Thought* (San Marino, CA: Huntington Library, 1967); and D. R. Woolf, *Reading History in Early Modern England* (Cambridge: Cambridge University Press, 2000). For studies that address *The Faerie Queene* in relation to historiography, see esp. Carrie Anna Harper, *The Sources of the British Chronicle History in Spenser's "Faerie Queene"* (Bryn Mawr, PA: Bryn Mawr College Monographs, 1910); Andrew Escobedo, *Nationalism and Historical Loss in Renaissance England: Foxe, Dee, Spenser, Milton* (Ithaca, NY: Cornell University Press, 2004); and Bart van Es, *Spenser's Forms of History* (Oxford: Oxford University Press, 2002).

6. In "Monuments and Ruins: Spenser and the Problem of the English Library," *ELH* 70 (2003): 6, Jennifer Summit argues that the choice of title terms, "monument" and "antiquity," links these two volumes to post-Reformation book collection efforts. For a detailed discussion of the word "monument," see van Es, *Spenser's Forms of History*, 23–30.

gating a simple reading of Spenser's historiographical politics. At the same time, the details that surround this historical account register the poet's shrewd awareness that relating the "countreys auncestry" necessarily invokes such strands of contention.[7] Similarly, as an allegory of memory and memorial function, Eumnestes's treasures of the past are notably material, and the fact that he maintains a library of books and "long parchment scrolls . . . all worm-eaten, and full of canker holes" (2.9.57.8–9) likens him to "an overworked Tudor antiquary."[8] Rather than aligning himself with one methodology or another, however, Spenser offers competing signals for the practice of assembling and relating national history, highlighting the concerns over credibility and verification that overshadowed the project of the past in Elizabethan England.[9]

Andrew Escobedo has argued that we are meant to understand *Briton moniments* as the lost, ancient Welsh source text that "Geoffrey [of Monmouth] claimed to have received from a friend and translated"[10]—an alluring proposition for a poem so concerned with origins. The book that Arthur finds suggests an opportunity for fulfilled desire, a chance for these missing links and questions of history and historiography to be filled in and fulfilled. However, I want to suggest that the framework surrounding Arthur's book—both in the poem and in its first printing—also signals that the chronicle canto marks an act of textual invention rather than textual recuperation. In book 2, canto 9, *Briton moniments* rises to Arthur's hand, and the poem even invites us to imagine our encounter with *Briton moniments* as ontologically distinct from our encounter with Spenser's poem. The typography of the poem's first edition (1590) contributes to this fiction. In the 1590 *Faerie Queene*, six of the twelve cantos of book 2 begin on a new page. However, canto 10 is the first both to begin on a new page and to follow a canto that ends with a printer's device (fig. 1).

---

7. At issue was the veracity of medieval historical accounts, notorious for their commingling of fact and fiction. For a discussion of the lack of distinction between such categories in medieval writing, especially chronicles, see Summit, "Monuments and Ruins," 10; Patricia Clare Ingham, *Sovereign Fantasies: Arthurian Romance and the Making of Britain* (Philadelphia: University of Pennsylvania Press, 2001); and Monika Otter, *Inventiones: Fiction and Referentiality in Twelfth-Century English Historical Writing* (Chapel Hill: University of North Carolina Press, 1996).

8. Escobedo, *Nationalism and Historical Loss*, 75.

9. In so doing, Spenser echoes the logic behind Sidney's notoriously unflattering description of the historian in the *Defence of Poesy*. Woolf points out the "internal contradiction" in Sidney's account, since "his historian was both obsessed with old records like the new-fangled antiquary *and* at the same time reliant 'for the most part . . . upon other histories' like the old-fashioned chronicler"; he concludes that Sidney "either did not see" the "obvious internal contradiction in [his] caricature" or "chose to ignore" it ("Erudition," 23).

10. Escobedo, *Nationalism and Historical Loss*, 52.

CHAPTER TWO

FIGURE 1. Edmund Spenser, *The Faerie Queene* (London, 1590). The Harry Ransom Center, The University of Texas at Austin.

Though it is not the last printer's device to appear at the end of a canto in book 2, it is the first printer's device to appear in the text since the woodcut of Saint George defeating the dragon concluded book 1.[11] As a result, the graphic layout offers a visual suggestion that the start of canto 10 could be the opening page of Arthur's book, a possibility heightened by the first line of the argument at the top of the page: "A chronicle of Briton kings."

Canto 9 concludes when the hosts "gladly graunted" the heroes' "desire" to "read those bookes" (2.9.60.9). However, the transition from finding the books to relating their content is far from seamless: the tenth canto begins not with the text of Arthur's chosen book, but rather with commentary supplied by the loquacious narrator. In the distance between one canto and the next, Spenser highlights the extent to which the poet mediates our access to the history. Despite the "feruent fire," we are denied direct access to Arthur's chosen book, finding instead four stanzas of introduction and apology

---

11. The same is true in the 1596 printing of *The Faerie Queene*, though a different printer's device is used.

beginning with a salient creative question: "Who now shall giue vnto me words and sound, / Equall vnto this haughty enterprise?" (2.10.1.1–2).[12] Spenser's poem is notoriously elusive in its election of a muse—Calliope and Clio seem equally to be candidates—but in canto 10 the question, rendered explicit, feels markedly out of place: Why is Spenser seeking a muse at all when Arthur has *Briton moniments* in hand? Hasn't Eumnestes already provided the "words and sound" by supplying the knights with their coveted books? The shift that occurs in the course of a canto change—from the book that Arthur selects to the narrator's anxiety about how he will approach this "haughty enterprise"—signals a potential divide between the text that Arthur reads and the text that we read.[13] It mimics the kind of slide that occurred between the description of Eumnestes's "infinite remembraunce" and the description of his "worm-eaten" historical records, and anticipates the poem's later moments of self-conscious narrative construction. In this case, the jarring shift at the start of a new canto foregrounds the person responsible for creating the history: the attention paid to the materiality of the recorded past and to the act of reading unsettle the fiction that canto 10 merely reproduces an ancient source text.

Apparently inspired by literary precedent, canto 10 opens with four stanzas devoted to the poet's anxiety and unworthiness: "How shall fraile pen, with feare disparaged, / Conceiue such soueraine glory, and great bountyhed?" (2.10.2.8–9).[14] The narrator's question brings to the fore the enterprise of writing history and the challenges of representing history accurately, not to mention Spenser's own abilities as both poet and "poet historicall." The mention of "soueraine glory, and great bountyhed" locates the anxiety in the task of rendering his Faerie Queene in words. Even as Spenser invokes an ambiguous worry—is the difficulty getting history right or representing majesty?—his modesty about literary creation is self-reflexive. His language recalls a moment of performed poetic doubt from the third canto of the same book: "How shall frayle pen descriue her heauenly face, / For feare through

---

12. The narrator's words closely echo the start of *Orlando Furioso*'s third canto where Ariosto prepares his own reader for an Italian prophetic history: "Who will give me the voice and eloquence to do justice to so lofty a subject? Who will lend wings to my verses that they might soar up to the height of my theme? ... I shall for the moment take my ill-suited chisel to chipping free a first rough outline; later, perhaps, with more practice, I shall be able to reduce my work to perfection" (Ludovico Ariosto, *Orlando Furioso*, trans. Guido Waldman [Oxford: Oxford University Press, 1974], 3.1; 3.4).

13. Though his conclusions and evidence are different, van Es follows a similar logical trajectory in thinking that the book Arthur finds and the chronicle that Spenser reproduces are different texts (*Spenser's Forms of History*, 37–38).

14. Escobedo notes that the first few stanzas closely echo Ariosto except where they diverge from Ariosto's "cautious" invocation of prophetic inspiration (*Nationalism and Historical Loss*, 76).

want of skill her beauty to disgrace?" (2.3.25.8–9). This earlier question falls halfway through a multistanza *blason* of Belphoebe, one of the poem's central figures for Elizabeth, and is answered by a stanza opened with one of the poem's worst lines: "So faire, and thousand thousand times more faire" (2.3.26.1). Spenser's stunning demonstration of the sins of the "frayle pen" initiates a stanza that leads to one of very few half lines to appear in *The Faerie Queene*, breaking off just as Spenser's *blason* reaches Belphoebe's hemline— "Was hemd with golden fringe" (2.3.26.9; see fig. 2). This earlier attempt to depict an image of Elizabeth affords Spenser an opportunity to demonstrate his strict control of the "frayle pen," whether through the feigning of poor artistry or through the masterfully timed omission.

When Spenser repeats "fraile pen" at the beginning of the chronicle canto, he aligns the difficulty of describing Elizabeth with the difficulty of describing the Elizabethan past. In repeating both the phrase and its attendant "feare," he emphasizes that the history that follows comes from his pen, not from some worm-eaten library volume. In other words, Spenser is not only, as Escobedo has suggested, "call[ing] attention to his inability to represent Elizabeth's ancestry," but simultaneously insisting that he is precisely the poet to do it.[15] Spenser gives us every reason to believe that this is his own attempt to write the past. History becomes subject to and mediated by the poetic imagination of Spenser, who denies us the chance to read over Arthur's shoulder just as he grants himself a voice in the telling and a hand in the making of his nation's history. With no more than a quick mention of that "old mans bookes" (2.10.4.9), Spenser launches into more than sixty stanzas on the history of Britain from Brute to Uther Pendragon, Arthur's father. Filled with information from chronicle sources, and a few Spenserian inventions, the chronicles, as Harry Berger Jr. has shown, do not quite celebrate Britain, but rather emphasize its turbulent past. Berger has rightly remarked the lack of "allegorical clarity" in the "muddiness" of this chronicle account.[16] Though the content of *Briton moniments* does not provide much direction, the framework that introduces it (and Spenser's insistence on his creative capacity) sheds light on his narrative strategies as well as his engagement with temporality. The chronicles may not establish the glorious beginnings and unadulterated line of England, but they do begin to provide a way of approaching Spenser's interest in narrative time through his investment in looking back and relating the past.

---

15. Escobedo, *Nationalism and Historical Loss*, 76.
16. Harry Berger Jr., *The Allegorical Temper: Vision and Reality in Book II of Spenser's* Faerie Queene (New Haven, CT: Yale University Press, 1957), 93.

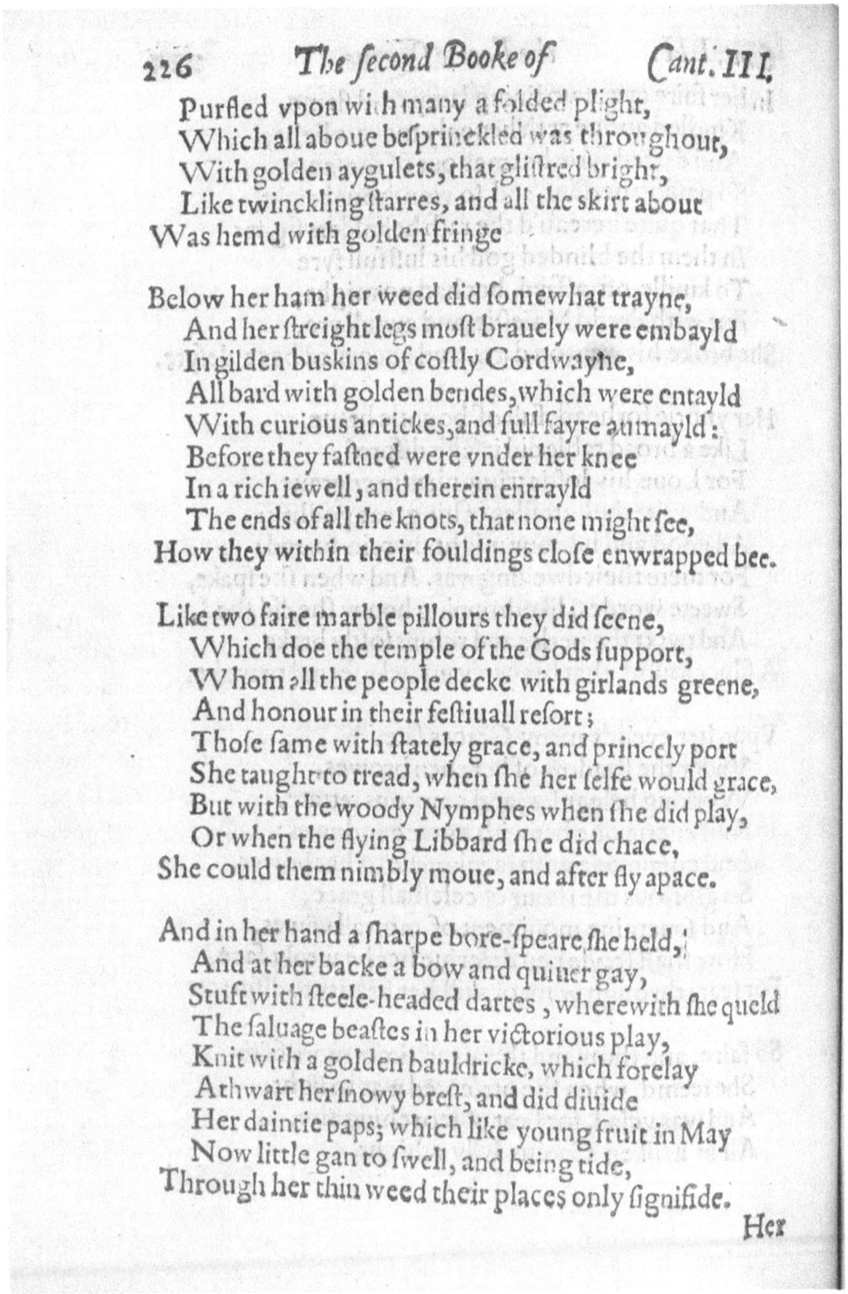

Purfled vpon with many a folded plight,
    Which all aboue besprinckled was throughout,
    With golden aygulets, that glistred bright,
    Like twinckling starres, and all the skirt about
Was hemd with golden fringe.

Below her ham her weed did somewhat trayne,
    And her streight legs most brauely were embayld
    In gilden buskins of costly Cordwayne,
    All bard with golden bendes, which were entayld
    With curious antickes, and full fayre aumayld:
    Before they fastned were vnder her knee
    In a rich iewell, and therein entrayld
    The ends of all the knots, that none might see,
How they within their fouldings close enwrapped bee.

Like two faire marble pillours they did seeme,
    Which doe the temple of the Gods support,
    Whom all the people decke with girlands greene,
    And honour in their festiuall resort;
    Those same with stately grace, and princely port
    She taught to tread, when she her selfe would grace,
    But with the woody Nymphes when she did play,
    Or when the flying Libbard she did chace,
She could them nimbly moue, and after fly apace.

And in her hand a sharpe bore-speare she held,
    And at her backe a bow and quiuer gay,
    Stuft with steele-headed dartes, wherewith she queld
    The saluage beastes in her victorious play,
    Knit with a golden bauldricke, which forelay
    Athwart her snowy brest, and did diuide
    Her daintie paps; which like young fruit in May
    Now little gan to swell, and being tide,
Through her thin weed their places only signifide.

Her

FIGURE 2. Edmund Spenser, *The Faerie Queene* (London, 1590). The Harry Ransom Center, The University of Texas at Austin.

The peculiarity of the status of Arthur's reading material is reinforced by the manner in which that book ends. *Briton moniments* stops short at Uther—that is, before the story can reach Arthur:

> After him Vther, which *Pendragon* hight,
> Succeeding There abruptly it did end,
> Without full point, or other Cesure right,
> As if the rest some wicked hand did rend,
> Or th'Author selfe could not at least attend
> To finish it: that so vntimely breach
> The Prince him selfe halfe seemed to offend,
> Yet secret pleasure did offence empeach,
> And wonder of antiquity long stopt his speach. (2.10.68)

This stanza is filled with puns that draw attention to both metrics and the physical break in Arthur's book. The second line begins with the word "Succeeding," which, it turns out, is the final word of the chronicle. "Succeeding" should presumably introduce an encomium to Uther's success, or at least should introduce the son who succeeds him, but instead, the word begins a thought that is never finished. However emphatic the puns on "Succeeding" and "Author,"[17] Spenser clouds the reason for the textual break, though his readers can understand it as a temporal matter—it occurs at the moment that the history intersects with characters alive in the narrative's present tense. The chronicle refrains from narrating any specifics of Uther's reign, leaving Arthur ignorant of both his lineage and his own place in the story. In a poem so notable for its overlapping and incommensurable time schemes, it is the telling of history that brings time most sharply to the reader's attention, emphasizing the temporal distance between the narrative chronology, the poem's reference time, and the reader's real-time existence in the 1590s.[18] Yet, Spenser's text does not admit to breaking off because of some quirky problem of simultaneity. Rather, he pointedly obscures the cause, and proposes two options by means of a noncommittal "As if . . . Or" structure. The

---

17. For a discussion of the pun on "Authour" and the depiction of the hero as a prince in the poem, see Kenneth Gross, *Spenserian Poetics: Idolatry, Iconoclasm, and Magic* (Ithaca, NY: Cornell University Press, 1985), 122–25. For a view that privileges Arthur's role as author, see also Sarah Wall-Randell, *The Immaterial Book: Reading and Romance in Early Modern England* (Ann Arbor: University of Michigan Press, 2013), 26.

18. See David J. Baker, *Between Nations: Shakespeare, Spenser, Marvell, and the Question of Britain* (Stanford, CA: Stanford University Press, 1997), 171–72 for an alternative account. He claims that the historical circumstances of the 1590s could never bear out the "heroic Britain" that the poem's projections anticipate (171–72).

first option—"As if the rest some wicked hand did rend"—offers a surmise about the physical status of the remainder of the book ("the rest"); the reference to a "wicked hand" rending the text offers the possibility that *Briton moniments* is physically compromised. Jennifer Summit has argued that in the post-Reformation era, "rending" text was an activity in which both "friends [and] enemies of history" participated, attempting either to cull the record in order to improve and correct it, or to censor it.[19] By contrast, the second option proposes a writer that "could not at least attend / To finish it," and thus conjures an image of hasty departure: someone left the codex midsentence.[20] Despite their ambiguity, these competing explanations reestablish Arthur's reading material as the ontologically distinct book from Eumnestes's chamber by drawing attention to what *Briton moniments* looks like: does Arthur face a blank page or a torn page? Just as Spenser emphasizes that we are separated from Arthur temporally, the words we read become divorced from him physically as well. His book and our book are decidedly distinct material objects.

As I noted earlier, *The Faerie Queene* notoriously includes a handful of half lines like the one at the edge of Belphoebe's skirt (fig. 2). These erasures have long eluded critics: are parts of lines intentionally absent, are the blank spaces printer's errors, or do Spenser's half lines attempt to make the poem look antique as if materially decayed? Notably, the "canker hole" in Arthur's book is not graphically reproduced; the poem continues even though *Briton moniments* has ended (fig. 3). His text ends "[w]ithout full point, or other Cesure right" because "Succeeding" signals a material break, not a metrical pause. Spenser's "full point" refers equally to the truncated matter of Arthur's book and the full stop graphically absent from *The Faerie Queene* itself, despite the retrospectively notable capital "T" present in "There" in the 1590 edition (2.10.68.2). The stanza calls attention to the lack of a graphic, material break through a series of puns that capitalize on the link between content and its poetic display. Despite the puns, however, the stanza reveals and heightens a misalignment of meter and meaning.

---

19. Summit, "Monuments and Ruins," 17–18.
20. Critics read the text as either incomplete, censored, or materially compromised, and routinely contend that "Cesure" is a reference to Caesar, which certainly resonates with the mention of "untimely breach." Summit, for example, suggests that the allusion invokes "one of the objections raised against Geoffrey of Monmouth, whose version of the British matter was damagingly perceived to differ from the one advanced in Caesar's authoritative historical writings" ("Monuments and Ruins," 17). See esp. Debra Fried, "Spenser's Caesura," *English Literary Renaissance* 11, no. 3 (1981): 262. Fried links the description of incompletion here to the metaphors Spenser uses in invoking Chaucer's *Squire's Tale* in book 4, and suggests that the agent of destruction in the poem is Time.

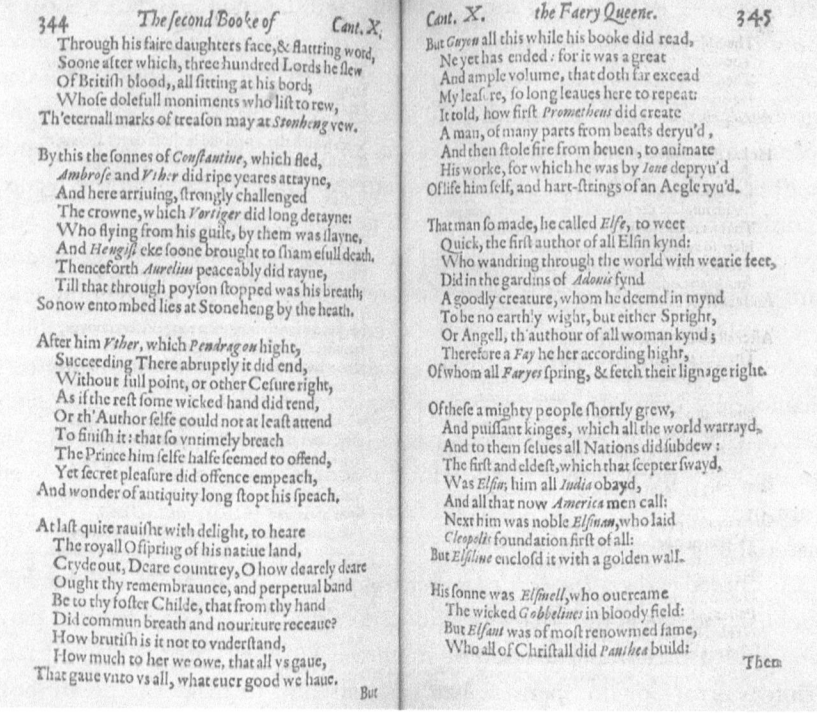

FIGURE 3. Edmund Spenser, *The Faerie Queene* (London, 1590). The Harry Ransom Center, The University of Texas at Austin.

Whereas the condition of the materials in Eumnestes's library—"all worm-eaten, and full of canker holes" (2.9.57.9)—invoked the antiquarian's enterprise of constructing history from the physical remnants of the past, Spenser absorbs the chronicle's material break into his poetics, communicating the history's "abrupt" ending through the interplay of prosody and content. Spenser highlights his role in the creation of this story by making metrics do a kind of work that could have been expressed through visual means. Rather than reproducing a lacuna, Spenser uses prosody to illustrate the disruptive force of the broken text. Though the chronicle comes to a halt one word into a line, it takes a few words, and even a second reading, to fully absorb that "Succeeding" is the final word of an unfinished thought. The meaning creates an intellectual rupture before the rhythm of the line can comfortably pause, but adjusting to accommodate that meaning alters and complicates the metrics. Before the sense of the line settles in, it reads quite naturally as regular iambic pentameter. However, as soon as we realize that "Succeeding" occasions a break, the meter must be adjusted to accommodate the pause between "Succeeding" and "There" that the meaning dictates. Yet, doing so requires a medial caesura to fall between the syllables of an iamb. *Briton moniments* may lack a "Cesure right," but the rupture in Arthur's text forces an awkward recess in Spenser's line just as "Succeeding" becomes an amphibrach that precedes a pause. As a result, the possibility of a spondaic close for the line—"did end"—enables the four beats that follow the pause to carry five stresses. Are the words after the pause masquerading as a full Spenserian line? Does the remainder of the line, beginning with "There," sonically try to squeeze five stresses—an approximation of Spenser's usual pentameter—into a line that already has a foot firmly planted in Arthur's curtailed book? Or is the entire second line masquerading as regular iambic pentameter, as though Arthur's book hadn't been interrupted at all? The line concludes with the word "end," but this is not the end of the sentence, and the lines that follow also keep pressure on the Prince's interrupted text, emphasizing the extent to which meaning and metrics are out of sync.[21]

"Succeeding" may not lead Britain's history anywhere, but the fourth line—"As if the rest some wicked hand did rend"—elaborates the stanza's prosodic self-consciousness. Spenser's diction suggests not only that the "wicked hand" has compromised the remainder of the historical content, but also that it has taken away the caesura. Spenser puns on "the rest" as both the remainder of Arthur's book and a synonym for "caesura" or "pause." The word play amplifies the poetic force of his stanza by stressing the material quality of Spenser's verse—the idea that a hand could "rend" a "rest," even punningly, suggests that the audible silence of caesura is also tangible. But, of course, Spenser himself has denied us a "rest" in the line where a physical break occurs. The regularity of the meter even works to conceal the rupture, and we have to reread and do work to insert the absence. Instead of a glaring graphical blank—a visual cue like a half line—we get an awkward, unnatural silence, or if we want to follow Spenser's usual metrical pattern, we are denied a silence. No matter who else it might refer to, that "wicked hand" also belongs to Spenser.

Curiously, the 1609 folio edition of the poem invents a compromise for this stanza by adding a graphic guide to the metrics that Spenser has made tangible to the ear (fig. 4). The 1609 compositor exaggerates the graphic tip-off provided by the capital "T" in "There" that has been present since the 1590 printing. This later edition of the poem adds several spaces between

---

21. I am grateful to Greg Londe for his help in discussing and scanning these stanzas.

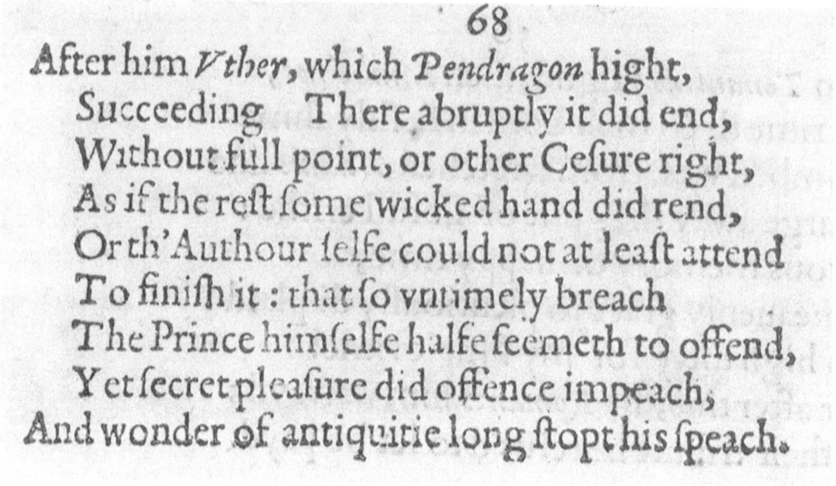

> 68
> After him *Vther*, which *Pendragon* hight,
> Succeeding   There abruptly it did end,
> Without full point, or other Cefure right,
> As if the reft fome wicked hand did rend,
> Or th'Authour felfe could not at leaft attend
> To finifh it : that fo vntimely breach
> The Prince himfelfe halfe feemeth to offend,
> Yet fecret pleafure did offence impeach,
> And wonder of antiquitie long ftopt his fpeach.

FIGURE 4. Edmund Spenser, *The Faerie Queene* (London, 1609). The Harry Ransom Center, The University of Texas at Austin.

the words "Succeeding" and "There" presumably to communicate the difference between Arthur's book and Spenser's own.[22] The change introduced in the printing process between editions alters the effect of the 1590 (and 1596) *Faerie Queene*, which simultaneously communicates physical rupture through the dissonance between meter and meaning, and through the creation of a poetics that mirrors materiality. In the poem as it originally appeared, Spenser heightens his experiment by staying silent about the more obvious reason for the break: the chronicle is incomplete because it has reached the present moment of its next historical subject. When Spenser marries the promotion of real time to prosodic measure, he shows how *poiesis* can answer physical loss. Jacques Le Goff has suggested that "history without the imagination is a mutilated, disembodied history";[23] Spenser provides us access to a quite literal encounter with this idea. Though the material rupture of *Briton moniments* is not simulated graphically, it is recreated metrically; material experience becomes metrical—accessible through an aspect of poetry that plays on a collapse between sound and touch, accessible not through what we can see, but through what we can hear.

---

22. The change suggests that at least one reader was being carefully instructed by Spenser's metrics, even if that reader doubted others would read as carefully. In the 1596 *Faerie Queene*, the typographical placement is identical to the 1590 version except that "succeeding" is misspelled (it appears as "Succeding").

23. Jacques Le Goff, *The Medieval Imagination*, trans. Arthur Goldhammer (Chicago: University of Chicago Press, 1988), 5.

Spenser's emphasis on the materiality of prosody heightens the disjointed ending of the chronicle, inviting his reader to wonder what would ever make a caesura "right." George Puttenham asserted in his *Art of English Poesy* (1589) that a caesura should come "in the midway, if the verse be even and not odd, otherwise in some other place, and not just in the middle."[24] The line that contains the end of *Briton moniments* might well be considered "odd"—both for its complexity and its pentameter—and perhaps the pause would have been more "right" at the center of the even, hexameter ninth line, that is, if the close of history came neatly at the end of a stanzaic thought.[25] But I take this to be part of Spenser's point: *The Faerie Queene* opts against presenting a measured version of time, narrative, or history. Whether through the strategic deferral of a "yitt" or crafting verse that obviates material text (despite the 1609 compositor's superfluous, exaggerated assist), Spenser has amply demonstrated his poetic control. In this case, prosodic time is skillfully manipulated just as the untidiness of real time is brought to light. In *The Faerie Queene*, the distance in time is communicated through the physical remains of the past, calling into question the relationship between time, space, and experience. The poet will bridge the history that he has split up and scattered across the poem through repetition and prosody, encouraging a reading process that moves forward and back between episodes.[26]

Though the chronicle itself was unqualified in tone, the stanza that concludes it, navigating the transition between past and present, known and unknown, is characterized by doubt. In addition to the "As if . . . Or" explanations for the text's ending, the unfinished chronicle the "Prince him selfe halfe seemed to offend, / Yet secret pleasure did offence empeach" (2.10.68.7–8). Spenser's language frustrates precision, leaving uncertain what it is that offends Arthur and why it does so only by halves, a confusion stressed by the tentative language of what "seemed." Arthur's "wonder of antiquity long stopt his speach," a notably decisive quiet at the end of a stanza characterized by vacillation.[27] The following stanza clarifies the power of the "pleasure"

---

24. George Puttenham, *The Art of English Poesy*, ed. Frank Whigham and Wayne A. Rebhorn (Ithaca, NY: Cornell University Press, 2007), 164.

25. See Paul Fussell Jr., *Poetic Meter and Poetic Form* (New York: Random House, 1965), esp. 27–30 and 77.

26. For an excellent discussion of this episode, see David Lee Miller, *The Poem's Two Bodies: The Poetics of the 1590* Faerie Queene (Princeton, NJ: Princeton University Press, 1988). In The Faerie Queene *and Middle English Romance: the Matter of Just Memory* (Oxford: Clarendon Press, 2000), Andrew King assumes that the whole poem takes place during Uther Pendragon's reign.

27. Wall-Randell's fascinating study of *The Faerie Queene* reads these cantos in a different, though often complementary, light. Focused on the "wonder" produced by a "deep, monumental unknowing" in the act of reading that Spenser fictionalizes in his poem, she shows how the "fascination" of

that mitigates the offense, but Spenser does not specify what is "secret" about it—is Arthur secretly pleased (and if so, by what?), or is he explicitly pleased by a chunk of missing text that contains something secret? Or does the rhetoric of doubt, incompletion, and thrill indicate that Arthur experiences a somatic response to his unconscious, "secret" understanding that the story he has just heard relates to him? His pleasure is surrounded by words—"secret," "offence," "empeach"—whose etymologies bespeak splitting, stumbling, and stopped feet, linking his enjoyment back to the material metrics that worked to recuperate the past even when his own material text failed him. Just as the stanza of rupture exposed the relationship between knowledge, time, and space, Arthur's sense of "wonder," which renders him "rauisht with delight" (2.10.69.1), derives from a chronicle that provides him access to the past at the same time that it suspends his geographical isolation from England, a correlation of fictive time and physical space that Spenser exhibits through a cheap pun—"How brutish is it not to vnderstand" (2.10.69.7)—that conjoins the British with the Brutus myth.

Arthur becomes an invested and enraptured armchair traveler as fictive time and space coalesce—British characters traverse a mythical space, which both offers and alters time. The language of Arthur's silent rapture—"wonder," "rauisht"—resonates in the poem's later historical scenes, and Spenser relies on prosody and repetition, as well as content, to link them all together. On a more local level, Arthur's reading engenders repetitive, painful poetry: "Deare countrey, O how dearely deare" (2.10.69.3). David J. Baker has suggested that Spenser's reader would have had the same relationship to *The Faerie Queene* that Arthur has to *Briton moniments*. That is, that *The Faerie Queene* provides an incomplete portrait of Britain, and the rupture provides a source of "secret pleasure." Baker claims that to be "between nations"—aware of but still on the verge of a not-yet-realized perfected Britain—is the source of such thrill. However, I think we take Spenser too literally if we suppose that his treatment of British history aims solely to define his British nationalism.[28] On the contrary, rather than trying to settle a link to the past, Spenser creates a space in which the past can be thought of as not yet settled. Where we expect Spenser to resolve or fill in a gap, he seems to be opening and expanding one, and the end of *Briton moniments* puts the emphasis on the poet's role in creating history through poetry. Arthur's repetitive outburst calls attention to the act of poetic creation, just as the textual rupture is embodied through its

---

a book like *Briton moniments* "might lie not in potent totality, but in incompleteness" (Wall-Randell, *The Immaterial Book*, 32, 22).

28. Baker, *Between Nations*, 173.

prosodic intricacies. The textual break quite literally displays its own novelty, forged from the neologism "abruptly."[29] Spenser marks it as a moment of creation, and links *poiesis* to an excitement—a "secret pleasure"—associated equally with not knowing and accessing the possibility of knowing.[30] The past, and its attendant national concerns, become the province of the present through the exercise of poetic creation.[31]

Upon the "abrupt" end of *Briton moniments*, Spenser turns from Arthur to find that Guyon is still reading. Critics have wrestled over Guyon's *Antiquitee of Faery lond*, observing movements within it that link it to Arthur's reading material, and also marking it as fundamentally different, particularly because it tells the invented history of the fictional Faerieland. At the same time, elements of its contents, especially toward the end, seem to stand in for a British history more proximate to Elizabeth's reign, while earlier parts of the book seem to encompass the history of the world, starting with Promethean creation. Spenser's presentation of the history of Faerieland gains momentum because it is not actually reproduced. Whereas Arthur's text became conclusively independent from Spenser's poem because its material rupture was not reproduced on the page, Guyon's text enacts the reverse principle. His history of Faerieland is offered only in summary form, hinting at the relationship between the history he reads and *The Faerie Queene* itself, described elsewhere as "this famous antique history" (2.pr.1.2). That "*Guyon* all this while his booke did read, / Ne yet has ended" (2.10.70.1–2) suggests simultaneously that Spenser has wearied of long chronicles and that Guyon currently reads the interminable history of Faerieland, a "great / And ample volume, that doth far excead / My leasure, so long leaues here to repeat" (2.10.70.2–4). Spenser's mention that Guyon's reading "[n]e yet has ended" also draws attention to the fact that the Faerie history, unlike the chronicle that Arthur reads, *does* take its reader into the 1590 present moment. Spenser takes the claim that the history exceeds his "leasure" to "repeat" seriously, and offers only a seven-stanza redaction of that "ample volume"—what Chloe Wheatley has persuasively argued is an "epitome" of the full text.[32] Citing

---

29. Spenser, *The Faerie Queene*, 258n68.1–2; and Summit, "Monuments and Ruins," 17.
30. See Angus Fletcher, *The Prophetic Moment: An Essay on Spenser* (Chicago: University of Chicago Press, 1971).
31. For a different view, see van Es, *Spenser's Forms of History*, 47–48 and 52–53. He links the materiality of the poem's historical objects to Camden and antiquarianism. For the relevance of this to antique objects, see van Es, 45–46. King claims such items get placed in Faerieland (*Middle English Romance*,160–88).
32. Chloe Wheatley, "Abridging the *Antiquitee of Faery lond*: New Paths through Old Matter in *The Faerie Queene*," *Renaissance Quarterly* 58, no. 3 (2005): 857–80.

both "his appropriation of the rhetoric of time management found in many epitomes" as well as his gestures to "rhetorical and print practices associated with the creation of epitomes," she suggests that Spenser is playing on the profusion of "more readily marketable . . . octavo or smaller texts that claimed to summarize . . . large folio histories."[33] Her argument aids our consideration of Spenser's presentation of himself as historiographer, and his engagement with the practices of antiquarianism and history. Spenser's interest in and awareness of these forms and debates suggest that both are quite different from his own representation of history. His engagements with historical form and content enable him to experiment with the temporality of his own narrative.

The delight that Arthur betrayed at the mere possibility of knowing resurfaces in Guyon's reading. In the narrator's seven-stanza synopsis, he skips "seuen hundred Princes" in the middle, claiming they "were too long their infinite contents / Here to record" (2.10.74.3, 5–6). What remains is a history that begins at the beginning, with Prometheus's creation of "Elfe" (71), and ends with Gloriana (76). Though critical attention has long attempted to map the pieces of this allegorical history onto English history, recently scholars have paid particular attention to the history because it links present-day Faerieland with a history of imperial domination:

> Of these a mighty people shortly grew,
> And puissant kinges, which all the world warrayd,
> And to them selues all Nations did subdew:
> The first and eldest, which that scepter swayd,
> Was *Elfin*; him all *India* obayd,
> And all that now *America* men call:
> Next him was noble *Elfinan*, who laid
> *Cleopolis* foundation first of all:
> But *Elfiline* enclosd it with a golden wall. (2.10.72)

Taken together, the analogy of a remote historical existence of the New World and the claim that the rule of Faerieland has reached to geographies as distant as India and America have occasioned intriguing critical analysis. David Read, for example, argues that through Faerieland "Spenser is not writing the past history of regions that are known to the visionary poet in the present and will be revealed to those less clairvoyant in the future. He is writing the history of the future itself, of the as-yet-undiscovered inheritance

---

33. Ibid., 861–62.

of England."³⁴ Read takes this as an imperial gesture, that Spenser's "indication of a genuinely New World already bestowing its abundant gifts on the Old World lends his words the quality of *prophetia ex eventu*; the success of the Elizabethan adventure is (or ought to be) a foregone conclusion."³⁵ Similarly, Wheatley argues that the events in Guyon's history "seem to be projected into England's future."³⁶ On her account, the epitome form underscores the futurity of the gesture, since it suggests an empire "so secure, so total, that it will be possible to epitomize it in a casual, nonprophetic, and distinctly bureaucratic manner."³⁷

I want to resist these two provocative readings, in part to suggest that it is precisely the treatment of temporality in *The Faerie Queene*'s historical episodes that invites the kind of speculation offered by Read and Wheatley. They use the New World references to imagine Faerieland as an undiscovered country that exists not just in Spenser's poem, but in the reader's world, one that provides a glimpse of an impending British imperial future.³⁸ As Read puts it, "As part of Spenser's ahistorical history, America is also part of England's promised future."³⁹ Spenser's *The Faerie Queene* writes a history of the future, but rather than defining that future in terms of a projected imperial interest, the poem imagines itself as reinventing the history it offers to the reader. In so doing, Spenser scrutinizes the project of history writing, and even the feasibility of such writing, not by suggesting the inevitability of Elizabethan conquest, but by imagining that poetic narrative has a role to play in the creation of the historical imagination, rendering the poetic future responsible for the impending past.

In Alma's castle, the chamber that leads to Eumnestes's repository of memory contains allegories of the present and the future. The future belongs to Phantastes, a "man of yeares yet fresh" (2.9.52.3), who sits in a chamber

---

34. David Read, *Temperate Conquests: Spenser and the Spanish New World* (Detroit: Wayne State University Press, 2000), 21–22.
35. Ibid., 22.
36. Wheatley, "Abridging," 869.
37. Ibid.
38. However, the manner in which Britain as a nation is fictional and unreachable in the poem mirrors the ineffability of the geographical Faerieland. See also Ingham, who argues that Spenser "view[s] Arthur as the genealogy necessary for imagining a British national future; those imaginings depend upon the losses and the antagonisms crucial to [an] earlier romance tradition" (*Sovereign Fantasies*, 7).
39. Read, *Temperate Conquests*, 42.

filled with some things "as in the world were neuer yit" (2.9.50.4), as well as "flyes," "idle thoughtes and fantasies,"

> Deuices, dreames, opinions vnsound,
> Shewes, visions, sooth-sayes, and prophesies;
> And all that fained is, as leasings, tales, and lies. (2.9.51.6–9)

The description of the future jars with the textual matter of the past that Guyon and Arthur encounter. Phantastes's chamber also contains things "as in the world were neuer yit"—an explanation that undercuts the notion of material novelty. However, it is not entirely clear how seriously we are to take this allegory of the future, which links "[s]hewes, visions, sooth-sayes, and prophesies" with lies in a poem that will put precisely these endeavors in Merlin's capable hands in book 3. Spenser continually uses time to investigate the complexities of the relationship between history and narrative imagination. He underscores this by linking history with reading, a temporally absorbing enterprise. Guyon and Arthur almost miss dinner because of their reading: "So long they redd in those antiquities, / That how the time was fled, they quite forgate" (2.10.77.3–4). Ironically, reading chronicles from memory's chamber makes these readers forget time. Arthur loses track of time just as the reader encounters the poem's most prominent admission of chronological specificity. The concentration that the two knights exhibit in their enraptured reading also marks distraction—dwelling on the past comes at the expense of having new adventures and fulfilling quests. Arthur and Guyon, figures of avid reading, reveal a present moment characterized by an absorption in the past, which Spenser resists by showing repeatedly that he uses the present moment to invent history.

II

Spenser's historical episodes tug on temporal frameworks, gaining traction especially through fractured report—the British history curtailed in book 2 continues in Merlin's prophecy in book 3. The poem asserts an overt manipulation of past and future when it turns to engage in prophetic figuration because of *The Faerie Queene*'s timeline: Arthur cannot reasonably be both a character in the present tense of the text and simultaneously "enrold" in the annals of history. As a result, anything that occurs during or after Arthur's lifetime becomes the domain of the future fictionally, even if the events related are also familiar history for Spenser's contemporary audience. By making the narrative's present tense the pivot point from which to delineate "past" from "future," Spenser inserts into his poem a structure that both depends on linear historical structures and promotes a sense of ordered stasis. However, the figure of Arthur as the logical point of orientation between past, present, and future offers a false sense of temporal stability that the poem constantly works to undo.

The complexity of narrative time in the poem is apparent even within the initial chronicle: though *Briton moniments* ends "abruptly" at the moment that the chronology reaches Arthur, the sixty stanzas themselves contain at least one loose thread. In a brief, prophetic reference at 2.10.49.8, the chronicle mingles projection and hindsight: England's subjection to Rome persists "[t]ill *Arthur* all that reckoning defrayd." Though Arthur is the text's fictional reader, this temporal wrinkle does not gain his notice. In an analogous muddle of linearity, Merlin's prophecy resurrects the telling of British history begun in book 2, but does so in the midst of an extended flashback. Indeed, Spenser's narrative is fueled by temporal confusion, most poignantly felt in book 3's commitment to the *entrelacement* typical of romance, and the structure—Arthur's history, Britomart's prophecy—heightens the chaos created by narrative fracture. As a result, the present provides the illusion of a simple, singular temporal perspective, but the narrative itself jostles the present and even unsettles the certainty of the narrative ahead especially through the alteration of the story of the past.

Despite the presence of magical instruments and mystical visions, the episode in Merlin's cave is slowed by repetition, a persistent backward looping that coexists alongside his future forecasting. In the thick of the romance, the revelation of Britomart's prophetic history comes by way of a brief introduction to Merlin—what one might, were it not so impossibly convoluted, call an epitome. Spenser provides his quick history of Merlin via a set of stanzas repeatedly qualified by what David O. Ross might call the "Alexandrian footnote."[40] Over four different stanzas in this seven-stanza summary, Spenser tells us twice what "they say," once what "some say," and once what "men say" (3.3.7–13). Stephen Hinds has suggested that, as a rhetorical strategy, the "Alexandrian footnote" means that "the poet portrays himself as a kind of scholar, and portrays his allusion as a kind of learned citation."[41] Here, however, despite Merlin's medieval literary frame, the "they say" construction,

---

40. David O. Ross Jr., *Backgrounds to Augustan Poetry: Gallus, Elegy and Rome* (Cambridge: Cambridge University Press, 1975), 78.

41. Stephen Hinds, *Allusion and Intertext: Dynamics of Appropriation in Roman Poetry* (Cambridge: Cambridge University Press, 1998), 2.

which appears only twice in the entire chronicle canto, strikes a tentative note when compared to the manner of telling the history that came a book before or the prophecy immediately to follow, though both pepper details out of Geoffrey of Monmouth with Spenser's own inventions.[42]

In what A. C. Hamilton describes as a "whimsical interlude," Spenser begins by recounting Merlin's whereabouts with the nearly nonsensical "whylome wont . . . / To make his wonne," or so "they say" (3.3.7.5–6).[43] He exhibits his trust in external wisdom when he advises the reader to "go to see that dreadfull place . . . if thou euer happen that same way" (3.3.8.1–2), duly supplying directions that come courtesy of what "they say." However, at the close of the same stanza, the narrator cautions against entering Merlin's abode, calling into question both his confidence in outside authority and his own reliability as a guide, since the narrative soon makes the descent he disavows. Just before that journey begins, Spenser provides another description that relies on temporality to undercut and establish imaginative credibility: the narrative moves from relying on what "they say" to reporting what "some say." Spenser's Galfridian adventure is preceded by a rehashing of the story of the Lady of the Lake, and the implication is that "some" are decidedly less reliable than "they." Merlin's imminent appearance in the cave, alive and intact, validates this distinction, leaving the reader to conclude that either the familiar legend is mere fantasy or that Spenser's poem predates this well-known literary moment.[44]

Britomart and Glauce's "entraunce bold" into Merlin's cave fails to "moue" him, since "of their comming well he wist afore," a foreknowledge emphasized by the narrator, who spends the following pair of lines insisting that nothing remains "hidden" or "vnknowne" to the wizard (3.3.15). The scene leans heavily on repetitive and superfluous narrative: Merlin asks that his visitors "vnfold" their purpose in stanza 15, and he bids them "tell on" in stanza 16, goading Glauce into continuing her false account until he breaks into laughter, unable to "beare her bord" any longer (3.3.18–19). He goes on to tell his prophecy twice, first in a two-stanza redaction that reveals

---

42. For example, as Hamilton notes, Spenser names Merlin's mother Matilda (*The Faerie Queene*, 313n13).

43. Spenser, *The Faerie Queene*, 312, note to lines 8–11.

44. Spenser also situates himself temporally against Ariosto at this moment: he subtly one-ups Ariosto by implying either that Britomart's prophetic visit predates Bradamante's, or that Bradamante's is the stuff of cloudy legend, not national history, the sort of thing that only "some say." For a discussion of unidentified external authority as a component of oral tradition, see Susanne L. Wofford, "Epics and the Politics of the Origin Tale: Virgil, Ovid, Spenser, and Native American Aetiology," in *Epic Traditions in the Contemporary World: The Poetics of Community*, ed. Margaret Beissinger, Jane Tylus, and Susanne Wofford (Berkeley: University of California Press, 1999), 244.

that from Britomart's "wombe a famous Progenee / Shall spring, out of the aunceint Troian blood" (3.3.22.5–6), and then in a full-blown account of British history after Uther.[45]

In Eumnestes's library, Arthur's chronicle ended abruptly, devoid of "Cesure right," and Merlin's prophecy is similarly truncated:

> But yet the end is not. There *Merlin* stayd,
> As ouercomen of the spirites powre,
> Or other ghastly spectacle dismayd,
> That secretly he saw, yet note discoure:
> Which suddein fitt, and halfe extatick stoure
> When the two fearefull wemen saw, they grew
> Greatly confused in behaueoure;
> At last the fury past, to former hew
> Hee turnd againe, and chearfull looks did shew. (3.3.50)

Hamilton notes that Merlin's final words echo "Christ's words to his disciples telling them of the things that must come to pass before the end of the world: 'but the end is not yet.'"[46] In book 3, the words of the gospel are rearranged to right the pentameter.[47] Though in this case, "yet" enjoys a slot early in the line, it announces the same inventive poetic control as the "yitt" that deferred indefinitely Arthur's discovery of his own lineage. The eschatological resonance highlights the fact that Merlin knows more than he reports, and his announcement of time's continuation simultaneously marks the end of his speech. The mage's sudden silence often attracts critical attention because the mention of the "ghastly spectacle" suggests Elizabeth's childlessness will result in a tumultuous British future. However, the force of the scene can also be located in its links to its earlier historical partner. Merlin's silence stands apart from the broken *Briton moniments* because his is true *aposiopesis*—though he might say more, he breaks off into silence. Yet the language and mechanics of the stanza share common ground with the close of Arthur's book: Spenser repeats the word "There" to signal the narrative break, even though cessation in Merlin's cave does not find physical form in a fictional book. The poet again explains the silence through an ambiguous "As ... Or" construction, refusing, or perhaps unable, to provide

---

45. In *Revisionary Play: Studies in the Spenserian Dynamics* (Berkeley: University of California Press, 1988), 120, Harry Berger Jr. points out that even though Spenser goes to the trouble of enumerating Merlin's magical abilities, he resigns him to a more benign prophecy.

46. Spenser, *The Faerie Queene*, 319n50.1.

47. The word order that Hamilton cites is standard in versions of the Bible from at least 1535 to 1612, including the Great Bible, Bishop's Bible, Coverdale Bible, Geneva Bible, and King James Bible.

a definitive reason. Considering Merlin's break by looking back to book 2, rather than forward to the unknown content of his omission, reveals that Spenser's poetry in the cave finally grants a satisfying caesura, punctuated by a "full point" at the very moment it reintroduces interruption—ending the prophecy before it requires Spenser actually to predict the future. This time, the majuscule "T" in "There" draws attention to the terminal punctuation—a period—that occurs three feet into the line. In this case, the mismatch of meaning and punctuation attempts to contain the wizard's fury with controlled prosody. The announcement that reorders the gospel of Matthew—"but yet the end is not"—precedes a period, and introduces a medial caesura that clearly ascribes the apocalyptic phrasing to Merlin. His reaction to the vision recalls the vocabulary of Arthur's response—whatever he "secretly" sees sends him into a "halfe extatick stoure" reminiscent of the Prince's "secret pleasure."

Merlin rounds out the history begun at Alma's, employing the familiar epic construction of legitimizing history by telling it prophetically, thus validating events to readers who already understand the narrated events as part of their national past. Spenser emphasizes the providential implications of this historiographical method:

> It was not, *Britomart,* thy wandring eye,
> Glauncing vnwares in charmed looking glas,
> But the streight course of heuenly destiny,
> Led with eternall prouidence, that has
> Guyded thy glaunce. (3.3.24.1–5)

Merlin's words simultaneously offer an appealing paradigm for viewing the poem as a whole, capitalizing on the early modern understanding of prophecy as an act of interpretation rather than mystical access to an unknowable road ahead. *The Faerie Queene* hardly provides a "streight course," but the second scene of history does work to "guyde" the reader's "glaunce." For example, Merlin's prophecy, born of a vision that already reaches back to the magic mirror, sprinkles some retrospective mystical dust into Eumnestes's library where first Arthur and then Guyon "chaunce" upon the narratives that tell their histories. In his note to these lines—"There chaunced to the Princes hand to rize, / An auncient booke, hight *Briton moniments*" (2.9.59.5–6)—Hamilton glosses "rize" as "happen; come to hand," and Berger argues that the poet's "phrasing stresses the purposiveness beneath the chance."[48] Berger's view of the text anticipates a link between Eumnestes's chronicles and Merlin's

---

48. Berger, *Allegorical Temper,* 80n3.

"streight course of heuenly destiny" (3.3.24.3), but his intuition does not take the lines quite far enough. Whereas Hamilton's is surely the dominant register of meaning, the text twinkles, however briefly, with the image of the "aunciend booke" floating toward Arthur. Yet, the mystical bridge built between serendipity and destiny, paved with a dash of magic, *depends* on Merlin, who discusses the phenomenon explicitly, and it is through the wizard that we can satisfy ourselves with a return to Eumnestes's chamber, attentive to the repetition of the word "chaunce" when "Sir *Guyon* chaunst eke on another booke, / That hight, *Antiquitee* of *Faery* lond" (2.9.60.1–2). I am only slightly disingenuous when I suggest that the image of a book floating in midair gains purchase in Merlin's cave.

Merlin may stop at the moment when the real 1590s future is at stake, but his prophetic history begins without Arthur. It is only by treating the two historical episodes together that we can see that the poet has cut Arthur out of his historical narrative, leaving the Prince to exist entirely in Spenser's fiction. He silently corrects the long-standing problem of the issueless king by introducing Artegall ("equal to Arthur," and similarly ignorant of his own history), the half brother through whom he reroutes the British line. As a result, Merlin's manner of telling—history in the guise of prophecy—does more than merely rewrite history in the future tense.[49] The fractured historical record between Eumnestes's book and Merlin's prophecy tells us *when* the poem takes place, and also repeats the rupture of narrative to jolt us into awareness of how and when we gain such knowledge. To be attentive to looking both forward and back in this poem is to notice that Spenser's historical episodes invite aggregation.[50] It shows us how to navigate the poem, both demanding that separate episodes be read together and drawing attention to the poem's treatment of time.

Susanne Wofford points out that epics "seek to represent cause and to tell a story of origins, and an important subset of epic also seeks to make that story into a national history, providing a surrogate memory for the nation," even though epics also regularly display an anxiety about their inability to do just that.[51] Most Renaissance editions of *The Aeneid* included an additional book of the poem in order to provide the epic with a gentler close.[52] In Spenser's narrative, the project of "perfecting" comes

---

49. See van Es, *Spenser's Forms of History*, 164 for this claim.
50. For an analysis of a similar phenomenon in the Arthurian tradition, see Ingham, *Sovereign Fantasies*, 6.
51. Wofford, "Epics and the Politics of the Origin Tale," 241.
52. According to Burrow, *Edmund Spenser* (Plymouth: Northcote House Publishers, 1996), Mapheus Vegius penned this thirteenth book, regularly appended to the poem because it concluded

90   CHAPTER TWO

from the opposite direction—rewriting the beginning of the story. The flickering possibility for a book's mystical "rize" in Eumnestes's chamber gets instantly extinguished, in part because the poem's temporal structures are preempted by an undercurrent of Galfridian legend that the text never explicitly engages. As soon as his prophecy ends, Merlin refers to the wars against pagans that Uther is engaged in "now," but his insistence on the present moment reasserts the poem's manipulation of temporality—this is the "now" of flashback, after all.

Merlin's cave, introduced by structures of hearsay, continually questions narrative credibility and helps to illuminate book 2's interest in narrative origins, which in turn unsettle future stories. Indeed, it is fitting that it is Arthur who unwittingly encounters his future self in the book he reads, given his role as a weathervane between past and future in the poem.[53] In her study of medieval Arthurian romance, Patricia Ingham cites both the "wide circulation of Arthurian traditions in the late Middle Ages" and the "difficulty in recognizing some of those stories as history" as evidence that tracing such stories elucidates "contestations over the ownership of a British imaginary past, indeed of Britain itself."[54] The chronicle canto revealed that for Spenser the "ownership of a British imaginary past" is inextricably linked to the project of poetry. In a similar vein, the poet opts not to rewrite the story of King Arthur, unlike many other writers, but instead makes his "antique history" a story of anteriority—that is, not solely a story about the past, but also a story of what happened *before*. Middle English tales of Arthur often focused on the loss and death of Arthur,[55] and as soon as he appears in *The Faerie Queene* the hero's death is invoked: Merlin made the shield, sword, and armor for "this young Prince, when first to armes he fell, / But when he dyde, the Faery Queene it brought / To Faerie lond, where yet it may be seene, if sought" (1.7.36).[56]

Yet Spenser's engagement with this typical feature of Galfridian literature aims to alter narrative time, not to follow precedents. The fantasy of the legendary Arthur—*Rex quondam, Rexque futurus*—notoriously cheats time. The once and future king grants Arthur a life in multiple temporal

---

the epic "in a manner that is aware of the mildness appropriate to a Christian hero"—that is, with Aeneas's marriage to Lavinia (30).

53. See Summit for a comprehensive account of how Matthew Parker et al. were particularly focused on Arthur in their library plans; she also outlines what Leland and Prise conceded in their effort to defend the veracity of Arthurian history ("Monuments and Ruins," 14).

54. Ingham, *Sovereign Fantasies*, 3.

55. See Ingham, *Sovereign Fantasies*, passim for a treatment of this facet of the tradition.

56. Hamilton points out that the same is said of Caesar's sword at 2.10.49.5 (Spenser, *The Faerie Queene*, 99n36.8–9).

registers, especially as his story absorbs Britain's past into an ex post facto providential history popular with Tudor propagandists. Spenser turns this temporal trick on its head; he rewrites the story of Arthur's origins. By telling the backstory of the King, Spenser's invention is an act of pretelling, one that simultaneously calls the usual, future story into question by making his creative imprint on the moments that *precede* the standard narrative. Contra Wofford's claim that Spenser makes clear "the need to evade direct representation of origin," he writes a new story of Arthur, the story of Prince Arthur.[57] Spenser's creation of Arthur raises some of the same creative questions that will arise when Scudamour recounts his own narrative in book 4, canto 10; in both cases, the reader is invited to wonder how looking backward will affect the ride forward. Indeed, the abrupt end of *Briton moniments* proves less innocent—by sixteenth-century England, there was a wealth of material relating the story of King Arthur, and genealogies that could move beyond Uther. Arthur's story moves past this moment, and while he understandably stops here because the character cannot reasonably find himself lurking in a set of chronicles, the stopping point also reminds the reader that Arthur's story, which begins with backstory, is under Spenser's own control.

The poet establishes the poem in time through the meeting point of Arthur and history, but *The Faerie Queene* also invents an unknown history of Arthur.[58] Arthur's other history, the well-known but uncomfortably flawed story of King Arthur, is invoked without ever appearing in Spenser's text. Within the question of narrative time and the question of future history, Spenser's main character also makes the most overt gesture to a story of origins, one that might parallel the Elfin history that stretches back to Promethean creation. It is a choice that lends *The Faerie Queene* a claim to being a story of origins. To leave off at the moment preceding Arthur in book 2, canto 10, and to pick up just beyond him in book 3, canto 3, allows Spenser to play with the notion of a story never told, even as that story is being told. The "they say" and "some say" constructions bring credibility to the fore, but they also tempt us to wonder about Spenser's flirtation with literary fatalism—will all the signal princely virtues of *The Faerie Queene*

---

57. Wofford, "Epics and the Politics of the Origin Tale," 258. Ingham has argued that "late Middle English Arthurian romance offers a fantasy of insular union, an 'imagined community' of British sovereignty," claiming that the Arthurian tradition was able both to "encode utopian hopes for communitarian wholeness" and "poignantly narrate the impossibilities, the aggressions, and the traumas, of British insular community" (*Sovereign Fantasies*, 2). See also Wofford, 253 for a discussion of the risks that epics face in employing etiologies.

58. See King for a discussion of the broken ancestral link between Arthur and Elizabeth (*Middle English Romance*, 196).

inevitably dissipate once Arthur becomes king and settles into his more familiar, and much more problematic, role? Is Arthur doomed to a qualified, negative exemplarity, the kind of picture painted by popular works such as Richard Lloyd's *A briefe discourse of the most renowned actes and right valiant conquests of those puisant Princes called the Nine worthies* (1584)? Or does Spenser's portrayal of Prince Arthur, and his hints at the narrative that he precedes, cause the reader to wonder what the history of Arthur's future holds?

Spenser's poem illustrates that any story might be different than what we have been told, or even that it awaits its own revision. In reproducing a sense of the contingency of the received story, Spenser also leaves ambiguous the source of that contingency: is it located in the happening, the telling, or both? I would suggest that rather than merely retelling and reshaping the familiar parts of Arthur's story, Spenser invents a most innovative and far-reaching history by intersecting origins—by writing up to a moment of rupture to suggest he will close the fissure, and then not doing so. He relies on mythography to construct history through narrative imagination, and calls into question that familiar future story. Ultimately, the engagement with history and backstory suggests that changing the story of the past can invalidate an inevitable outcome and a future story; looking backward in the service of moving forward has the power to alter the future.

III

The prophetic history that Merlin offers Britomart concludes a lengthy flashback that began much earlier in book 3. That first canto of analepsis opened on a perplexing historical note:

> Here haue I cause, in men iust blame to find,
> That in their proper praise too partiall bee,
> And not indifferent to woman kind,
> To whom no share in armes and cheualree,
> They doe impart, ne maken memoree
> Of their braue gestes and prowesse martiall;
> Scarse doe they spare to one or two or three,
> Rowme in their writtes; yet the same writing small
> Does all their deedes deface, and dims their glories all,
>
> But by record of antique times I finde,
> That wemen wont in warres to beare most sway,

And to all great exploites them selues inclind:
Of which they still the girlond bore away,
Till enuious Men fearing their rules decay,
Gan coyne streight lawes to curb their liberty,
Yet sith they warlike armes haue laide away,
They haue exceld in artes and pollicy,
That now we foolish men that prayse gin eke t'enuy. (3.2.1–2)

The narrator's claims about the "prowesse martiall" of the fairer sex pave the way for his celebration of Britomart, but his account of gender politics comes via a muddled view of history. "Men" are guilty of denying "woman kind" not only a "share" in chivalric undertakings, but also of proper valorization for the courageous "deedes" they do perform. Far from book 2's allegory of memory—the "infinite remembraunce" granted Eumnestes, keeper of national chronicles—these undifferentiated males "maken memoree" without much concern for accuracy, and they omit women's "braue gestes," or distort them in their writing. Yet the evidence for assigning "iust blame" comes from the "record of antique times." In the space of two stanzas, the narrator attempts to have it both ways—men corrupt the written record of valiant deeds, which can, in turn, be found uncorrupted in the historical record, a register that implies, no less, that ancient women were better warriors than men. Spenser's hyperbolic claims about the effect of envy on both "lawes" and historical writing dazzle with statements so unfamiliar that the contradictory assumptions about historical fallibility might easily glide by unnoticed. The pair of stanzas also draws an implicit temporal distinction between men in the present tense and the "record of antique times." How can the record be simultaneously fallible and infallible? Spenser's paradoxical stanzas playfully present a logical fallacy in which history remains at the center of his inquiry, but also bring to the fore a set of questions relevant to the recounting of history: Is the "record of antique times" more reliable because it is older? If so, how has Spenser vetted it, and what is wrong with the writings of his contemporaries? And, more to the point, what does it suggest about the reliability of the story that Spenser is in the midst of telling?

Though book 3, canto 2, focuses on personal history rather than national history, the internal contradictions that initiate the canto set the tone for the question of credibility in the stanzas that follow. Spenser's narrative begins its loop backward because the Redcrosse Knight decides "[t]o ask this Briton Maid, what vncouth wind, / Brought her into those partes, and what inquest / Made her dissemble her disguised kind" (3.2.4.5–7). Redcrosse's unremarkable attempt at small talk renders Britomart speechless.[59] She quakes and blushes, the victim of "hart-thrilling throbs and bitter stowre" (3.2.5.3). When she finally regains her composure, she answers her companion with a fabricated history constructed to elicit news of Artegall, the true object of her quest. It is the mere thought of her amorous endgame that occasions her "passion" (3.2.5.9); the narrator's description of Britomart's "hart-thrilling throbs" recalls the "secret pleasure" and "wonder" that "long stopt [Arthur's] speach" at the end of his chronicle reading, while her "bitter stowre" anticipates the "halfe extatick stoure" that ends Merlin's prophecy a canto later. The repeated language strengthens the conceptual links between these episodes, but it is through Britomart that Spenser explicitly connects the process of thinking back and recounting a story of origins with *eros*, a development that works to recast and elucidate the personal, emotional engagement common to the fragments of history scattered throughout the poem.

Redcrosse obliges her request for a full description of Artegall: "And him in euerie part before her fashioned" (3.2.16.9). Though Redcrosse's words are not reproduced, Spenser refers to them as an almost *enargeiac* conjuration—he brings Artegall "before her," "fashion[ing]" his virtual presence so that it can appear in Britomart's imagination. The line is nearly repeated in the following stanza—"Yet him in euerie part before she knew" (3.2.17.1)—but the word "before" no longer indicates mental space. Rather, Spenser's repetition employs the temporal register of "before" as the bridge to a narrative dissolve that launches the multicanto flashback. With this turn on the doubled word, Spenser separates the function of time and space.

The narrator recounts how Britomart discovered Merlin's "mirrhour playne" (3.2.17.4) in which she found Artegall reflected: "By straunge occasion she did him behold, / And much more straungely gan to loue his sight, / As it in bookes hath written beene of old" (3.2.18.1–3). The initiation of Britomart's love for Artegall has dynastic implications for British national history, as Merlin will detail at length in canto 3. At this moment, however, Spenser clouds historical import by foregrounding the instability of the relationship between history and poetic invention. What exactly has been written in these old books? Spenser's contorted syntax admits two possibilities: either love at first sight, though "straunge," is normalized by being the familiar fare of old stories, or it is the story of Britomart's glance in Merlin's mirror that is the tale as old as time. In the latter case, the story Spenser is in the midst of inventing

---

59. For an analysis of the ubiquitous "introductory tale" in the poem, see Merrilee Cunningham, "The Interpolated Tale in Spenser's *The Faerie Queene*, Book I," *South Central Bulletin* 43, no. 4 (1983): 99–104.

concomitantly would lay claim to a place in a well-known tradition.[60] As I argued earlier, the union of Britomart and Artegall corrects the problem of an heirless Arthur common to most medieval accounts, and provides the most efficient means for unsettling the medieval traditions of Arthuriana—that is, his future. Though the chronicle canto was heavily indebted to sources such as Geoffrey of Monmouth and Holinshed, Spenser went out of his way to position himself as the author of that account of history. In Britomart's flashback, by contrast, at the moment that he tweaks British destiny by inventing Britomart's history, Spenser implies that his inventions are old news, already available in the unquestioned "record of antique times."

On the other side of Merlin's cave, British history is told a third time in a narrative invited by Hellenore and provided by Paridell. In book 3, canto 9, Paridell plans to tell the story of his history in order to communicate to Hellenore his plans for their own private, amorous future—that is, as a means of seduction. Heather Dubrow argues that "Paridell's conflation of boasting and wooing" itself alludes to a counternarrative to the mainstream account of epic, citing Helen's rebuff in the *Heroides* when she chides Paris: "But you boast your birth, your ancestry, and your royal name.... Go now, and loudly tell of remote beginnings of the Phrygian stock, and of Priam with his Laomedon."[61] In this canto, however, it is Hellenore who requests lineage: "Purpose was moued by that gentle Dame, / Vnto those knights aduenturous, to tell / Of deeds of armes, which vnto them became, / And euery one his kindred, and his name" (3.9.32.2–5). Paridell's account of his genealogy takes the connection between kindred and name awfully seriously: he charts a family tree that leads from Paris to Parius to Paridas to Paridell. The repetition looks and sounds precious, if not contrived. However, by considering Spenser's historical episodes together, we cannot help but notice that Paridell's account is built on the same phonemic principles as Guyon's history, alive and resonant with its morphologies of "elf" (2.10.71–75). Through Paridell, Spenser foregrounds and parodies his own historical *poiesis*, emphasizing the poem's habit of both rewriting history and laying claim to an originary moment. The commingling of glances back with questions of source, invention, and credibility reveals the nuanced layers of Spenser's claim that *The Faerie Queene* is itself an "antique history."

---

60. For a discussion of Merlin as a figure for the artist, see William Blackburn, "Merlin," in *The Spenser Encyclopedia*, ed. A. C. Hamilton et al. (Toronto: University of Toronto Press, 1990), 470–71.

61. Heather Dubrow, "The Arraignment of Paridell: Tudor Historiography in *The Faerie Queene*, III.ix," *Studies in Philology* 87, no. 3 (1990): 322.

Paridell dubs his ancestor Paris the "Most famous Worthy of the world" (3.9.34.1)—a particularly absurd claim for the Greek character best known for his amorous exploits. Paridell's account of origins warps a set of literary facts well known to Spenser's original readership—it was Paris's brother, Hector, who earned a spot among the nine.[62] Paridell's claim to descend from a worthy is not in much danger of being believed, but his attempt to rest his present identity on a lineage of altered history warrants notice because his family tree contains another of the poem's rare half lines: "The which he dying lefte next in remaine / To *Paridas* his sonne. / From whom I *Paridell* by kin descend" (3.9.37.4–6). Is Paridas Paridell's father? Does the fifth line mark an omission, a rupture, a trailing off? Is this another "canker hole"? Paridell's account does not enjoy an overabundance of credibility, so it is particularly difficult to determine whether or not an important piece of Paridell's lineage is missing. What is most striking is that it does not much affect the story. Unlike ruptures in the other histories of Britain, this one is barely noticeable.

The interruptions that do merit attention in this episode belong to Britomart. In an attempt to correct Paridell's version of history, Britomart asks Paridell "backe agayne / To turne [his] course" (3.9.40.5–6) to fill in the details of his account of Aeneas. Far from inspiring novel discovery, Britomart's request, though couched in navigational language, casts the heroine as Dido, entreating her Aeneas to tell his tale twice over. Britomart calls attention to the enterprise of presenting and representing history as she begs Paridell to alter his version of the past. Spenser's readers know that Paridell's account is pure fabrication, a realization that simultaneously calls into question the fictionality of the account he gets wrong. Moreover, the exchange emphasizes the act of literary creation in the act of looking back. She interjects:

> There there (said *Britomart*) a fresh appeard
> The glory of the later world to spring,
> And *Troy* againe out of her dust was reard,
> To sitt in second seat of soueraine king,
> Of all the world vnder her gouerning.
> But a third kingdom yet is to arise,
> Out of the *Troians* scattered ofspring,
> That in all glory and great enterprise,
> Both first and second *Troy* shall dare to equalise. (3.9.44)

---

62. As did Arthur; Paridell's false history hints yet again at the Arthurian legend that shadows Spenser's text without ever being explicitly told.

Britomart's language is immediately confusing—the story she cites predates all of the history so far recounted in the poem, but she introduces Troynovant in future terms: "yet is to arise." Hamilton identifies her excited interjection—"There there"—as *epizeuxis*, but the word she chooses to repeat is not merely rhetorical.[63] Instead, it points to a specific *location* in a prophetic story that she repeats by rote, rendering the familiar tale material even as she enacts its currency in the present moment through repetition. The story should also sound familiar to readers of *The Faerie Queene* not just because of its general fame, but also because Britomart's assertion that this great empire "yet is to arise" bespeaks a kind of "are we there yet" sentiment, since Troynovant first appears in *Briton moniments,* when Hely's son Lud "did reædifye" its "ruin'd wals" (2.10.46). The elusive nature of temporality resonates with the "reædify[ing]" of London's walls—Spenser emphasizes the repetition and retelling of history, and the momentum of a beginning forever jostled by the possibility of an earlier moment. It also echoes both the withheld "yitt" that separated Arthur from his lineage and Merlin's concluding "yet," which deferred the end even as it reordered a familiar biblical verse. The gesture is underscored by the phrase "scattered ofspring," since in the sixteenth century, "offspring" could mean both "source" and "progeny."[64]

In this poem, history is never told just once. Indeed, though Britomart and Paridell offer two different versions of epic history, her desire to hear Aeneas's story reminds us not only of Dido, but also of the threat that Dido traditionally poses to the teleological drive of epic narrative. Paridell overtly turns the fall of Troy into a romantic plot as he attempts to ignite a romance with Hellenore. But are we to extend Paridell's overtly parodied lineage to Britomart's claims for British origins in the Troynovant schema? Spenser might well have chosen to couch this contested story in such muddy terms, protecting himself with a defense of potential irony. But the more striking detail is that Britomart's interest in her national history and destiny aligns her with Dido—that is, with the narrative mode of delay and stasis par excellence: romance. While the chronicle mode already blurs the line between romance and history, the passion evoked by reading is usually associated with the dangers of romance reading; here, however, the idea that reading is dangerous gets mapped onto history. In fact, it is through the technique of

---

63. Hamilton marks this as *epizeuxis*, a rhetorical device where a word is repeated to mark vehemence or emphasis (Spenser, *The Faerie Queene*, 377n44.1). Van Es points out the change in tense in these stanzas and claims it is Spenser's attempt to "anticipate the glory of Brutus, Arthur, and Elizabeth equally" (*Spenser's Forms of History*, 147).

64. See *OED*, s.v. "offspring, *n.*," defs.1a, 2a, 2b, and 4.

entrelacement that a continuous history is knit across the fracture—a process that depends on the reader. Dubrow notes that both in Merlin's cave and at Malbecco's table, Spenser describes Britomart as "empassiond" and "sighing" as she listens to the stories of her national past and future, thus tying the two scenes together.[65] The connections do not end there—Britomart also sighs when Redcrosse asks about her background, and the affective vocabulary of "wonder," "hart-thrilling throbs," and "stoure" resurfaces repeatedly at these historical moments. These outpourings of emotion also tie her to the "fervent fire" with which Guyon and Arthur "burn." In all these episodes, even if history is meant to convey the "just memory" of public, political lives and deeds, Spenser moves into the realm of intensely private moments of retelling. Arthur and Guyon, the most passionate of readers, enjoy that imaginative engagement *as* readers—they are intensely antisocial, each grabbing his own book and reading silently to himself. Britomart's request to Paridell might similarly remind us that at the end of book 2, canto 10, both Arthur and Guyon are "beguyld" by their reading, linking their "thrill" with Merlin's magic. At this third historical moment, the strands of all the histories are drawn together because the presentation of history throughout time is described through paradigms familiar to the reading of romance. Spenser's weaving together of history and the intensely emotional, magical reaction to their past suggests that history, regardless of one's temporal starting point, is born of back-and-forth motions, a movement that bears comparison with another kind of reading practice: if biblical typology links texts by revealing how stories in the Old Testament prefigure those in the New, Spenser's historical accounting suggests a similar expectation that episodes benefit from being considered in tandem.[66] The poem, however, also places an emphasis on simultaneity, and on the act of trafficking back and forth between episodes without privileging a particular end.

IV

The dual motion of forward and back slows its pace considerably in book 4. At the very end of the ninth canto, Amoret, a figure for chaste, married love, famously and inexplicably disappears from the poem just as her paramour, Scudamour, offers to tell the story of how he and Amoret first met. As Jonathan Goldberg has noted, the opening of the following canto is filled with such banal commonplaces about love that it takes several stanzas for the

---

65. Dubrow, "The Arraignment of Paridell," 315–16.
66. See Fletcher, *The Prophetic Moment*, 57–76.

reader to realize that it is Scudamour, and not the narrator, who is speaking.[67] At the instant that the two lovers are unmistakably and inexplicably denied reunion, Scudamour narrates—in an instance that is absolutely unique in this regard—an entire canto of the poem.[68] This peculiar canto recalls the narrative disorientation that preceded the chronicle canto at book 2, canto 10, similarly foregrounding the person responsible for crafting the history.

Scudamour's canto is an exercise in sustained backstory, and the unlikely interim narrator crafts the narrative of his own amorous history. Scudamour describes the various impediments that barred his entrance into the Temple of Venus, giving special mention to the porter at the outer gate: "His name was *Doubt*, that had a double face, / Th'one forward looking, th'other backeward bent, / Therein resembling *Ianus* auncient" (4.10.12.3–5). It is only in the narratorial hands of Scudamour that Spenser's pervasive image of moving forward while looking back invokes Janus, the god of gates and doors and beginnings and endings, by name.[69] The Roman deity was regularly associated with temporality, and Scudamour's comparison hinges on the two-faced god's currency in time—Janus is able to look in opposing directions simultaneously, just as he can serve as a point of reference in the present moment and as an "auncient." At the same time, the mythical figure normally championed for his doubled perspective is absorbed into an allegory of mental paralysis, and Spenser stresses the hazards of back and forth by pairing Doubt with Delay.

As a character who frequently exhibits rash boldness, Scudamour is not the most obvious choice as the poem's mouthpiece for multidirectionality. He proceeds to face Daunger, guardian of the "*Gate of good desert*," a "hideous Giant . . . dreaded ouer all," a monster so gruesome that "oftentimes faint hearts at first espiall / Of his grim face, were from approaching scard . . . soone as they his countenance did behold, / Began to faint, and feele their corage cold" (4.10.16–18). In other words, facing Daunger is more likely to inspire hasty retreat than contemplative hesitation or dual motion. But

---

67. Goldberg's observation is part of his larger claim about narrative desire. His reading of book 4, heavily engaged with Chaucer's *Squire's Tale*, explains this episode as a moment in the poem when recursive narration hinders the fulfillment of something that is right in front of Scudamour: "He goes back to a troubled beginning when a happy ending seems to stand before him" as a movement toward "permanent loss" (Jonathan Goldberg, *Endlesse Worke: Spenser and the Structures of Discourse* [Baltimore: Johns Hopkins University Press, 1981], 62–64).

68. Goldberg notes that this is the "only canto in book IV in which one entire story corresponds to one marked unit of narration" (*Endlesse Worke*, 67).

69. Ignaro may represent half of Janus just "deprived of his younger, forward-looking face (i.e., foresight, circumspection), for he is given a staff and keys, the typical emblematic signs" of Janus. However, "double-faced figures" generally "personify not Ignorantia but Prudentia (wisdom), as represented by Janus." Wilhelm Füger, "Ignaro," in Hamilton et al., *The Spenser Encyclopedia*, 388.

Scudamour, armed with his magic shield, aligns himself with a dual perspective only after he has passed Daunger:

> So as I entred, I did backeward looke,
> For feare of harme, that might lie hidden there;
> And loe his hindparts, whereof heed I tooke,
> Much more deformed fearefull vgly were,
> Then all his former parts did earst appere.
> For hatred, murther, treason, and despight,
> With many moe lay in ambushment there,
> Awayting to entrap the warelesse wight,
> Which did not them preuent with vigilant foresight. (4.10.20)

Scudamour explicitly connects his look back to an allegory of hidden danger, as figured by the giant's monstrous "hindparts." However, because Scudamour's entrance happens in the midst of a look back, it also seems to lay claim to an allegorical engagement with the menace of retrospection. Scudamour's view of Daunger's posterior—literal hindsight—occasions commentary on the prospect of foresight, but his syntax obscures the function of a prudent look ahead, leaving the reader to wonder whether danger strikes as a result of a lack of foresight or in spite of such vigilance. Though he is a figure of Janus, we are only granted a brief glance at Doubt's face; Daunger, on the other hand, appears in three dimensions, exaggerating his duality as a figure of the body made temporal.

The flood of contradictory images of twinned perspective, retrospection, and foresight, does not do much to relieve the discomfort produced by Scudamour's love life—the backstory he offers begins with a backward glance just as a narrative reunion is replaced by an account of originary events. Why does Scudamour, granted the space to provide a narrative, choose to go back and add this story of his first amorous sally? When Busirane holds Amoret captive at the end of book 3, Scudamour complains in two successive stanzas, "My Lady and my loue is cruelly pend" (3.11.11.1), articulating his beloved's physical imprisonment through a pun that also lays blame on Spenser's pen and the cruel storyline it has invented. So, why, when Scudamour gets a stanza-long chance at retaliation, does he choose to use his own pen to insert the story that came *before* Spenser's? Does this new knowledge of amorous abduction alter our understanding of the events that come after it? Does it change our view of the Amoret-Scudamour story or of their pairing? By taking over the story, Scudamour brings the main narrative methods of the historical episodes into the poem's fictions, highlighting the idea of contingency as he subverts order in his self-conscious act of telling. We will never know if a completed poem would have included the reunion of Scudamour and Amoret, but in book 4, cantos 9 and 10, their imminent meeting is clumsily replaced by Scudamour's account of origins. The canto he narrates generates more questions than it answers, most notably because it ends in abduction. In crafting an account of his own ardent beginning, Scudamour encourages reflection on the contingent nature of the poem we have been reading.

Goldberg argues that the "fundamental quality of narration" in book 4 is deferral. Indeed, book 4, the subject of Goldberg's analysis, begins with the "displacement" of book 3's original ending, and includes Scudamour's canto that appears in lieu of romantic reunion, engaging and sustaining the balance of forward and back in part because it never comes to a close. Goldberg's formulation sheds light on the temporal considerations that emerge from the poem's treatment of the past. These moments, explicit in their denied endings, are not so much "perfected" when the next installment of history appears as they are a demonstration of the creative activity of the poem. They are not notable for the way that they generate a need for further narrative, but rather for the creative activity they generate in being interpreted together, suggesting that temporal structures add to the procedures of "endlesse worke."[70]

The 1590 edition of *The Faerie Queene* ends with the joyous reunion of Amoret and Scudamour, rendered silent ("No word they spake") by their "pleasure" and "sweete rauishment" in embrace (3.12.45). The narrator assures the reader that

> Had ye them seene, ye would haue surely thought,
> That they had beene that faire *Hermaphrodite*,
> Which that rich *Romane* of white marble wrought,
> And in his costly Bath causd to bee site:
> So seemd those two, as growne together quite. (3.12.46.1–5)

Melded together at this happy moment, the lovers enjoy the jointure of hermaphroditism, rather than the dual perspective—whether doubt or wisdom—of Janus. Yet, of course, the 1596 *Faerie Queene* changes the 1590

---

70. Goldberg explains his reading through Roland Barthes's conception of the "writerly text" (*Endlesse Worke*, 8–10). He points out that the Temple of Venus episode is "explicitly embedded in texts." He claims the episode is overshadowed with reading of a directive—reading and rereading, and sees Scudamour as the "embodiment of the already written text" (65). Considering a concept such as "endlesse worke" as a function of temporality works to pinpoint an interpretive activity predicated on the idea of multidirectional thinking.

ending, ripping apart that union for the purpose of narrative generation. Critics regularly refer to the "canceled" ending of the 1590 poem, but I would argue that the change is more emblematic of the way that histories and stories change, and undergo alteration, even silently.[71]

Even as Scudamour merrily relates his abduction of Amoret in book 4, canto 10, his canto ends with an incomplete allusion to the story of Orpheus and Eurydice.[72] The reference omits the infamous moment of looking back, that is, the moment when looking back results in loss. Hamilton has suggested that Spenser might have drawn on a lesser-known version of the myth,[73] but I am inclined to read Scudamour's omission as a more pointed reminder that narrative acts, whether mythographical, historical, or personal, are the province of the present and future even if their scope glances back. In Spenser's narrative, looking back does not necessarily result in a painful reminder of a lost, inaccessible past, but rather it regularly results in thrill, and even proves generative when reconsidered in conjunction with later textual moments.

In Alma's castle, the figure for the present is never named. The "man of ripe and perfect age" (2.9.54.2) is only identifiable as the present because his chamber is located in between Eumnestes's and Phantastes's, between the past and the future. The present moment, its room filled with law and policy, conjures the kind of judgment associated with the interpretation of prophecy, as an enterprise of both understanding the past and foreseeing the future.[74] How can this model for the present possibly work in a poem in which time is so insistently confused? When the present moment is so difficult to locate? And even then time might slip by, as one reads, without one's notice. Part of Spenser's investigation of narrative and narrative time comes about as he manipulates temporality in the telling of history, as he

---

71. This critical tendency, of course, borrows its vocabulary from bibliographic convention. In the printing process a cancel (*cancellans*) replaces a canceled leaf (*cancellatum*) as a means of error correction. However, the idea that the original ending of book 3 is a *cancellandum*—erroneous stanzas in need of replacement—is importantly speculative. My point is that a critical terminology that leans on typographical convention in this instance is necessarily imprecise: the relationship between the original 1590 ending and the new ending to the book of Chastity that appears in 1596 is much stranger and more ambiguous than this technical vocabulary admits.

72. Goldberg sees this as a "suppresse[d]" ending, whereby Orpheus gains a "story of loss to tell"; he claims that "rereading, recounting" are Scudamour's "only prize": "the story progresses only by denying endings that were earlier possible" (*Endlesse Worke*, 66).

73. Spenser, *The Faerie Queene*, 49n58.4–5.

74. For a discussion of providence, and the treatment of Arthurian heroism in the poem, see Richard A. McCabe, *The Pillars of Eternity: Time and Providence in "The Faerie Queene"* (Blackrock, Ireland: Irish Academic Press, 1989), esp. 51.

investigates the complexities of both telling and verifying history, as well as the imaginative role that both writer and reader might play in the process. Spenser's repeated treatment of accounts of Britain's origins betrays a shrewd recognition that the future controls the events of the past through writing. Spenser offers a model for narrative born of the same double vision that his backward-headed characters enjoy. In *The Faerie Queene*, the written, historical record does not depend upon the physical existence of fanciful geography, but rather it depends on the literary imagination, underscoring the role of the reader in both preserving and projecting future memory. The future's history includes both the transmission of the present moment, and the tools with which the past can be recuperated and interpreted. Looking backward while moving forward engenders a simultaneity that encourages the reader to join disparate episodes together, and also emblematizes the notion that the history of the future requires an understanding of the present moment as an act of narrative construction.

Chapter 3

The Fiction of the Future
Dangerous Reading in Titus Andronicus

When Titus Andronicus first encounters his mutilated, violated daughter Lavinia, he exhibits understandable grief, outrage, and resolve: "Let us that have our tongues / Plot some device of further misery / To make us wondered at in time to come" (3.1.134–36).[1] At this moment, the most familiar logic of revenge—an eye for an eye—gives way to a different kind of calculation: for Titus, the appropriate retribution is one that will be "wondered at" in the future. Titus's appeal to posterity foregrounds the irony of the drama: onstage, a Roman no one has ever heard of muses about what the future will think of him. In the previous two chapters, I charted strategies for approaching the future that relied on temporal reflexivity. Both Sidney's and Spenser's fictions work to destabilize the mechanisms upon which secure and dependable teleologies depend. In the *Old Arcadia*, Sidney grounded his investigation by challenging the gap between the presumed fixity of art and the flux of experience. In *The Faerie Queene*, Spenser used the contested space of the Elizabethan historical imagination to make the future a consequence of artistic production. For Spenser, making history is the poet's prerogative, and his poem demonstrates how a fiction's present tense can productively unsettle both past and future.

---

1. All references are to William Shakespeare, *Titus Andronicus*, ed. Jonathan Bate, 3rd ser. (London: The Arden Shakespeare, 2002).

In chapters 1 and 2, the future illuminated the elasticity of the past, and imaginative literature demonstrated how looking to the future prompts us to reconsider seemingly reliable assumptions about our relationship to the past. My focus turns now to the Shakespearean stage. Shakespeare's earliest tragedy takes up the intersection of historical and poetic license on rather different terms. *Titus Andronicus* stands out in this book for a number of reasons. Unlike the other literary texts I treat, it makes no claims to the category of romance; it is a revenge tragedy. It has a complicated textual history and an even more complicated authorial history.[2] It is also the only core fiction in *Untold Futures* that does not include a soothsayer, oracle, or prophetic voice. I turn to *Titus Andronicus* in this chapter, despite these singularities, to initiate an argumentative arc that considers Shakespeare's treatment of the future in light of his career-long interest in antiquity. In this regard, I treat *Titus* as the first in a series. Not incidentally, that series includes three of Shakespeare's Roman plays.[3] In this chapter, however, my interest is not in classical allusion per se, but in the relationship between narrative paradigms and the practice of hermeneutics. Unlike the other dramas classified as Roman plays, in *Titus* history is a convenient fiction. Not only do Titus and the play's other protagonists fail to ring any bells in the collective Elizabethan historical consciousness, but the very present from which Titus invokes a projected "time to come" also evades historical placement. Remarkably, however, in the play the past in question is not unsettled. On the contrary, the past, especially the literary past, is so stable that characters use it as a reliable road map for the future.

Titus Andronicus takes place in a Rome populated by invented Romans, Goths, and a single Moor, but *when* does it represent?[4] Admittedly,

---

2. *Titus Andronicus* has never enjoyed an uncomplicated place in Shakespeare's canon. Although it has not been universally accepted, many scholars support the recent case made for George Peele's collaboration. Brian Vickers offers a comprehensive account of both the long history of doubting Shakespeare's authorship and evidence of coauthorship in *Shakespeare, Co-Author: A Historical Study of Five Collaborative Plays* (Oxford: Oxford University Press, 2002). My argument stresses a continuity between Shakespeare's first and last Roman plays that aims to highlight the importance of his use of classical allusion, and especially his interest in Ovid's *Metamorphoses*, evident in *Titus Andronicus*. I do not insist upon Shakespeare's sole authorship, but for the sake of simplicity and consistency, I refer throughout the chapter to *Titus* as Shakespeare's play. See Patrick Cheney, *Shakespeare's Literary Authorship* (Cambridge: Cambridge University Press, 2008), 70–71 for an illuminating discussion of this issue.

3. Robert S. Miola's influential *Shakespeare's Rome* (Cambridge: Cambridge University Press, 1983) was the first to include *Titus Andronicus* in a discussion of "the works of Shakespeare's Roman canon" (14).

4. Katharine Eisaman Maus, "Titus Andronicus," in *The Norton Shakespeare* (New York: W.W. Norton & Company, 1997) discusses historical sources for the action in *Titus*. On the accuracy of *Titus*'s Rome, and the lineage of empire, see Naomi Conn Liebler, "Getting It All Right: *Titus*

Elizabethan drama has never been known for its attachment to chronological fidelity; the abundance of unremarked anachronism on the Renaissance stage does not suggest that questions of precise historical placement much troubled the sixteenth-century playgoer. Nevertheless, *Titus Andronicus* stands out for the resemblance it bears to real Roman histories. The play traffics between the succession crisis with which it opens and a Goth invasion near its close, inviting assumptions about the relation of the play to the notable events that *do* appear in the pages of Plutarch and Livy, or even to the birth of Christ.

Gordon Braden has argued that this "Rome of no particular period" lends the play's "brutalities a sinister feel of timelessness"; other critics have been interested in the political purchase a declining Rome might afford Shakespeare's implicit commentary on the Elizabethan state.[5] But I begin this chapter by asserting that a puzzlingly atemporal ancient Rome differs markedly from the kind of "timelessness" established by a play whose characters orient themselves through their engagement with literature. Shakespeare's play constructs its present tense on literary-historical terms: not only is the play overwhelmingly devoted to classical allusion and imitation, but its characters also constantly and overtly refer to these texts.[6] In alluding to, reading, and seeking to interpret plays, poetry, and history, the characters onstage also reveal that Titus's ancient Rome is a Rome in decline because this "wilderness of tigers" (3.1.54) exists after all the major works of classical Latin literature (the poems of Virgil, Ovid, and Horace; Seneca's plays; Livy's histories) have already been written.[7] Because his characters fashion their

---

Andronicus and Roman History," *Shakespeare Quarterly* 45, no. 3 (1994): 263–78. For a possible source text for the play, see G. Harold Metz, *Shakespeare's Earliest Tragedy: Studies in* Titus Andronicus (Cranbury, NJ: Associated University Presses, 1996), 150–89.

5. Gordon Braden, "Shakespeare's Roman Tragedies," in *A Companion to Shakespeare's Works: The Tragedies*, ed. Richard Dutton and Jean E. Howard (Oxford: Blackwell Publishing, 2003), 1:200. For a compelling political claim about the play as a comment on English national identity, see Heather James, *Shakespeare's Troy: Drama, Politics, and the Translation of Empire* (Cambridge: Cambridge University Press, 1997).

6. Little criticism on the play fails to note its classical allusions. For attention to Ovid in particular, see, for example, Jonathan Bate, *Shakespeare and Ovid* (Oxford: Clarendon Press, 1993). For a discussion of distinctions between *aemulatio* and *imitatio* in the period, see G. W. Pigman III, "Versions of Imitation in the Renaissance," *Renaissance Quarterly* 33, no. 1 (1980): 1–32; and Vernon Guy Dickson, "'A Pattern, Precedent, and Lively Warrant': Emulation, Rhetoric, and Cruel Propriety in *Titus Andronicus*," *Renaissance Quarterly* 62, no. 2 (2009): 376–409. For allusive theory more generally, see Charles Martindale, *Redeeming the Text: Latin Poetry and the Hermeneutics of Reception* (Cambridge: Cambridge University Press, 1993).

7. For a comprehensive discussion of Rome and Ovid's status as school text in the play, see Grace Starry West, "Going by the Book: Classical Allusions in Shakespeare's *Titus Andronicus*," *Studies in Philology* 79, no. 1 (1982): 62–77.

actions in the present according to models gleaned from literary texts that the play insists are already antique, already so canonical that they have been relegated, in this imaginary Rome, to libraries and grammar books, Shakespeare pens a present moment bound to a problematically certain future. Ovid enjoys pride of place, not least because a codex of his *Metamorphoses* appears onstage in the fourth act. That poem's ubiquity calls into question Titus's aim to "plot some device" because Titus himself does not plot much of anything; rather he and his fellow characters follow Ovid, and brilliantly, gruesomely reenact his stories. As a result, Titus's conception of the future ends before it begins—the future is inherently foreclosed because prewritten plots prescribe its outcome.

Literary history sets the temporal scene, but it is the *interpretation* of that literature that proves crucial to the play. Titus's own obsession with the material text extends beyond the superficial gesture of producing an actual *Metamorphoses* onstage.[8] In this chapter, I show how Shakespeare's characters challenge and limit future possibility by employing Ovid's text as though it were a practical handbook for revenge. Titus's appeals to "plot" and "wonder" expose a wider rift between the characters' awareness of their tireless adherence to literary texts and their troubled interpretive practice, which ignores the consequences those same texts anticipate. I argue that their hermeneutic derives from the medieval tradition of moral commentaries, a link that sheds light on the play's comments on both pagan antiquity and post-Reformation England: Shakespeare critiques the tradition of Christian attempts to moralize Ovid's *Metamorphoses* by placing those interpretive techniques in the hands of ruthless pagan characters who pervert that text's narratological underpinnings. They conflate beginnings and endings and force etiologies to become teleologies. In so doing, they enable Shakespeare to expose the dangers of a moralizing hermeneutic. He shows that a reading practice that flattens the complexities of artistic production restricts the future; such an approach to the literary is what renders pagan poetry truly dangerous for Renaissance England. The playwright explores the implications of a future inevitably compromised, leaving only the narrowest of openings for an alternative, which he voices through the fleeting, but markedly Christian, appearance of a clown.

---

8. Shakespeare's countrymen and his fictional Romans share intriguing literary common ground: Shakespeare imagines a late antique world in which the ancients are just as obsessed with classical texts as the moderns. So while Shakespeare's classical allusions may be in keeping with an Elizabethan interest in antiquity, they also tempt us to believe that little has changed in that regard *since* antiquity.

I

As Titus announces, classical texts provide a "pattern, precedent, and lively warrant" for the play's plot (5.3.43), and even the bold and violent acts of revenge in *Titus* call into question the value of a present moment that effectively rehearses the past. Imitation might help to situate the play historically, but it does so at the expense of the future. The play's brand of innovation operates via amplified, hyperbolic allusion that results in "mythology viewed in the competitive mode."[9] Ovid's story of Philomela provides the chief example of classical reference at its most dynamic and mobilizing, both communicative and dialogic, beginning with Aaron's prediction that Bassianus's "Philomel" (i.e., Lavinia) "must lose her tongue today" (2.2.43).[10] Chiron and Demetrius both follow and improve upon Ovid's story: Philomela outwits Tereus by transmitting the tale of his wrongs via tapestry, so after raping her, Tamora's sons cut off Lavinia's hands as well as her tongue, thereby denying her Philomela's means of communication. Lavinia's uncle Marcus immediately understands the trick: "A craftier Tereus, cousin, hast thou met" (2.3.41). Yet Shakespeare highlights the limits of *amplificatio* by deferring any kind of active response until an actual copy of Ovid's *Metamorphoses* appears onstage and enables the family to understand the crime and Titus to devise a revenge "patterned by" that poet (4.1.57). Despite the edits and amplifications, the future, though it technically still lies ahead, derives from a pattern established in the literary past, one that anticipates an inevitable outcome.[11] So when, just before baking them into pies he will feed to Tamora, Titus explains to Chiron and Demetrius, "[W]orse than Philomel you used my daughter, / And worse than Progne I will be revenged" (5.2.194–95), hyperbole and allusion begin to jar: what exactly makes it "worse"? If Titus follows Procne's lead to the letter, then isn't his revenge really just equivalent? Should we understand that it is worse because of the repetition, because no lesson was learned from Ovid's brutal tale? Shakespeare includes two rapists where Ovid had one, puts two boys in pies instead of one. However, within the play's grotesque atmosphere of exaggeration, this literal doubling strikes a superficial

---

9. Leonard Barkan, *The Gods Made Flesh: Metamorphosis & the Pursuit of Paganism* (New Haven, CT: Yale University Press, 1986), 244.

10. Cf. Barkan's contention that Ovid provides "a series of paradigms for the act of communication" (*Gods Made Flesh*, 247).

11. Stanley Fish helpfully details the idea that the set of possibilities for discourse are inevitably limited by the standards of play in "The Law Wishes to Have a Formal Existence," in *The Fate of Law*, ed. Austin Sarat and Thomas R. Kearns (Ann Arbor: University of Michigan Press, 1991), 159–208. In "Allusion and Sacrifice in *Titus Andronicus*," *SEL* 49, no. 2 (2009): 311–31, Danielle A. St. Hilaire addresses the question of the future, but focuses on future generations and offspring.

note; the outdoings seem gratuitous. I contend that the playwright suggests a register for "worse" that bears directly on the play's relationship to the future: worse because it will not go down in history; worse because it lays bare a future fundamentally curtailed—because of its willful reliance on the literary past, the present has a wholly predictable outcome, one that Chiron and Demetrius can recognize as soon as Titus mentions Procne, and that they should have expected as soon as they dragged Lavinia into the woods.[12]

Admittedly, the notion of bounded narrative potential is not limited to classical allusion. The structure of revenge tragedy is also prone to foreclosing the future. As John Kerrigan notes, "When a revenger accepts the task imposed on him, he limits the flexibility of his life-responses in order to focus on a single aim."[13] In *Titus*, however, classical patterns insert themselves precisely where the script for revenge ought to go. Whereas traditionally "the revenger is prevented from originating an action,"[14] *Titus*'s initial catalyst for revenge—Alarbus as sacrifice—provides a motivation but not a template for revenge. Instead of following a pattern of abuse, characters in *Titus* rely on a literary pattern, and, more particularly, an Ovidian myth that encodes its own script for revenge.[15] As a result, the moment of origination comes in the act of literary choice, in *turning* to follow a literary precedent. Where we expect the revenger to seek an eye for an eye, in *Titus* the revenge structure has shifted to an eye already plotted by a myth. The problem is the foreclosure of outcomes (and the ethical determination of outcomes) because of the standard practice of a plot teleology that must be followed *to the letter*. The type of future-oriented, memorializing gesture with which the play began—Titus burying his sons at the tomb of the Andronici—marks a road not taken. As classical myth begins to steer the play's patterns, memorial structures and "originary" grievances give way. In their stead, patterned "plotting" charts the course of events, and revenge holds it steady.[16]

---

12. St. Hilaire usefully tries to distinguish between the Goths' classicism and Titus's ("Allusion and Sacrifice," 319).

13. John Kerrigan, *Revenge Tragedy: Aeschylus to Armageddon* (Oxford: Clarendon Press, 1996), 201.

14. David Scott Kastan, "'His Semblable Is His Mirror': *Hamlet* and the Imitation of Revenge," *Shakespeare Studies* 19 (1987): 113. In his argument about Hamlet's exceptionalism, Kastan provides a valuable discussion of the tension between the imitative structure of revenge and Renaissance writers' predilection for imitation.

15. In "Lavinia's Message: Shakespeare and Myth," *Renaissance Papers*, 1981, 65, Barbara A. Mowat suggests a further element of allusive layering—that allusions to the Philomela story actually function within a larger "revenge structure" modeled on Hecuba's story.

16. The election of mythical templates goes hand in hand with the initial irony of Titus as a forgotten historical figure who comes onstage to emphasize his plans for memorable action. In their

Far from suggesting a nuanced relationship to the future, Shakespeare's prophetic foreshadowing demonstrates the stronghold of the Ovidian web in which his characters are caught. Bassianus, doomed to the pit that would have been his beloved's salvation, initiates a string of references to Ovid's Pyramus and Thisbe story, which get reiterated until a character comments on the tale explicitly. Assuming that a lion has killed his beloved Thisbe, Pyramus commits suicide, and the "leaves that were upon the tree besprincled with his blood."[17] When Quintus approaches the hole that Martius has just fallen into, he asks, "What subtle hole is this, / Whose mouth is covered with rude-growing briers / Upon whose leaves are drops of new-shed blood" (2.2.198–200). As in Ovid's description, Quintus's words are followed by brutal realization, and just as Pyramus misidentified the mountain lion as a murderer, both Quintus and Martius are wrongly blamed for the death of Bassianus, who lies in the pit. The allusion is a bubble beneath the surface that rises to view a few lines later when Bassianus's ring illuminates "the ragged entrails" of the pit, revealing his dead body to Martius, who remarks, "So pale did shine the moon on Pyramus / When he by night lay bathed in maiden blood" (2.2.230–32).[18] The extended reference to the Pyramus and Thisbe story, a myth that would hold some fascination for Shakespeare in his early career, enjoys a partner in the play's various references to Diana and Actaeon. At the beginning of this exchange in the woods, occasioned by a hunt, Tamora notes that the "babbling echo mocks the hounds," and forty lines later, tells Bassianus and Lavinia, "Had I the power that some

---

adherence to classical precedents, characters in *Titus* act in a way that suggests a desire to become exemplary, never focus on themselves *being* imitated, but rather loyally follow literary models. Though Titus's desire to be "wondered at in time to come" seeks to indicate a revenge producing unspeakable "misery," his language never even flirts with the idea of inspiring imitators.

17. Golding, *Metamorphoses* 4.150. All references are to Ovid, *Ovid's Metamorphoses: The Arthur Golding Translation, 1567*, trans. Arthur Golding and ed. John Frederick Nims (Philadelphia: Paul Dry Books, 2000).

18. An echo of this story returns two scenes later when Marcus describes Lavinia's wounds as "a conduit with three issuing spouts" (2.3.30), recalling Golding's rendition of Pyramus's wounds: "And cast himselfe upon his backe, the bloud did spin on hie / As when a Conduite pipe is crackt, the water bursting out / Doth shote it selfe a great way off and pierce the Ayre about" (Golding, *Metamorphoses* 4.147–49). In *Ovid Renewed: Ovidian Influences on Literature and Art from the Middle Ages to the Twentieth Century*, ed. Charles Martindale (Cambridge: Cambridge University Press, 1988), 12, Charles Martindale cites this moment in the Pyramus and Thisbe story as classic evidence that "Ovid cannot be tied down to one set of static attitudes.... When he tells the story of Pyramus and Thisbe, the tone is pathetic, until the outpouring of blood of the dying Pyramus is compared to water spurting out of a drainpipe (*Met.* 4.121ff). But this unexpected moment of grotesque wit, while it may undercut, does not destroy the pathos of the tale as a whole, which is certainly not merely a parody of a tragic love story."

say Dian had, / Thy temples should be planted presently / With horns, as was Actaeon's, and the hounds / Should drive upon thy new-transformed limbs" (2.2.61–64).[19] Shakespeare embeds Ovid into his language in a manner that conflates prescience and inevitability; the impetus to "plot some device" never stood a chance.

Ovid's *Metamorphoses* bears significant responsibility for making things "worse" in this play; because Ovid often tells source stories—etiological legends—about objects that already exist in the world, his narrative paradigm proposes that we live in a world dictated by mythological consequence. Arachne, spinning her tapestry, is always already arachnid: she transforms to fit her name, and the spider carries that name because of the woman she once was. If Ovid's etiologies, fundamentally past-oriented, suggest that we live in a world of endings, Shakespeare's use of the *Metamorphoses* in this play allows him to create a Rome that exists without the possibility of new beginnings. At the same time, Shakespeare mimics another Ovidian structure: rather than offering a single, linear narrative, the *Metamorphoses* delights in underscoring connections between stories, creating not only a past-oriented collection of myths, but also an interconnected web of stories. Still, in Ovid, a reader might, however briefly, follow the trail back far enough to an originary moment or an originary rape. Not so in Shakespeare, since the playwright's point of origination is the *Metamorphoses* itself. Being inseparable from Ovid complicates both interpretation and the future because Ovid's own text inspires a hermeneutic that implicates every textual moment simultaneously. In his 1567 translation of the *Metamorphoses*, Arthur Golding compares the poem to a "cheyne" in which "eche linke within another wynds," adding that "every tale within this booke dooth seeme to take his ground / Of that that was reherst before, and enters in the bound / Of that that folowes after it."[20] As Jonathan Goldberg notes, Echo's and Philomela's stories are "entwined" because of their emphasis on voice, just as Echo and Narcissus become forever linked through Ovid's rendering.[21] When Shakespeare's characters use the *Metamorphoses* as a manual after which to "pattern" action,

---

19. Anthony Brian Taylor points out that Tamora's statement that the "babbling echo mocks the hounds" recalls Golding's description of Echo as a "babling Nymph" in "Golding's 'Metamorphoses' and 'Titus Andronicus,'" *Notes and Queries* 223 (1978): 118. See also Douglas E. Green, "Interpreting 'Her Martyr'd Signs': Gender and Tragedy in *Titus Andronicus*," *Shakespeare Quarterly* 40, no. 3 (1989): 323 for a view of Lavinia's role in the Actaeon exchange.

20. Golding, preface to *Metamorphoses*, 205, 207–9.

21. Jonathan Goldberg, *Voice Terminal Echo: Postmodernism and English Renaissance Texts* (New York: Methuen, 1986), 11.

they also explicitly burden the compound nature of Ovidian myth. Not only are his text-obsessed characters terminally stuck in a past that is an all-consuming web in which both "that that went before and that that followes binds," but any gesture toward the future must wrangle with this doubled pull of backward momentum weaved out of etiology and internal resonance.[22] What results is a web in which characters repeatedly get caught—one by which Shakespeare's Ovid is "worse" than Ovid's own. Shakespeare amplifies this web by bringing language from Ovid into his allusions. For example, Philomela's original threat, "Yea I my selfe rejecting shame thy doings will bewray," resounds in Chiron's prattle: he co-opts Philomela's verb when he taunts Lavinia to "[w]rite down thy mind, bewray thy meaning so" (2.3.3).[23] In so doing, he calls attention to his textual innovation—cutting off Lavinia's hands: her inability to write means she cannot "bewray" the identities of her assailants. Philomela's threat prompts Tereus to remove her tongue—Chiron not only reenacts the story, but also harasses Lavinia with Philomela's words.

The problem compounds when details from one Ovidian myth spill over into an allusion to another. Philomela's story, like other Ovidian rape narratives, contains within it the originary story of Apollo's attempted rape of Daphne. Upon finding his mutilated niece, Marcus bids her, "Speak, gentle niece, what stern ungentle hands / Hath lopped and hewed and made thy body bare / Of her two branches, those sweet ornaments" (2.3.16–18), and Lavinia becomes inscribed as Daphne: in the absence of her hands, these appendages become metaphorical "branches," "lopped and hewed" as a tree might be. Marcus's words do not merely rewrite Lavinia's suffering alive to the stronghold of Ovid's narrative technique, they also bear comparison to the moralized afterlife of the *Metamorphoses*, that is, to the tradition in which the poem had been read for a thousand years.[24] Since the early Middle Ages, Ovid had been engaged by readers bent on explaining his poems in a Christian context, reading them "as if they were allegorical and as if their

---

22. Golding, preface to *Metamorphoses*, 206.
23. Golding, *Metamorphoses* 6.694. This resonance contributes to the store of scholarly evidence that Shakespeare knew Golding's translation.
24. For medieval uses of Ovid, see, for example, Ralph J. Hexter, *Ovid and Medieval Schooling* (Munich: Arbeo-Gesellschaft, 1986); A. J. Minnis, *Chaucer and Pagan Antiquity* (Cambridge: D.S. Brewer; Totowa, NJ: Rowman & Littlefield, 1982); and Frank T. Coulson, *The 'Vulgate' Commentary on Ovid's* Metamorphoses: *The Creation Myth and the Story of Orpheus* (Toronto: Pontifical Institute of Mediaeval Studies, 1991). For a detailed reading of Golding's translation, see Raphael Lyne, *Ovid's Changing Worlds: English* Metamorphoses, *1567–1632* (Oxford: Oxford University Press, 2001).

sentiments were morally elevated rather than erotically charged."[25] These texts were often commentaries on, rather than rewritings or translations of, Ovid's text—companion texts "obviously intended to be read in conjunction with a copy of the Latin text."[26] To be sure, Shakespeare's characters "put their knowledge of the classics to destructive use," but why should this be the case?[27] If a well-worn interpretive approach peddled the assumption that Ovid's infelicities could be repurposed by writers looking "to warne euery man to auoyde the perill," as one sixteenth-century writer put it, then what accounts for the Ovidian mayhem in *Titus Andronicus*?[28] Both the misprision and the mischief in *Titus* can be understood as a response to the allegorical tradition.

Among these texts, the anonymous *Ovide moralisé*, written in the early fourteenth century, stands out in the tradition both for its length relative to Ovid's poem—it is roughly 60,000 lines longer—and because it provides not only moralized, Christian commentary, but also the first complete translation into French.[29] In the *Ovide moralisé*, the brutal tale of Philomela is one of very few stories for which the anonymous poet claims to offer another writer's vernacular translation.[30] Chrétien de Troyes's *Philomena* is intriguing as much for its rendering as for its departures from the Ovidian source. In

---

25. Bate, *Shakespeare and Ovid*, 25. See also Daniel Javitch, "Rescuing Ovid from the Allegorizers," *Comparative Literature* 30, no. 2 (1978): 98–99 for an overview of Pierre Bersuire's [Petrus Berchorius's] *Ovidius moralizatus*, the "seminal, representative treatment of Ovid's poem."

26. Ann Moss, *Ovid in Renaissance France: A Survey of the Latin Editions of Ovid and Commentaries Printed in France Before 1600* (London: Warburg Institute Surveys, 1982), 50. According to Bate, popular Continental commentaries from the variegated mythographical tradition were translated into English during Shakespeare's lifetime (*Shakespeare and Ovid*, 27).

27. Bate, *Shakespeare and Ovid*, 112.

28. Stephen Gosson, *The Schoole of Abuse* (London: Thomas Woodcocke, 1579), ☞4v.

29. Renate Blumenfeld-Kosinski, *Reading Myth: Classical Mythology and Its Interpretations in Medieval French Literature* (Stanford, CA: Stanford University Press, 1997), 90–91.

30. For a history of this attribution, see Roberta L. Krueger, "*Philomena*: Brutal Transitions and Courtly Transformations in Chrétien's Old French Translation," in *A Companion to Chrétien de Troyes*, ed. Norris J. Lacy and Joan Tasker Grimbert (Cambridge: D.S. Brewer, 2005), 87–102. The anonymous French poet insists upon the sufficiency of Chrétien's de Troyes's text:

Mes ja ne descrirai le conte
Fors si com Crestiens le conte,
Qui bien en translata la letre.
Sus lui ne m'en vueil entremetre.
Tout son dit vous raconterai
Et l'alegorie en trairai. (6.2211–16)

But I will not recount the story other than as Chrétien told it, for he has translated the letter of the text very well. I do not wish to supersede his version. I will relate his whole poem to you, and then I will extract the allegory.

expanding Ovid's tale from 262 Latin hexameter lines to 734 French octosyllabic couplets, Chrétien adds, among other things, "authorial interventions that present narrative signposts, proverbs and moralizations," and a "focus on moral questions."[31] Notably, on Philomena's first appearance in the narrative, the unfortunate heroine comes into Tereus's greedy view via a long description that is unique to the moralized account. In Chrétien's version, the poet exaggerates Ovid's foreshadowing asides by adding even more colorful interjections: "Ha! What a scoundrel! See him lie now!"[32] By contrast, the prescience of Philomena's portrait is relatively understated. After insisting upon her indescribable beauty, Chrétien begins a long *blason* that pays special attention to her mouth:

> Fresche color ot an son vis
> De roses et de flor de lis;
> Boche riant, levre grossettes,
> Et un petitet vermeillettes
> Plus que samiz vermauz an grainne,
> Et plus soef oloit s'alainne
> Que pimanz ne basmes n'ançans.

> Her face was freshly colored like roses and lilies. Her mouth smiling, with full lips, slightly crimsoned, somewhat more than scarlet-dyed silk. And her breath smelled sweeter than spices, balms, or incense.[33]

The description of the "boche riant" builds over the course of three lines, a detail that Alice M. Colby dubs "overdrawn" even before the poet "increases the exaggeration" of the lip color "by adding the rhyme-stressed phrase *an grainne* 'dyed with cochineal' to show that he has in mind the particularly handsome shade of red produced by this costly dye."[34] By likening Philomena's lips to dyed fabric, Chrétien's description points toward later plot points: the impending excision of her tongue and the tapestry that ultimately

---

As translated by and qtd. in Rita Copeland, *Rhetoric, Hermeneutics, and Translation in the Middle Ages: Academic Traditions and Vernacular Texts* (Cambridge: Cambridge University Press, 1991), 118.

31. Krueger, "Brutal Transitions," 92. For a discussion of Chrétien as a "medievalization" of Ovid, and an anticourtly rewriting of the tale, see Edith Joyce Benkov, "*Philomena*: Chrétien de Troyes' Reinterpretation of the Ovidian Myth," *Classical and Modern Literature* 3, no. 4 (1983): 201–9.

32. "Ha! Del felon! Come or li mant!" Raymond Cormier, ed. and trans., *Three Ovidian Tales of Love (Piramus et Tisbé, Narcisus et Dané, and Philomena et Procné)* (New York and London: Garland Publishing, 1986), 224–25. Krueger refers to these moments as the "narrator's rhetorical cross-examination," which "warns" of lurking danger ("Brutal Transitions," 93).

33. Cormier, *Three Ovidian Tales*, 206–7.

34. Alice M. Colby, *The Portrait in Twelfth-Century French Literature: An Example of the Stylistic Originality of Chrétien de Troyes* (Geneva: Librairie Droz, 1965), 128.

allows her to communicate Tereus's gruesome assault. The portrait bristles with such ominous details, early warnings that set the *Ovide moralisé* poet up to "extract the allegory" ("l'alegorie en trairai") from Chrétien's tale.[35] As the story proceeds, Philomena's violations uncomfortably deliver on these hyperbolic claims about her beauty.

In Shakespeare's play, the raw material of Chrétien's addition is taken to its logical extreme. Emphasizing Lavinia's resemblance not just to Daphne, but also to Philomela, Marcus offers a *blason* routinely labeled chilling, if not a "point of rupture in the history of literary taste":[36]

> Alas, a crimson river of warm blood,
> Like to a bubbling fountain stirred with wind,
> Doth rise and fall between thy rosed lips,
> Coming and going with thy honey breath.
> But sure some Tereus hath deflowered thee
> And, lest thou shouldst detect him, cut thy tongue.
> Ah, now thou turn'st away thy face for shame,
> And notwithstanding all this loss of blood,
> As from a conduit with three issuing spouts,
> Yet do thy cheeks look red as Titan's face,
> Blushing to be encountered with a cloud. (2.3.22–32)

For all the Ovidian details that Chrétien either truncates or omits in the course of his version of the story, his portrait of Philomena is pure invention. The prescience of Philomena's dyed red mouth serves a cautionary function, but it also suggests that Ovid's tale requires additional signposting; this foreshadowing bolsters an already self-referential myth by acting as added protective apparatus. Marcus's speech exposes the uselessness of such defensive groundwork by staging a confrontation between rhetorical excess and physical suffering.

Though I take some liberties in putting the *Ovide moralisé* in Shakespeare's allusive storehouse, bringing these descriptions into conversation helps to clarify the stakes of classical literature in *Titus Andronicus*.[37] The (suggestively

---

35. Krueger points out that though the author of the *Ovide moralisé* "betray[s] the meaning" of Chrétien's translation by "willfully appropriat[ing] the story and forcefully re interpret[ing] it," Chrétien's rendering lends itself to such manipulation because he already significantly recasts Ovid's myth ("Brutal Transitions," 90). See also Benkhov, "*Philomena*," 202.

36. Lynn Enterline, *The Rhetoric of the Body from Ovid to Shakespeare* (Cambridge: Cambridge University Press, 2000), 8.

37. There is no question about the vast influence of the *Ovide moralisé*. Blumenfeld-Kosinski goes so far as to claim that it "replaced Ovid as a source for future vernacular writers," citing Machaut, Froissart and Christine de Pizan as writers particularly under the influence of the old French text

uncanny) resonances between the two portraits illustrate the moralizing tendency to buttress Ovid through overdetermined prefiguration. Chrétien's invention presumably aims to provide protection for the reader, but how effective is the warning? Critical accounts of Marcus's speech have ably attended to the kinds of violence at work in his words. Lynn Enterline demonstrates the extent to which the scene shows Lavinia subjected to a male reading practice commonly found in the "dismembering rhetoric" of Petrarchan poetics.[38] Jonathan Bate posits the speech as a "critique of humanism," exposing the extent to which "having all the rhetorical tropes at your fingertips doesn't actually help you to *do* anything."[39] Heather James argues that Shakespeare here "analyzes poetic devices which distort and fragment the female body and may lead teleologically to rape," but points out that the scene operates via "striking reversal" because the Petrarchan language appears *after* Lavinia's rape.[40] Shakespeare's uncomfortable description certainly engages Petrarchan poetics, but it also resembles the kind of protective discourse intended to *supplement* Ovid's story. Both Chrétien and Shakespeare add to Ovid's account through verbal portraiture, but by having Marcus linger in this overwrought language after the attack, Shakespeare exposes how easily warnings can become directives. Language appropriate to the realm of simile and metaphor, though ominous in Chrétien, proves unseemly when applied to Lavinia's literal wounds. Marcus's speech exposes the futility of the kind of cautionary apparatus that Chrétien's portrait attempts to supply, and, ultimately, marks a failure of *moralizatio*.

In looking at Marcus's speech in the context of moralizing precursors, we begin to see how Shakespeare's play mounts its critique of moralizing hermeneutics. This does not, however, suggest that Shakespeare spurns foreshadowed discourse—he simply redraws the lines. When Lavinia

---

(*Reading Myth*, 136). Chaucer's indebtedness to the poem has also been well documented; however, tracking the place of the poem in England introduces complications. William Caxton claims to have printed his own translation, but only a manuscript survives. Moreover, this manuscript translates a prose redaction of the poem (one that omits the Philomena portrait). In "Gascoigne's *Phylomene*: A Late Medieval Paraphrase of Ovid's *Metamorphoses*," in *Elizabethan Literature and Transformation*, ed. Sabine Coelsch-Foisner (Tübingen: Stauffenburg Verlag, 1999), 71–81), Mike Pincombe makes a case for verbal echoes in *The Complaint of Phylomene* (1576) that suggests George Gascoigne was familiar with the *Ovide moralisé*.

38. Enterline, *Rhetoric of the Body*, 8.
39. Bate, *Shakespeare and Ovid*, 112.
40. James, *Shakespeare's Troy*, 66–67. See also Eugene M. Waith, "The Metamorphosis of Violence in *Titus Andronicus*," in *Shakespeare Survey* 10 (Cambridge: Cambridge University Press, 1957), 39–49; and Jonas Barish, "Shakespearean Violence: A Preliminary Survey," in *Violence in Drama*, ed. James Redmond (Cambridge: Cambridge University Press, 1991), 101–21.

begs Tamora to kill her before her sons drag her away, her pleas prove portentous:

> 'Tis present death I beg, and one thing more
> That womanhood denies my tongue to tell.
> O, keep me from their worse-than-killing lust,
> And tumble me into some loathsome pit. (2.2.173–76)

Shakespeare's language contributes to a heightened sense of Ovidian inevitability: Lavinia's mention of her denied tongue prophesies a fate that audiences should already expect.[41] Instead of gesturing to the future, such presaging shimmers reiterate a well-known literary past. The play flirts with a literary determinism that would seem providential had Ovid not *already* been established as a pattern. Shakespeare puts pressure on sequence as the characters' strict adherence to the text defines the difference between foreshadowing and allusion; what results is an inability properly to delineate past, present, and future. So, when Marcus refers to Lavinia's mouth as "that pretty hollow cage / Where, like a sweet melodious bird" her tongue used to sing (3.1.83–87), he invokes the image of the nightingale. In the *Metamorphoses*, the hope and redemption of the Philomela story rests in her transformation into the nightingale; the bird becomes a symbol of poetry almost as pervasive as the laurel wreath. Bate points out that Ovid allows Philomela to be "released *into* song," whereas Lavinia "must submit" to a "terrible combination of silence and shame."[42] I want to suggest that this difference results from the play's habit of putting its characters in an anterior, Ovidian frame: Marcus suggests that Lavinia's tongue was like a nightingale *before* she was ever attacked. According to his discourse, Lavinia always was what she becomes; the etiological narrative paradigm reveals a circularity to her fate that inscribes her as characteristically Ovidian, but also emphasizes a fate that exists fundamentally in the past. Such a reliance on literature limits the set of available future possibilities, redoubling the Ovidian web in which both "that that went before and that that follows binds." However, as Bate's observation suggests, *Titus*'s use of Ovid includes everything but metamorphosis. Lavinia

---

41. Enterline reads this moment as evidence that "the failure to persuade throws thought back upon how readily words escape control of the one who utters them," such "conditions of becoming a speaking subject," she argues, are "deeply Ovidian" (*Rhetoric of the Body*, 14).

42. Bate, *Shakespeare and Ovid*, 111.

has undoubtedly been "translated into petrarchan rhetoric," but more is at stake than literary origins, whether Ovidian or Petrarchan.[43] Rather, we can locate the center of Shakespeare's critique not just in source texts, but also in the manner of approaching and interpreting them. Shakespeare privileges the act of interpretation in order to show the dangers introduced by a moralized hermeneutic.

II

In the last century, the literary scholarship on Ovid in sixteenth- and seventeenth-century England has ranged from critical claims that the medieval mode was the only way that English writers engaged Ovid to fervent assertions that the moralized style had long since been abandoned by the time Shakespeare encountered the poem.[44] Whether or not Shakespeare "bothered to read"[45] any moralizing Ovidian commentaries, there is no reason to doubt that he would have been acutely aware of the tradition. My argument assumes that the practice was at least familiar enough to attract critique in the late sixteenth century. Indeed, its procedures are in evidence in all the early English translations of Ovid's *Metamorphoses*, and in the schoolroom.[46] Mary Thomas Crane has made a persuasive case for the cultural and pedagogical centrality of

---

43. See James, *Shakespeare's Troy*, 66. See also Enterline, *Rhetoric of the Body*.

44. See, for example, Richard F. Hardin, "Ovid in Seventeenth-Century England," *Comparative Literature* 24, no. 1 (1972): 44–62 for the former. For the latter, see Bate, *Shakespeare and Ovid*. Lyne offers an alternative account—he reads Golding's "paratexts" as wholly separate from the moralizing tradition. See esp. Lyne, *Ovid's Changing Worlds*, 32–53. In *The Survival of the Pagan Gods: The Mythological Tradition and Its Place in Renaissance Humanism and Art*, trans. Barbara F. Sessions (Princeton, NJ: Princeton University Press, 1972), Jean Seznec notes that the "jeers" thrown at the moralizing tradition by such notables as Martin Luther and Rabelais do not indicate a cessation in this mode of reading, nor do they support the misimpression that the Renaissance "must have wished to banish allegory" because of its approach to "classical literature as a source of pleasure, aesthetic as well as sensuous" (96). Minnis discusses "'classicizing' scholars, i.e. clerics who sought to show how pagan science, history and mythology could serve and support Christian doctrine" (*Chaucer and Pagan Antiquity*, 11) while also endeavoring to establish "that fable moralization is not to be confused with, or seen as a mere appendage of, Scriptural exegesis" (16). For a discussion of the ways in which the "Middle Ages notoriously moralised Ovid" and the "habit continued into the Renaissance and beyond," see Martindale, *Ovid Renewed*, 8–9.

45. Bate suggests that "Golding's Epistle probably constituted Shakespeare's only sustained direct confrontation with the moralizing tradition," and imagines that the playwright might well have "skip[ped] straight to the English text of his admired Ovid" (*Shakespeare and Ovid*, 31).

46. Golding produced the first full translation of the poem into English, but there were translations of individual myths earlier, such as the anonymous poem *The Fable of Ovid Treting of Narcissus* (1560) and Thomas Peend, *The Pleasant Fable of Hermaphroditus and Salmacis* (1565). George Sandys produced the next full translation, complete with commentary, in 1632.

easily digested, fragmentary *sententiae*, and has demonstrated the extent to which "commonplace ideas generally contribute to a kind of moral framing" in the schoolroom that "indoctrinat[es] students with values ... that would support the humanist project."⁴⁷ Grammar-school education privileged sustained engagement with small pieces of text, as in the composition of "themes" in which "schoolboys were taught to deploy all their imaginative resources to transform the simplest of narratives into sophisticated moral and political disquisitions."⁴⁸ Richard Halpern points to several Renaissance texts that promote poetry as "inventories of rhetorical styles and tropes, not as sources of instructive content," and such methodology finds its reflection in educational texts like Thomas Elyot's *The Boke Named the Governor* (1531), which urges caution where Ovid is concerned:

> But by cause there is litell other lernyng in [Ovid] concernyng either vertuous maners or policie I suppose it were better that as fables and ceremonies happen to come in a lesson it were declared abundātly by the maister than that in [the *Metamorphoses* and the *Fasti*] a longe tyme shulde be spente & almost lost: which mought be better employed on suche autors that do minister both eloquence ciuile policie and exhortation to vertue.⁴⁹

Elyot goes on to call Ovid the "moste of all poetes lasciuious," though he admits that the poet's "mooste wanton bokes hath righte cōmendable and noble sentences."⁵⁰ His emphasis on Ovid's "sentence" reinforces his recommended schoolroom technique, which leaves the bulk of the interpretive work in the hands of the teacher; the schoolmaster's

---

47. Mary Thomas Crane, *Framing Authority: Sayings, Self, and Society in Sixteenth-Century England* (Princeton, NJ: Princeton University Press, 1993), 80.

48. R. W. Maslen, "Myths Exploited: The *Metamorphoses* of Ovid in Early Elizabethan England," in *Shakespeare's Ovid: The* Metamorphoses *in the Plays and Poems*, ed. A.B. Taylor (Cambridge: Cambridge University Press, 2000), 17–18. See also A. B. Taylor, "Introduction," in the same volume for a discussion of the medieval exegetical influence on the grammar school curriculum. See also Crane, *Framing Authority*, 79–92. Though he does not attend to the importance of the *moralisé* tradition, Dickson provides a useful analysis of the play's debts to humanist education and questions of good judgment, implying even that the play is a "kind of schoolboy's revenge on his own education" ("Pattern, Precedent," 380). See also Lynn Enterline, *Shakespeare's Schoolroom: Rhetoric, Discipline, Emotion* (Philadelphia: University of Pennsylvania Press, 2012). The classic critical work on early modern English pedagogy is T. W. Baldwin, *William Shakspere's Small Latine and Lesse Greeke*, 2 vols. (Urbana: University of Illinois Press, 1944).

49. Richard Halpern, *The Poetics of Primitive Accumulation: English Renaissance Culture and the Genealogy of Capital* (Ithaca, NY: Cornell University Press, 1991), 46. Thomas Elyot, *The Boke Named the Gouernour* (London: Thomas Bertheleti, 1531), E2r.

50. Elyot, G3r.

abundant declarations would presumably shield students from Ovidian verse by providing appropriate textual summary. Along similar lines, John Brinsley's translation of the first book of the *Metamorphoses*—written, as the title page announces, "chiefly for the good of Schooles"—introduces Ovid across four typographical columns. At the center, he provides a literal translation of the poem and the three surrounding columns offer various instructional aids, including grammatical information, vocabulary, and moral commentary.[51] Having established Apollo as "pure, because the Sun is pure from all grossnesse or corruption," Brinsley's conclusion to the Daphne story evinces the subtlety of the interpretive ethos undergirding grammar-school instruction.[52] The literal translation reads: "Apollo had [thus] ended [his speech] the Laurell assented wth [her] boughs so lately made, & seemed to haue mooued [her] top euen as [her] head." In the innermost column, Brinsley provides a gloss so similar as to seem redundant except, crucially, that it strips Ovid's text of its ambiguity.[53] "[S]eemed to haue mooued" silently transforms into "by mouing" and Daphne's "assent" becomes an uncomplicated transition that allows the laurel, in the outermost column, easily to figure "victorie and triumph" (fig. 5).[54]

Whereas the moralizing tradition in general proceeded via interpretive multiplicity—in Pierre Bersuire's fourteenth-century treatment of the poem, for example, Daphne is by turns "the glory of the world," the "Christian soul," a virgin comparable in steadfastness to an English nun (reminiscent of Saint Lucy) who "plucked out her eyes" and sent them to the king, her suitor, "so his concupiscence would be calmed," and the laurel, which "signifies the cross"; Apollo is first the devil and then "Christ the sun of justice"[55]—both sixteenth-century English translations of Ovid and schoolroom exercises

---

51. For a discussion of similar instructional texts, such as John Palsgrave's *Acolastus* (1540), see Crane, *Framing Authority*, 87–88.

52. John Brinsley, *Ouids Metamorphosis Translated Grammatically, and also according to the propriety of our English tongue, so farre as Grammar and the verse will well beare* (London, 1618), N2r.

53. James glosses the Ovidian episode as follows: "Branches blowing in the wind may signify consent (as the verb *adnuo* implies), as Apollo and some critics assume, or dissent. On the other hand, their agitation (*agitasse*) may mean nothing at all, since the viewer is required to create meaning from their movement (as the phrase *visa est* implies). Ovid's tale dramatizes the ambiguity of signs and exposes the motives for variable readings: power and passion affix meaning to words, bodies, and gestures" (*Shakespeare's Troy*, 46).

54. Brinsley, N3r.

55. William Donald Reynolds, "The *Ovidius Moralizatus* of Petrus Berchorius: An Introduction and Translation" (PhD diss., University of Illinois at Urbana-Champaign, 1971), 138–41.

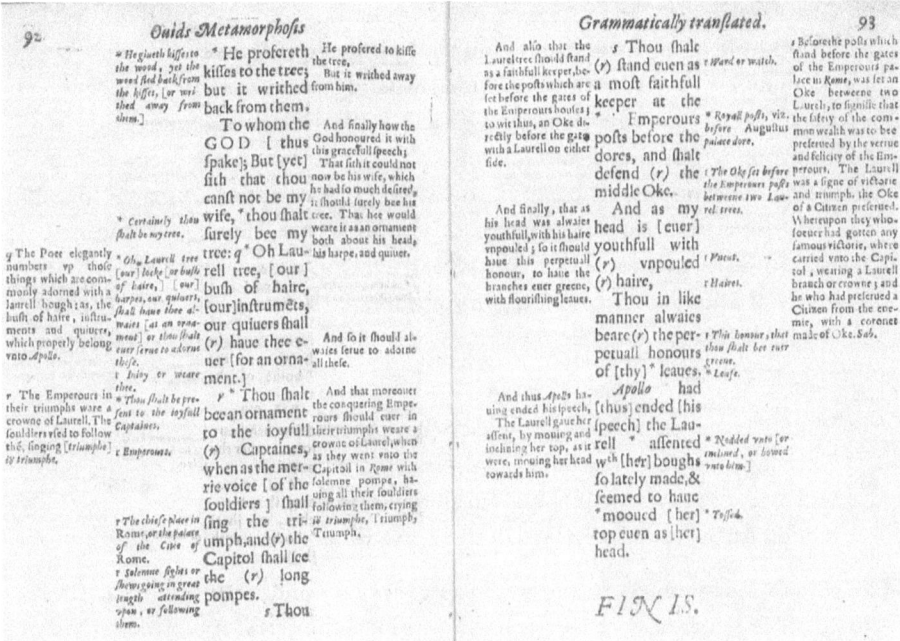

FIGURE 5. John Brinsley, *Ouids Metamorphosis Translated Grammatically, and also according to the propriety of our English tongue, so farre as Grammar and the verse will well beare* (London, 1618). FSL Collection: STC 18963. Used by permission of the Folger Shakespeare Library under Creative Commons License CC Y-SA 4.0.

inclined toward privileging particular moral lessons.[56] Golding's 1567 translation, for example, incorporates a moralizing apparatus into the prefatory material. In the dedicatory epistle to Robert Dudley, the Earl of Leicester, Golding seeks to offer an approach to a text written by an author who "[k]new not the true eternall God." He advocates a redemptive interpretive methodology that hinges on "reduc[ing]" the "Paynims . . . sense to ryght

---

56. As Bate (*Shakespeare and Ovid*, 25–32) notes, in the sixteenth century, Ovidian moralization tends to favor general morals over specific exegetical links. However, such treatments should also be distinguished from strands of *moralizatio* that privileged allegoresis at its most wide-ranging. Certainly, in the Renaissance schoolroom, the emphasis on classical literature had shifted away from unabashed Christian moralization. Halpern argues that the "humanist program . . . tended to displace Christian training" (*The Poetics of Primitive Accumulation*, 22). He specifically contrasts Renaissance copia, which "neutralize[d] textual content" by "decompos[ing]" the "disturbing alterities of classical texts" into "harmless, inert atoms," with older allegorical constructions that "subsumed dangerous contents within a larger ideological unity" by reinterpreting the text "with an officially sanctioned (Christian) narrative." In his view, "copia represented a decisive innovation in ideological control" (22, 47).

of Christian law."[57] He provides a book-by-book summary of Ovid's work intended to help his reader draw out the "pitthye, apt and playne / Instructions" that Ovid's stories contain. The instructions, he assures us, "import the prayse of vertues and the shame / Of vices, with the due rewardes of eyther of the same."[58] The nature of Golding's summaries vary: book 1 enjoys only four lines of synopsis, all devoted to Daphne's transformation to a "[b]ay." Golding describes her as a "myrror of virginitie.... Which yeelding neyther unto feare, nor force, nor flatterye, / Doth purchace everlasting fame and immortalitye."[59] Other books inspire longer readings, and often touch on multiple stories; at their most heavy-handed, they relate Ovid's stories directly to the Bible:[60]

> Moreover by the golden age what other thing is ment,
> Than Adams tyme in Paradyse, who beeing innocent
> Did lead a blist and happy lyfe untill that thurrough sin
> He fell from God? From which tyme foorth all sorrow did begin.[61]

Golding's indebtedness to the tradition of moral commentary comes across partly in showing how self-evident he considers the relation between Ovid's golden age and the book of Genesis. "[W]hat other thing is ment?" he asks rhetorically, revealing a confidence in his interpretation no doubt bolstered by a mode of reading Ovid that had been in use for a millennium.

The confidence in interpretation expressed in these English texts suggests the influence of the *Ovide moralisé*, whose anonymous author "consider[ed] himself as much a biblical exegete as an arts commentator"

---

57. Golding, epistle, *Metamorphoses*, 312, 321–22.
58. Ibid., 64–66.
59. Ibid., 67–70.
60. The Philomela story attracts a relatively lengthy explanation:
    The tale of Tereus, Philomele, and Prognee dooth conteyne
    That folke are blynd in thyngs that to their proper weale perteyne.
    And that the man in whom the fyre of furious lust dooth reigne
    Dooth run to mischeefe like a horse that getteth loose the reyne.
    It also shewes the cruell wreake of women in their wrath
    And that no hainous mischiefe long delay of vengeance hath.
    And lastly that distresse doth drive a man to looke about
    And seeke all corners of his wits, what way to wind him out.
                    (Golding, epistle, *Metamorphoses* 135–42)

    It is difficult to puzzle out Golding's analysis since the "man" in "distresse" who relies on "his wits ... to wind him out" is surely the tapestry artist herself, yet Golding's lesson obscures Philomela's gender. At the same time, neither her loyalty to her sister nor her attempts to preserve her virginity garner mention while she is implicated in "the cruell wreake of women in their wrath."
61. Golding, epistle, *Metamorphoses*, 469–72.

and stood out for his tendency to privilege Christian significations above other interpretive options by means of a consistently relative vocabulary—"'plus noble' (nobler), 'meillour' (better), 'plus digne' (worthier), and even 'plus saine' (healthier or more reasonable)."[62] The uncouth elements of Ovid's text engendered spirited exegeses that relied on creative metaphor to reinscribe the tales into a Christian framework, and thereby "assume[d] that allegorical interpretation is essentially an exercise in metaphorical thinking."[63] Moralization regularly involves explaining away the supernatural and unseemly aspects of Ovid's text by dubbing them mere metaphor. The anonymous French poet, for example, insists that Ovid's poetic contribution operates only at the literal level, so the *Metamorphoses* requires commentary to extract "another sense, another meaning" ("autre sen, autre entendement") for the reader's edification. Rita Copeland argues that

> the *Ovide moralisé* proposes a Christian theological significance that claims its origin, not unlike the allegory of the theologians, in the letter of the text itself ... [Ovid's] pagan fables ... have no claim to veracity in their literal sense, only achieve their value through the offices of a good reader who recognizes them as integuments, and who, through the wisdom invested in him by God, can in turn disclose the divine wisdom concealed in them.[64]

The moralizing approach not only denies Ovid's ability to play with metaphorical registers, but also strips metaphor of its impact by making it undifferentiated.

Titus Andronicus intervenes in this mode of interpretation because Shakespeare's pagan characters unexpectedly employ the interpretive techniques of moral commentators. Though moralizing readers intended to redeem the pagan poem, not inspire vice, Shakespeare demonstrates that reducing Ovid to a purely literal text is what makes his poetry a threat.[65] My claim

---

62. Copeland, *Rhetoric, Hermeneutics*, 112; Blumenfeld-Kosinski, *Reading Myth*, 119–20. For a discussion of an "underlying polemic" that contrasts the poem with "earlier unsuccessful attempts at interpreting Ovid," see Blumenfeld-Kosinski, 99ff. Krueger interprets this evidence differently ("Brutal Transitions," 90).

63. Moss, *Ovid in Renaissance France*, 25. As Barkan notes, "To 'explain,' as Arnulf does, Jupiter's metamorphosis into a flame as a way of asserting that he used a cook as a go-between" reveals an "overenthusiasm about metaphor" (*Gods Made Flesh*, 107).

64. Copeland, *Rhetoric, Hermeneutics*, 124–26.

65. Shakespeare is by no means the first in this regard. Other literary texts absorb the apparatus of *moralizatio* into their own fictions to critique the practice. See Javitch, for example, who argues that Ludovico Ariosto, "embodies a manifesto [in *Orlando Furioso*] about proper ways of reading and

here should seem initially counterintuitive—doesn't the trouble that Ovid "patterns" in the play arise from precisely the type of bad reading that moral commentators feared would lead to immoral action? For example, in his 1555 edition, one of the "most widely used" in the period, Georgius Sabinus suggested that "the transformation of men into beasts should be viewed metaphorically as an image of monstrous human behaviour."[66] Golding takes the claim a step further, admonishing his reader that beastly humans are actually "[m]uch woorse than beasts, bicause they doo abace theyr owne degree."[67] By extension, Shakespeare's Rome must be a "wilderness of tigers" (3.1.54) because its human inhabitants, devoted readers of Ovid, act so bestially. However, such logic starkly alters Ovid. Where beastliness or monstrousness is concerned, etiology and teleology are brought into uncomfortable proximity—after all, Ovid's stories depend on transformation (often into animals) for their completion. To assume a moral inevitability to the debasement inherent in men's becoming beasts means Ovid's etiologies have been transformed into teleologies. Such a transformation operates contrary to Ovid's own methodology: teleology is inherently end-driven, and as a result it is future-oriented, whereas etiology provides backstory, and sets in motion a circularity that constantly returns and reaches into the past.[68]

Rather than simply learning bad morals from Ovid, Shakespeare's characters, diligent readers, literalize the fantastical in Ovid—as a Christian moralist would—in order to use the narration as a script. Ovid's text is routinely employed as a how-to guide—an excruciatingly flat, literal mode of reading. At the same time, Shakespeare's characters still allow for the imposition of a metaphorical register once the text has been taken literally, just not in the service of moral behavior. In *Titus*, moral reading actually *enables* the practical handbook mode: reducing Ovid's stories to mere metaphor reflects a system of interpretation that need not be limited to the moral commentators. Shakespeare combines the most essential elements

---

using the *Metamorphoses*" ("Rescuing Ovid," 101). Minnis claims of Chaucer's *Maniciple's Tale* that through "the Manciple's *moralizatio* . . . Chaucer has highlighted the arbitrary nature of this moral, thereby showing . . . how the technique of *moralizatio* can be misused or abused by a moralizer of dubious moral standards" (*Chaucer and Pagan Antiquity*, 20).

66. Bate, *Shakespeare and Ovid*, 26, 28.
67. Golding, epistle, *Metamorphoses*, 62.
68. Shakespeare begins to expose this fundamental unraveling when he takes away Lavinia's voice at the moment that he aligns rhetoric and oratory with civilization, as Lawrence Danson, *Tragic Alphabet: Shakespeare's Drama of Language* (New Haven, CT: Yale University Press, 1974), 6–7; and S. Clark Hulse, "Wresting the Alphabet: Oratory and Action in 'Titus Andronicus,'" *Criticism* 21, no. 2 (1979): 106–18, demonstrate.

of Ovidian metamorphoses with the most essential assumptions of Ovidian moralization. With both registers in play, the authority that has been granted to the metaphorical begins to wreak havoc on the literal. To return to an earlier example, Lavinia is repeatedly referred to as a tree, making her relation to Daphne uncomfortably explicit. It is Ovid's narrative mode that allows her to be Daphne at the moment that she is Philomela, and it is the mode of moralizing metaphor that allows Marcus to discuss her in arboreal terms. Aaron reinforces this troubled conflation when he joyfully recalls that Tamora's sons "cut thy sister's tongue and ravished her / And cut her hands and trimmed her as thou sawest" (5.1.92–93). Like Marcus, who declared that Lavinia's "branches" had been "lopped and hewed," Aaron invokes the language of forestry: she was "trimmed" as though she were a tree.[69] Aaron and Lucius quibble over this word for a few lines:

> LUCIUS   O detestable villain, call'st thou that trimming?
> AARON   Why, she was washed and cut and trimmed, and 'twas
>   Trim sport for them which had the doing of it. (5.1.94–96)

The word "trim," relentlessly repeated, carries with it both the sense of herbaceous pruning and a slang reference to sexual intercourse.[70] Lucius has license to be doubly outraged: Aaron refers both to mutilation as winsome garden sport and to gang rape as mere copulation. Aaron's reply introduces a third sense of "trim," this time referring to the pleasure the two boys took in their attack. The force of the exchange, an echo of Marcus's initial reaction, derives from its Ovidian underpinnings. Because of Ovid, the two languages—of rape and of trees—are inseparable, enabling Aaron's coarse wordplay. However, it is only through an "overenthusiasm about metaphor" that Lavinia can be the subject of the entwined rape/tree discourse. She receives none of the benefits of transformation: the metaphor remains a metaphor, while Lavinia herself remains a mutilated, violated woman. By applying the procedure of *moralizatio*, literary legacy is redefined on the body of Lavinia.

Despite the fact that the ends that *Titus*'s Romans, Goths, and Moor seek could not be further from Christian morality, reading Ovid complicates Titus's Rome in ways that reveal the limits of reading Ovid for any

---

69. Such wordplay also brings to light the pun available in "sawest," which conjures not just the past tense of "to see," but also that of the verb "to saw," adding to the image of hacked and cut tree limbs.
70. Shakespeare, *Titus*, 248n93. See also *OED*, s.v. "trim, *v.*," def. 2: "to get (land) into condition for cropping, to till; to cultivate (a tree)."

predetermined Christian outcome. Shakespeare plays upon the fear that Golding articulates in his dedication to Leicester:

> The use of this same booke therfore is this: that every man
> (Endevoring for to know himself as neerly as he can,)
> (As though he in a chariot sate well ordered,) should direct
> His mynd by reason in the way of vertue, and correct
> His feerce affections with the bit of temprance, lest perchaunce
> They taking bridle in the teeth lyke wilfull jades doo praunce
> Away, and headlong carie him to every filthy pit
> Of vyce, and drinking of the same defyle his soule with it:
> Or else doo headlong harrie him uppon the rockes of sin,
> And overthrowing forcibly the chariot he sits in,
> Doo teare him woorse than ever was Hippolytus the sonne
> Of Theseus when he went about his fathers wrath to shun.[71]

The resonance between this passage and *Titus* is striking: readers who fail to "use" Ovid's work correctly end up in "every filthy pit / Of vyce," eventually dismembered like Hippolytus. Shakespeare provides a literal enactment of Golding's metaphorical warning by fashioning characters whose spectacularly bad reading derives from the techniques of *moralizatio*, urging a fundamental question: is reading dangerous when it is too metaphorical, or when it is too literal?[72] Augustine addresses such problems of misapplication in his consideration of 2 Corinthians:

> To begin with, one must take care not to interpret a figurative expression literally. What the apostle says is relevant here: 'the letter kills but the spirit gives life' [2 Cor. 3:6]. For when something meant figuratively is interpreted as if it were meant literally, it is understood in a carnal way.[73]

Intelligence should elevate men's souls above the animals, Augustine writes, so subjecting it "to the flesh by following the letter" constitutes a "death of the soul."[74] Golding's hyperbolic metaphors about what happens to readers who "use" Ovid inappropriately underscore the way in which moral commentators might misuse a text for its divine message. The danger derives not

---

71. Golding, epistle, *Metamorphoses*, 569–80.
72. I follow Barkan and Moss in using metaphor rather than allegory.
73. Saint Augustine, *On Christian Teaching*, trans. R. P. H. Green (Oxford: Oxford University Press, 1997), 3.4–6.
74. Ibid.

from reading too literally or too metaphorically, but rather from engaging Ovid on a confused middle ground.

The mode of interpretation employed by Shakespeare's characters derives from a mode of reading Ovid, but it is not limited to an engagement with the *Metamorphoses*. Metaphors in this play frequently transform into horrific realities; as Gillian Murray Kendall puts it, "In this text, to lend one's hand is to risk dismemberment." Although I agree with Kendall that "reality wreaks a terrible vengeance, finally, on those who confuse it with art," I would suggest that the problem stems not from a confusion of art and life, but from a hermeneutic intended to dismantle art.[75] In fact, exposing and manipulating the "fragile boundaries between literal and figurative" allows Shakespeare to critique the moralizing mode. To suggest that everything is a metaphor invites the characters in *Titus* to ignore consequences, which means the register of the "real" bears the burden of the liberties taken by the literary. Shakespeare critiques the moralizing tradition by staging the enactment of its hermeneutic, and showing that it can be used without the imposition of a moral. In so doing, he delivers an uncomfortable excess of materiality by displaying the consequences: a victimization of the real in the service of the metaphorical, one in which literal body parts become casualties of text.

The tradition popularized by the *Ovide moralisé* prompts a new, problematic way of reading for non-Christian purposes. In *Titus*, Shakespeare relates redemptive metaphor to the practice of employing metaphors, which exposes a danger in reading that results from a confusion of the literal and the metaphorical. If Ovid's poem pretends that we live in a world of endings, where natural objects mark the *result* of a story, then Shakespeare's characters exacerbate Ovid's narrative attention to sequence by curbing the potential for new narrative. By using Ovid as a how-to guide or handbook, the characters subscribe to the "what other thing is ment" school of reading, which means that they follow a hermeneutic that neutralizes Ovid's text by literalizing the supernatural elements of metamorphic transformation while still believing in the power of metaphor. This center of critique proves ever more

---

75. Gillian Murray Kendall, "'Lend Me Thy Hand': Metaphor and Mayhem in *Titus Andronicus*," *Shakespeare Quarterly* 40, no. 3 (1989): 299, 303. See also Albert H. Tricomi, "The Aesthetics of Mutilation in 'Titus Andronicus,'" *Shakespeare Survey* 27 (1974): 11–19. While I agree with both Kendall's and Tricomi's brilliant analyses of the literalization of metaphor—particularly engaging head and hands—I believe these moments of literalized metaphor are part of a larger technique of critique at work in the play. Rather than suggest, as Tricomi does, that the play "deliberately 'exposes' the euphemisms of metaphor" ("Aesthetics," 13), I want to suggest that Shakespeare depicts characters who literalize metaphor in order to critique a technique particular to a tradition of problematic reading.

shocking as death pervades a stage littered with body parts: Shakespeare, initiating a career-long interest in the relationship between the ancients and the moderns, suggests that the real tragedy is the entrapment of a future predetermined by allusion, particularly when it is chained to a dangerously limiting interpretive tradition.

III

On the one hand, *Titus Andronicus* repeatedly foregrounds the fluidity of both signification and interpretation. For example, Marcus manages to quell his brother's rage and even earn his praise through a simple recasting of the act of swatting a housefly:

> MARCUS Alas, my lord, I have but killed a fly.
> TITUS   'But'?
>   How if that fly had a father and a mother?
>   How would he hang his slender gilded wings
>   And buzz lamenting doings in the air.
>   Poor harmless fly,
>   That with his pretty buzzing melody
>   Came here to make us merry, and thou hast killed him.
> MARCUS Pardon me, sir, it was a black ill-favoured fly,
>   Like to the empress' Moor. Therefore I killed him.
> TITUS   Oh, Oh, Oh!
>   Then pardon me for reprehending thee,
>   For thou hast done a charitable deed. (3.2.59–71)

This strange scene provides a paradigm for the act of interpretation, and the nature of metaphor. It is one the scene has been elaborating with its absurdist play on "hands." Titus first understands Marcus's act as murder; the slaughter of an innocent inciting expulsion from Titus's company introduces a viable alternative hermeneutics. By simply reframing the fly as "[l]ike to the empress' Moor," instead of as "[p]oor harmless fly," Marcus is able to reconstruct the situation. The reinterpretation changes neither the act nor the dead fly on the table, but rather the register for reading both. The exchange brings the act of interpretation and the function of metaphor to the fore: in this fleeting parable, the literal fly has always suffered the same fate, but his metaphorical afterlife (as innocent or as villain) enjoys an ambiguity that furnishes the action with a second meaning, and validates both interpretations. The playwright simultaneously highlights the fragility of meaning and the potential for

THE FICTION OF THE FUTURE 129

hermeneutic multiplicity, insisting upon the power that can be granted to the act of interpretation.

On the other hand, central characters interpret and make sense of their lives and the events unfolding in their Rome by mapping them onto a past they have encountered in literary texts, and Titus proves himself particularly beholden to the material text. Yet, they misunderstand the havoc this wreaks on their relation to the future. Marcus teaches Lavinia, in the aftermath of her mutilation, to act like Ovid's Io and make an inscription revealing the identity of her rapists and their crime. With both violation and violators written in the sand, Marcus asks his family to swear, like Junius Brutus, "[m]ortal revenge upon these traitorous Goths" (4.1.93), and Titus suggests that he will transfer Lavinia's message from sand to brass:

> And come, I will go get a leaf of brass
> And with a gad of steel will write these words,
> And lay it by. The angry northern wind
> Will blow these sands like Sibyl's leaves abroad,
> And where's our lesson then? (4.1.102–6)

Citing M. P. Tilley's *A Dictionary of the Proverbs in England in the Sixteenth and Seventeenth Centuries*, Bate explains Titus's impulse toward engraving with the proverb "Injuries are written in brass."[76] While this may certainly be one register of meaning, I would argue that Titus's words also echo the beginning of a Horatian ode:

> I have finished a monument more lasting than bronze, more lofty than the regal structure of the pyramids, one which neither corroding rain nor the ungovernable North Wind can ever destroy, nor the countless series of the years, nor the flight of time.

> Exegi monumentum aere perennius
> regalique situ pyramidum altius,
> quod non imber edax, non Aquilo impotens
> possit diruere aut innumerabilis
> annorum series et fuga temporum.[77]

---

76. Shakespeare, *Titus*, 217, note to lines 102–3.
77. Horace, *Odes and Epodes*, ed. and trans. Niall Rudd, Loeb Classical Library (Cambridge, MA: Harvard University Press, 2004), book 3, ode 30, 216–17. This passage is "so regularly echoed in the Renaissance that it is impossible and unnecessary to guess whether a poet who uses [it] had [it]

130 CHAPTER THREE

If the brass itself does not immediately conjure Horace's "monumentum aere perennius," then Shakespeare's "angry northern wind" surely removes any temptation to dismiss it. For Horace gives us "Aquilo impotens" as yet another challenge over which his poetic monument will triumph. Horace's ode famously suggests that his poetry is the very monument he describes—one more durable and important than any physical structure could ever be, regardless of the material from which it is crafted.

I have yet to find a reference to Horace in this speech in any edition of *Titus Andronicus*, and I believe that part of the reason the connection has been overlooked lies in the logic of Bate's notion that an "inscription on brass should endure, unlike writing on sand."[78] Certainly, that is the intent behind Titus's preservationist suggestion that Lavinia's words be re-recorded via "gad" onto "brass." However, Titus invokes Horace just as he misreads him. We have no reason to doubt Titus's familiarity with Horace—in the play's very next scene, Titus quotes another ode in the letter he sends Chiron and Demetrius—but at this moment of planned reinscription, Titus mistakes the medium for the message. To invoke Horace in this way is ironic: longevity is hardly important if readers are going to misunderstand the meaning altogether. Titus's desire to preserve and immortalize words results in an allusion to Horace's poem that divorces the poet's words from the message they convey. In his fixation on the future perpetuation of those words scratched in sand, Titus elevates the physical text even as he compromises it through misinterpretation.

Titus's obsessive tie to the written, material text throws into high relief the play's pervasive concern with slavish adherence to source texts, and its attendant interpretive dangers. After vowing revenge via Ovid, Titus sends Chiron and Demetrius a "bundle of weapons" wrapped in a scroll on which he has written lines from another Horatian ode: "Integer vitae, scelerisque purus, / Non eget Mauri iaculis, nec arcu" (4.2.sd; 4.2.20–21).[79] Chiron immediately identifies it: "O, 'tis a verse in Horace, I know it well: / I read it in the grammar long ago" (4.2.22–23). Even at a moment when Chiron's interpretive fatuity prevents him from understanding Titus's provocative missive, he is able to participate in the play's mode of classical allusion. Unfortunately for Chiron, his claim to "know it well" bespeaks a reliance

---

at first hand or not," according to Stephen Booth, ed., *Shakespeare's Sonnets* (New Haven, CT: Yale University Press, 1977), 227.

78. Shakespeare, *Titus*, 217, note to lines 102–3.

79. From Horace *Odes* 1.22.1–2: "The man of upright life and free from crime does not need the javelins or bows of the Moor," as qtd. in Shakespeare, *Titus*, 219, note to lines 20–21.

on text over message: he exhibits no interest in understanding the meaning once he has identified it.[80] Of course, his interpretive shortcomings also reveal Aaron's strengths. The Moor remarks in an aside, "Now what a thing it is to be an ass. / Here's no sound jest! The old man hath found their guilt" (4.2.25–26). As Aaron notes, Horace's lines indicate that Titus thinks that the boys need the javelins and the bows of the Moor (he did send them weapons after all), which implies that they are neither *integer vitae* nor *sceleris purus*.

Together, the two Horace scenes emphasize the hegemony of Titus's Rome—Rome proves culturally dominant outside the city limits, and its texts are central as far as the empire reaches.[81] At the same time, in both scenes Horace emblematizes a divide between the text and its message. Titus's letter to the boys is a warning—he specifically denies his grandson's recourse to murder: "No, boy, not so; I'll teach thee another course" (4.1.119)—but "knowing" and understanding are held apart by interpretive capacity. Despite an implicit comment on the pervasiveness of reading Roman texts beyond Rome's cultural and geographical boundaries, Shakespeare underscores the divide between leaning on a text and accessing its meaning.

By having a character drag the codex of the *Metamorphoses* onstage, Shakespeare foregrounds the problem of a material text that has been divorced from its meaning. The irony of reducing Ovid's *Metamorphoses* to the status of handbook, of course, is that anyone can use it. Chiron's and Demetrius's ingenious amplification of the Philomela story never really works: hands or no hands, Lavinia does not need to sew a tapestry, since she can simply gesture at Ovid's book.[82] Indeed, the play's tendency to privilege

---

80. In *The Third Citizen: Shakespeare's Theater and the Early Modern House of Commons* (Baltimore: Johns Hopkins University Press, 2007), Oliver Arnold presents an illuminating analysis of an uncomfortable moment of identification this scene creates for some audience members: they would not understand the Latin text either. For a reading of these scenes as a statement that cultural authorities like Horace have become nothing but a "dead metaphor, apt only as a figure for lifeless Roman virtue," see James, *Shakespeare's Troy*, 72.

81. We learn from Chiron's reactions that Goths read Latin, know classical literature, and even go to grammar school. Consequently, we learn that the domain of classical literature is available to Romans, Goths, and Moor alike. Notably the "barbarians have been educated in Roman ways—as so many barbarians really were—through Roman literature" (West, "Going by the Book," 74). Thus while Rome's literary greatness (i.e., the Augustan age that is memorialized in school texts) is clearly marked in the past, the fact that the Goths have read and memorized the Roman classics points to Rome's pervasive cultural domination. West offers an alternative reading of Ovid as a teacher at odds with moralization (see esp. 73–77).

82. For an alternative, though related, discussion of Lavinia as "a metonym for the whole history of the book in which Shakespeare found her story," see Barkan, *Gods Made Flesh*, 246–47.

the physical text over the meaning it contains might provide some relief for the long-standing readerly discomfort with the logical break between Marcus's instant recognition that Lavinia's attack stems from the Philomela myth—"A craftier Tereus, cousin, hast thou met"—and the entire family's inability to understand the nature of the attack until she brings them a codex of the *Metamorphoses* and "busily . . . turns the leaves" in search of the relevant story (4.1.45). Words, as Horace well knows, transcend materiality, thus Marcus could *immediately* identify Lavinia as Philomela. Yet, despite Marcus's familiarity with the story demonstrated at the initial moment of discovery, her family requires the material text to link the pieces together. More to the point, they need it to "plot" their revenge; without this script, all will be, as it has been, stasis.

The reliance on material text over, and often at the expense of, message owes to the moralizing tradition, because texts like the *Ovide moralisé* proceed by aligning wrong and right with letter and spirit, respectively. These commentaries insist that the letter of the text cannot properly signify without intervention, that interpretation figuratively lifts a veil.[83] Shakespeare, however, critiques such strict adherence to an inflexible interpretive agenda by showing that it need not result in Christian instruction. Titus reaffirms his attachment to the material text when Tamora arrives at his study door dressed, rather redundantly, as Revenge. Titus is not interested in buying Revenge's wares:

> Is it your trick to make me ope the door,
> That so my sad decrees may fly away
> And all my study be to no effect?
> You are deceived, for what I mean to do
> See here in bloody lines I have set down,
> And what is written shall be executed. (5.2.10–15)

Concerned that a gust of wind might carry away his papers, Titus again suggests that without access to the material text, his study will "be to no effect." When Titus states that "what is written shall be executed," he implies that without the text, there is no action. Titus's unabashed reliance on text as script derives from his confused hermeneutic, and recalls his misguided sense that a borrowed plot might merit "wonder." His wording— "what is written shall be executed"—adds a new contour to the notion

---

83. See, for example, Blumenfeld-Kosinski's discussion of the Veronica story in the *Ovide moralisé* (*Reading Myth*, 130–31).

that a moralized approach initiates *Titus*-style abuses, because Titus's statement perverts Romans 15:4: "For whatsoever things were written aforetime were written for our learning." Paul's words play no small role in the moralizing tradition—the *Ovide moralisé* opens with this very reference: "If Scripture doesn't lie to me, all that is written in books, whether good or evil, is for our instruction. For anyone who really wants to pay attention, evil is presented there so that one may guard against it, and good so that one may imitate it." (Se l'escripture ne me ment, / Tout est pour nostre enseignement / Quanqu'il a es livres escript, / Soient bon ou mal li escript.)[84] In Titus's mouth, Shakespeare's critique reveals itself as the difference between "learning" and "execut[ion]," the latter a kind of uncritical rote repetition, as when a text has already been digested, and manipulated, on the reader's behalf.

On the face of it, divine revelation and texts should not seem such peculiar bedfellows—the practice, known as *sortes Virgilianae*, of casting lots to read the future through Virgil's works, is just one example in a long tradition of divination practices that privileged biblical and literary texts. Shakespeare redraws these lines: characters in *Titus* seek answers from outside the text they follow, but when the gods fail to answer, the text is considered an acceptable substitute. As a result, the characters' strict adherence to the text doubles this divine replacement by allowing literary determinism to seem suddenly providential. Though prophetic structures in this play offer hollow glimpses of the future, they do highlight the peculiar temporalities established by narrative commitments. Since the characters follow stories that have already been written, asking those same texts to stand in for divine messages provokes a circularity mimetic of and enabled by the temporal frameworks established by Ovid—that is, by the etiological narrative's powerful backward pull. In threatening that Bassianus's "Philomel must lose her tongue today," Aaron set in motion a chain of prewritten events that allowed Lavinia's fate as Philomela to be sealed before she was ever touched by Chiron and Demetrius. Shakespeare's characters, then, cheat the notion of prophecy as they make Ovid's text at once a guide for action and a predictor of it.

Titus's Horace scenes demonstrate that a text and its meaning can be uncomfortably detached, and Shakespeare turns to Ovid for his overarching

---

84. As qtd. in Copeland, *Rhetoric, Hermeneutics,* 109–10. According to Copeland, the French poet "takes what had become a traditional critical rationale borrowed from St. Paul (Romans 15.4)," one especially popular with discussions of the *Heroides*, and goes on to argue that this reference bolsters his role as both compiler and exegetical commentator (110).

comment on the practices of textual interpretation. Shakespeare exposes the disconnect between text and meaning, literal and metaphorical, letter and spirit, that Ovidian moralization breeds. In so doing, the playwright mounts a larger statement on interpretive paradigms: Ovid and Christianity do not belong together, nor do they belong in dialogue. As I suggested earlier, Elizabethans and Romans draw upon the same set of classical texts. Surprisingly, however, Christian moralizers use Ovid just as badly as Shakespeare's Romans. The playwright exposes a danger in the reading practices of moralizers, and Elizabethan practitioners prove no exception. This holds true at both extremes—though their express purposes are vastly different (revenge; redemptive sermonizing), both sets of readers must strip Ovid of his most essential elements to wrench his words into another context. And if the similarity of these two modes of reading, despite their different purposes, illustrates the extent to which Ovid and Christianity don't mix, then what does that say about the availability of a Christian message in *Titus Andronicus*? In the next section, I consider how the critique of reductive reading practices sharpens because the play repeatedly denies expressions, even those crafted in the vocabulary of Christianity, of hope for the future.

IV

Shakespeare's play shows how Christian traditions of interpretation add to the pagan doom, rather than providing an exit from it. To pinpoint the force of *Titus*'s hermeneutic critique, I want to conclude this chapter by turning to a minor character who is excluded from, and falls victim to, the play's destructive classicizing. In act 4, as Titus is pursuing his revenge scheme, a clown wanders haplessly across his path, a misstep that sends the rustic man to Saturninus's doorstep—the audience barely has time to register this stock character before he is sent to be executed. A glaring misfit, he surpasses the bounds of his comic register by remaining inassimilable. He represents a nexus of competing discourses: he demonstrably fails to speak the play's language of literary allusion; he most closely resembles an Elizabethan rustic; he originates a variety of Christian references. By the time the Clown enters the stage, Aaron has aptly demonstrated his interpretive abilities in reading and understanding through Horace, and has exhibited unique shrewdness in his capacity to shape action and manipulate agents via Ovid. The inclusion of the play's Moor in the classical literary mode of communication bespeaks not only Aaron's intelligence, but also suggests that a knowledge of classical literature could be available to anyone in Titus's Rome. Nonetheless, Shakespeare introduces the Clown, a comic character who meets a tragic end because he is explicitly incapable of participating in the play's dialogue via classical allusion. Not only is he not classical, but he also bears easily identifiable Christian signs and messages, even if he does not understand the resonance of his own transmissions. The literalizing Clown's miscommunications emphasize the ill fit of classical literature and Christian morality previously exposed by modes of interpretation in the play. He seems hopelessly alienated both from reading practices and from Ovid.

This "ignorant, rude, uncouth, ill-bred man"[85] signals cultural clash because he resembles an untutored Elizabethan far more closely than he does a Roman. At the same time, he makes good on his stock role as fool or jester when he enters carrying a basket of pigeons, which he intends as a peace offering to the "tribunal plebs":

Enter the Clown with a basket and two pigeons in it.

TITUS	News, news, from heaven! Marcus, the post is come. Sirrah, what tidings? Have you any letters? Shall I have justice? What says Jupiter?
CLOWN	Ho, the gibbet-maker? He says that he hath taken them down again, for the man must not be hanged till the next week.
TITUS	But what says Jupiter, I ask thee?
CLOWN	Alas, sir, I know not Jubiter, I never drank with him in all my life.
TITUS	Why, villain, art not thou the carrier?
CLOWN	Ay, of my pigeons, sir – nothing else.
TITUS	Why, didst thou not come from heaven?
CLOWN	From heaven? Alas, sir, I never came there. God forbid I should be so bold to press to heaven in my young days. Why, I am going with my pigeons to the tribunal plebs to take up a matter of brawl betwixt my uncle and one of the emperal's men. (4.3.77–93)

Titus mistakes him for Jupiter's messenger (i.e., Mercury), and asks him specifically "art not thou the carrier?" The Clown responds, "Ay, of my pigeons, sir – nothing else" (4.3.86–87). The two speak at cross-purposes, yet they seem complicit in ignoring an obvious possible use for the

---

85. *OED*, s.v. "clown, *n.*," def. 2.

birds—pigeons act as message carriers.[86] Titus magnifies this oversight when he asks the Clown to deliver a letter to the emperor on his behalf, and commissions a round-trip journey: "[Y]ou must kneel, then kiss his foot, then deliver up your pigeons" (4.3.110–11), then "[W]hen thou hast given it to the emperor, / Knock at my door and tell me what he says" (4.3.117–18). Titus asks the Clown to act as a carrier pigeon, delivering a message and then returning to the sender. The comedy of the interaction exhibits a redundancy reminiscent of the interpretive practice of moralization. If the pigeons are the text, then the Clown carries the hidden message. At the same time, the pigeons provide only a metaphor for message carrying, while the Clown is the literal agent of delivery. The trouble derives from the middle ground: both pigeons and the Clown are onstage, so the metaphor becomes literalized, and by having both, Shakespeare draws attention to the superfluity.

The scene offers further insight into modes of interpretation and miscommunication precisely because the Clown does not understand classical reference. Unluckily, he enters the play carrying his "basket and two pigeons in it" while Titus is shooting missives addressed to the gods into Saturninus's court. Titus's fantasy is elaborately strange: the classical gods have become his pen pals. He treats the Clown as a messenger delivering "post" that contains written responses to his supplicant missives; his greeting is effusive as he expects his "news ... from heaven!"[87] But "the post" is instantly forgotten; Titus wants the Clown to relay the written message. The redundancy is starting to grate: why must the Clown be both letter and spirit, both medium and message? Titus anxiously asks, "What says Jupiter?" and the Clown mistakes "Jupiter" for "gibbeter," replying, "Ho, the gibbet-maker?" The classical god Jupiter is assuredly a far cry from the Elizabethan hangman, but the phenomenon underlying the homonymic joke has implications that prove serious: the Clown does not recognize the name Jupiter, does not speak the play's language of classical allusion. Titus persists, asking, "But what says Jupiter, I ask thee?" and the Clown replies, "Alas, sir, I know not Jubiter, I never drank / with him in all my

---

86. The *OED* cites *Titus Andronicus* as the first place that "carrier" is used to mean "a bearer of a message, letter, etc." (s.v. "carrier, *n.*," def. 1b) rather than the more general "bearer" or "person who or thing that carries" (def. 1a).

87. In "Topicality and Conceptual Blending: *Titus Andronicus* and the Case of William Hacket," *College Literature* 33, no. 1 (2006): 131, Nicholas R. Moschovakis notes that this pair of lines is attributed to Titus only in the Folio (F) and second quarto (Q2) texts; Q1 (1594) attributes them to the Clown. Contra Moschovakis, my argument provides further evidence that modern editors have good reason to follow the later, emended editions.

life." His misunderstanding, which hinges on a lack of classical understanding, is also an apt metaphor because Jupiter *is* the Clown's gibbeter; the metaphor becomes literal as his mistake of "gibbeter" for "Jupiter" proves cruelly prophetic. Titus sends the Clown to deliver a message to Saturninus, the Roman emperor, and is immediately sentenced to death. Francis Barker has suggested that there is a particular tragedy to this unexpected, swift, and inexplicable death by hanging. Although, as Molly Easo Smith has pointed out, the threat of hanging haunts Aaron's scaffold scene until Lucius dubs it too "sweet" a fate to answer such villainy (5.1.146), Barker singles out the Clown's silent, unnoticed sentence of hanging as particularly poignant even amid the play's bloodshed because hanging really was a commoner's punishment in Elizabethan England.[88] Indeed, this glaringly Elizabethan figure calls to mind Shakespeare's own present day, but the critical aspect of the Clown scenes lies in the moments of misinterpretation. The Clown seems unable to understand classical allusions—cultural clues that he fatally misses—and he initiates biblical allusions that set him markedly apart from the rest of the play.

Literalizing the Clown's mistake engenders violence, and his situation emblematizes the moralizers' interpretive mode. The Clown's prophetic words mirror Shakespeare's Ovidian textual operations; the etiological narrative structure persists in the face of a glaringly absent Ovid (that is, a lack of classical knowledge) because the reading practices derived from, and subsequently misapplied to, Ovid are still in place. By demonstrating total ignorance of a classical god (and by extension of classical mythology), the Clown immediately is positioned as different from the other characters. It is specifically this critical lack of knowledge that prevents him from identifying Titus as a madman and responding to him accordingly. His speech amplifies his traditional generic role because "repeatedly it is the figure of the fool who provides this link [between stage and audience]. No other actor stands so clearly on the threshold between the play and the community occasion." Robert Weimann suggests the figure

---

88. Francis Barker, "Treasures of Culture: *Titus Andronicus* and Death by Hanging," in *The Production of English Renaissance Culture*, ed. David Lee Miller, Sharon O'Dair, and Harold Weber (Ithaca, NY: Cornell University Press, 1994), 226–61; Molly Easo Smith, "Spectacles of Torment in *Titus Andronicus*," *SEL* 36, no. 2 (1996): 316. Smith offers a discussion of the importance of the Clown's death as an indicator of the inefficacy of political authority in the play. For compelling readings of these scenes as topical references to two distinct contemporary events, see Moschovakis, "Topicality," 131ff.; and Jina Politi, "'The Gibbet-Maker,'" *Notes and Queries* 236 (1991): 54–55. See also Maurice Hunt, "Compelling Art in *Titus Andronicus*," *SEL* 28, no. 2 (1988): 197–218; and Anthony Brian Taylor, "The Clown Episode in *Titus Andronicus*, the Bible, and Cambises," *Notes and Queries* 46, no. 2 (1999): 210–11.

of the Clown exists in a spatial/temporal world discrete from that of the represented action (and closer to that of the audience).[89] Not only do his words and references appear anachronistic, but his Elizabethan cadences make him ana*topi*stic as well: to an absurd degree he is in the wrong place at the wrong time.

Though the Clown cannot participate in the play's Ovidianism, he initiates a series of Christian allusions. In the first place, he is carrying a basket of pigeons. In the Renaissance, the words "dove" and "pigeon" were often used interchangeably.[90] Because pigeons and doves were twins in Elizabethan theological ornithography, the Clown's pigeons silently invoke the Holy Spirit and the Noah story.[91] The Clown, lacking text, is all message; he represents not simply illiteracy and an aural tradition, but also the opportunity for a Christian message that persists in the absence of the material text. The Clown cannot understand that he is in danger. In fact, he cannot even understand the registers of his own representation: he requires interpretation. Denied access to the text, he can no more read the deadly message Titus asks him to deliver than he could Titus's classical reference.

Yet, the Clown's particular death sentence only reiterates the extent to which this glaringly Elizabethan stock character already calls to mind Shakespeare's own present day. The unexpected urgency of the Clown scenes lies in their misunderstandings because these moments ground the dialogue in classical reference while simultaneously introducing explicitly Christian allusion into the play's discourse. Titus initially asks the Clown, "Why, didst thou not come from heaven?" Because the Clown does not understand the classical allusion, he does not realize that Titus has cast him as Mercury, and instead assumes Titus means Christian heaven. He replies, "From heaven? Alas, sir, I never came there. / God forbid I should be so bold to press to heaven in my / young days" (4.3.88–91). This recourse to religious terminology is repeated

---

89. Robert Weimann, *Shakespeare and the Popular Tradition in the Theater: Studies in the Social Dimension of Dramatic Form and Function*, ed. Robert Schwartz (Baltimore: Johns Hopkins University Press, 1978), 43.

90. See, for example, Anthony Copley's *A Fig for Fortune* (London, 1596): "What Iesus erst had planted with his blood / This Pigion gaue it grace-full liuelihood" (K1r). See also *OED*, s.v. "pigeon, *n.*," defs. 1a and 2.

91. Noah uses a dove to search out dry land specifically because the dove can fill a carrier role (going out and coming back in): "the Arck . . . From whence the hopeful Noe, a pigeon did let flee" (Richard Verstegan, *Odes in Imitation of the Seaven Penitential Psalmes* [1601], D2v). The third time Noah sends the dove out, it does not return, indicating it has found dry land on which to nest (Genesis 8:8–10, *The Holy Bible* [London, 1584], A4v). The Christian allusions cited in this chapter are certainly not exhaustive.

when the Clown interprets Titus's question—"[C]an you deliver an oration to the emperor with a grace?"—in a Christian framework: "Nay, truly, sir, I could never say grace in all my life" (4.3.97–100).[92] Oliver Arnold suggests that "saying grace" in the context of execution would strike a particular chord with an Elizabethan audience, since in Shakespeare's England demonstrating a reading knowledge of Latin meant avoiding capital punishment:

> The neck verse had originally been a benefit of clergy.... But the requirement of reading from Scripture in Latin—typically from the Fifty-first Psalm—to obtain grace and pardon preserved the religious resonance of the practice. With this context and his end on the gallows in mind, we can see that the Clown's fate is both sealed and foreshadowed in the way he first betrays his illiteracy.[93]

If the "way he first betrays his illiteracy" calls to mind a specifically Elizabethan context—his scriptural shortcomings guarantee his execution—it also powerfully resituates illiteracy as a matter of allusive register. The inability to say grace echoes and reinforces the Clown's prescient appeal to the "gibbet-maker."

Whereas the Clown's initial Christian references seem accidental or self-alienating in his first scene, at the palace they become a more naturalized feature of his parlance:

Enter Clown.

TAMORA	How now, good fellow, wouldst thou speak with us?
CLOWN	Yea, forsooth, and your mistress-ship be emperial.
TAMORA	Empress I am, but yonder sits the emperor.
CLOWN	'Tis he. God and Saint Stephen give you good e'en. I have brought you a letter and a couple of pigeons here.

[Saturninus] reads the letter.

SATURNINUS	Go, take him away and hang him presently!
CLOWN	How much money must I have?
TAMORA	Come, sirrah, you must be hanged.
CLOWN	Hanged, by'Lady? Then I have brought up a neck to a fair end. *Exit.* (4.4.39–48)

---

92. See Arnold, *Third Citizen*, 137 for a compelling argument demonstrating why these lines, often cut by editors, are an essential part of the scene.
93. Arnold, *Third Citizen*, 136–37.

The Clown's casual Christian mentions stand apart from both his classical ignorance and his comic malapropisms ("emperal"; "tribunal plebs"). His unorthodox salutation—"God and Saint Stephen give you good e'en"—invokes the first martyr,[94] and when he accepts his fate without struggle, he acts in accordance with Stephen, who, as he was being stoned to death, asked God to "lay not this sin" to the "charge" of his assailants.[95] Stephen is described as being "full of the holy Ghost," a designation that seems at least technically applicable to the Clown given his "couple of pigeons." With two pigeons instead of just one dove, his Christian resonance is surprisingly in keeping with the play's superlative ethos. The Clown's unannounced Christian register is quite sophisticated, since so many of his jokes rely on misunderstood classical reference. His explicit mention of Stephen nods toward the play's signature outdoing—in referring to him while carrying pigeons, the Clown supplies his own script for execution. His miscommunications over Christian heaven and the act of "saying grace" alongside his references to God, Saint Stephen, and the Virgin Mary ("Hanged, by'Lady?") gain purchase in the aggregate even as he demonstrates an inability to function in or to interpret his deadly situation. More importantly, his allusions go unremarked by his classics-loving interlocutors. Here I diverge from Arnold's salient point that "those who cannot say grace will find none on the gallows" to suggest that the Clown's end on the gallows provides instead a comment on the *availability* of grace.[96] Ironically, grace proves more available to an illiterate rustic than it does to those who both speak and read Latin in the play. Yet, even given this exception, Shakespeare portrays a Rome that accommodates neither saying nor receiving grace.

The Clown's counterstrand invites comparison to biblical paradigms for message delivery. The Annunciation as reported by Luke and the preceding story of Gabriel's announcement of a son to Zacharias offer the most obvious examples.[97] Both stories seem inverted in *Titus*: when the Clown arrives, Titus reverses Mary's position by revealing that he has been expecting a messenger: "News, news, from heaven! Marcus, the post is come" (4.3.77). In *Titus*, it is the messenger who exhibits confusion, and though his language and iconography suggest it, he does not seem to know that he is delivering the message of Christianity. Confusion of

---

94. Moschovakis makes a similar point ("Topicality," 134–35).
95. Acts 7:48–60, Ttt5r.
96. Arnold, *Third Citizen*, 138.
97. Luke 1:19–38.

this magnitude gets cleared up in Luke—when Mary learns that the Holy Spirit will join her in the form of a son, she agrees to be God's servant. Titus, on the other hand, expects a pagan message, and effectively rejects a Christian one by not responding to the Clown's allusions.[98] Similarly, when Zacharias questions the veracity of Gabriel's news that he will have a son, he is punished for his doubt—Gabriel takes away his ability to speak for the remainder of Elizabeth's pregnancy. These details are recalled in *Titus*, but the situation has been turned around, its implications reversed. In the Bible, questioning God's message leads to the loss of communication, but for the Clown it is a lack of communication that prevents him from understanding Titus's messages in the first place. This rustic character pushes the questions of interpretation and future potential beyond the register of classical allusion. Fittingly, Christian reference cannot function as amplified allusion in the way that the *Metamorphoses* does in *Titus*: Christian parallels remain mere shimmers as their means and messages get turned upside down in a world that operates in a different referential register.

Whereas *Titus*'s core characters communicate via classical allusion, the Clown offers an unacknowledged counternarrative in Christianity. What is the significance of locating both classical ignorance and Christian proficiency in the Clown character? On the one hand, only high or royal characters actually demonstrate facility with classical literature. On the other, the play's most foolish, rustic, and uneducated character is also the most connected to the audience, and the most loaded with Christian references (a phenomenon in scant supply in the rest of the play). It seems then that there is something complicated going on in this moment of miscommunication. After all, Christ is God's messenger who takes on flesh in order to offer the news of man's deliverance: the gospel that sinful man would be saved by God's mercy. The notions of mercy, pity, and piety have been present from the opening of the play, when Tamora begs Titus to spare Alarbus, telling him that "[s]weet mercy is nobility's true badge" (1.1.122). When he ignores her pleas, she curses his "cruel, irreligious piety" (1.1.133). Their interaction fuels the resulting revenge and violence in the play, but the specific notion of Christian redemption enters only with the Clown. Because of their flawed reading of Ovid, which has so much in common with moral readings of Ovid, the concepts of grace and mercy seem absent from the play's world,

---

98. It is impossible to determine whether Titus does not or simply will not understand the Clown's Christian allusions. We can only know definitively that he never acknowledges any of them.

reinforcing the mismatch between a hermeneutic tradition and the pagan text it sought to correct.

In a play so concerned with pity and piety, perhaps the distance between Jupiter and gibbeter is actually not so vast. Perhaps it is a death that comes along with pagan religion—Jupiter seems specifically set apart from the Christian God, who offers redemption instead of death. Moreover, the Clown introduces the Christian message of grace or forgiveness—grace and martyrdom—just as Titus embarks on his vicious, barbaric revenge. Titus does not receive the pagan "news ... from heaven" that he was expecting, but rather gets bombarded with "good news"—Christian reference and the message of grace.[99] Whereas the Clown cannot understand Titus's classicizing, Titus never answers the Clown's Christianity, but his subsequent actions implicitly reject the Christian message that the Clown quietly invokes. From early on in the play, the type of reading that the characters engage in serves as a critique of moral commentaries, and the principle pays off when even a minor character demonstrates that Christian messages and classical literature are held firmly apart. Even the biblical parallels in the Clown scenes get derailed by Titus's insistent classical fantasy: the Clown is entirely unread by Titus. The Clown highlights the way in which *moralizatio* bypasses the messages it should champion, and provides a final limit case even though he does not offer a successful alternative.

The violence done to the *Metamorphoses* by moralizing commentators is doubled back upon in the Clown scenes. Being unread, misinterpreted, or read out of context are problems with fatal consequences, and yet, this already misses the point of a concept such as God's grace. Titus's future is problematically constrained, but the same is true for the moralizers. The Clown's iconography is too subtle to reorient a play marked by repetitive textual structures. And without a script to follow, he also ends up dead. The moralized mode comes under fire in this play, and the Clown's hapless Christianity does not really fare any better. Yet the Clown does offer a glimpse of an alternative, a glimpse of a way out of the play's recursive temporal movements. He introduces a truly unpredictable future, even if, though more muted, his fate is the same as that of the other characters on Shakespeare's stage.

The Clown, who embraces his death and martyrdom, is entirely outside the system; he escapes the temporality associated with narrative paradigms

---

99. Moschovakis suggests that the very phrase "'news from heaven' would have primed for access the concept of Christian revelation, or traditionally 'the good news' (Greek *evangelion*)" ("Topicality," 134).

of both etiology and teleology. Though he provides a message of which he seems entirely unaware, he counters the play's versions of temporality, not only by literally appearing more Elizabethan than Roman, but also by invoking a divine temporality, which serves as an alternative to the options aligned with the contrary registers of reading and interpreting Ovid. As he moves toward the gallows, he shifts out of the play's temporal traps at the very moment that he reveals a message that has transcended text.

In Ovid, the Philomela story begins with an owl, one of many bad omens at Procne and Tereus's wedding:

> And on the house did rucke
> A cursed Owle the messenger of yll successe and lucke.
> And all the night time while that they were lying in their beds,
> She sate upon the bedsteds top right over both their heds.[100]

Despite its eagles, ravens, pigeons, and swallows, there is no owl in *Titus*'s Rome to offer auguries, an omission in keeping with a cast of characters who prefer text to portent or prophecy. The owl is never named in *Titus Andronicus*, but neither is the nightingale. This latter absence merits more notice in a play that so consciously cleaves to and depends on Philomela's tale. Because of Ovid's etiological project, the myth both begins and ends with the nightingale. Philomela's trials result in redemptive metamorphosis, but Lavinia never flies from her fate. Almost everyone dies in *Titus Andronicus*. Yet the play does end with birds. In its final lines, Lucius mandates that Tamora be denied burial:

> No mournful bell shall ring her burial,
> But throw her forth to beasts and birds to prey:
> Her life was beastly and devoid of pity,
> And being dead, let birds on her take pity. (5.3.196–99)[101]

At the end of their story, Philomela, Procne, and Tereus are all turned into birds—metamorphoses that free them from their human plight. Birds are no less central to Shakespeare's conclusion, but they represent retribution rather than redemption. Lucius intends the birds to prey on Tamora's

---

100. Golding, *Metamorphoses* 6.552–55.
101. In *Biblical References in Shakespeare's Tragedies* (Cranbury, NJ: Associated University Presses, 1987), 72, Naseeb Shaheen suggests that the story of Jezebel in 1 and 2 Kings and Seneca's *Thyestes* are possible sources for these lines.

unburied body.¹⁰² He says her life was "beastly" (conjuring the world of allegorical readings of the *Metamorphoses*) and thus necessarily "devoid of pity." As a result, justice dictates that in death she should be devoured by birds of prey that will decidedly not "on her take pity." Lucius's final act, exaggerated by the repetition of the words "birds" and "pity," illustrates that the play's movement is circular—death offers poetic justice rather than salvation. Moreover, Lucius's direction to "throw her forth to beasts and birds to prey" confines possibility to a pun. While he intends "beasts and birds" to "prey" on her, the audience might briefly imagine Tamora not as scavengers' prey, but as a woman praying for pity. But only briefly—not simply because she is already dead, but also because Shakespeare has long since established that petitions for Christian mercy have been denied a place in this play. In the absence of the nightingale, we might also notice that the birds Lucius twice mentions are not the Clown's pigeons. Unlike those birds, Lucius's birds only offer "pity," not grace. These lines allude only by antithesis, while the ethos of cruelty and vengeance remains amplified.

With Lucius's discordant closing words, the play ends deprived of the hopeful birds of both Ovid and the Bible. As I have attempted to show, their exclusion highlights the play's insistence that classical materials and Christian topoi do not mix. The matter of reading underscores this essential incompatibility. The play's repeated signals toward a future foreclosed by textual models, and its emphasis on the problematic interpretation of source texts, suggest the dangers of a present moment that insists too strongly on models from the past. The matter of allusion casts a long shadow on Lucius's final gestures. The textual history of the play's ending lengthens that shadow. In 1905, a sole surviving first quarto of the play (printed in 1594) was discovered, and it stopped at "pity." That is, the text did not include four final lines that had appeared, with minor variations, in editions beginning with the second quarto (printed in 1600).¹⁰³ The editorial explanation for that difference makes *Titus Andronicus* look more than a little like Spenser's *Briton moniments*. According to the prevailing account, the editor of Q2 based that text on a damaged copy of Q1; its final leaves compromised four passages,

---

102. For a discussion of an implicit denial of Christian (specifically Catholic) funeral rites in this speech, see Nicholas R. Moschovakis, "'Irreligious Piety' and Christian History: Persecution as Pagan Anachronism in *Titus Andronicus*," *Shakespeare Quarterly* 53, no. 4 (2002): 466.

103. See Vickers, *Shakespeare, Co-Author*, 148.

including the closing speech.[104] That editor assumed the play's final lines were missing and invented these:

> See iustice done on *Aron* that damn'd Moore,
> From whom our heauie haps had their beginning:
> Then afterwards to order well the state,
> That like events may nere it ruinate.[105]

These lines close the play with proper rhyme, but the "justice" to which they explicitly refer does little to distinguish itself from Lucius's vengeance. Instead, they amplify the dangerous impulse to look back. Attentive to "beginning," these lines deny the future Lucius attempts to establish, because they keep the scripts of the past so squarely in view. In them, Lucius's emphasis falls to "like events," even as he proclaims that such models are to be avoided. One of the play's very few survivors, Lucius represents a restoration of order to Rome, emphasized by the stirring endorsement he receives: "Lucius, all hail, Rome's gracious governor!" (5.3.145). However, far from ending the play with rousing rhetoric about Rome's bright future in the aftermath of war and vicious slaughter, Lucius allows vengeance the last word. If these added lines close the play, Rome's future looks even dimmer because they furnish a vision fixated on prevention. To avoid "like events," to hope to sidestep ruination, such positions sketch out a future very limited indeed. The future imagined by negation does little to protect against the link suggested by formal pairing: "state" rhymed with "ruinate." If, with the discovery of Q1, we are restored to an ending that lands instead on "pity," even as Lucius denies it, then the close more forcefully echoes the attention to "pity" and "piety" with which the drama began. Over Tamora's dead body, both terms seem beside the point; mercy or redemption derives neither from mining the past nor from deterministic overreading. The closest the play gets to God's grace is an illiterate clown, but even he falls tragically short of relieving a tradition of entrapment. Shakespeare's engagement with classical allusion manages to undercut the dangers that uses of the past pose. The end of the play sounds a warning that reiterates the limitations of looking back. The play advocates

---

104. Joseph S. G. Bolton, "The Authentic Text of *Titus Andronicus*," *PMLA* 44, no. 3 (1929): 765–88. Bolton argues that "if the particular copy of the first quarto that came into the hands of the second printer had happened to lose the lower parts of its last two leaves, one could understand how four of the passages, recurring at almost exact page-intervals, came to be rewritten. And when one compares the two versions of these four passages one notes that in each the later version is distinctly lacking in poetic power" (776). Bate and Vickers both incorporate this account into their own.

105. See Shakespeare, *Titus*, 277.

a reading practice suspicious of totalizing morals (one strangely replayed in that textual puzzle). Instead, we might use this heightened attention to the relationship between looking forward and looking back to extend the critique enabled by this particular hermeneutic: the danger of being too beholden to the past informs strategies for its reappropriation in Shakespeare's later Roman plays. In the next two chapters, I consider a variety of competing approaches to the future, and the resources furnished by grammar, narrative, and poetic form out of which such gestures are made.

Chapter 4

Shakespeare's Second Future
Anticipatory Nostalgia in Cymbeline

Like *Titus Andronicus*, Shakespeare's *Cymbeline* opens with the threat of a succession crisis: Cymbeline's daughter, Imogen, has secretly married Posthumus Leonatus, a "poor but worthy gentleman" to dire effect (1.1.7).[1] "She's wedded, / Her husband banish'd; she imprison'd" (1.1.7–8), an unnamed gentleman reports. The king deems the match unsuitable because of Posthumus's dubious and obscure lineage—he cannot be "delve[d]" to the "root" (1.1.28). His name, however, can be. Cymbeline himself bestowed it on his charge after the boy's mother died in childbirth; his valiant father, whose deeds earned him the surname Leonatus, had already expired. Imogen's husband began his life etymologically linked to his own belatedness, his estrangement from his family reinforced by a name that communicates a disordered temporal sequence ("after death").[2] Because Posthumus cannot boast himself the latest member of a worthy family line, Cymbeline perceives him as a threat to the prospect of royal issue. Posthumus's new father-in-law seeks to banish not just his person, but also the particular future that he promises. That Imogen is heir to her father's throne is itself the result of a previous succession crisis—twenty years earlier, Cymbeline's two sons

---

1. All references are to William Shakespeare, *Cymbeline*, ed. J. M. Nosworthy, 2nd ser. (1995; repr., London: The Arden Shakespeare, 2000).

2. The *OED* entry on "posthumous" offers a discussion of the "folk-etymological" associations of this postclassical Latin word, which link "humus" to the earth and to burial.

were abducted. As their kidnapper, Belarius, later notes, "I stole these babes, / Thinking to bar [Cymbeline] of succession" (3.3.101–2). In stealing his male heirs, Belarius steals the king's posterity and troubles the prospects of the British crown well beyond his own lifetime. Despite their antipathy, Cymbeline and Belarius share in their presumption that such inevitable consequences require no guesswork; certain futures tend to signal doomed endings.[3] Like Posthumus's name, Belarius's proleptic perspective on loss brings to the fore the temporal dimensions of a problem like lineage. Yet the play simultaneously illuminates the complexity of a structure as seemingly dependable as linear time by testing out and acknowledging more flexible futures. As in the previous chapters, I demonstrate the extent to which narrative offers a resource for unsettling the future. In *Titus Andronicus*, highlighting the temporal implications of structures like etiology and teleology pried revenge tragedy's conventional focus on ends apart from the dangers of a reading practice that aimed to dismantle art's power to open up unscripted futures. Whereas in that play, narrative reinforced a hermeneutic that resulted in a future stripped of possibility, in *Cymbeline*, voicing alternatives to certain futures entails narrative and even grammatical choices. Shakespeare's characters themselves look forward to looking back when they imagine the link between present experience and its eventual reconstitution in words.

No sooner does Imogen's exiled husband arrive in Rome than he enters into a heated exchange about his new wife, resulting in a wager that powers much of the play's plot. At his Roman host Philario's house, Posthumus is greeted by a motley collection of foreigners eager to dispute his contention that Imogen is "more fair, virtuous, wise, chaste, constant, qualified and less attemptable than any the rarest" women in France or Italy (1.5.56–58).[4] The

---

3. For an excellent argument that traces the concepts of fortune and luck through the use of those words in the period to show how "Shakespeare, in creating such a complex world of chance in Hamlet, was not reacting against [the culture's] theological sensitivity, he was participating in it," see Brian Cummings, *Mortal Thoughts: Religion, Secularity & Identity in Shakespeare and Early Modern Culture* (Oxford: Oxford University Press, 2013), 235. Cummings has argued that *Hamlet* is "situated" at the "nexus of the knowability and the unknowability of the future, of certainty and uncertainty." He traces the word "luck" in an effort to uncover how this "nexus is part of the ordinary language of sixteenth-century Protestantism" (214). This chapter proceeds in sympathy with his interest in pulling such concepts out of the language, and its changes, of the period. Cummings's approach is particularly compelling in that he attempts to "work outwards from the language of the play rather than inwards from what we might think we know about Shakespeare's biography" (213). Though I share an interest in methods of such "working outwards," I don't share his emphasis on religious culture.

4. In "Romancing the Wager: *Cymbeline*'s Intertexts," in *Staging Early Modern Romance: Prose, Fiction, Dramatic Resource, and Shakespeare*, ed. Mary Ellen Lamb and Valerie Wayne (New York: Routledge, 2009), 163–87, Wayne suggests that this points toward the various international versions of this familiar tale.

rivalry, reminiscent not just of an earlier argument but also of the opening lines of Shakespeare's *The Rape of Lucrece* (1594),[5] begins on national terms—Posthumus's interlocutors seem affronted that Imogen is claimed to outshine their countrywomen by any standard—but patriotic pride quickly gives way to a more basic epistemological concern:

> Post.   I would
> abate her nothing, though I profess myself her
> adorer, not her friend.
>
> Iach.   As fair, and as good—a kind of hand-in-hand
> comparison—had been something too fair, and too good
> for any lady in Britany. If she went before others
> I have seen, as that diamond of yours outlustres
> many I have beheld, I could not believe she
> excelled many: but I have not seen the most
> precious diamond that is, nor you the lady. (1.5.64–73)[6]

Alongside his boasts that he could easily bed Imogen given half a chance, Posthumus's Italian rival, Iachimo, casts doubt on the possibility of knowing that any woman is actually a paragon. Whereas in Shakespeare's key source text, Boccaccio's *Decameron*, this is a misogynistic ontological doubt—there's no such thing as a chaste woman—Iachimo challenges Posthumus's access to an epistemological limit point. His claim, "I have not seen the most precious diamond that is, nor you the lady," suggests that Iachimo takes issue with the very notion that Posthumus could know with certainty that he has encountered the superlative case.[7]

In beginning his play with a concern about succession and moving into a debate over virtue that turns on epistemological certainty, Shakespeare echoes a culture well versed in attempts to determine likelihood and to

---

5. Cf. "When Collatine unwisely did not let / To praise the clear unmatched red and white" and "in Tarquin's tent, / Unlocked the treasure of his happy state, / What priceless wealth the heavens had him lent / In the possession of his beauteous mate" (William Shakespeare, "The Rape of Lucrece," in *The Complete Sonnets and Poems*, ed. Colin Burrow [Oxford: Oxford University Press, 2002], lines 8–18).

6. See Nosworthy for a discussion of editorial responses to "could not believe," and the practice of changing it to "could not but believe" (22n71).

7. In the *Decameron*, the Iachimo figure (Ambroginolo) pushes questions concerning possibility, certainty, and epistemology so hard that the exasperated Posthumus figure (Bernardo) responds, "I am a Merchant, and no Philosopher," and Boccaccio shuts down where Bernardo does. Giovanni Boccaccio, *The Decameron Containing An hundred Pleasant Nouels*, trans. John Florio (London: Isaac Jaggard, 1620), N3v.

presuppose the realm of what "will be," practices that seemed to cohabitate with unequivocal expressions about the workings of providence.[8] Though mathematical probability as we know it was not "invented" until around 1660, instruments for assessing and protecting against risk existed alongside tracts about the ills of gambling in Renaissance England.[9] Scholars in the past few decades have disputed the seemingly late rise of probability on theological terms, assessing whether the move from God to gambling was slowed or hastened by religious principles.[10] We, too, might be tempted to consider the extent to which these two contexts—God and gambling—bristle together especially in a play that offers both a wager and various glimpses of a divine realm—an onstage visit from Jupiter in the play's fifth act and a vague sense

---

8. For example, in "Drama and Marine Insurance in Shakespeare's London," in *The Law in Shakespeare*, ed. Constance Jordan and Karen Cunningham (Basingstoke, UK: Palgrave Macmillan, 2007), 135, Luke Wilson documents "lost or not lost" policies available from the 1580s in the early modern marine insurance market in London, which allowed speculators to buy insurance for a ship that had already begun a voyage. In such cases, the pricing and availability of the policies depended on whether or not any reports about potential shipwreck had been received. Shakespeare's pairing might remind us of such coincidences in the culture more broadly: in early modern England, "hazard" was the name of a dice game. In *The Emergence of Probability*, 2nd ed. (Cambridge: Cambridge University Press, 2006), 6, Ian Hacking notes that the word's origin is Arabic. The "term 'adventurer' was applied to both gamblers and venture capitalists," according to Linda Woodbridge, "'He Beats Thee 'Gainst The Odds': Gambling, Risk Management, and *Antony and Cleopatra*," in *Antony and Cleopatra: New Critical Essays*, ed. Sara Munson Deats (New York: Routledge, 2005), 196–97. See also Douglas Lane Patey, *Probability and Literary Form: Philosophic Theory and Literary Practice in the Augustan Age* (Cambridge: Cambridge University Press, 1984), who offers a counter to the underlying assumption of what he calls the "Foucault-Hacking hypothesis."

9. See Hacking, *Emergence of Probability*. The first English lottery was held in 1569, and financial "speculation on futures was born during this period" (Woodbridge, "'He Beats Thee,'" 196). Texts that treated gambling in the period tended to be more forgiving of games that depended on skill rather than chance. In James Balmford's *A Short and Plaine Dialogve Concerning the vnlawfulnes of playing at Cards or Tables, or any other game consisting in chance* (London, 1593), for example, the preacher cautions against using lots "in sport" because "we are not to tempt the Almightie by a vaine desire of manifestation of his power and speciall prouidence" (A5r). That is, the vice lies in the *vanity* of games of chance because such games call on providence frivolously, not because of any doubt about providential design.

10. Hacking claims "theological views of divine foreknowledge were being reinforced by the amazing success of mechanistic models" (*Emergence of Probability*, 2–3); Peter L. Bernstein claims that the "idea of risk management emerges only when people believe that they are to some degree free agents" (*Against the Gods: The Remarkable Story of Risk* [New York: John Wiley and Sons, 1996], 35). Reinhart Koselleck identifies "rational forecast" as a sea change whereby the "future became a domain of finite possibilities, arranged according to their greater or lesser probability" (*Futures Past: On the Semantics of Historical Time*, trans. Keith Tribe [New York: Columbia University Press, 2004], 18). See also Cummings, who finds in Hacking the useful proposition that our assumptions about "modern philosophical doctrines of determinism" have been used "to understand earlier, theological models (both pagan and Christian) in more rigid ways" than those to which people in the period actually subscribed (*Mortal Thoughts*, 210).

that, historically, Christ is being born somewhere just offstage.[11] In *Cymbeline*, the future is imagined at the crux of these kinds of distinctions. If Iachimo's wager against Posthumus's "confidence" (1.5.108) proves a guide by challenging epistemological certainty, the play exploits the certainty of future outcomes as a narratological and linguistic problem. The wager introduces the possibility that hazard, chance, and divination provide means for investigating future certainty, but the play broaches such pathways only to turn away from them.

Instead, *Cymbeline* illuminates a complex temporal perspective whereby the usual triad of time—past, present, and future—becomes characterized not by discrete, linear difference, but rather, by the overlap of the three, and the projection of how each can be redefined in terms of the others. In the play's first strokes, we encounter time in terms of both grand-scale hereafters and individual aftertimes as Shakespeare directs our attention to a page out of British history that he will fill with an investigation of the future. The playwright gives voice to a temporal orientation founded on the unstable interrelation of past, present, and future. In so doing, he shares intellectual common ground with English grammar books, which first emerged in the early modern period. Such texts struggled to explain and define verbal moods and tenses, and offered categorical descriptors such as "future perfect" and "second future"—the verb tense concerned with what *will have been*—to record knotty, even fluctuating, conceptions of futurity. The developing understanding and expression of such a grammatical category invite comparison with Shakespeare's treatment of the mutual implications of future and present, and particularly with the concept of looking forward to looking back that he establishes in this play.[12] In *Cymbeline*, narrative emerges as the preeminent strategy for distinguishing between different *kinds* of futures. Characters choose and construct the stories they want to tell, and even mold their actions with an eye toward the narratives their deeds will yield. In examining

---

11. Wilson argues that "in earlier ways of thinking, uncertainty was framed in terms of belief, and thus of truth; the new forms of insurance represent a new way of thinking in which uncertainty is a matter of probability and thus of risk" ("Drama and Marine Insurance," 135).

12. In looking to English grammar books, I mean to call attention to a discourse that renders explicit both the struggle to communicate time in language and to describe the conventions of that communication. In this regard, I am attempting to situate myself in between two compelling approaches. Though neither quite aligns with my own position, each approximates an aspect of that which I am trying to pinpoint in Shakespeare's approach: on the one hand, Cummings's examination of particular words because "philological history impinges on profound philosophical issues, with which sixteenth-century culture was in general struggling to come to terms" (*Mortal Thoughts*, 216); on the other, Simon Jarvis's contention that "language is one of the materials of verse" ("For a Poetics of Verse," *PMLA* 125, no. 4 (2010): 934) and his insistence that "verse is not a subset of language, . . . poetics is not a subset of linguistics" (933–34).

and setting in contradistinction the forward-looking linguistic and narrative structures in the play, I show in this chapter how negotiating time becomes a matter of choosing a narrative strategy for the future it will secure, especially when that future will be spent telling stories about the past. The proliferation of futures examined in the drama is in keeping with a contemporary discourse, ranging from theology to economic risk, that reflects a broadening set of approaches for reckoning with the unknowability of the days ahead. However, *Cymbeline* generates a unique perspective—what I call anticipatory nostalgia—that privileges the role that grammatical and imaginative constructions can play in accessing possible futures.

Recent criticism that has considered time in *Cymbeline* has tended to read it as primarily bound up with questions of political sovereignty and national identity. For example, Andrew Escobedo has persuasively argued that this play refuses "to allow ancient and modern to coalesce," that the play valorizes "the severing of roots," and that "*Cymbeline* explores what it would mean to say that the condition of being posthumous, if not exactly a virtue, is also not a cause for shame."[13] By contrast, this chapter demonstrates that Shakespeare routes his investigation of the future's uncertainty through frameworks distinct from God, gambling, and national identity. Instead, the playwright's exploration foregrounds the planning and manipulation of narrative, and its attendant grammatical constructions. In *Cymbeline*, artistic production—figured prominently as narrative—nudges open a unique kind of future, one that makes apparent the flexibility of temporal boundaries. The disagreements that emerge over opportunity and its narrative consequences underscore the play's embrace of grammatical structures that might fashion aesthetic resources for reimagining linear time and the place of the future. In this chapter, I show how the future is embedded in the play's aesthetic, narrative, and grammatical dimensions, and argue that the question of temporality obtains powerfully on the level of artistic production.

I

In the third act of the play, the focus turns away from both Cymbeline's Ludstown court and Philario's Italian league of nations to Wales, where we find that future-stealer, Belarius, raising Cymbeline's two kidnapped princes, Guiderius and Arviragus. Shakespeare sets up this third geographical

---

13. Andrew Escobedo, "From Britannia to England: *Cymbeline* and the Beginning of Nations," *Shakespeare Quarterly* 59, no. 1 (2008): 84, 76, 87.

location to accommodate a struggle over approaches to time that emerges between Belarius and his foster sons. This Wales, as Rosalie L. Colie has noted, "is unmitigated hard pastoral, a rocky, difficult terrain training its inhabitants to a spare and muscular strength sufficient to wrest their nutriment from its minimal, ungenerous, exiguous resources."[14] The pastoral landscape, as Ken Hiltner has argued, often goes undescribed in Renaissance literature, but Belarius offers a charged overview of the space.[15] He instructs the kidnapped princes by means of pedantic prospect in order to reinforce allegorically a narrative paradigm structured on inevitability: he sends the brothers up a hill, urging that they "[c]onsider, / When you above perceive me like a crow, / That it is place which lessens and sets off, / And you may then revolve what tales I have told you / Of courts, of princes; of the tricks in war" (3.3.11–15). On Belarius's account, Welsh topography furnishes an allegorical representation of the hierarchy and fragility of the court politics he often recounts—the landscape that "sets off" high and low underscores "tales" of power relations and uncertain fortune at court, and, by extension, reflects the doomed teleology that Belarius associates with that life.

Through Belarius, Shakespeare introduces the "long classical tradition, largely stoical, . . . of a harsh but reliably supportive external nature which trained man in endurance and in self-knowledge."[16] In allegorizing Wales in this way, Belarius uses the landscape to reinforce gloomy, deterministic lessons that he culls from his own painful history:

> two villains, whose false oaths prevail'd
> Before my perfect honour, swore to Cymbeline
> I was confederate with the Romans: so
> Follow'd my banishment (3.3.66–68)

The unjust sentence provoked his outlook; on his account, courtly favor is a mountain "whose top to climb / Is certain falling" (3.3.47–48). Notably, his insistence on an unrelenting teleology springs from his suspicion of sequence; he casts his wrongful banishment in terms of causal perversion: "Having receiv'd the punishment before / For that which I did then. Beaten for loyalty / Excited me to treason" (5.5.344–46). He commits the

---

14. Rosalie L. Colie, *Shakespeare's Living Art* (Princeton, NJ: Princeton University Press, 1974), 295.
15. Ken Hiltner, *What Else Is Pastoral?* (Ithaca, NY: Cornell University Press, 2011). See also Patricia Parker, "*Cymbeline*: Arithmetic, Double-Entry Bookkeeping, Counts, and Accounts," *Sederi* 23 (2013): 100 for a discussion of the future-oriented vocabulary of surveying land.
16. Colie, *Shakespeare's Living Art*, 302.

crime of kidnapping because he has already been punished, and spends his days in Wales warning his foster sons about the cruel, but inevitable, mismatch of cause and effect: "oft a sland'rous epitaph" serves as "record of fair act" (3.3.52–53). For Belarius, the corruption of life at court represents a particular future, one that drives toward an assured doom: "Nay, many times, / Doth ill deserve by doing well: what's worse, / Must court'sy at the censure" (3.3.53–55). Belarius's account of inversion—that good deeds might *deserve* ill—is compounded not just by the indignity of "must"—the injunction to curtsy—but also by its habituation: corruption at court stings through repetition, through its capacity to occur "many times." Not only did this inverted temporality spur his revenge-driven plot to steal Cymbeline's heirs, but it also shaped his own approach to the future. In emphasizing the unavoidable perils of court, he also consciously limits the possible future paths available to his foster sons. His account of the future is directed by the events of his own past, constantly threatened by the peril of a haunting past repeated, and it is this view that informs his critique of court in favor of the stasis of Wales. The future is robbed of its variety because one can depend upon courtly injustice. As a result, he is a figurative memento mori, a near double for the conventional death's head, and despite the pastoral tradition's ability to accommodate the "image of the snake hidden in the grass" and accept "death as a law of nature,"[17] his present moment is forever compromised.

Despite Belarius's rhetoric, however, Shakespeare is not content merely to make "spatial trespass figure aesthetic trespass" or for the genre to "allegorize [its] own narrative."[18] Rather, he uses pastoral convention to exaggerate the reach of Belarius's temporal approach, and to set the stage for its dismantling. Belarius stands out for reading Wales in terms of haunting memories that cause him to fixate on deterministic outcomes; Shakespeare simultaneously invokes literary tradition to establish Wales as a softer pastoral space, rather than merely an allegorical mirror of brute nature. The playwright's employment of a wellspring of literary conventions highlights pastoral's various temporal meditations. For example, Shakespeare insists upon the seasons in Wales, detailing "freezing hours" when "rain and wind beat dark December" (3.3.37–39), the "heat o' th' sun" and "furious

---

17. Renato Poggioli, *The Oaten Flute: Essays on Pastoral Poetry and the Pastoral Ideal* (Cambridge, MA: Harvard University Press, 1975), 20.
18. Heather Dubrow, "'I Would I Were at Home': Representations of Dwelling Places and Havens in *Cymbeline*," in *Shakespeare and Historical Formalism*, ed. Stephen Cohen (Aldershot, UK: Ashgate, 2007), 70–71.

winter's rages" (4.2.258–59), as well as the "pinching cave" (3.3.38) in which Belarius and his foster sons live. In so doing, this third world echoes Ovid's silver age:

> And aunceint Spring did Jove abridge, and made therof anon,
> Foure seasons: Winter, Sommer, Spring, and Autumne off and on:
> Then first of all began the ayre with fervent heate to swelt.
> Then Isycles hung roping downe: then for the colde was felt
> Men gan to shroud themselves in house. Their houses were the thickes,
> And bushie queaches, hollow caves, or hardels made of stickes.[19]

A few scenes later, the ages seem once again at the fore as Imogen (disguised as Fidele, a male page) enters the pastoral landscape. Uninvited, she is discovered in the cave, and when she offers to pay for the food she has taken, she sparks a heated reaction:

> GUI.   Money, youth?
> ARV.   All gold and silver rather turn to dirt,
>   As 'tis no better reckon'd, but of those
>   Who worship dirty gods. (3.7.25–28)

Fidele's offering is flatly rejected, and the brothers' answers serve to set their existence apart from that of the Ludstown emissary. Money has no place in the pastoral: it is a telltale sign of the iron age. The boys' responses unsettle even the earlier echo of the silver age; the upshot of their reply is, as J. M. Nosworthy has noted, utopic.[20] Such motley allusions to the schema of the ages resound in their dissonance. Rather than inviting his audience to map Wales neatly onto one age or another, or to settle into a singular vision of pastoral, Shakespeare creates a "green world" that collapses the ages. Belarius's future stealing born of inverted temporality is merely one ingredient in the wilderness of Wales, in which pastoral space proves less contentious than pastoral time.

Wales becomes a brief hotbed of activity when Cloten arrives from court in search of Imogen. Quick to insult and threaten his Welsh interlocutors,

---

19. Ovid, *Ovid's Metamorphoses: The Arthur Golding Translation 1567*, ed. John Frederick Nims (Philadelphia: Paul Dry Books, 2000) 1.133–38.

20. Nosworthy cites More's *Utopia*: "In the meane time golde and sylver, whereof money is made, they do so use, as none of them doeth more esteme it, then the very nature of the thing deserveth" (111n25–28). See also Colie, who reads the boys as "nature's noblemen," charting tensions between Belarius's "stoic moral instruction" and the brothers' "mysterious elevations beyond their present condition" that register their birthright (*Shakespeare's Living Art*, 296).

he loses a fight with Guiderius and is beheaded by him; the disguised Fidele, meanwhile, feels not quite herself and takes a powerful sedative that she mistakenly believes is a cure-all potion. When Arviragus, Guiderius, and Belarius find Fidele in a deep sleep, they think that their new friend has died. Shakespeare pairs Cloten's gruesome beheading with Fidele's apparent death to turn the action toward funeral elegy, invoking a pastoral tradition characterized as working "not merely to convey the individual grief of the survivor, but also man's recurrent sense of the everlasting presence of death."[21] Shakespeare alludes to Virgil's ninth eclogue, modeled on Theocritus, in which the "shepherds and the poet himself question the extent to which [speech and song are] possible."[22] Political calamity, as Anita Gilman Sherman has noted, robs the shepherd Moeris "not only of memory but of voice."[23] Death's everlasting presence is intensified by Guiderius and Arviragus's frame of reference for funeral rites—they repeatedly invoke the death of their foster mother, heightening the scene's atmosphere of ritual memory.

Specifically, they intend to "sing [Fidele] to th' ground, / As once to our mother" (4.2.236–37).[24] Shakespeare devotes several lines to a discussion of technical difficulties that result in an absence of singing. Even though their "voices / Have got the mannish crack," Arviragus entreats his brother to "sing [Fidele] to th' ground" (235–36), but Guiderius declines: "I cannot sing: I'll weep, and word it with thee; / For notes of sorrow out of tune are worse / Than priests and fanes that lie" (240–42). Shakespeare initially denies the elegiac act, and the discussion ends with the omission of song—Arviragus acquiesces that they will "speak it then" (242). The inflated cost attributed to bad singing draws attention to the expectation for song only to amend it.[25] If in Virgil, "tyranny produces a crisis of memory,"[26] in *Cymbeline*, that crisis comes to the fore in the content of the boys' song; Belarius slinks his jaded perspective into their funeral elegy. "Fear no more," their song begins,

---

21. Poggioli, *The Oaten Flute*, 20.
22. Paul Alpers, *What Is Pastoral?* (Chicago: University of Chicago Press, 1996), 6.
23. Anita Gilman Sherman, *Skepticism and Memory in Shakespeare and Donne* (New York: Palgrave Macmillan, 2007), 69.
24. Yet, their plan to "use like note and words / Save that Euriphile must be Fidele," (237–38) is complicated—what sounds at first like a matter of simple substitution proves more curious, since neither name appears in the song itself. See Nosworthy, 131n238.
25. Cf. *Lucrece*: "These means, as frets upon an instrument, / Shall tune our heart-strings to true languishment" (lines 1140–41). That is, "tuning sorrows" is usually linked to a capacity for compassion.
26. Sherman, *Skepticism and Memory*, 69.

repeating the encouragement as it introduces and enumerates the harsh realities of the mortal world:

SONG
GUI. Fear no more the heat o' th' sun,
 Nor the furious winter's rages,
 Thou thy worldly task has done,
 Home art gone and ta'en thy wages.
 Golden lads and girls all must,
 As chimney-sweepers, come to dust.
ARV. Fear no more the frown o' th' great,
 Thou art past the tyrant's stroke,
 Care no more to clothe and eat,
 To thee the reed is as the oak:
 The sceptre, learning, physic, must
 All follow this and come to dust.
GUI. Fear no more the lightning-flash.
ARV. Nor th' all-dreaded thunder-stone.
GUI. Fear not slander, censure rash.
ARV. Thou hast finish'd joy and moan.
BOTH. All lovers young, all lovers must
 Consign to thee and come to dust.
GUI. No exorciser harm thee!
ARV. Nor no witchcraft charm thee!
GUI. Ghost unlaid forbear thee!
ARV. Nothing ill come near thee!
BOTH. Quiet consummation have,
 And renowned be thy grave! (4.2.258–81)

Guiderius and Arviragus might well have thought to fear the sterner elements of nature—"heat o' th' sun," "winter's rages," "lightning-flash"—those features of hard pastoral living from which death might offer a reprieve. But mingled in the song's inventory is a more curious set of fears: death, it turns out, also provides release and relief from "the frown o' th' great," "the tyrant's stroke," "slander," and "censure rash." This list of earthly burdens suggests that Belarius penned the dirge, or at least that his incessant warnings precipitate a compelled ventriloquism. Belarius's heavy-handed, signature complaints about tyranny haunt the boys' pastoral, too often reiterated to be forgotten. Even the song's refrain insists upon mortality's inevitability in a manner that pushes beyond the pastoral tradition's capacity to accept "death as a law of nature."²⁷ The couplet refrain echoes the enforced habituation upon which Belarius established his determinism by linking "must" to "dust." The couplet heightens rhyme's usual capacity for prediction—a resource founded on a scarcity of options—by translating form's habit into content's necessity: "must" denies an alternative.²⁸ The play's most conventional pastoral gesture offers a song meant to honor the deceased with the comforts of the world beyond that operates outside of time. Despite those elements that suggest Belarius's influence, the dirge's account of death as "[q]uiet consummation" distinguishes between the afterlife and the future; the former affords a reprieve from earthly burdens in a manner that evokes "consummation" as it was sometimes used in biblical contexts—an indication of final judgment and the end of the world.²⁹ Death, unlike a lived future based on Belarius's obsessive worldly inevitability, offers a release from "fear." At the same time, "[q]uiet consummation" also introduces a more placid perspective on the future by suggesting completion and perfection in a manner that signals an outcome, an end point according to an earthly time scale.³⁰ Even as the song's string of negative incantations promises to leave the deceased in peace, the scenes in Wales invite us to investigate what kinds of futures remain in a context that foregrounds, on the one hand, Belarius's sequestering protections against injustice, and, on the other hand, elegy as a way to look beyond time. The song, of course, ends by implying an active future role for the mourners: "And renowned be thy grave!"

If Belarius's gloss of Welsh topography registers a relentless, inevitable vision, his version of prospect also entails an inability to speculate. His commitment to particular outcomes and a doomed teleology resurfaces over Fidele's (presumed) dead body: "Thou blessed thing, / Jove knows what man thou mightst have made: but I, / Thou diedst a most rare boy, of melancholy" (4.2.206–8). In short space, Belarius's grammar refuses guesswork. Mourning Fidele's premature death, he reserves any assurances about the lost future—the kind of person Fidele might have become—for the realm of the divine. In Belarius's hands, the word "might" reinforces the

---

27. Poggioli, *The Oaten Flute*, 20.

28. Various poetic treatises in the period offer instructions for constructing makeshift rhyming dictionaries, and stress that listing "all the words of the selfsame sound by order of the alphabet" produces a limited set of words. See, for example, George Gascoigne, "Certain Notes of Instruction (1575)," in *Sidney's "The Defence of Poesy" and Selected Renaissance Literary Criticism*, ed. Gavin Alexander (London: Penguin, 2004), 242. See chapter 5 for a discussion of rhyme as a predictive structure often discussed in the early modern period in terms of its certainty.

29. *OED*, s.v. "consummation, *n*." def. 3a.

30. "A fitting, crowning or inevitable outcome" (*OED*, def. 4), a "conclusion, end, or death" (def. 3b), "an act of completing, accomplishing, or finishing" (def. 2a), an "act of perfecting" (def. 1a).

uncertainty of an alternative future that will never come to pass. The conditional phrasing draws attention to what Renaissance grammar books called the potential mood, a classification that was "present in neither Roman nor medieval grammars" and was added in the sixteenth century to "the classical five [moods] of indicative, imperative, optative, subjunctive, and infinitive."[31] As Margreta de Grazia notes, "Before [Thomas Linacre's sixteenth-century Latin grammar], the potential mood would not have been distinguished from the optative, the wishing mood that covered wishes put to God and wishes dependent on the speaker's resources. Sixteenth-century grammarians, however, separated possibility resting in God's hands from possibility residing in individual power."[32] Belarius, however, maintains a strict distinction between his firmly indicative knowledge and God's access to counterfactual potential. But before we can attribute to Shakespeare a theological view or to Belarius an extreme deference to the mysteries of providence, Belarius's part in the assertion highlights the dangers of his credulity about his own sphere of knowledge: "but I, / Thou diedst a most rare boy."[33] Fidele, as the audience knows, is both female and still alive: the irony of Belarius's statement redoubles his aversion to speculation—we know his certainty is wrong. When he notes, "I stole these babes, / Thinking to bar [Cymbeline] of succession" (3.3.101–2), he reveals that he stole Cymbeline's future because the king had stolen his, and the ensuing ripples expose that exile is not merely about being shorn of geographical, social, and economic possessions, but also about an overdetermined relationship to certainty.

As with the ventriloquism evident in the funeral song, Belarius's outlook infects a broader set of counterfactual statements uttered in Wales. In his 1586 *Bref Grammar for English*, William Bullokar labeled such formulations the "Dout-ful-preter,"[34] but in *Cymbeline* they do not tend to communicate much doubt. Instead, the conditional utterances consistently voice a sense of inevitability and threat in the perceived alternative: they suggest dead ends. Fidele,

---

31. Margreta de Grazia, "Lost Potential in Grammar and Nature: Sidney's *Astrophil and Stella*," *SEL* 21, no. 1 (1981): 22.

32. Ibid. See also Brian Cummings for a discussion of Linacre's influence on Lily, and also for the ways in which English auxiliaries proved such difficult cases for grammarians that they became places where grammarians had to take or develop positions simply because of the structural differences between Latin and English (*The Literary Culture of the Reformation: Grammar and Grace* [Oxford: Oxford University Press, 2002], 208–9).

33. How seriously should we take the assertion that God has access to a future that will never come to pass? "Jove knows what man thou mightst have made" sounds like a matter for theological debate, and indeed in the years leading up to *Cymbeline*'s first production, claims made by a Spanish Jesuit Luis de Molina—that God had *scientia media*, or "middle knowledge" of counterfactual outcomes—were under review by the pope.

34. William Bullokar, *A Bref Grammar for English* (1586), D1r.

for example, offers such a defense for stealing food from the Welsh cave: "Know, if you kill me for my fault, I should / Have died had I not made it" (3.7.29–30). This conditional construction—"should have died"—explains the motivation for action even in the face of the equivalent future outcome: death. The consequences assumed by these statements reveal that action is spurred by thinking that the imagined alternative is deadly. Repeatedly, these formulations—joining *should*, *would*, or *could have* with the past participle— express not only an event that is contrary to fact, but also the fatalism of having nothing to lose.[35] As Guiderius says after killing Cymbeline's troublesome stepson, Cloten,

> not Hercules
> Could have knock'd out his brains, for he had none:
> Yet I not doing this, the fool had borne
> My head, as I do his. (4.2.114–17)

What begins as a counterfactual at Cloten's expense—no amount of force could produce nonexistent brains—becomes one about the peril of inversion. By claiming such a starkly parallel alternative outcome, Guiderius calls upon a singular future to justify action in the present. I pointed to Bullokar's terminology—the "Dout-ful-preter"—to suggest that in *Cymbeline* these counterfactual statements are notably free of doubt.[36] Yet, turning to a grammatical account that removes doubt overcorrects in a manner resisted by these Welsh utterances: "*Might, Would,* or *Should,* have no relation in the least to the Time past, but rather to the Time to come; unless they be followed with *Have,* the Sign of a Preter Tense."[37] The play's conditional statements capitalize on the variety reflected in these competing grammatical explanations—they are characterized by certainty, but that certainty about an imagined alternative does not reside precisely in the past, as the "sign of a preter tense" would indicate. Rather, Shakespeare's conditional formulations are interesting for a fatalism that renders distinct time frames irrelevant—a character pursues an alternative to avoid a threat only to arrive at the very threat that led him to pursue that alternative. When Belarius expresses distress over the slaying of Cloten, Guiderius notes bluntly: "Why, worthy father, what have we to lose, / But that he swore to take, our lives?" (4.2.124–25). In the counterfactual,

---

35. "The auxiliaries *should haue* plus past participle refer to an event which has not taken place" (N. F. Blake, *A Grammar of Shakespeare's Language* [New York: Palgrave, 2002], 128).

36. See Cummings for a discussion of Bullokar on ambiguity. Cummings notes that Bullokar's "'doubtful' tenses" come about because the grammar "is confused" (*The Literary Culture,* 212).

37. Guy Miège, *The English Grammar; or, the Grounds, and Genius, of the English Tongue* (London, 1688), F4r–v.

what ought to provide a temporal and imaginative agility underscores instead the end of options. These instances of verbal construction—"should have" or "would have" joined to the past participle—mark out territory that is, at least rhetorically, doubly compromised. Repeatedly, these conditional statements traffic between an imminent threat and a retrospective account of the relationship between risk and certainty.

In offering counterfactuals that resonate with Belarius's approach to time, does Shakespeare suggest that the future can be laid open because it is not open-ended? The possible outcomes represented in these counterfactuals assume a circumscribed future. In saying, "[W]hat have we to lose, / But that he swore to take, our lives?" the play embeds fatalism into its rhetoric by making the alternative outcome indistinguishable from choices made in the absence of alternatives. In isolating this approach to time and the future through narrative and grammatical constructions, we gain purchase on the competing approach on offer in Wales—that is, the conceptually powerful terrain marked out by the "future perfect" or "second future," what I call anticipatory nostalgia.

II

Stealing futures is not the only game in town. Wales also offers access to a philosophical orientation bracketed off from the meditations on futurity that Belarius introduces into the play, because the scenes in Wales attend particularly to temporality.[38] I will turn back shortly to the two kidnapped princes to consider their unexpected suggestion that they are bored, a consequence of their uncomfortably circumscribed options. I will suggest that Guiderius and Arviragus express a desire to circumvent an all-too-certain future, and, in so doing, reproduce considerations of the future that puzzled grammarians. We can understand the play's most peculiar engagement with time—and its relationship to narrative—by first looking even more closely at the future tense as treated in the grammar books of the period. A subject at both the university and school levels, grammar was the first part of the trivium, "the universal educational practice of the Christian West," a primacy echoed in

---

38. Gérard Genette makes a compelling case for the centrality of time, rather than space, in narrative production: "By a dissymmetry whose underlying reasons escape us but which is inscribed in the very structures of language (or at the very least of the main 'languages of civilization' of Western culture), I can very well tell a story without specifying the place where it happens, and whether this place is more or less distant from the place where I am telling it; nevertheless, it is almost impossible for me not to locate the story in time with respect to my narrating act, since I must necessarily tell the story in a present, past, or future tense. This is perhaps why the temporal determinations of the narrating instance are manifestly more important than its spatial determinations." Genette, *Narrative Discourse: An Essay in Method*, trans. Jane E. Lewin (Ithaca, NY: Cornell University Press, 1980), 215.

the very term "grammar school."³⁹ Grammar was foundational, encompassing a logical system as well as the "interpretation of linguistic meaning or of literary theory and the study of authoritative Latin texts."⁴⁰ Brian Cummings makes the case that grammar became "newly controversial" in the sixteenth century, and points particularly to the "relation between grammar and logic, or between linguistic and literary theory on the one hand and theology and biblical interpretation on the other," as the centers of these tensions.⁴¹ Though Latin grammars existed in England in the Middle Ages, the first English grammar was not published until the sixteenth century.⁴² In these texts, the future tense appears in sections on verbs, and is routinely divided into two categories: as Michael Maittaire puts it in an English grammar published about a century after *Cymbeline*, "The Present is but one Point of time, and therefore indivisible.... The Futur is twofold."⁴³

English grammar books of the early modern period are a messy affair. To begin with, they draw from two distinct traditions, though many English grammarians mix the two strands. The first comes down through the highly influential Latin grammars in use in England: William Lily's *A Shorte Introduction of Grammar* (1567) and Thomas Linacre's *Rudimenta Grammatices* (1556), both of which follow a Priscian model.⁴⁴ Lily's grammar, developed with John Colet around 1510, became the "only authorized grammar" "by official decree of Henry VIII" in 1540.⁴⁵ The second tradition, from Petrus Ramus, was based on a Varronian model.⁴⁶ Latin grammars were standard fare in the Renaissance schoolroom, whereas "English grammar does not appear on the curricula of English schools before 1650."⁴⁷ Latin grammars were often written in English, English grammars in Latin, but the most pronounced obstacle to clarity was that the vernacular grammars often mapped English onto classical forms, despite some glaring structural mismatches. As a result, there is quite a bit of variety in these grammatical texts. Notably, these grammarians have difficulty explaining, understanding, and describing

---

39. Cummings, *Literary Culture*, 20.
40. Ibid., 22.
41. Ibid., 23. See Cummings also for an in-depth treatment of theology, and its implications for translation.
42. Emma Vorlat, *The Development of English Grammatical Theory 1586–1737* (Leuven: Leuven University Press, 1975), 2.
43. Michael Maittaire, *The English Grammar: or, an Essay on the Art of Grammar, Applied to and Exemplified in the English Tongue* (London, 1712), E8r–v.
44. From the Stoics and Dionysius Thrax to Donatus and Priscian (Vorlat, *The Development of English Grammatical Theory*, 6–8, 302).
45. Vorlat, *The Development of English Grammatical Theory*, 7.
46. Ibid., 302.
47. Ibid., 3.

time through tenses. The descriptions of the future—especially in terms of mood and aspect—put on display the difficulties of dealing with differences between Latin and English, and the clunkiness of those distinctions abates only over the course of a century and a half of English grammar books.

Most early modern grammarians split the future into two categories, though the terms of that breakdown are dizzying rather than standardized. What I want to highlight is that the distinction between a first and second future allows us to draw out notions of both certainty and future possibility. To simplify the matter, today we call one the "future" ("Posthumus will repent"), and the other the "future perfect" or, following French, the "future anterior" ("Posthumus will have repented"). As I have noted, the "future perfect," a grammatical category of future tense and perfect aspect, was often referred to in early modern grammar books as the "second future." As a grammatical construction, this "will have done" is now and was then a rare construction. Unlike the correspondence between counterfactuals and a fatalistic rhetoric that denies imagined alternatives, Shakespeare seldom employs the future perfect.[48] As a category to think with, however, it provides exclusive access to an enabling condition for speculating about the future.

The "second future," sometimes called the "future perfect" or "future praeteritum," is always described relative to the first. Depending on the grammarian, the two tenses are, respectively, "absolute" and "conditional" (Miège, 1688), "determinate" and "indefinite" (Jones, 1724), and "imperfect" and "perfect" (Jonson, 1640; Maittaire, 1712); and grammarians are not always in agreement about which one is primary and which one secondary. The English grammars' descriptions of what we would call the "future perfect" get more clearly articulated by the early eighteenth century: the "Future Perfect imports a Thing's being past or finish'd at some future Time."[49] With few exceptions, grammarians consistently explain that the second future records the "past hereafter" (Jones, 1724)—a more anterior imagined "hereafter" or "future" time that will be seen as completed from some even more future vantage point, as opposed to the future that is "imperfect" because it lays no claims to completed action. Maittaire explains:

> The Futur is twofold; the first may be truly call'd Imperfect, when the thing meant by it is merely Future, still to come and to be done : the

---

48. For example, consider these utterances in Shakespeare: Paulina, in *The Winter's Tale*, says: "Besides, the gods / Will have fulfill'd their secret purposes" (5.1.35–36); and Coriolanus: "But we will drink together; and you shall bear / A better witness back than words, which we, / On like conditions, will have counterseal'd" (5.3.203–5).

49. William Turner, *A Short Grammar for the English Tongue* (London, 1710), A7v.

second Perfect, partly Future, partly Perfect, when one thing, though it is yet To come, is however supposed to be Passed, with comparison to another thing, which is To come after it. The First belongs to the Indicative mood, the Second to the Potential.[50]

The future perfect registers as fact a past that has not happened yet as seen from the perspective of the future—it is, then, the past tense of another time frame. Bullokar calls it the "Dout-ful Futur" to indicate that it records what is possible though not yet true.[51] I will focus on the "second future," but part of my point in referring to the grammatical treatises is to highlight how much variety and confusion surrounded the descriptions of the future tense. John Wilkins (1668), for example, distinguishes between "absolute" and "conditional" possibility, between "absolute" and "conditional" liberty.[52] Guy Miège (1688) stands out in defining the second future as using not the past participle, but rather "might, should, would or could":

> This tense I call a *Future*, contrary to the Genius of other Grammarians, who place it in the Subjunctive Mood, and call it a Preter Tense. An Errour that proceeds from a fond Way of modelling right or wrong our Vulgar Speeches to the Latine Tongue. . . . *Might, Would,* or *Should,* have no relation in the least to the Time past, but rather to the Time to come; unless they be followed with *Have,* the Sign of a Preter Tense.[53]

The diversity of these accounts also suggests the seriousness and attempted precision that went into categorizing the future in early modern England.

The second future traffics between prospect and retrospect, and reveals an important intricacy to future certainty.[54] For example, Angus Fletcher has claimed that

> Calvinists were living in the future anterior tense, acting now (in their present) so that they *will have been saved* (in their future). They

---

50. Maittaire, *English Grammar*, E8v.
51. Bullokar, *Bref Grammar*, D1r.
52. John Wilkins, *An Essay Towards a Real Character and a Philosophical Language* (London, 1668), SS2v.
53. Miège, *English Grammar*, F4r–v.
54. The concept of the future perfect, or *futur antérieur*, has attracted special attention in psychoanalysis where "the future perfect is the tense of *undoing*, not only the pathological negation of the past Freud isolated as an obsessional symptom (*Ungeschehenmachen*) but also its homeopathic antidote, the undoing that occurs during the process of analysis. . . . Here the reference is to the past rather than to the future, but the resemblance in structure suggests that the desire of undoing may be inextricably intertwined with the more positive impulses to autothanatography. The future perfect is at any rate its operative tense, because it governs the mediated transactions between correspondents separated from each other by space and time (Harry Berger Jr., *Imaginary Audition: Shakespeare on Stage and Page* [Berkeley: University of California Press, 1989], 121).

were compressing the future into the present moment of choice, and as we shall see with alchemical formulations, they in fact were attempting to accelerate time in order to look back upon its future effects. Faustus is a Calvinist gambler betting against the absolute *latering* of time.⁵⁵

Fletcher understands behavior in the present moment as a way for Calvinists to check for (or even manufacture) evidence of a determined outcome (salvation). However, I want to distinguish between what Fletcher ascribes to theology and grammarians' notions of the "future anterior tense." Fletcher rightly notes that Calvinists operate as though they could make manifest in the present moment signs that could (theoretically) later be retrospectively read as indicators of future salvation. The formulation "will have been saved" does attempt to capture with grammar an outcome that is already set, but because the point of reference in Fletcher's example is the present, the "future anterior tense" does not properly apply: their outlook does not represent the back formulation of an even farther ahead future. Crucially, Calvinists are saved (or not) in the present, they just don't know it. But their attempt to access that already-determined-though-not-yet-disclosed information doesn't really represent an acceleration of time or a strategy for looking back on the "future effects" on the present. Such an explanation unduly privileges the future perfect, a category that proves superfluous in its overlap with the present tense. The decision about salvation has already happened, of course, but its revelation is deferred to a future time. As a result, a future tense articulation—"will be saved"—would problematically forestall enactment. Nonetheless, the fantasy about the present merely serves to reinforce one future that is already fixed. Contra Fletcher, the second future proves more complex than merely imagining access to certainty about the future from the vantage of the present moment. I hasten to add, however, that language provides few resources for making iron-clad distinctions between the present and the second future. Saint Augustine's meditations on time help to articulate the basis of the difficulty:

> If we can think of some bit of time which cannot be divided into even the smallest instantaneous moments, that alone is what we can call 'present.' And this time flies so quickly from future into past that it is

---

55. Angus Fletcher, *Time, Space, and Motion in the Age of Shakespeare* (Cambridge, MA: Harvard University Press, 2007), 57. Contra Fletcher's account, Koselleck identifies "the increasing speed with which [the future] approaches us" and "accelerated time" as key components of the progress that precipitates modernity (*Futures Past*, 22).

an interval with no duration. If it has duration, it is divisible into past and future. But the present occupies no space.[56]

His description goes a long way toward explaining why the line between the present and the second future requires so much tending if we hope to keep it from blurring.

The full significance of the second future comes to the fore in Shakespeare's Wales. Before Fidele arrives, before Cloten dies, we find those two kidnapped princes, Guiderius and Arviragus, grumbling that they are bored. Dissatisfied with the Welsh pastoral space they call home, they chafe at Belarius's pronouncement that court life is "no life to ours" (3.3.26). "[T]his life," Guiderius counters, is both a "cell" and a "prison" (3.3.29–34). Worse still, the boredom of the present promises a dull future:

> What should we speak of
> When we are old as you? When we shall hear
> The rain and wind beat dark December? How
> In this our pinching cave shall we discourse
> The freezing hours away? (3.3.35–39)

Arviragus's questions pose rather convoluted counterfactuals that express his desire to avoid the all-too-inevitable answers, "Nothing" and "We won't be able to." He betrays a subtle temporal anxiety, realizing what kind of past the present will become, and his proleptic perspective simultaneously calls the straightforward nature of linear time into question.

Arviragus's vision of the future depends upon two clearly defined features: first, that "freezing hours" of "dark December" lie ahead; second, that, huddled in a "pinching cave," those hours will be filled with "speak[ing]" and "discourse." His account of the threat posed by present boredom in Wales draws attention to forward-looking linguistic and narrative structures; they reveal that negotiating time is a matter of choosing a literary strategy. As the brothers worry about the boredom that looms ahead, they usher an anticipatory nostalgia into the play—they aspire to a future from which they will look back on their present moment and find it worth remembering. Arviragus's questions—"What should we speak of?" and "How shall we discourse?"—place narrative at the heart of his concern: because old age is the time to tell stories about the past, the future is imagined in terms of future memory. Because the present they are now

---

56. Saint Augustine, *Confessions*, trans. Henry Chadwick (Oxford: Oxford University Press, 1991) 11.20 (232).

experiencing is inadequate, their vision of the ideal future depends upon having a second future distinct from their current condition. The mention of "discours[ing] / The freezing hours away" introduces a novel winter of discontent; "dark December" is no longer a seasonal fact of life, but a grim vision of an old age devoid of nostalgic pleasure. To imagine the future, then, is to privilege the second future by imagining the capacity for present time to become the past, and to register an awareness about the remote potential of reminiscing. Consequently, the brothers' criterion for judging the merit of action in the present (or, more precisely, the immediate future—that space most valuable for its status as second future) lies in the potential for that action to become the content of a pleasurable, exciting story. As the boys offer a present concerned with the options for its impending narrative rehearsal, they foreground an overriding question: how can the present moment negotiate its relationship to both the future and the past? Once the present becomes conceptually transformed into a "future hereafter" and nostalgic retelling becomes the characteristic feature of the even more distant future, the "second future" obtains because it is imagined as the enabling precondition for nostalgia. The boys *will have done* something that will be the substance of stories in that even later future. Guiderius and Arviragus seem content to look forward to a modest future, one filled solely with looking back—so long as the stories of their youth are worth telling. Though they worry that their lives lack material worth recounting later, they initially long neither for a particular future narrative nor for a particular present experience—neither ambition nor martial heroism nor duty drives their complaint. Rather, they anticipate narrative for the sake of narrative, and imagine a future without content. In insisting that the present is less important than the story they plan to tell about it, the brothers privilege an approach to past, present, and future that exposes the difficulty of keeping those categories intact.

Unlike the other gestures to the future in the play, anticipatory nostalgia provides a vision of the future that is uniquely open-ended and nonapocalyptic. In psychoanalysis, Jacques Lacan locates in the "mirror stage" the formation of what in the future will be an antecedent: "[T]he self is constituted through anticipating what it will become, and then this anticipatory model is used for gauging what was before."[57] For Lacan, a person's history is always constructed; the future perfect reflects one's ability to absorb moments of one's past into one's future narrative self-understanding. The future perfect marks

---

57. Jane Gallop, *Reading Lacan* (Ithaca, NY: Cornell University Press, 1985), 81; Jacques Lacan, *Écrits*, trans. Bruce Fink (New York: W.W. Norton, 2006), 247.

the formation of what will have been a "rootstock," or originary moment—a retroactively constructed narrative of identity formation. As Linda Charnes notes, "For the individual subject, the truth of the past always arrives from the future, that history is always constructed retroactively."[58] Lacan writes:

> What is realized in my history is neither the past definite as what was, since it is no more, nor even the perfect as what has been in what I am, but the future anterior as what I will have been, given what I am in the process of becoming.[59]

This account of identity formation resonates with Guiderius's later self-evaluative life-philosophical statement: "Than be so, / Better to cease to be" (4.4.30–31), but Lacan's rubric intrigues me more for its narrative implications than for its claims about subjecthood. Peter Brooks, in a study of the novel sympathetic to psychoanalysis, uses such a perspective to expound how we might understand ourselves as readers:

> If the past is to be read as present, it is a curious present that we know to be past in relation to a future we know to be already in place, already in wait for us to reach it. Perhaps we would do best to speak of the *anticipation of retrospection* as our chief tool in making sense of narrative, the master trope of its strange logic.[60]

Brooks's proposition attends to the effect fiction's unruly temporality has on its readers in a manner that helpfully models the precision required to think through the mental gymnastics involved. Both Lacan and Brooks foreground temporality as a means of managing our revisionary impulses (as subjects, as readers). In this regard, these two approaches expect what we see in Fletcher's problematic account of the "future anterior": the degree to which the present is collapsed with the second future. What is more, in approaching the future on terms that might best be described as providential, such models disavow uncertainty. The kind of inevitability that results—however active and self-consciously fictional its construction—accords readily with Belarius's fatalism, and with the play's flurry of dead-end counterfactuals. All three options, however, fall short of accounting for those statements about boredom and flattened opportunity in Wales. Narrative, the power to tell stories,

---

58. Linda Charnes, "Anticipating Nostalgia: Finding Temporal Logic in a Textual Anomaly," *Textual Cultures* 4, no. 1 (2009): 76.

59. Lacan, *Écrits*, 247.

60. Peter Brooks, *Reading for the Plot: Design and Intention in Narrative* (Cambridge, MA: Harvard University Press, 1984), 23. He notes, of plotted fiction, that "what remains to be read will restructure the provisional meanings of the already read" (23).

sits at the center of Guiderius's and Arviragus's complaint, and anticipatory nostalgia introduces a way of engaging action sensitive to future uncertainty. For the brothers, lived experience is a moving target, most important in the present for its narrative afterlife, and most important in the future for its ability to furnish nostalgia's content. The second future, because it boasts a status simultaneously speculative and completed, recasts the question of certainty on new grounds, furnishing speculation with an additional level of remove.

As a result, the curious aspect of Guiderius's and Arviragus's complaint is that they want to act with an eye to the future, yet they are more interested in anticipating the present moment from that imagined future than they are in the experience that second future will contain. Their anticipatory nostalgia registers a future project to be sure, but it also profoundly affects the present by essentially approaching it as a "past hereafter," as a second future: their plans for the present are at once highlighted and short-circuited in such a future-oriented narrative model. If in this play, as Bradin Cormack has provocatively suggested, "the present only is the place of action and being," it is curious that the boys produce even the fantasy of that present without furnishing any particulars.[61] They signal a preference for the adventure of the unknown—something outside of the circumscription of "home," but the substance of Guiderius and Arviragus's second future is empty except by negation—they don't initially specify the something memorable they "will have done"; rather, they simply insist that it is *not this*.

The interest in remodeling the present moment engenders speculation, not about how to fill that time—discussions of particular action come up only in later scenes—but rather about the stories they will be able to tell when they are "old as [Belarius]." Rather than a performance of the familiar *carpe diem* cry or even a testament to Francis Bacon's claim that "the care of posterity is most in them that have no posterity," the content of the amended present is passed over—regarded, that is, only as abstract action in the future perfect tense.[62] The second future negotiates a desire to control the uncontrollable, and offers a way of shaping uncertainty. While anticipatory nostalgia requires a second future

---

61. Bradin Cormack, *A Power to Do Justice: Jurisdiction, English Literature, and the Rise of Common Law, 1509–1625* (Chicago: University of Chicago Press, 2007), 236. Cormack offers a sustained consideration of time in the play that is admirably sensitive to Shakespeare's manner of teasing out temporal operations. Though my reading proceeds in sympathy with and endorsement of his attention to time, our different emphases produce notably different readings of the play. Because Cormack seeks to show that Shakespeare's approach to time and the notion of "temporal limit" reinforces the playwright's interest in political accommodation—the threshold that divides sovereign entities—the efficaciousness of the present moment supersedes a consideration of the way that the play reimagines or questions how art's intervention might extend beyond a representation of time.

62. Francis Bacon, "Of Parents and Children," in *The Major Works*, ed. Brian Vickers (Oxford: Oxford University Press, 1996), 352.

that is up to the task, the "past hereafter" is nonetheless mere middleman, the gateway to future memory. Shakespeare uses Guiderius's and Arviragus's gripping to discover this unique kind of future, one that gestures to the notion that the present should be worth remembering, but ultimately denies an interest in posterity even as it privileges narrative and the act of narration.

The second future displaces the potential for present pleasure. Anticipatory nostalgia disregards pleasure in the moment of experience, favoring the potential for retrospective enjoyment. Narrative boasts a privileged place, which helps to explain the formative role that even Belarius's sour memories take: "When on my three-foot stool I sit, and tell / The warlike feats I have done, [Guiderius's] spirits fly out / Into my story ... [he] puts himself in posture / That acts my words" (3.3.89–95). Belarius's tales do not deter his sons, do not have their desired admonitory effect; rather, his listeners are brought to life by narrative. Despite his best efforts, Guiderius and Arviragus see in Belarius what they will one day be—"when we are old as you"; his sons perceive his cautionary tales as their model for remembering. Belarius attributes his sons' mimetic reactions to their true identities:

> How hard it is to hide sparks of Nature!
> These boys know little they are sons to th' king,
> ... and though train'd up thus meanly,
> I' th' cave wherein they bow, their thoughts do hit
> The roofs of palaces, and Nature prompts them
> In simple and low things to prince it. (3.3.79–80, 82–85)

In other words, he assumes that it is the content of his stories about "warlike feats" that animates them, because valor is somehow innate. Belarius's confession proposes a crux between imagination, embodiment, and action—his account of narrative, which causes "spirits" to "fly" as his listener "acts [his] words," suggests that narrative invites embodiment. He continues that Arviragus "[s]trikes life into my speech, and shows much more / His own conceiving" (3.3.97–98). In this case, the imaginative effects of narrative go beyond mere reenactment, also inspiring innovation crafted from the listener's "own conceiving." It is the very assumption that narrative can inspire such personalized tailoring for its audience that makes Guiderius's and Arviragus's initial words so striking: in act 3, scene 3, action exists only in the abstract. Action gives way to the story it will yield in a future devoted to narrative reminiscence. Yet, it is hard to deny that acting out the story links imagination and embodiment in a manner that echoes the idea that narrative controls the future.

Belarius may succeed in allegorizing the Welsh landscape, but the obsessive, continual recounting of his past undermines the lesson. Had he stuck to allegory, he might have succeeded in circumscribing his foster sons' futures, but by pathologically rehearsing his own history, he unwittingly communicates the importance of having a story to tell. And this seems to be the crucial consideration: Belarius has no shortage of stories to offer during those freezing hours, so why do Arviragus and Guiderius worry over their narrative prospects? Arviragus's questions stress personal experience, the ability to speak, as his brother puts it, from "proof" (3.3.27). The brothers are not content simply to spend those dark Decembers spinning Belarius's old yarns. Rather, they insist that their stories must be their own, and that they must derive from experience. Yet, their emphasis on experience seems at odds with their disinterest in the present—they are, as I have been arguing, more focused on anticipating the present moment from the future than they are on the present itself. The future retrospection and anticipatory nostalgia that I have been outlining might sound akin to something like the logic of the Saint Crispin's Day speech from Shakespeare's *Henry V*, in which Henry motivates his troops by claiming that their present action will grant them a place in the nation's collective future memory: "And Crispin Crispian shall ne'er go by / From this day to the ending of the world / But we in it shall be remembered" (4.3.57–59).[63] The promises of that speech—"He that shall see this day and live old age / Will yearly on the vigil feast his neighbours. . . . Then will he strip his sleeve and show his scars, . . . he'll remember, with advantages, / What feats he did that day" (4.3.44–51)—contradict Mikhail Bakhtin's claim that "[i]t is impossible to achieve greatness in one's own time. Greatness always makes itself known only to descendents, for whom such a quality is always located in the past (it turns into a distanced image)."[64] Guiderius and Arviragus find motivation in being fed up with a habituated present moment in which nothing happens, but what sets them apart from a figure like Henry V is the modesty of their claim. Bakhtin distinguishes "[c]ontemporaneity for its own sake (that is to say, a contemporaneity that makes no claim on future memory)" from "contemporaneity for the future (for descendents)," and insists that for the latter the

> valorized emphasis is not on the future and does not serve the future, no favors are being done it (such favors face an eternity outside time);

---

63. William Shakespeare, *Henry V*, ed. T. W. Craik, 3rd ser. (London: The Arden Shakespeare, 1995).
64. M. M. Bakhtin, *The Dialogic Imagination: Four Essays*, trans. Caryl Emerson and Michael Holquist (Austin: University of Texas Press, 1981), 18.

what is served here is the future memory of a past, a broadening of the world of the absolute past, an enriching of it with new images (at the expense of contemporaneity)—a world that is always opposed in principle to any *merely transitory* past.[65]

Shakespeare, by contrast, negotiates a window onto a different approach to the future, and a different kind of future. Belarius is engraved with enduring reminders of the wrongs he has suffered: "O boys, this story / The world may read in me: my body's mark'd / With Roman swords" (3.3.55–57). But if he figures his scars in narrative terms—a "story" to be "read"—the boys have taken a very different lesson from the school text. They understand this kind of codex to provide the content of the future—and that content *is* narrative. Despite Belarius's comment about the "sparks of Nature," in imagining the future, the boys cite neither ambition nor glory nor collective duty; instead, the future provides a stage for the stories they will tell in their cave, to each other. Guiderius and Arviragus exhibit a commitment to neither national service nor national identity. Shakespeare's anticipatory nostalgia introduces a vision of future memory more interested in private recollection than patriotic duty. The privilege to tell future stories about what will have been outweighs ambition, audience, and is even evacuated of content. Paradoxically, in providing access to a conception of shaping outcomes by attending to the second future, Guiderius and Arviragus privilege a modest, past-oriented future, one occupied in the pleasure of telling their own story. They may stand in for a more modest futurity—the cozy cave for two where the teller's pleasure forms the center of the narrative enterprise—but in so doing, they upend an account of aesthetic pleasure that reaches back to the Horatian dictum, which privileges poetry's power to edify, by delighting, its *listener*. This unexpected overturning is reinforced by the static quality of a future like the one Brooks proposed as fiction's operating structure, a future "already in wait for us to reach it." The modesty of the boys' fantasy is communicated in that they never imagine that the content of the future perfect might secure for them a future outside of the cave.[66]

The brothers finally shift their focus to shaping their own present moment when the battle literally invades their pastoral home. Standing "*Before the Cave of Belarius*" (4.4.sd), it is only with "[t]he noise" of war "round about" them (4.4.1) that Arviragus suggests entering the fray: "What pleasure, sir, we

---

65. Ibid., 19.
66. The play, of course, furnishes precisely this shift in location. Moreover, since the play ends with the princes reinstalled at court, we might imagine that their unusual upbringing becomes the subject of nostalgic recollection.

find in life, to lock it / From action and adventure" (4.4.2–3). Though the context more than implies that Arviragus is eager to join the fight, the syntax here is counterintuitive, prompting later editors to make the lines interrogative: "What pleasure *find we* in life, to lock it / From action and adventure?" I don't want to insist that the unamended, declarative line—"What pleasure ... we find in life, to lock it / From action and adventure"—holds open the possibility of valorized inaction. But it is the case that barring the prompt of a battle on one's cavestep, action matters only notionally, not for its experience, but for the pleasure it will yield to its teller in a future devoted to narrative reminiscence.

A few scenes later, the play offers a reprise, a window onto the potential afterlife of this second future—what we might have expected the boys' anticipatory nostalgia to boast as its center. The fight that finally shifts Guiderius's and Arviragus's focus, however, finds voice through another narrator. Posthumus, embarked upon a desperate search for death, encounters a Briton lord, a deserter, and recounts for him how Belarius and his foster sons turned the tides of the battle against Rome:

>   Post.   These three,
>   Three thousand confident, in act as many,
>   For three performers are the file when all
>   The rest do nothing, with this word 'Stand, stand,'
>   Accommodated by the place, more charming,
>   With their own nobleness, which could have turn'd
>   A distaff to a lance, gilded pale looks;
>   Part shame, part spirit renew'd, that some, turn'd coward
>   But by example (O, a sin in war,
>   Damn'd in the first beginners) 'gan to look
>   The way that they did, and to grin like lions
>   Upon the pikes o' th' hunters. Then began
>   A stop i' th' chaser; a retire: anon
>   A rout, confusion thick: forthwith they fly
>   Chickens, the way which they stoop'd eagles: slaves,
>   The strides they victors made: and now our cowards
>   Like fragments in hard voyages became
>   The life o' the need: having found the back-door open
>   Of the unguarded hearts, heavens, how they wound!
>   Some slain before, some dying, some their friends
>   O'er-borne i' th' former wave, ten, chas'd by one,
>   Are now each one the slaughter-man of twenty:

174   CHAPTER FOUR

>   Those that would die, or ere resist, are grown
>   The mortal bugs o' th' field.
> LORD   This was strange chance:
>   A narrow lane, an old man, and two boys.
> POST.   Nay, do not wonder at it: you are made
>   Rather to wonder at the things you hear
>   Than to work any. Will you rhyme upon't,
>   And vent it for a mock'ry? Here is one:
>   Two boys, an old man twice a boy, a lane,
>   Preserv'd the Britons, was the Romans' bane. (5.3.28–58)

To Posthumus's ears, the lord's rejoinder threatens to debase his vivid account of the battle. Posthumus loses his temper, it seems, over poetic decorum; "Will you rhyme upon't, / And vent it for a mock'ry?" sounds like an aversion to doggerel.[67] If, however, a control over narration implies a sensibility about form, his question also communicates a pressing concern about the unsteady relationship between creating narrative content—to "work" things rather than merely "wonder at" them—and the privilege of recounting it.

Posthumus continues to muse on the Briton lord's words, and he links the properties of narration and survival:

> This is a lord! O noble misery,
> To be i' the field, and ask 'what news?' of me!
> To-day how many would have given their honours
> To have sav'd their carcasses? Took heel to do't,
> And yet died too! I, in mine own woe charm'd,
> Could not find death where I did hear him groan,
> Nor feel him where he struck (5.3.64–70)

Though Posthumus's focus is the elusiveness of death, his words also highlight the clash between action ("be[ing] i' th' field") and narrative potential (needing to "ask 'what news?'"). The matter of desertion works to pinpoint the value of experience. Posthumus's words cast experience—and its non-coincidental connection to an evasion of death—in terms that anticipatory nostalgia enables: experience mitigates the dangers of the remove threatened by merely telling someone else's story, or having someone else not merely script yours, but, worse yet, tell it. In implicitly rebuffing Belarius's storehouse

---

67. Parker suggests that Posthumus's "summing up" resonates with a disapproving discourse about "commercial arithmetics" ("Arithmetic," 101).

of fireside tales, Arviragus and Guiderius privileged "proof"; Posthumus expands this emphasis. His words reveal that, more than content, it is lived experience that is crucial to embarking on a future of narrative pleasure.

III

In its final act, *Cymbeline* favors resolutions that accommodate the play's more pronounced tensions, going so far as to pay the disputed tribute and redress Cymbeline's stolen future via restored succession. Still, the play's end bears reminders of the viewpoints I've been tracing. Likewise, the remainder of the second future and its attendant anticipatory nostalgia can be heard in Guiderius's defense: "I cut off's head, / And am right glad [Cloten] is not standing here / To tell this tale of mine" (5.5.295–97). The announcement might echo those earlier dead-end counterfactuals I discussed, but Guiderius no longer speaks in the conditional, though he references a life-or-death decision. Instead, his reason offers more texture than a mere acknowledgment that he would otherwise be dead. His grammar grants his present moment access to a lived future. Notably, he foregrounds narrative, and in a moment that grimly encapsulates the dominance inherent in the victor's prerogative to script history—his living on is predicated on murder—he also reminds us that it is the pleasure and privilege of the teller that is at stake.[68]

Anticipatory nostalgia—for all it was introduced as subordinating action to narration—also raises the question of whether or not there are boring stories worth telling. Perhaps Imogen is best positioned to provide an answer, since the restoration of Cymbeline's rightful heir dislodges her from the line of succession. In so doing, her marriage to Posthumus is validated, and also answers the subjunctive exclamations she has been uttering since the play's opening: "Would I were / A neat-herd's daughter" (1.2.79–80) and "would it had been so, that [Guiderius and Arviragus] / Had been my father's sons, then had my prize / Been less, and so more equal ballasting / To thee, Posthumus" (3.7.48–51). Those wistful counterfactuals whereby she might be a nobody are now closer to reality than mere grammatical fantasy, and the future that lies open to her at the play's conclusion operates outside of royal succession's plotted path. It is hard to locate the afterlife of anticipatory nostalgia here because the play works so hard to tie up loose ends. At the play's

---

68. The notion here of the wish for the perspective of the end of life, of death as finitude, is worth comparing to Walter Benjamin's "The Storyteller." But Arviragus also wants to deny this model: "I had rather / Have skipp'd from sixteen years of age to sixty: / To have turn'd my leaping time into a crutch, / Than have seen this" (4.2.198–201).

resolution, possibilities have been disciplined. Are these resolved plot strands analogous to a control over discourse or a measure of grammatical mastery? Do they mimic the way that musings about future narrative slip into the pleasure of telling tales that depend on murder? This seems to be the point of the elaborate implications of these grammatical constructions and categories. The restoration of the past requires otherworldly accommodation—Jupiter's visit and the visit of Posthumus's ghostly family—but finding the future doesn't require an equivalent voyage to utopia.

When the wager over chastity lands Iachimo in Imogen's bedchamber, he abandons the certain outcome of familiar stories from literary history (end points glossed through allusions to Philomela and Lucrece) in favor of future narrative, but he does not enjoy an equivalent certainty in return. Rather, his future narrative offers only the probability that he will win the bet—the likelihood that his deception-by-narrative will fully convince Posthumus. Shakespeare's play highlights time's ability to offer multiple kinds of futures, even modest ones. In operating outside of frameworks like probability and determinism, the brothers in Wales provide an index of what artistic production works to advance. In this play, linguistic constructions and the imaginative constructions that language games offer open up the future without requiring more space. Far from a "cause for shame," artistic production—most conspicuous, as I have suggested, as narrative—is a central force in the play—one that works actively for all categories of the future, but is most interesting, perhaps, for its claims to an awareness of the flexibility of temporal boundaries.

 CHAPTER 5

Imminent Futures
*Absent Art and Improvised Rhyme
in* Antony and Cleopatra *and* Cymbeline

                      This chapter considers two plays—*Antony and Cleopatra* and *Cymbeline*—in which artistic forms, whether absent and fleeting or, conversely, too permanent, organize Shakespeare's investigations. Both plays balance the transitory nature of art with its potential staying power through their approaches to time. In the previous two chapters, I focused on the means by which Shakespeare explored alternatives to dead-end futures. This chapter draws together the playwright's interest in antiquity and the forms through which alternative futures can be accessed. As in the previous chapter on *Cymbeline*, I recover a preoccupation with near-term, lived futures. However, beginning in *Antony and Cleopatra*, the strategies employed to avoid unwanted futures reveal a perspective on the present that troubles the allure of anticipatory nostalgia. I use this difference to argue that the playwright's engagement with the ancient past allows him to lay claim to agency and authority in artistic production in seventeenth-century England.

   This chapter begins with *Antony and Cleopatra* to show how Shakespeare explores artistic forms that undergird unique versions of the future. I focus on a division between a fear of a future imagined in terms of the present and a sense of enduring legacy that crystallizes in the repeated references to Octavius Caesar's triumph, and the role that Cleopatra would play in it. Octavius claims that Cleopatra's "life in Rome / Would be eternal in our triumph" (5.1.65–66), but his grandiose, "eternal," mythologizing vision of the future is not the play's vision of it.¹ The link that he makes between triumph and immortality marks only one perspective on the power of this particular future event. By contrast, Cleopatra's interpretation of herself in triumph focuses on what she will herself experience, introducing to the discussion an immediate, lived future. For Cleopatra, it is the extemporaneous performance embedded in that triumph that threatens not some far-ahead hereafter, but rather an "imminent future," a formulation I borrow from Georges Poulet's compelling account of the compression of present and future experience. In writing about Marivaux, Poulet describes

> a *fore-living*, a *fore-feeling*; the feeling of being on the threshold of a future instant and a new mode of being. The passage from the present to the future is so prompt, the allurement so irresistible that one lives as it were simultaneously both the one and the other.... One finds oneself thrown into a present so transitory that it vanishes, and out of a past still so warm that one falls into an unknown, imminent future already almost actual.²

Articulations about triumph in *Antony and Cleopatra* regularly prompt an image of a future "already almost actual" because imagined as though a present moment. Of course, the play's famous abundance of messengers and insistence upon the urgency of up-to-the-minute reports put particular emphasis on the present moment—"time" regularly means the present time, the present state of affairs. Even as its characters insist upon the *mythos* afforded by the past, the quick pace of its forty-two scenes and over 200 entrances and exits reinforces a distinctive vision of the future imagined in terms of that present moment.³ Though characters from antiquity frequently gesture to legacy on the Jacobean stage, as when they contemplate "earn[ing] a place

---

1. All references are to William Shakespeare, *Antony and Cleopatra*, ed. John Wilders, 3rd ser. (London: The Arden Shakespeare, 1995). Critics of the play have usefully pointed out that *Antony and Cleopatra* witnesses the erosion of Antony's identity and, more broadly, that the plot's political and military crises are spurred because "Roman virtues of valor and heroism in the play are distinctly in the past tense" (Janet Adelman, *The Common Liar: An Essay on* Antony and Cleopatra [New Haven, CT: Yale University Press, 1973], 132). Yet, such accounts assume that the past is rendered unavailable in the process.

2. Georges Poulet, *The Interior Distance*, trans. Elliott Coleman (repr., Ann Arbor: University of Michigan Press, 1964), 21. I borrow some of what Poulet's language elegantly points to, though I do not pursue the affective psychology that prompts his analysis.

3. When Shakespeare's Mark Antony complains that Octavius Caesar "harp[s] on what I am, / Not what he knew I was" (3.13.147–48), he offers an example of an exalted, mythic past that keeps bumping up against the play's present-tense reality, and the play regularly sets outrageous mythic claims alongside their minority reports. Adelman has claimed that "Cleopatra finds in Antony's death the signs of the great Apocalypse," and that this account is corroborated by the guardsmen who "greet Antony's suicide as an apocalyptic event" (*Common Liar*, 162). Yet, though the exchange between the two guards—"The star is fallen"; "And time is at his period" (4.14.107–8)—emphasizes

i'th' story" (3.13.47) and "earn[ing] our chronicle" (3.13.180), Shakespeare's approach to a well-known Roman history attempts to do more than merely draw attention to the fragility of historical account. He intervenes in Roman history on artistic and aesthetic terms.[4] In calling attention to a temporal overlap that is unusually unstable, Shakespeare offers a perspective on what it will be like to experience the future, and develops a mode for constructing the future in terms of present-tense immediacy.[5] What emerges is the consideration of a future that is characterized not exactly by its durability, but by those qualities that render it reliably, even permanently, ephemeral.

I then turn to Cleopatra's brief reappearance in *Cymbeline*, where she is depicted on a tapestry, to argue that this woven afterlife of Shakespeare's character allows him to comment on his own artistic craft, and claim independence, not to mention superiority, for that art. Shakespeare's intervention is intriguing for what this future might tell us about any present moment, and because it acts as an index of the playwright's capacity to insert himself into an emerging artistic story. He offers his own body of work as a replacement for classical sources. That is, he highlights the role of art and artistic medium as tools for negotiating both past and future. Shakespeare uses his classicism to develop a theatrical practice predicated on his capacity to appropriate and refashion the literary past. The playwright situates conceptions of the future

---

the magnitude of the event, their claims are offset by the staged agony of Antony's slow, botched suicide attempt.

4. Linda Charnes and Heather James have each made a persuasive case for how Shakespeare positions himself in this play in relationship both to Virgil and to Augustan sensibilities in accounts that foreground politics and identity. As they show, by inserting himself into a literary lineage, Shakespeare can preempt and complicate a figure like Virgil. Charnes claims that Shakespeare writes Octavius in anticipation of the Augustus he will become in order to undercut the emperor's "authority" over literary and historical legend. See Linda Charnes, *Notorious Identity: Materializing the Subject in Shakespeare* (Cambridge, MA: Harvard University Press, 1993), esp. 107–8, 145–47. James has argued that Shakespeare undermines an Augustan-sanctioned history by forcing Octavius to "modify the historical record" in making his political success depend on the revised narrative in which Antony and Cleopatra are best known for their romance. See Heather James, *Shakespeare's Troy: Drama, Politics, and the Translation of Empire* (Cambridge: Cambridge University Press, 1997), 122.

5. The tension between present and past is reproduced in critical accounts of *Antony and Cleopatra*'s most obvious binaries, which break across geographical lines: Egypt stands out for its damaging, distracting qualities; Rome for its stoicism. See, for example, Rosalie L. Colie, *Shakespeare's Living Art* (Princeton, NJ: Princeton University Press, 1974). Cleopatra physically pulls Antony away from Rome, and critics have shown how she also pulls him away, irretrievably, from a Roman sensibility and identity—from himself. See Garrett A. Sullivan Jr., *Memory and Forgetting in English Renaissance Drama: Shakespeare, Marlowe, Webster* (Cambridge: Cambridge University Press, 2005) for an interesting argument about Antony's "self forgetting." The distinction proves palpable even on a basic temporal level: Egypt as timeless in a strikingly lethargic sense of the word; Rome as a regimented culture in which we might comfortably calculate just how much time Antony is wasting as he dallies with Cleopatra. Yet, neither geographical nor temporal divisions adequately describe the play's treatments of the future.

in terms that stress its immediacy. He experiments with time, and introduces a concept of futurity, an imminent future, to render the ancient past subordinate to the literary enterprise of his own present moment.

I

There are no less than six references to Octavius's dreaded victory parade in Shakespeare's play, and they set us up to understand what the experience of this future event will be like. As I have suggested, Octavius announces his anticipated triumph in mythologizing terms when he claims that Cleopatra's "life in Rome / Would be eternal in our triumph" (5.1.65–66). At first glance, Shakespeare seems to take his cue from Plutarch's *Lives*. In that ancient account, the triumvir

> sent *Proculeius*, and commaunded him to doe what he could possible to get *Cleopatra* aliue, fearing least otherwise all the treasure would be lost: and furthermore, he thought that if he could take *Cleopatra*, and bring her aliue to ROME, she would maruelously beawtifie and sette out his triumphe.[6]

As Russell Jackson has pointed out, unlike Shakespeare's Octavius, Plutarch makes no mention of immortality. Whereas Plutarch's would-be triumphator emphasizes the importance of capturing Cleopatra "alive," accounts of Roman triumphs were often more concerned with the everlasting. They held that a triumphator would be reminded by "an attendant at his shoulder ... that he was not immortal, even as he held a crown over his head" as the procession advanced.[7] The context of "eternal" is Shakespeare's addition. He takes every opportunity to draw our attention to temporality as he investigates lasting and fleeting futures. *His* Octavius offers a perspective decidedly unchastened by a tradition intended to keep a victor in check, emphasizing instead the legacy of the imagined event. If it was, traditionally, the victor who was in danger of falling prey to the allure of his own mythology, Octavius Caesar's phrasing shifts these terms to suggest that immortality is also at stake for his would-be captive, Cleopatra.[8]

---

6. Plutarch, "The Life of Marcus Antonius," in *The Lives of the Noble Grecians and Romanes, compared together by that graue learned Philosopher and Historiographer, Plutarke of Chæronea: Translated out of Greeke into French by James Amyot . . . and out of French into English by Thomas North* (London, 1579), PPPP6r.

7. Russell Jackson, "The Triumphs of *Antony and Cleopatra*," *SJH*, 1984, 130. Anthony Miller makes a similar point in *Roman Triumphs and Early Modern English Culture* (New York: Palgrave, 2001), 20. But see Beard, who debunks this as something of an urban legend in studies of triumph (Mary Beard, *The Roman Triumph* [Cambridge, MA: Belknap Press of Harvard University Press, 2007]).

8. Jackson makes a similar point ("Triumphs," 144).

The concern that Cleopatra voices about triumph does not originate with Shakespeare's play. According to "an ancient commentator," Cleopatra "used to repeat, again and again, 'I shall not be led in triumph.'"[9] That an aversion to Roman display prompted the Egyptian queen's suicide became a commonplace feature of her legacy from antiquity onward.[10] In *Antony and Cleopatra*, that high-stakes aversion to triumph provides a guide to a fear of a future imagined in terms of the present, rather than through a sense of enduring legacy. This emphasis runs counter to Cleopatra's inclination to mythologize the past. *That* was a time when "[e]ternity was in our lips and eyes" (1.3.36); or after Antony's death, when her hyperbolic account of him uses the language of dreams—"I dreamt there was an emperor Antony"—to render the past mythic only to proclaim him "past the size of dreaming" (5.2.75, 96). Octavius's claim that her "life in Rome / Would be eternal in our triumph" puts his vision of the future in terms that resemble such immortalizing approaches to the past. So it is all the more notable that Cleopatra's vantage on the impending triumph introduces a future characterized by immediacy rather than immortality.[11] In distinguishing her view of triumph from Octavius Caesar's we can see that the play also uses triumph to think about (and avoid) a different kind of future, providing a kind of elaboration of the historical Cleopatra's alleged mantra.

The majority of references to Octavius Caesar's triumph in *Antony and Cleopatra* highlight Cleopatra's display in the procession. The Egyptian queen herself echoes this emphasis when she refuses to leave her monument to visit the dying Antony for fear of triumph:

> I dare not
> Lest I be taken. Not th'imperious show
> Of the full-fortuned Caesar ever shall
> Be brooched with me. If knife, drugs, serpents, have
> Edge, sting or operation. (4.15.23–27)

---

9. Beard, *Roman Triumph*, 114–15. The Horatian commentator provides a reference to a lost portion of Livy's history of Rome.

10. Beard, *Roman Triumph*, 115. This is an aspect of accounts of her in Plutarch, Florus, and Dio Cassius as well. The would-be trophy who commits suicide was "one of the commonest tropes of Roman triumphal narratives" (Beard, 115).

11. I resist critical accounts, then, which have suggested that time does not matter (Eugene M. Waith, as qtd. in Rackin), or that Shakespeare "repudiates Time" in this play (Phyllis Rackin, "Shakespeare's Boy Cleopatra, the Decorum of Nature, and the Golden World of Poetry," *PMLA* 87, no. 2 [1972]: 201, 207).

Threatening to kill her, an angry Antony anticipates her death in terms of its cost to Caesar's procession:

> Vanish, or I shall give thee thy deserving
> And blemish Caesar's triumph. Let him take thee
> And hoist thee up to the shouting plebeians!
> Follow his chariot like the greatest spot
> Of all thy sex; most monster-like be shown
> For poor'st diminutives, for dolts, and let
> Patient Octavia plough thy visage up
> With her prepared nails! (4.12.32–39)

Antony's diction—"hoist[ed]" and "shown"—makes clear Cleopatra's role in the triumph: she would be a central component of the spectacle.[12] She seeks to avoid becoming a piece of ornamentation, and maintains this focus when she extends her warning to her attendant, Iras:

> Thou an Egyptian puppet shall be shown
> In Rome as well as I. Mechanic slaves
> With greasy aprons, rules and hammers shall
> Uplift us to the view. (5.2.207–10)

The emphasis repeatedly falls on Cleopatra's display, and the sensory terms in which it is described communicate the immediacy of the dreaded view. The visceral experience of her triumphal future includes the noise of "shouting plebeians," the uncomfortably tactile "thick breaths" and "greasy" accoutrements of the "[m]echanic slaves" that will taunt her from the crowd, and the damage that Octavia's sharp nails will inflict.[13] The threats are as encompassing as surround sound, but they are also threats of the instant. Such details underscore the dissimilarity with the more grandiose, monumentalizing afterlife that Caesar hopes to enjoy—rather than suggesting Cleopatra will be "eternal in [his] triumph," they illuminate an immediate and present-tense quality to Cleopatra's version of her anticipated role in the spectacle.

---

12. Cf. Cleopatra's own words: "Shall they hoist me up / And show me to the shouting varletry / Of censuring Rome?" (5.2.54–56). See also Ruth Nevo, *Tragic Form in Shakespeare* (Princeton, NJ: Princeton University Press, 1972), 346–47 for a claim that Cleopatra's lines here soften the degradation that Antony has imagined for her in triumph.

13. Nevo has pointed out a "significant verbal echo" between "shouting plebeians" and "shouting varletry," both of which descriptions encapsulate the "lewd jeering of the despised populace" (*Tragic Form*, 348).

Implicit in Octavius's view, by contrast, is a victory parade that yokes her to a future legacy of subjection and defeat.[14]

What I have set out to isolate so far intensifies in one of the play's most memorable speeches. According to Cleopatra's final description of the anticipated triumph,

> Saucy lictors
> Will catch at us like strumpets, and scald rhymers
> Ballad us out o'tune. The quick comedians
> Extemporally will stage us and present
> Our Alexandrian revels; Antony
> Shall be brought drunken forth; and I shall see
> Some squeaking Cleopatra boy my greatness
> I'th' posture of a whore. (5.2.213–20)

Understandably, the description of the squeaking Cleopatra and Shakespeare's striking use of the word "boy" as a verb—"boy my greatness"—have received the lion's share of the attention in the critical literature. There is a boy actor on Shakespeare's stage, and he predicts himself even as he performs Shakespeare's play, potentially drawing the audience out of the fiction at the same moment that the character insists upon her own authenticity.[15] This moment announces theater's capacity to put past and present on simultaneous view and cries out for contemplation of the relationship between ancient Rome and its afterlife in Jacobean performance. We confront, as Catherine Belsey has put it, the "gap between the future performance that Cleopatra imagines and fears on the one hand, and the play we are watching on the other."[16] However, attending to that gap has caused us to overlook the complexity of the former term: "the future performance that Cleopatra imagines and fears." Shakespeare's powerful self-referentiality has put us too much in mind of the play *Antony and Cleopatra* itself, and has thereby distracted us from Cleopatra's revulsion at what *she* "shall see." Critical accounts have too readily subscribed to a temporality that attaches the future to legacy and the "eternal." I offer a corrective by showing that Cleopatra's expected performance also brings a different kind of future into view because she projects forward the perspective of the play's preeminent "now."

---

14. Neither account, however, mentions the threat of execution at the end of the triumph.

15. As Charnes and others have discussed, this moment further amplifies Cleopatra's position as consummate actress, which has been operative since the play's opening scenes.

16. Catherine Belsey, "Cleopatra's Seduction," in *Alternative Shakespeares*, ed. Terence Hawkes (London: Routledge, 1996), 2:46.

Writing about a twentieth-century performance of the play, theater critic Walter Kerr claimed that "we are—now—looking at the very play that Cleopatra is killing herself to avoid seeing. She is already an actress playing herself, expressing the hope that she will never see herself played."[17] Juliet Dusinberre has countered that "Kerr's account misses an important point. Cleopatra killed herself to avoid seeing a *boy* perform."[18] Dusinberre usefully emends Kerr in an attempt to draw attention to the complexities of gender identity at work in this speech. However, her correction also implicitly endorses the view of an "eternal" future that I have been aligning with Octavius Caesar. Dusinberre's emphasis on the word "boy" obscures the speech's multiple valences because it renders Cleopatra's fears inextricable from Shakespeare's play as a sign of immortality's success. Both Kerr and Dusinberre are wrong about one crucial detail: Cleopatra does not care about Shakespeare's play, despite the irony toward which she unwittingly nods. Critical accounts of the boy Cleopatra have tended to assume that Shakespeare asks his Jacobean audience to imagine their present as the future anticipated by characters from the past. I am suggesting that that temporal overlay, though certainly at issue, is not Shakespeare's primary interest in this moment. I aim to maintain the distinction between Shakespeare's "very play" and the triumph that Cleopatra imagines because they are markedly different performative events.

Crucially, this particular speech shifts the focus assumed in the play's other mentions of triumph: this is no longer a matter of Cleopatra's display. Though the immediacy of the description is maintained, in this future, she will not be a "brooch," but an audience. Iras reinforces this shift in focus when she recasts the nails that Antony first conjured with his threat about Octavia: "I'll never see't, for I am sure my nails / Are stronger than mine eyes" (5.2.222–23). That Cleopatra worries about watching herself performed rather than displayed pinpoints an important aspect of her speech. Rather than fearing a future play or the boy that will play her, Cleopatra's aversion to an imminent future is communicated through the word "extemporally." Whether on display or as spectator, her future is a lived, visceral future. It is a future imagined through the context of "now." In imagining herself as a "brooch," Cleopatra lingered on sensory experience by emphasizing the grossness of plebeian proximity. When she shifts to

---

17. Kerr, reviewing Michael Langham's production in Stratford, Ontario in 1967 (as qtd. in Juliet Dusinberre, "Squeaking Cleopatras: Gender and Performance in *Antony and Cleopatra*," in *Shakespeare, Theory, and Performance*, ed. James C. Bulman [London: Routledge, 1996], 52).

18. Dusinberre, "Squeaking Cleopatras," 53.

become an audience in that final speech, however, she voices anxiety about an anticipated confrontation with a very particular performative set: rhymers and comedians. The impromptu performance that she predicts sums up the horror of the spectacle; rhymers and comedians presage a rendition enacted on the spur of the moment. Moreover, in a future consisting of being audience to one's own representation, what is imagined is facing a caricature in the future that is derived from a mockery of one's past behavior.[19] Whereas critical accounts of Antony have tended to focus on his loss of self, Cleopatra finds most alarming the prospect of a reenactment that debases her perfectly clear sense of herself, which helps to explain why the "extemporal" and its performance context become the vocabulary through which she invokes a future that prompts suicide.

II

The word "extemporally" ties Cleopatra's future-oriented speech to the play's newsy sense of time by linking her description to particular forms of artistic expression, both impromptu and topical. Etymologically, "extemporally" derives from the Latin *extemporālis*, "arising out of the moment," from out of the time.[20] In short space, Cleopatra's diction—"quick comedians"; "extemporally"—draws attention to the improvisatory quality of the Roman reenactment she dreads, a characteristic that ought to highlight its ephemerality. Patrick Cheney has tallied Shakespeare's uses of this word (and its variants), and notes ten appearances of "extempore," "extemporal," and "extemporally" in the playwright's canon.[21] Seven of these ten, Cheney notes, "pertain to an actor's improvization of his speech."[22] I want to think about Shakespeare's reference to this form—impromptu performance—to isolate the terms of Cleopatra's revulsion not merely by assuming that this anticipated "grand

---

19. See James for a discussion of "Caesar's ideological rewriting of [Cleopatra] as a whore and political travesty" (*Shakespeare's Troy*, 146). Charnes insists that this is a matter of character (*Notorious Identity*, 131–34); see David A. Brewer, *The Afterlife of Character, 1726–1825* (Philadelphia: University of Pennsylvania Press, 2005) for a compelling discussion of the stakes of establishing character. Despite the richness of these studies, this chapter aims to show that the artistic stakes are far from incidental.
20. *OED*, s.v. "extemporal, *adj.*" Like the *OED*, the *Chambers Murray Latin-English Dictionary* traces the etymology of "extemporālis" to "ex tempore"; the entry for the latter offers "on the spur of the moment," or, from Cicero, "according to circumstances"; Sir William Smith and Sir John Lockwood, *Chambers Murray Latin-English Dictionary* (1933; repr., Edinburgh: Chambers, 1995), 257, 746.
21. Patrick Cheney, *Shakespeare's Literary Authorship* (Cambridge: Cambridge University Press, 2008), 16–17.
22. Ibid., 17.

theatrical event" will be Cleopatra's travesty, but by teasing out the terms on which she understands the imminent future.[23]

Two common associations for extemporizing in the period were clowns and rhymes. On the Elizabethan stage, Richard Tarlton was, famously, the "*extempore* genius" of the theater, though the taste for improvisatory "wit" was "on the wane by the time of his death in 1588."[24] Improvisation was "given free rein at the end of a play, when members of the audience throw up clever rhymes with the aim of outwitting the comedian, whose task it is to give an instant riposte."[25] In *Thalia's Banquet* (1620), Henry Peacham offers an epigram "To Sir Ninian Ouzell" that testifies to Tarlton's storied popularity and effect:

> As *Tarlton* when his head was onely seene,
> The Tire-house doore and Tapistrie betweene,
> Set all the mulltitude in such a laughter,
> They could not hold for scarse an houre after.[26]

In so doing, he reproduces the couplet form commonly associated with extemporizing even as he emphasizes that Tarlton's link to comedy was so strong that he came to inspire laughter without requiring recourse to words. Clowns like Tarlton and his successors implicitly emphasized the unrehearsed nature of extemporizing by noting their lack of ability in memorizing theatrical parts.[27] The preference for a form that could be improvised to combat an unreliable memory was standard fare in jokes about acting throughout the period. For example, in *A Midsummer Night's Dream*, Snug asks Quince to give him the lion's part in advance since he is "slow of study," and Quince

---

23. Charnes, *Notorious Identity*, 131. James sees these as "low-class analogues" for the high art that Virgil, Ovid, and Horace will produce (*Shakespeare's Troy*, 121). See Miller for a claim that the "burlesque theatricality [Cleopatra] envisage[s] . . . equates Caesar's Roman triumph and Shakespeare's English play" and thus "appropriat[es]" triumph for England (*Roman Triumphs*, 135).

24. Brian Walsh, *Shakespeare, The Queen's Men, and the Elizabethan Performance of History* (Cambridge: Cambridge University Press, 2009), 33. Theatrical "extemporizing" was so closely aligned with this famous jesting clown that the practice was often invoked via a synonym: Tarltonizing. In *Rehearsal from Shakespeare to Sheridan* (Oxford: Clarendon Press, 2000), Tiffany Stern notes that "[John] Aubrey's chief heroes of extemporization are Jonson and Shakespeare—'A grace by Ben Johnston extempore, . . .'; 'at the Tavern at Stratford . . . [Shakespeare] makes . . . this extempore Epitaph'" (101).

25. David Wiles, *Shakespeare's Clown: Actor and Text in the Elizabethan Playhouse* (Cambridge: Cambridge University Press, 1987), 14.

26. Henry Peacham, *Thalia's Banquet* (London, 1620), C8r.

27. Stern makes a case for a link between Clown and playwright by considering how together they were "extemporizing" the play's script (*Rehearsal*, 101–2). She points out that parts were learned separately, so did not afford much chance for actor development (70).

replies that he "may do it extempore since it is nothing but roaring" (1.2.62–63).[28] Likewise, in *The Travels of the Three English Brothers* (1607), a character named Will Kemp (historically, Tarlton's successor) claims: "I am somewhat hard of study . . . but if they will invent any extemporal merriment, I'll put out the small sack of wit I ha' left in venture with them."[29] Curiously, the fashion for wit also prompted its opposite: memorizing material in the hopes of faking spontaneity. Cripple in *The Fair Maid of the Exchange* (1607) boasts that he can "[m]ake [him]self famous for a sudden wit" by using the "quire / Or two of paper, fill'd with songs and ditties, / And here and there a hungry epigram" that a dead poet has "bequeath[ed]" to him. He claims to

> pater-noster-like, have conn'd them all.
> I could now, when I am in company
> At ale-house, tavern, or an ordinary,
> Upon a theme make an extemporal ditty
> (Or one at least should seem extemporal)
> Out of the abundance of this legacy,
> That all would judge it, and report it too,
> To be the infant of a sudden wit,
> And then I were an admirable fellow.[30]

He registers an impulse toward even an appearance of the quickness of mind—sudden wit—that inhered in the capacity to produce "an extemporal ditty." Peculiarly, the context of memory coordinates these problems by effecting a collapse between the fleeting and the durable: to "seem extemporal" the impostor learns by heart a skill that the clown claims to rely on because of the elusiveness of "study."

Discussions of rhyme in late sixteenth-century England often mention extemporizing, and the two activities are often treated together in reverent terms in rhetorical and poetic treatises, even when the treatise writer betrays hostility. In *A Discourse of English Poetrie* (1586), William Webbe claims writers "who can with facility intreate at large, and as we call it *extempore*, in good and fencible ryme, vppon some vnacquainted matter" are "right worthy of

---

28. William Shakespeare, *A Midsummer Night's Dream*, ed. Russ McDonald (1968; repr., New York: Penguin, 2000).

29. John Day, William Rowley, and George Wilkins, *The Travels of the Three English Brothers*, in *Three Renaissance Travel Plays*, ed. Anthony Parr (Manchester: Manchester University Press, 1995) scene 9.77–79.

30. Thomas Heywood, *The Fair Maid of the Exchange*, ed. Barron Field (London: Shakespeare Society, 1845) 3.2, 49–50. Tarlton is associated with Paternoster Row in three separate jests.

admiration, for their readines and plenty of wytt and capacity."[31] In explaining his method for counterfeiting impromptu wit, Webbe even offers a layman's option for memorization. An author can "ende [a line of verse] with what word you wyll: then what soeuer the word is, you may speedilie runne ouer the other wordes" that rhyme with it. He reckons the odds that one word on the list will "fitte the sense" are "twenty to one." He continues:

> And indeede I thinke, that next to the Arte of memory, thys is the readyest way to attaine to the faculty of ryming well Extempore, especially if it be helped with thus much paynes. Gather together all manner of wordes especially *Monosillables*, and place them Alphabetically in some note, and either haue them meetely perfectly by hart (which is no verye laboursome matter) or but looke them dilligently ouer at some time, practising to ryme indifferent often, whereby I am perswaded it wil soone be learned, so as the party haue withall any reasonable gyft of knowledge and learning, whereby hee want not bothe matter and wordes altogether.[32]

Although Webbe details an approach more "laboursome" than merely "con[ning]" someone else's verses "pater-noster-like," he and Cripple both emphasize that *extempore* rhyming is "right worthy of admiration." Webbe also anticipates Cripple when he explains his method: he may not shy away from diligence and practice, but the "readiness and plenty of wytt and capacity" that he admires prompt a "readiest way" that sounds like a short cut. To some degree, both examples reproduce the advice that George Gascoigne offers a would-be poet, Eduardo Donati, the addressee of *Certain Notes of Instruction* (1575). He warns him to "beware of rhyme without reason" for fear it might "lead" him from his "first invention," like writers who are "drawn sometimes by rhyme to forget it." Lest rhyme cause a writer to stray from his topic, Gascoigne recommends that Donati choose a word to end a line of verse and then "count over all the words of the selfsame sound" by making an alphabetical list. Once this makeshift rhyming dictionary has been compiled, he urges his reader to "take that [word] which best may serve your purpose, carrying reason with rhyme, and if none of them will serve so, then alter the last word of your former verse, but yet do not willingly alter the

---

31. William Webbe, *A Discourse of English Poetrie*, ed. Edward Arber (London: English Reprints, 1870), 64.
32. Ibid., 64–65. Quintilian makes the link between extemporizing and the art of memory even more explicit. See Terence Cave, *The Cornucopian Text: Problems of Writing in the French Renaissance* (Oxford: Clarendon Press, 1979), 126–56.

meaning of your invention."[33] Gascoigne's practical advice provides some insight into how the mechanics that Heywood and Webbe claim can power studied "extemporizing" might operate.

Thomas Campion in his *Observations in the Art of English Poesy* (1602) concedes, "I am not ignorant that whosoever shall by way of reprehension examine the imperfections of rhyme must encounter with many glorious enemies, and those very expert and ready at their weapon, that can, if need be, extempore (as they say) rhyme a man to death."[34] Impromptu rhyme can be divine—Don Adriano de Armado makes a plea to "some extemporal god of rhyme" in *Love's Labour's Lost*—but it can also be dangerous, if not deadly.[35] It can also be a mark of extraordinary skill. In his *Art of English Poesy* (1589), George Puttenham suggests an exercise, an "example of a ditty written extempore" whereby a poet might prove to be "his craft's master." In the exercise, he recommends that his reader

> ye yourself make one verse, whether it be of perfect or imperfect sense, and give it [to the poet] for a theme to make all the rest upon. If ye shall perceive the maker do keep the measures and rhyme as ye have appointed him, and besides do make his ditty sensible and ensuant to the first verse in good reason, then may ye say he is his craft's master. For if he were not of a plentiful discourse, he could not upon the sudden shape an entire ditty upon your imperfect theme or proposition in one verse. And if he were not copious in his language, he could not have such store of words at commandment as should supply your concords. And if he were not of a marvelous good memory, he could not observe the rhyme and measures after the distances of your limitation, keeping with all gravity and good sense in the whole ditty.[36]

This description links the generative possibility connected to verse "upon the sudden" to a preexisting bedrock foundation of "plentiful discourse."

In the oratorical tradition, writers like Quintilian made explicit the principle that extensive rhetorical training enabled extemporaneous speech. By contrast, discussions of extemporaneous rhyme introduce a much less

---

33. George Gascoigne, "Certain Notes of Instruction (1575)," in *Sidney's "The Defence of Poesy" and Selected Renaissance Literary Criticism*, ed. Gavin Alexander (London: Penguin, 2004), 241–42.
34. Thomas Campion, "Observations in the Art of English Poesy (1602)" in Alexander, *Sidney's "The Defence,"* 282.
35. See also Sidney, "to be rhymed to death, as is said to be done in Ireland," ("The Defence of Poesy," in *Sir Philip Sidney*, ed. Katherine Duncan-Jones [Oxford: Oxford University Press, 1994], 142).
36. George Puttenham, *The Art of English Poesy*, ed. Frank Whigham and Wayne A. Rebhorn (Ithaca, NY: Cornell University Press, 2007), 179.

flattering shadow discourse. We need only think back to the terms of Posthumus's rant in *Cymbeline*, which I discussed in the previous chapter, for an example. After the battle in Wales, Posthumus registers disgust with his accidental interlocutor, the Briton lord, who has answered his lengthy account of the conflict with a puzzled recap of the narration: "This was strange chance / A narrow lane, an old man, and two boys" (5.3.51–52). Enraged by his listener's "wonder," Posthumus asks, "Will you rhyme upon't, / And vent it for a mock'ry?" Not only does he align rhyme with a capacity for parody ("a mock'ry"), but he also goes so far as to produce an improvised couplet in response: "Two boys, an old man twice a boy, a lane, / Preserv'd the Britons, was the Romans' bane." In so doing, he reshapes the material of the lord's reaction to highlight the feature—rhyme—that most readily primes it for debasement (5.3.53–58).[37] In other words, Posthumus reiterates period attitudes that tended to link extemporaneous rhyme to the kind of lowbrow performance that Cleopatra has in mind. Along similar lines, when, in his dedication to his translation of Virgil (1584), Richard Stanyhurst claims he offers up his work in print to educate poets and provide an antidote to "*wooden rythmours*," those "drones" that need to be "slap[ped]" from the "sweet scenting hives of *Poetry*," he calls upon the

> learned to apply them selves wholly . . . to the true making of verses in such wise as the *Greeks* and *Latins*, the fathers of knowledge have done and to leave to these doltish coistrels their rude rhyming and balducketome ballads.[38]

Stanyhurst's examples of bad verse presage the artistic terms of the reenactments and representations of herself that Cleopatra imagines; her focus falls to the "scald rhymers" and "quick comedians."[39] Though her phrase "Ballad us out o'tune" means "in or out of order or proper condition; in or out of harmony with some person or thing,"[40] in casting the "scald rhymers" in this

---

37. All references are to William Shakespeare, *Cymbeline*, ed. J. M. Nosworthy, 2nd ser. (1995; repr. London: The Arden Shakespeare, 2000).

38. As qtd. in Eric Nebeker, "Broadside Ballads, Miscellanies, and the Lyric in Print," *ELH* 76, no. 4 (2009): 1009–10.

39. Given the succession of performers that Cleopatra lists, the "saucy lictors" conjure both a musical context and a physical activity as they "catch at" the queen. That verbal phrase, often used figuratively, shows up in the *OED* among examples of the word in the sense of "to snatch at; to make a quick or eager attempt to lay hold of." "Catch" is also a musical term that refers to a song composed for multiple, overlapping voices (a "round"). The word was "subsequently specially applied to rounds in which the words are so arranged as to produce ludicrous effects, one singer catching at the words of another." *OED*, s.v. "catch, *v.*," def. 23; "catch, *n.*," def. 1.14.

40. *OED*, s.v. "tune, *n.*," def. 3b.

way, she emphasizes the mismatch of medium and content—from a musical perspective, a ballad would be sung "in tune" (and likely "to the tune of" a familiar song), but Cleopatra puns on musical vocabulary to offer a metaphor about the ballad's words, presumably penned to mock, humiliate, and debase her. In this regard, the ballad she imagines also reiterates formal critique of which Stanyhurst is typical.

The period association between rhyme and the extempore reinforces the importance of Cleopatra's diction in conjuring the imminent future. A player in Robert Greene's *Groats-worth of witte* (1592), for example, refers to his time as a "countrey Author," and signals that his couplet—"The people make no estimation / Of Morrals teaching education"—is meant to impress: "Was not this prettie for a plain rime extempore?"[41] When writing about Tarlton, people often comment on the difficulty of producing couplets. Improvised couplets may be wholly spontaneous, but, as Gascoigne's method indicates, the potential pairs are not unlimited; the labor of listing "all the words of the selfsame sound by order of the alphabet" is not an exercise in the infinite.[42] Moreover, Tarltonizing depends upon rhyme's capacity for prediction: rhymes entail the future because they point toward what is coming next. It is on this basis that Samuel Daniel, in his *Defence of Ryme* (1603) that sets out to defend rhyme against those adversaries who call it "grosse, vulgare, barbarous,"[43] claims for rhyme the capacity to organize the "vnformed Chaos" of imagination.[44] He claims that the "knowne frame" of rhyme offers

> due staies for the minde, those incounters of touch as makes the motion certaine.... For this kinde acquaintance and continuall familiarity euer had betwixt our eare and this cadence, is growne to so intimate a friendship, as it will now hardly euer be brought to misse it. For bee the verse neuer so good, neuer so full, it seemes not to satisfie nor breede that delight as when it is met and combined with a like sounding accent: Which seemes as the iointure without which it hangs loose, and cannot subsist, but runnes wildely on, like a tedious fancie without a close.[45]

---

41. Robert Greene, *A Groats-worth of witte, bought with a million of Repentance* (London, 1592), E1r.
42. Gascoigne, "Certain Notes of Instruction," 242. See Cave for Quintilian's discussion of this matter in terms of oratory (*The Cornucopian Text*, 126–49). Samuel Daniel praises rhyme for "consisting of an agreeing sound in the last silables of seuerall verses, giuing both to the Eare an Eccho of a delightfull report, and to the Memorie a deeper impression of what is deliuered therein" (*A Defence of Ryme* [London, 1603], F2v).
43. Daniel, *A Defence of Ryme*, E8v.
44. Ibid., F7v.
45. Ibid., F4v–F5r.

Nature, Daniel asserts, "desires a certainty, & cõports not with that which is infinit, to haue these clozes, rather than, not to know where to end, or how far to go, especially seeing our passions are often without measure."[46] Rhyme can "satisfie the eare of the world" (unlike "Latine numbers") because of its "Harmonicall cadence."[47] Couplets—what Puttenham called rhymes in the "first distance"—"do pass so speedily away and so often return again, as their tunes are never lost, nor out of the ear, one couple supplying another so nigh and so suddenly."[48] Despite Daniel's defense, it is the predictive capacity inherent in couplets that prompts him to "confesse" that he finds "continuall cadences of couplets . . . very tyresome, & vnpleasing." He charges them with "stuff[ing]" rather than "intertain[ing]" the "delight" because "they runne on, with a sound of one nature, & a kinde of certaintie." He repeats this charge of "ouer-glutting the eare" by referring to rhyme as "alwayes certaine," and recommends an "alternate or crosse Ryme" to "ease" the ear of the "continuall burthen" of couplets.[49] As Sidney put it in his *Defence of Poesy*, "one word so, as it were, begetting another, as, be it in rhyme or measured verse, by the former a man shall have a near guess to the follower."[50] The satisfaction peculiar to the "near guess" makes extemporal performance laudable, but also susceptible to counterfeit through intensive study. Cleopatra's simultaneous invocation of "extemporally" and ballads helps to train focus on the paradox of a future that, because it is filled with unscripted performance, signals a kind of artistic reception that is painfully certain. This is the tension that Cleopatra brings to light: a future that is extemporal is a future always generated in the present ("out of the time"), but it is powered by a form that ties her—no matter the context or occasion of that future—to an assured interpretation ("I'th' posture of a whore").

Like Stanyhurst, Puttenham derides forms such as ballads as lowbrow, low-quality verse: "[T]he poet must know to whose ear he maketh his rhyme, and accommodate himself thereto, and not give such music to the rude and barbarous, as he would to the learned and delicate ear."[51] But Cleopatra's complaint also suggests a dependability of form that provides her the vocabulary with which she can implicitly condemn its content. The charges against rhymers and comedians might qualify them to taunt Cleopatra, but by invoking ballad form she affixes to their production a firm classification.

---

46. Ibid., F7v–F8r.
47. Ibid., F3v.
48. Puttenham, *The Art of English Poesy*, 175.
49. Daniel, *A Defence of Ryme*, H6r, H6v, H7r.
50. Sidney, "The Defence of Poesy," 124.
51. Puttenham, *The Art of English Poesy*, 176.

Plays in this period were often published in close proximity with other forms like ballads and broadsides, which treated the same subjects. In Shakespeare's time and often even at his theater, the very production and selling of ballads would have been an ephemeral, itinerant affair.[52] The attendant printed material was often topical, whereby Cleopatra's Egyptian lifestyle would be at risk of negative representation. As Ruth Nevo puts it, "Their Alexandrian revels can be debased by scurrilous burlesque."[53] Nonetheless, there seems to be more at stake than merely a distaste for being parodied, or even witnessing one's own parody. Cleopatra depends on the formal fact that a ballad will pillory her; both her diction and prediction echo the discourse describing marketplace performances in Shakespeare's own day that advertised such forms to potential customers: the "Ballad-monger" "squeakes" his ballad's story to the "attentive rout," "chant[ing]" because he is reluctant to "sing it out."[54] As a result, her future's certainty is tied to an artistic form that is wedded to the instant. It is dangerous because it is not fleeting enough.

That Cleopatra fears an imminent future that entails watching extemporal performance casts the matter in terms familiar to discussions of theater. Performance theorists such as Peggy Phelan have usefully emphasized that theater has an inherently transient quality: performances end, and no two are ever identical.[55] Though Cleopatra's vision stands in contrast to Octavius's "eternal," her complaint points to a paradoxical problem: an experience derived from the instant that is not sufficiently ephemeral. Joseph Roach has pointed out that "the most intriguing point about the ubiquity of improvisation in performance, especially Eurocentric performance, is that its memory is so often erased by its very success"; by Roach's account, improvisation's ephemerality happens because the "present stabilizes the past by representing itself as the inevitable consummation of deliberate steps, but to do this it must smooth over the unbidden eruptions necessary to its own creation."[56] Not only is extemporaneous performance wedded to the instant, but any present moment might give rise to the same thing, whereby a fleeting form becomes durable because it offers recurring ephemerality so predictable that it borders

---

52. Tessa Watt, *Cheap Print and Popular Piety, 1550–1640* (Cambridge: Cambridge University Press, 1991), 5.

53. Nevo, *Tragic Form*, 352.

54. William Brown, *Britannia's pastorals. The second booke (1616)*, as qtd. in Watt, *Cheap Print and Popular Piety*, 23–24.

55. Peggy Phelan, "Introduction: The Ends of Performance," in *The Ends of Performance*, ed. Peggy Phelan and Jill Lane (New York: New York University Press, 1998), 1–19.

56. Joseph Roach, "Kinship, Intelligence, and Memory as Improvisation: Culture and Performance in New Orleans," in *Performance and Cultural Politics*, ed. Elin Diamond (London: Routledge, 1996), 222.

on permanence. To survive, improvisation becomes script. Cleopatra's view of the triumphal future maintains improvisation's instantaneous quality, but cannot rely on it to fade away. What lies before her is an ephemeral form, but it also awaits her, ready to be derived from the instant. In this way, the imminent future she predicts both supplies couplets forged spontaneously and threatens the certain, predictive quality for which rhyme stands. Shakespeare uses Cleopatra to reveal that the future urgently encodes the capriciousness afforded to any present moment. Brian Walsh has recently suggested that the past, despite its inherent impermanence, can be resurrected by being staged, but that the revisitation is both fleeting and destabilizing.[57] Yet, Shakespeare uses Cleopatra to pose a rather different version of the past via a signature moment from antiquity—a past focused on the future that feels like the present, and, more troubling, even like a perpetual present. That imagined future is at once too unscripted and too unshakable. Poulet has described the "instant" as something that "surges out of nothingness," and echoing Augustine, he writes that "man never is, except in the moment; he is never in time."[58] Shakespeare gives to Cleopatra a version of the future that both expects an improvised "surge out of nothingness" of any future instant, and yokes such spontaneity to a creative form that will only have one thing to say. So, rather than the performance of the past alerting the Renaissance audience to the instability of the past, Cleopatra's idea of the contingency of history—its subjection to the instant—terrifies for its unwavering predictability.

III

The metatheatrical, ironic context inherent in "boy my greatness" arises because Cleopatra displays a fear about a kind of performance that is not sufficiently transient even as she enacts Shakespeare's scripted version. The real boy actor on the Jacobean stage plays in a performance markedly different from the one Cleopatra imagines being forced to witness. This reproduces a tension in the play—the traffic between improvisation and the staying power suggested by the predictive nature of its form. Because the performance

---

57. Walsh, *Shakespeare, The Queen's Men*, 11. Walsh argues that the past on the Elizabethan stage has the effect of pointing out the instability of the historical record because it can "foreground the representation of the past while using the language and playing practices that continually alert audiences to the present-tense reality of their performances. In other words, they initiate a stimulating dialectic between the 'pastness of the past' and the presentness of performance" (35); "that such narratives exist in the ephemeral context of a play shows how the wider concept of the past is likewise elusive and precarious" (68).

58. Poulet, *Interior Distance*, 16.

she imagines is extemporal, it is unscripted, and it is that lack of record that distinguishes it from the "eternal." But for Cleopatra, the problem inherent in being "extempore" lies in being continuously refashioned through a performance bound most strongly to its own moment in time. Cleopatra balks at the encounter between a thing and its parody, not because it is too unstable but because it is too predictable. The topical coincidence between ballads, broadsides, and plays in the period is also reinforced by formal discussions that insist certain verse forms are appropriate to certain subjects.[59] Gascoigne writes that rhyme royal is "a royal kind of verse, serving best for grave discourses," whereas ballads "derived of this word in Italian, 'ballare', which signifieth 'to dance'; and, indeed, those kinds of rhymes serve best for dances or light matters."[60] The horror of the imminent future is inextricably tied to its unscripted (and also low) creative forms. The context of extemporal rhyme serves as a reminder that this future is also iterative. In it, the "tunes are never lost," so performance drags on in perpetuity. Such "unbidden eruptions" cannot be contained—the extemporal suggests being subject to perpetual improvisation.

The wider context of impromptu generation that I have aligned with the forms that Cleopatra invokes (ballads, Roman comedy) is particularly appropriate to triumph, a context in which the "ex tempore" reinforces displacement. Nevo suggests:

> It is for the delectation of the despised rabble that the [triumphal] show is to be put on. It will be noticed that the members of the multitude, the many-headed monster, increasingly figure in Act V: the Roman mechanics, the saucy lictors, the mere boys and girls who are level now with men, the beggar, the maid that does the meanest chores. These figures punctuate the long reverie of Cleopatra like the tolling of a bell, for they are the petty contemptible life from which either she and Antony will be marvelously distinguished, or by whom they will be mocked, derided, and debased.[61]

Cleopatra fears a performance that is both shorthand for and too precariously derived from the present moment, which is also collapsed with popular opinion. If "ex tempore" means something derived from out of the time,

---

59. I will return in the next section to the question of multiple forms addressing the same material to consider Shakespeare's strategy of withholding spectacles in order to make verbal representation a resource for controlling the present and not being beholden to the past.
60. Gascoigne, "Certain Notes of Instruction," 244–45.
61. Nevo, *Tragic Form*, 348.

the etymology is also shadowed by a second idea: being dislodged from time. Roman triumphs staged the display of the conquered shorn of their treasure, but also of their home and proper context. The victory parade hosts the last flicker of a culture that has been extinguished, its splendor resurrected only to better emphasize how it has been stamped out of existence. Captives in ancient Rome were made to bear their finery in the procession because glorious attire reinforced what had been lost. For Cleopatra, being a historical figure conjured "extemporally" is to be a figure fundamentally dislodged from time, but forever yoked to interpretations of which she is spectator, not author.[62] In fighting against both being subject to a version of herself created out of the instant and being temporally displaced, Cleopatra transfers her triumphal role to her suicide. Even as she imagines what she "shall see," she is in the process of dressing just as the triumph would render her. She instructs her attendants: "Show me, my women, like a queen. Go fetch / My best attires. I am again for Cydnus / To meet Mark Antony" (5.2.226–28). In other words, her elaboration of a triumphal future accompanies "immortal longings" (5.2.273) that are recursive; she seeks a death that will return her to the past.

When Octavius sees Cleopatra adorned in her full glory after her asp-induced death, he notes that "she looks like sleep, / As she would catch another Antony / In her strong toil of grace" (5.2.337–39). His comment reproduces the play's competing temporal perspectives. Cleopatra's suicide communicates that she has no faith that the future would yield her "another Antony." Moreover, she shuns the future in favor of the past—the iteration she seeks is a retreat into an immortalizing, mythic past. She has no interest in "another Antony"; she seeks Antony himself, and the original exists only in that past. For her, the imminent future begets iteration. The fantasy that death will return her to a mythic past incorporates the insistence heard in the Horatian commentary: Cleopatra "used to repeat, again and again, 'I shall not be led in triumph.'"[63]

Octavius Caesar delivers the play's last speech, an encomium that also attempts to have the last interpretive word:

She shall be buried by her Antony.
No grave upon the earth shall clip in it
A pair so famous. High events as these
Strike those that make them, and their story is

---

62. See Charnes for the claim that Cleopatra does not consider being a spectacle and having control of her own reputation mutually exclusive (*Notorious Identity*, 131–33).

63. Beard, *Roman Triumph*, 114–15.

> No less in pity than his glory which
> Brought them to be lamented. Our army shall
> In solemn show attend this funeral,
> And then to Rome. Come, Dolabella, see
> High order in this great solemnity. (5.2.357–65)

Despite his claims in this speech that he has "made" the events, and that they lend him "glory," *Antony and Cleopatra* ends with Octavius's words, but not on his terms. We never see Octavius's triumph; we do not even hear the rhymes that Cleopatra dreads. Instead, Octavius produces his own couplets. In a rhyme-poor play, these four closing lines double the capping couplet common to Shakespearean drama. In each pair, Octavius's end-rhyme begins with a monosyllable that strains metrically to find an answer in a word that requires manipulation to offer masculine rhyme. In a complaint about meter, Daniel actually uses the word "funeral" to make his point:

> [A]ccording to our English March, wee must make a rest, and raise the last sillable, which falles out very vnnaturall in *Desolate, Funerall, Elizabeth, Prodigall,* and in all the rest sauing the Monosillables.[64]

What Daniel singles out about the results produced by the imposition of meter reinforces the strain under which Octavius labors to guarantee his "solemn show." The "unnaturall" emphasis required to yoke "shall" to "funerall" compromises the predictive force that Octavius relies upon to restore "high order." Daniel claimed rhyme commendable because it is "farre more laborious then loose measures," yet it also requires "wit and industry."[65] Rather than offering effortless rhyme, however, Octavius's couplets draw too much attention to their craft by requiring elevated diction born of manipulation. The use of the word "shall" in the first couplet reinforces the insistence on a future that cements one particular interpretation. Far from improvisatory wit, these laborious couplets mimic the forcible imposition of order. This is not the imminent future that Cleopatra feared, and the ponderous couplets show how unsuccessful Octavius's "eternal" future really is.

IV

Shakespeare ends his play with Octavius's couplets rather than the rhymes that Cleopatra dreads. Because those couplets claim the "solemn show" of

---

64. Daniel, *A Defence of Ryme*, H2r.
65. Ibid., F7v.

funeral rites will precede the journey home ("And then to Rome"), the lines also downplay the triumph that will celebrate that return. As a result, Shakespeare's ending sidesteps a well-known tradition in which Cleopatra's suicide fails to spare her from triumphal display. According to several classical accounts, she eluded triumph, but her *image* did not. Plutarch notes that Caesar "in his triumphe he carried *Cleopatraes* image, with an Aspicke byting of her arme."[66] Dio Cassius's less anodyne account suggests statuary: "[A]n effigy of Cleopatra upon a couch was carried by, so that in a way she, too, together with the other captives and with her children . . . was a part of the spectacle and a trophy in the procession."[67] In the sixteenth century, an ancient statue that Pope Julius II acquired for the Vatican's Belvedere courtyard was treated not only as a representation of Cleopatra, but also as "the very effigy carried in the post-Actium triumphs."[68] The association fueled Baldassare Castiglione's influential Latin verse monologue (1530) for this statue Cleopatra.[69]

The first half of Castiglione's poem focuses on the statue Cleopatra's inclusion in the triumph, and I quote here just a piece of it:

> namque triumphali invectus Capitolia curru
> insignes inter titulos gentesque subactas
> exstinctae infelix simulacrum duxit, et amens
> spectaclo explevit crudelia lumina inani.[70]

For indeed, having been conveyed to the Capitol in a triumphal chariot amidst the inscribed banners and the captives, the triumphator led the unfortunate image of the dead woman, and the demented man glutted his cruel eyes with the empty spectacle.

---

66. Plutarch, "Life of Marcus Antonius," QQQQ1v.

67. As qtd. in Leonard Barkan, *Unearthing the Past: Archaeology and Aesthetics in the Making of Renaissance Culture* (New Haven, CT: Yale University Press, 1999), 245. Barkan draws attention to Dio Cassius's insistence that "the queen was, in effect, present in the effigy," made more vivid by his suggestion that her sculpted presence is equivalent to the live inclusion of her children, who "were literally present in the procession" (245).

68. Barkan, *Unearthing the Past*, 246. How seriously anyone took this "hypothesis" at the time is not entirely clear. See Barkan for a comprehensive discussion of this statue, which was understood to figure Cleopatra during the Renaissance but was reclassified as Ariadne in later centuries (233–47).

69. Or perhaps the association was fueled by his poem. The poem was imitated by Italian poets such as Bernardino Baldi (1553–1617) and Agostino Favoriti (1624–82). It was later translated into English by Alexander Pope. For a fuller account of the Italian tradition, see Brian A. Curran, "Love, Triumph, Tragedy: Cleopatra and Egypt in High Renaissance Rome," in *Cleopatra: A Sphinx Revisited*, ed. Margaret M. Miles (Berkeley: University of California Press, 2011), 116–22.

70. Alessandro Peraso and John Sparrow, eds., *Renaissance Latin Verse* (Chapel Hill: University of North Carolina Press, 1979), 193–95 (lines 17–20). I am grateful to Philip Bixby and Dylan Davidson for their assistance with the translation.

The poet employs a vocabulary that relentlessly negotiates between life and lifelessness as he investigates Octavius Caesar's fantasy that Cleopatra's suicide has cost his glory nothing. The "simulacrum" he leads in the triumph is both an approximating image and a ghost in a manner that emphasizes its distinction from the real, dead Cleopatra for which it stands in, and thus undercuts Octavius's hopes that having her image present would seal for posterity her defeat and his victory. The splendor of the statue's artistry intends to correct the problem posed by Cleopatra's evasion, which has left him an "exstinctae infelix simulacrum" in place of a live captive. Castiglione suggests that Octavius commissioned a statue as lifelike as possible ("effigiem excudi spiranti e marmore") by making that liveliness a very property of the marble from which the artwork was carved. This ingenious substitution trades on the most familiar metaphors for art's capacity to animate in order to perform the triumphator's desperate CPR: in this fantasy, the marble's breath restores Cleopatra's. As Leonard Barkan has argued, "All the tropes that celebrate visual art objects—their verisimilitude, their ability to breathe or to speak—are precisely what defeat the queen's purpose by rendering her, in effect, alive to her humiliation in Rome."[71] On the one hand, Castiglione's poem endorses Caesar's success: he renders the statue so lively that it can speak. On the other hand, the words Castiglione provides attempt to empower the queen by restoring her agency in determining her own legacy. Castiglione's poem showcases the struggle over reputation in a manner that provides a strong check to Octavius Caesar's propagandistic victory. The vexed status of the statue Cleopatra as "independent work of art," however, is revisited not only by the poems and inscriptions, like Castiglione's, that ventriloquize it, but also by its Renaissance circumstance. Though the statue's enviable location and elaborate setting as a fountain in the Belvedere courtyard surely aim to celebrate rather than humiliate it (and, by extension, the woman depicted), the freedom these poems grant in celebrating the queen's evasion does not last long. As Evangelista Maddalena de' Capodiferro's (also known as Fausto Romano) slightly earlier epigrammatic verse has it, "I, who, conquered, refused by death to follow the triumphal procession of Augustus, now, stone, serve your waters, Julius."[72] Most sixteenth-century writings similarly echo the second half of Castiglione's poem, which restores a voice that begs favors of its new owners: pleading that she might be permitted to shed "eternal tears" ("aeternas lacrimas") for

---

71. Barkan, *Unearthing the Past*, 246.
72. As qtd. in and translated by Curran, "Love, Triumph, Tragedy," 118.

Mark Antony, Castiglione's Cleopatra implores Leo X to turn the fountain in which the statue is set back on.[73]

In Shakespeare's play, Octavius Caesar's closing words do nothing to acknowledge this tradition. Instead, the playwright takes a different tack in altering the case of immortality, and in doing so he also makes surprising use of the potential inherent not in an "empty spectacle," but in an absent one. He brings to the fore the cross traffic between ephemerality and durability that Cleopatra dreaded. That is, Shakespeare gestures toward and endorses *his* Cleopatra's final wishes by including her representation on a tapestry that hangs in the British princess's bedroom in *Cymbeline*. As I claimed earlier, Cleopatra's use of the word "extemporally" flags the predicament of being uncomfortably bound to the present moment at the end of a play that emphasizes both up-to-the-minute news and self-conscious mythmaking. In so doing, Shakespeare's dramatization of the past transports its audience back in time to a famous historical moment only to reveal that its star historical players were utterly preoccupied with the future. For Cleopatra, this means an imminent future, one experienced as a present moment, and it is a horror. For Shakespeare, this future glances at his own present moment, and it is a strategy. Through Cleopatra's cameo in *Cymbeline*, the playwright revisits her wish of return: "I am again for Cydnus." The context, however, has shifted from lowbrow, impromptu rhymes to expensive, unparalleled tapestry. Yet, both exist only imaginatively, exposing the playwright's stake in triangulating the classics, the future, and artistic production.

The tapestry in *Cymbeline* enjoys a lengthy description because Iachimo uses it as evidence that he has slept with Imogen. In an attempt to win the bet about her chastity, he uses ekphrasis to suggest to her exiled husband, Posthumus, that he was in her bedroom long enough to take in all its details. The catalogue of its contents in act 2, scene 4, recalls Iachimo's illicit visit to the bedroom in act 2, scene 2, in which he spied on the sleeping princess and took notes on her bedroom.[74] Iachimo's ekphrastic inventory wastes no

---

73. "lacrimas, Pater optime, redde. / Redde, oro, fletum; fletus mihi muneris instar, / improba quando aliud nil iam Fortuna reliquit" (lines 33, 43–45).

74. Rather than being highlighted in act 2, scene 2, however, these details were pointedly glossed over. Since the Renaissance stage was famously bare, there is no reason to believe that the items in Iachimo's catalogue, even if the stage were decorated according to the later scene, would have been actual props owned by Shakespeare's playing company. For discussions of the bareness of the Renaissance stage, see, for example, John H. Astington, ed., *The Development of Shakespeare's Theater* (New York: AMS Press, 1992); Andrew Gurr, *Playgoing in Shakespeare's London* (Cambridge: Cambridge University Press, 1987) and *The Shakespeare Company, 1594–1642* (Cambridge: Cambridge University Press, 2004); Bruce R. Smith, *Ancient Scripts & Modern Experience on the English Stage, 1500–1700* (Princeton, NJ: Princeton University Press, 1988). For a different perspective, and a claim

time in privileging the poignancy of Shakespearean memory. The catalogue begins with a tapestry that depicts Cleopatra on the very boat ride that Enobarbus lavishly describes in *Antony and Cleopatra*.[75] In that earlier play, references to the past established a vocabulary for the play's most immortalizing, mythologizing descriptions. In the case of the famous description of Cleopatra's first encounter with Antony, for example, Shakespeare communicates Cleopatra's elaborate display through Enobarbus's remembrance of the past:

> The barge she sat in, like a burnished throne,
> Burned on the water; the poop was beaten gold;
> Purple the sails, and so perfumed that
> The winds were love-sick with them; the oars were silver,
> Which to the tune of flutes kept stroke, and made
> The water which they beat to follow faster,
> As amorous of their strokes. For her own person,
> It beggared all description: she did lie
> In her pavilion, cloth-of-gold of tissue,
> O'erpicturing that Venus where we see
> The fancy outwork nature. On each side her
> Stood pretty dimpled boys, like smiling cupids,
> With divers-coloured fans, whose wind did seem
> To glow the delicate cheeks which they did cool,
> And what they undid did. (2.2.201–15)

Cleopatra's luxurious ride down the river closely follows the account recorded in Plutarch's *Lives*; it differs mostly in degree: in Enobarbus's version, the very elements of nature, like the lovesick winds and the water, fall under Cleopatra's sway.[76] Whereas in Plutarch's version, the Egyptian queen intentionally mimics representations of Venus ("apparelled and attired like the

---

about the place of textiles on the stage in particular, see Rebecca Olson, *Arras Hanging: The Textile That Determined Early Modern Literature and Drama* (Newark: University of Delaware Press, 2013), esp. 139. For a separate argument about hermeneutics in the play that includes an extended discussion of these two scenes, see J. K. Barret, "The Crowd in Imogen's Bedroom: Ethics and Allusion in *Cymbeline*," *Shakespeare Quarterly* 66, no. 4 (2015): 440–62.

75. Given that the tapestry likely wasn't present in act 2, scene 2, audience members might best consult memories made in the midst of a different play.

76. The speech is particularly indebted to Thomas North's translation of Plutarch. As Robert S. Miola points out in "Reading the Classics," in *A Companion to Shakespeare*, ed. David Scott Kastan (Oxford: Blackwell Publishers, 1999), 175, "Thomas North read Plutarch in Amyot's French version, itself indebted to a Latin translation."

goddesse *Venus*, commonly drawen in picture"),⁷⁷ in Shakespeare's rendering, it is Enobarbus who introduces the comparison, lending weight to the suggestion that Cleopatra effortlessly exceeds the goddess of love.⁷⁸ The speech secures the queen's mythic identity despite the fact that the play does not physically reproduce Cleopatra on the Cydnus. When Cleopatra exits *Antony and Cleopatra* in garb intended for her final, deadly theatrical display, she claims that she is "again for Cydnus." On the brink of suicide, the fate and future that she chooses for herself is one in which she is returned to the past both for its *mythos* and for its durability. In *Cymbeline*, Shakespeare seizes upon and reworks that durability by restoring her quite precisely to the Cydnus:

> First, her bedchamber,
> (Where I confess I slept not, but profess
> Had that was well worth watching) it was hang'd
> With tapestry of silk and silver, the story
> Proud Cleopatra, when she met her Roman,
> And Cydnus swell'd above the banks, or for
> The press of boats, or pride. A piece of work
> So bravely done, so rich, that it did strive
> In workmanship and value; which I wonder'd
> Could be so rarely and exactly wrought,
> Since the true life on't was— (2.4.66–76)

"Proud Cleopatra" revives the queen as she wished herself and her afterlife—she lives on as the subject of high art immortalized in a moment of her choosing.

In the tapestry in Iachimo's imaginary catalogue, she enjoys her chosen legacy because of an importantly ephemeral feature of these classical artistic treasures. The contents of Iachimo's tapestry bring with them a complex flood of images because Shakespeare's earlier play is so evidently entailed. Yet, notably, the tapestry depicts an episode never represented outside of Shakespeare's words.⁷⁹ Enobarbus's set piece, which encapsulated the penchant in

---

77. Plutarch, "The Life of Marcus Antonius," NNNN5r.

78. Some critics argue that Shakespeare refers specifically to Apelles's lost painting, *Venus Anadyomene*, placing the comparison in an even more ethereal intellectual register. For example, see Marguerite A. Tassi, "O'erpicturing Apelles: Shakespeare's *Paragone* with Painting in *Antony and Cleopatra*," in *Antony and Cleopatra: New Critical Essays*, ed. Sara Munson Deats (New York: Routledge, 2005), 291–307, esp. 295.

79. See Robert S. Miola, "*Cymbeline*: Shakespeare's Valediction to Rome," in *Roman Images: Selected Papers from the English Institute, 1982*, ed. Annabel Patterson (Baltimore: Johns Hopkins University Press, 1984).

Antony and Cleopatra to think of the past as mythic, was also an ekphrasis. So, in *Cymbeline* Iachimo describes an absent arras that reproduces a famous spectacle out of *Antony and Cleopatra* that the audience did not see, even if we saw that play.

Enobarbus's speech has been described as "the longest and most memorable" in *Antony and Cleopatra*, one in which Cleopatra is "the apotheosis of magnificence."[80] Phyllis Rackin has described it as a moment in which Enobarbus "suddenly abandons his characteristic ironic prose for the soaring poetry that creates for his listeners a Cleopatra who transcends anything they could see with the sensual eye or measure with the calculating and rational principle of the soul."[81] Iachimo's three, short ekphrastic lines reinforce the context of a description that stands in the place of a stunning visual spectacle, but with some notable alterations. Enobarbus's anthropomorphized winds and water resound in Iachimo's quick Cydnus, which "swells" with "pride" because Cleopatra rides upon it. Not merely ekphrastic, this description of the tapestry also captures the *enargeia*, the "vivid and lifelike reproduction in verbal art of natural detail," of Enobarbus's description.[82] At the same time, the tapestry ekphrasis is not exactly Enobarbus's speech in miniature. Rather, Shakespeare draws attention to the distance between the tapestry and its referent in temporal terms. Whereas in *Antony and Cleopatra*, Enobarbus's ekphrasis in the present conjured a pageant-like spectacle from the past, in *Cymbeline* the ekphrasis in the present refers back to a tapestry from a past that the audience witnessed, though the tapestry was not in it.[83] Although that past was a part of *Cymbeline*'s staged action, it emphasizes ontological distance by referencing an object no closer to hand than *Antony and Cleopatra*. Moreover, Iachimo's rhetoric insists upon the tapestry's artistic mastery, but the ekphrasis itself greatly reduces the image invoked in the earlier play. Unlike Enobarbus's investment in evocative similes, Iachimo's lines reveal an ambivalence about the images they generate. The description of the Cydnus, "swelling" with "pride" comes via an either-or structure. The river might swell with pride because it carries Cleopatra, but it might also be the "press of boats" that causes the displacement. Rather than a weak elision—Iachimo's poetic inability to imitate Enobarbus—the description functions to demonstrate how much words can convey within just a little space: is the river's "pride" a

---

80. Rackin, "Shakespeare's Boy Cleopatra," 202.
81. Ibid, 204.
82. Jean H. Hagstrum, *The Sister Arts: the Tradition of Literary Pictorialism and English Poetry from Dryden to Gray* (Chicago: University of Chicago Press, 1958), 62.
83. For an examination of technical textile vocabulary on the stage in this period, see Olson, *Arras Hanging*.

matter of arrogance, ostentation, pleasure, or sexual desire?[84] Or does "pride" refer to the eel-like fish, the lamprey, sometimes known by that name?[85] In the latter case, admittedly a momentary flicker at best, Iachimo offers an image of an overcrowded river that accounts for its high waters—either too many boats or too many fish. "Pride" also "swells" by echoing its other form in "Proud Cleopatra." For "proud" when applied to Cleopatra surely includes its lascivious valence in addition to a sense of arrogance and bearing.

According to Enobarbus, his description communicates his memory of Cleopatra; it also calls to mind the conventions of masque and pageant.[86] That is to say that embedded in the referential hall of mirrors reflecting off the river's water is the suggestion that the spectacle Enobarbus offered was a moment inherently theatrical, one that could have been produced on stage, and this may serve to remind us that Shakespeare withholds these spectacles. He uses instead verbal art to explore the limits of theatrical representation. Even as the tapestry engages in multiple conjurings—fake tapestry, real play, fake barge—the ambivalence in Iachimo's ekphrasis expresses both a capaciousness and an uncertainty inherent to verbal description and the complication of the relocation of the scene. Such equivocation also obscures a simple mapping between the ekphrasis and Enobarbus's speech: Is the "silk and silver" of Iachimo's tapestry a demotion from Cleopatra's "cloth-of-gold of tissue?" Or is it a reflection of the silver oars driving her barge forward? The packed descriptions Iachimo presents, despite their economical phrasing, allow the imagined tapestry to invoke the whole scene from Shakespeare's earlier play, that play in toto, and, of course, the barge ride itself. The episode is a testament to Enobarbus's *enargeia*. Rather than proving that "as a visual medium, *theater overpictures painting*,"[87] at this particular moment the verbal both conjures and replaces the visual, and for a second time. Theater does not overpicture painting at this moment, *words* do. Theater might outdo the plastic arts, but Shakespeare demonstrates that it is by no means limited to the visual axis. Iachimo's memory of an obscured tapestry depicts a moment in the story of Antony and Cleopatra simultaneously available as the memory of another ekphrasis of a singularly theatrical description, itself available only through Enobarbus's speech.

---

84. See *OED*, s.v. "pride, *n*.," defs. 1.2, 1.6a, 1.5, and 1.11, respectively.

85. See *OED*, s.v. "pride, *n*.2."

86. See, for example, J. R. Mulryne, "Cleopatra's Barge and Antony's Body: Italian Sources and English Theatre," in *Shakespeare, Italy, and Intertextuality*, ed. Michele Marrapodi (Manchester: Manchester University Press, 2004), 197–215. See Miller for a discussion of various "processions" within *Antony and Cleopatra* that "allude to the Roman triumph" (*Roman Triumphs*, 133).

87. Tassi, "O'erpicturing Apelles," 295.

The ekphrasis in *Cymbeline* foregrounds absence and fleeting objects by insisting upon an inaccessible, or at least no-longer-material, past. Cleopatra's status as an absent art object in *Cymbeline* baldly reveals Shakespeare's means of negotiating antiquity's history on the Renaissance stage, and his relationship to the classics by placing ancient art treasures in Britain. The past is evoked as a set of ephemeral images that can be brought forth powerfully in the present to the mind's eye, but that depends on the present for that resurrection. Iachimo's memory recalls a moment unavailable to the audience, one that calls forth an image to the mind's eye even as it highlights an ever-receding vision of the actual Cleopatra. In *Antony and Cleopatra*, Cleopatra confronted the imminent future on terms that spoke to this problem. She feared a performance that was both shorthand for and too precariously derived from the present moment (and its popular whims). *Cymbeline* shows us—by removing it from view—how such a fleeting quality also enables Shakespeare to lay claim to his version of antiquity as the durable, official story. Iachimo's advancement of a complex, imagistic summoning occurs in a mere three lines; the rest is *paragone*. At this point, for Shakespeare to call the tapestry a "piece of work / So bravely done, so rich, that it did strive / In workmanship and value" (2.4.72–74) is an exercise in self-congratulation. Iachimo goes on to suggest that the tapestry matches the event—"so rarely and exactly wrought"—a more subtle win for Shakespeare's verbal art as the visual, which overpictured nature, is itself overpictured by Shakespeare's (doubled) words. The playwright's use of ekphrasis not only demonstrates theater's ability to transcend mere visuality, but also uses verbal representation to reveal a complex interplay between the verbal and the visual. Iachimo's paired scenes highlight visuality's capacity to operate within language. Whether or not words emerge victorious over images, the staging of the struggle opens the way to considering the boundless potential of theatrical representation by virtue of a theatrics built from powerful rhetoric. Representation not only mediates our access to classical stories, but also operates beyond the limits of sight and sound.

In *Antony and Cleopatra*, Cleopatra wants to escape an imminent future by returning to an immortalizing past, and to do so she commits suicide. Her outlook invites comparison to Stoic practices of the self for managing time. According to some Stoics, for example, viewing the present from as broad a temporal perspective as possible evacuates the present of its significance. Marcus Aurelius, for example, notes "each of us lives only in the present, this brief moment.... Little the life each lives, ... little even the longest fame hereafter, and even that dependent on a succession of poor mortals."[88] Likewise, he suggests that the present might be isolated from both future and past: "the gulf of time behind and another infinite time in front."[89] Such approaches aim to cultivate an aesthetics of existence via time management—anxiety drains away, and life is restored to its natural beauty. The case for Cleopatra is quite different; because she is subject to an imminent future—because she cannot sever present from future—she adopts another tactic. In this regard, Cleopatra's fear of an imminent future echoes other Shakespearean characters who anticipate their future artistic representations and emphasize the threat inherent in such representations. Tarquin, the central male character in *The Rape of Lucrece*, for example, warns Lucrece that her "trespass" will be "cited up in rhymes, / And sung by children in succeeding times."[90] Tarquin's couplet prefigures the bad verse that Lucrece should fear, that occasions Posthumus's "mock'ry," and that Cleopatra commits suicide to avoid. However, Shakespeare repeatedly suggests that this dark side of the immortality topos—to be remembered badly, or, worse yet, to be forgotten—is the burden of the character, not the playwright. Shakespeare dazzles with the metatheatricality of an *Antony and Cleopatra* precisely because he reconceives and represents these iconic characters just as they worry about their fictive futures. In Cleopatra's case, the formal features of the queen's look forward reveal how this operates even when that future seems absolutely certain. Those instants that had disturbing staying power inform how Shakespeare sets up the question of artistic agency and the matter of whose authority takes precedence.

In comparing Cleopatra's perspective against the models provided by Stoicism, we begin to see how these different strategies also imply different models of aesthetics. In committing suicide, she suggests that she can escape the imminent future in favor of an iteration of an immortal, mythic past. Shakespeare seems to endorse her impulse, but he does so by returning her to a past of his own making. He exercises an analogous control to make claims about his own art. The implications for Shakespeare's dramatic art began to reveal themselves back in Imogen's bedchamber. There, the audience finds a national move doubled: in addition to aligning himself with his fellow Roman, Iachimo employs the plural possessive—"our Tarquin"—in the

---

88. Marcus Aurelius Antoninus, *The Meditations of Marcus Aurelius Antoninus*, ed. R. B. Rutherford and trans. A. S. L. Farquharson (Oxford: Oxford University Press, 1989), 20.

89. Marcus Aurelius, *Meditations*, 33.

90. William Shakespeare, "The Rape of Lucrece," in *The Complete Sonnets and Poems*, ed. Colin Burrow (Oxford: Oxford University Press, 2002), lines 524–25. If she refuses him, Tarquin threatens he will stage Lucrece's dead body in the embrace of a male page and claim their infidelity spurred the slaughter.

British princess's bedroom at the same moment that he invokes one of Shakespeare's own literary creations (*Cymbeline* 2.2.12). Moreover, when Iachimo retells his adventures in the bedroom, he does so in Rome. As Barkan notes,

> [Shakespeare's] audience sits in London watching a bare stage and hears a verbal description of classical pictures in words while, as a perfect complement, Posthumus sits in Rome and is treated to an ekphrastic rendering of the art work decorating Imogen's bedroom back in Britain. In effect, Shakespeare is staging the drama of cultural absence and poetic recuperation in the spaces that separate picture from word and Italy from England.[91]

I would like to push this provocative formulation even further to suggest that Shakespeare forwards a cultural recuperation with national implications. That is, in *Cymbeline*, Shakespeare imagines "cultural absence" in reverse—as Iachimo begins his complicated retelling, he posits England as the original. And what an original it is: not only does the British princess decorate her bedroom with the exploits of Roman myth and history, but they are "bravely done," "rich," produce "wonder" (2.4.73–74). The *paragone*, or competition between verbal and visual representation, communicated by those descriptors—"figures / So likely to report themselves; the cutter / Was as another Nature, dumb; outwent her" (2.4.82–84)—reveals that Iachimo—a character that critics regularly refer to as an early modern Italian despite the play's earlier setting—claims to see art in England that is not merely splendid, but possessed of qualities he "never saw" elsewhere (2.4.82). Iachimo's "never" necessarily includes his native Italy; his report concedes that the most peerless cultural objects and artistic treasures can and do exist in Britain. At the same time that Iachimo's trip to Britain and his memory of it allow Shakespeare to illustrate the boundless potential of theatrical representation, he performs a reversal that surrenders cultural and artistic originality and authority to England instead of Rome.

Shakespeare plays on the fact that remembering art is already at the heart of the project of recovering ruins when he makes the view of Imogen's art dependent on Iachimo's description of it. After all, even when Imogen's art objects exist in England, they do so only in reported speech. *Cymbeline* shows that making the past "a vividly present reality" is not a process unique to memory, but rather one unique to imagination. For the playwright, this might involve the predictive capacity of a formal feature like rhyme, but it escapes, and provides an escape from, the imminent future.

---

91. Leonard Barkan, "Making Pictures Speak: Renaissance Art, Elizabethan Literature, Modern Scholarship," *Renaissance Quarterly* 48, no. 2 (1995): 344.

The Cleopatra tapestry, then, provides an important alternative to the tradition that Shakespeare does not take up—the statue Cleopatra in Octavius Caesar's triumph. Castiglione's ventriloquism aims to spare Cleopatra from humiliation in triumph by allowing the statue the power of reclamation. The Cleopatra tapestry in *Cymbeline* replicates this by highlighting *paragone*. We might profitably consider the Cleopatra tapestry a substitute for that humiliating statue despite the assistance that Castiglione's ventriloquisim attempts to provide it. Rather than supplying her voice, however, Shakespeare's change recasts the potential of artistic afterlife. It is no longer Octavius Caesar's prerogative, but his own. In *Cymbeline*, the "empty spectacle" becomes an absent spectacle, and absence is precisely the resource to which Shakespeare lays claim. By privileging Iachimo's ekphrasis of the tapestry (rather than the stage prop that may or may not have appeared two scenes earlier), Shakespeare refashions the divide between permanence and ephemerality. The imagined tapestry Cleopatra exceeds any statue that would speak on her behalf even as Shakespeare uses her compromised reappearance to affirm his role in providing access to antiquity. The notion of embodying the past—especially the antique past—is under duress just as there is a transitory aspect to these classical artistic treasures, which are available only through Iachimo's words. Imogen's bedroom contains a modern Lucrece, Ovid's *Metamorphoses*, and a tapestry of Cleopatra, all cultural objects familiar to England through Shakespeare's own literary representations of them. Shakespeare demonstrates that ancient Rome is lost equally to Renaissance Italy and Renaissance England, and offers a mode of recuperation that simultaneously frees art from any obligation to pay tribute to antiquity, just as *Cymbeline* cedes Britain the power to *choose* to pay Rome the monetary tribute it seeks.[92] For Shakespeare, elaborating on different kinds of futures allows the playwright to set the terms of its recuperation by thinking about artistic production with respect to temporal categories, even if the imminent future ultimately prompts the most extreme avoidance. The instability of physical ruins presents an opportunity, and it is one upon which *Cymbeline* adeptly capitalizes. If the greatest artistic treasures reside in a British bedroom, they do so because their contents, though remnants of ancient Rome, are properties penned by Shakespeare. The present renovates the past, and the future is under new management.

---

92. And here, as in *Antony and Cleopatra*, the invocation of the *pax romana* also undercuts it. See Paulina Kewes, "'A Fit Memorial for the Times to Come . . .': Admonition and Topical Application in Mary Sidney's *Antonius* and Samuel Daniel's *Cleopatra*," *Review of English Studies* 63, no. 259 (2011): 243–64 for a discussion of period materials that link Octavius to Philip II.

 **Afterword**

Circles of the Future
Memory or Monument in Paradise Lost

Of all the fallen angels in *Paradise Lost*, John Milton registers unique disdain for those who sit "on a hill retired" and occupy themselves

> In thoughts more elevate, and reasoned high
> Of providence, foreknowledge, will, and fate,
> Fixed fate, free will, foreknowledge absolute,
> And found no end, in wandering mazes lost.
> Of good and evil much they argued then,
> Of happiness and final misery,
> Passion and apathy, and glory and shame,
> Vain wisdom all, and false philosophy (2.557–65)[1]

Though Milton derides such rumination as "vain wisdom" and "false philosophy," he also recognizes its perceived merits: "Yet with a pleasing sorcery could charm / Pain for a while or anguish, and excite / Fallacious hope" (2.566–68). The qualifications—"for a while," "fallacious"—do not entirely check the quasi-medicinal enchantments of the falsehood that stems from

---

1. All references are to John Milton, *Paradise Lost*, ed. Alastair Fowler, 2nd ed. (London: Longman Group, 1998).

"discourse...sweet" on topics as broad as "good and evil" (555, 562). Milton's attention falls especially to the conversation concerning divine destiny. In hell, the capacious list of providential subjects under discussion mimics the charges the poet levels against such heady chatter. The "wandering" that he chides resonates in his verse—he introduces a set of terms in one line only to reverse and repeat almost all of them in the next (559–60).[2] That second line, bereft as it is of providence, adopts adjectives that dilate the terms under discussion, but the additions render the repetitions no less perplexing: sorting out the fine distinctions between "foreknowledge" and "foreknowledge absolute" might well require eternity. Indeed, though he goes on to censure the vanity and deception of intellectualizing in general, his targeted distaste for discussions of fate derives not only from their futility, but also, ironically, because such reason "found no end." Such conundrums prove both inscrutable and infinite: lines 559–60 may contain the most "elevate" rubric for discussing the links between present and future, but Milton only mentions temporality insofar as he implies that philosophical contemplation is a poor use of time. The items on the demons' repetitive list treat knowledge of the future, yet Milton's paired lines emphasize the "wandering," timeless aspect of such contemplation. Such spurious debating may waste time, but these ruined souls have plenty to spare, and the speculations that draw Milton's opprobrium rather conspicuously overlap with motivating preoccupations of the epic itself.

Why, then, does Milton dismiss these cerebral gambols by employing both the language and poetic structure of error? The poem repeatedly revisits the problematics that these ruminative fallen angels introduce. The question of what is to come, and the inevitability of that future, is marked as a contemplative activity that delays progress and squanders time, a concern plausibly relevant to the relation between Milton's subject matter and his manner of telling it.[3] Milton, writing late if not last in the line of English Renaissance poets, chooses and justifies an epic on the Fall of Man. It is difficult to imagine a story with a more straightforward or more familiar teleology, and *Paradise Lost* labors under the burden of the inevitable ending it began by announcing. Yet Milton simultaneously manages to render epic progress dilatory as he relates the first three chapters of the book of Genesis in a poem over 10,000 lines long.[4]

---

2. I am indebted to Jeff Dolven for this insight.

3. In *Epic Romance: Homer to Milton* (Oxford: Clarendon Press, 1993), 268, Colin Burrow regards these philosophizing fallen angels as inhabiting the "metaphorical" version of "familiar spaces of romance" that have been "attenuated into speculation."

4. On the differences, often self-conscious, between epic and romance in the Renaissance, and the ways that romance is defined in the course of *Paradise Lost*, see Burrow, *Epic Romance*, esp. 3, 268, 273–74. Burrow argues that in *Paradise Lost*, Milton productively revises the romance tradition (5–6,

The fallen angels' endless contemplation initiates an emphasis that runs throughout the poem: pondering temporal matters occasions a loss of time. Yet, even amid the poem's interest in causation and inevitability, and the intellectual disorientation associated with matters of futurity, *Paradise Lost* maintains a sense of creative possibility and narrative potential. The poet links such matters more directly to his own narrative at the opening of book 9:

> No more of talk where God or angel guest
> With man, as with his friend, familiar used
> To sit indulgent, and with him partake
> Rural repast, permitting him the while
> Venial discourse unblamed: I now must change
> Those notes to tragic. (9.1–6)

Milton's conversion—"notes to tragic"—inspires a lengthy justification of his "argument" by asserting its preeminence. In particular, he sets his own enterprise apart from the works of his literary predecessors not merely to suggest that the religious nature of his task lends it greater weight, but also because its trajectory differs from the genre of romance.[5] He casts such generic aspersions even on the *Iliad*, claiming his is a "sad task, yet argument / Not less but more heroic than the wrath / Of stern Achilles on his foe pursued / Thrice fugitive about Troy wall" (9.13–16). Alastair Fowler points out that Milton implies the superiority of his Christian epic by purposefully choosing the Homeric episode "selected by Aristotle to exemplify epic's incorporation of what in another genre would be ridiculous."[6] Likewise, Milton disparages mythical subjects and mortal wars by offering a catalogue of images typical of chivalric romance:

> races and games,
> Or tilting furniture, emblazoned shields,

274–75). In *Inescapable Romance: Studies in the Poetics of a Mode* (Princeton, NJ: Princeton University Press, 1979), 128, Patricia A. Parker argues that the poem, despite Milton's repudiation of romance, "takes romance beyond the strictly generic." For a discussion of defining features of romance in terms of "error" and "wandering," see Parker, 140–41.

5. As Barbara Kiefer Lewalski notes in *Paradise Lost and the Rhetoric of Literary Forms* (Princeton, NJ: Princeton University Press, 1985), 220, the epic here turns "from the pastoral scene of 'rural repast' and the comedic symposium of 'venial discourse,'" but Milton's attention also sets heroic action in contradistinction to the genre of romance.

6. Milton, *Paradise Lost*, 468n16. For an alternative account, which locates the difference between "private life" and the "public, political world," see David Quint, *Epic and Empire: Politics and Generic Form from Virgil to Milton* (Princeton, NJ: Princeton University Press, 1993), 282–83. Quint argues that Milton "famously bids farewell to the traditional epic of war in the *recusatio* at the beginning of Book 9" in favor of a "private realm."

> Impresses quaint, caparisons and steeds;
> Bases and tinsel trappings, gorgeous knights
> At joust and tournament; then marshalled feast
> Served up in hall with sewers, and seneschals. (9.33–38)

This is not, he contends, the kind of activity that "justly gives heroic name/ To person or to poem" (9.40–41). The poet's vexation emphasizes the elongation of pace in these "less...heroic" works—"thrice fugitive about," "long and tedious" (30). Indeed, his critique of demonic musings about fate and futurity and of the literature of time spent going in circles seems to be cut from the same logical cloth. Though the conversation has changed to the judgment and repetition of heroic deeds, as with his philosophers, Milton seems attuned to the passage of time, unsettled to find it wasted.[7]

How seriously are we to take Milton's generic distinctions at the moment he suggests he will change the type of his tune—reaching for his tragic pipe in a vocabulary that recalls the turn to epic in the works of many of his forebears—to recount the story of "man's first disobedience" (1.1)?[8] Even if we have yet to reach the advertised event, hasn't precisely that tragedy been the purpose of the poem since its opening line? Milton's countless poetic debts to both classical epic and Renaissance romance render his seeming derision doubtful. He sets his own "higher argument" apart from the slow dalliance he ascribes to romance in the same set of lines that abruptly remind us of the end of his story, emphasizing that all other narrative options have been foreclosed. It is, therefore, particularly striking to find that Satan must be incorporated into the melody's purposeful minor key. Achilles may have "his foe pursued / Thrice fugitive about Troy wall" (9.15–16), but in the time since he was first detected in and tossed out of Eden, Satan has done the famous Greek four better:

> The space of seven continued nights he rode
> With darkness, thrice the equinoctial line
> He circled, four times crossed the car of Night
> From pole to pole, traversing each colure; (9.63–66)

Satan more than doubles Achilles's loops, yet like those philosophical fallen angels, his circles are grand gestures that do nothing more than spin his

---

[7]. For a discussion of the persistent concern with wasting time, as well as an ungenerous attitude toward romance, in Milton's juvenilia, see Burrow, *Epic Romance*, 246–47.

[8]. Stanley Eugene Fish provides a comprehensive and influential account of the tension between the poem's announced teleology and its effect on the fallen reader in *Surprised by Sin: The Reader in Paradise Lost*, (1967; repr., Berkeley: University of California Press, 1971).

wheels.⁹ The Argument to book 9 recounts that "Satan having compassed the earth, with mediated guile returns as a mist by night into Paradise," but the summary feels too determined, and the poem belies the notion that Satan's compassing was a prerequisite for action. Milton's verse marks the orbiting idle and uneventful—Satan does not sternly pursue any foe; he merely passes the time in which he waits.¹⁰ His motion recalls not only Achilles, but also scenes from *Gerusalemme Liberata* and *Orlando Furioso*. In these Italian romances, however, knights do not circle the globe because they are "full of anguish driven" (9.62), but rather because circumnavigation affords an opportunity to trumpet and celebrate New World discovery and imperial destiny.¹¹

The book of *Paradise Lost* that recounts the Fall denigrates romance in favor of the "higher argument" of "patience and heroic martyrdom / Unsung" (9.42, 32–33), elevating and linking epic progress with tragic action.¹² Yet, in the wake of a discussion of the frivolities of lesser poetic subjects, Milton reveals that Satan's intermediary days have been spent in a circular motion that seems to match the course of romance even if his travels prove markedly less productive than comparable journeys. On the one hand, as Milton gears up to march toward his inevitable Fall, Satan's "meanwhile" trajectory seems both risible and superfluous. On the other hand, a Satan whose antics echo the frivolity of "tinsel trappings,"¹³ absorbed in the errancy that Milton aligns with both romance and contemplation, seems wonderfully harmless. The poet's severe distinctions between "wandering" motion and "heroic" drive appear to privilege moving forward toward an end point, but they also admit of some sobering merits of the relatively benign safety of lingering.

Milton waffles on the danger and even importance of intermediary space. For the poem's demons, philosophizing and circling both immorally and innocuously waste time; for Adam, however, the interval between Eve's "fatal trespass" (9.889) and his own marks the crucial reckoning between "free will" and "fixed fate." Remarkably, Adam's decision to join Eve coincides

---

9. Anne Ferry offers an extended analysis of circling in the poem in *Milton's Epic Voice: the Narrator in "Paradise Lost"* (Cambridge, MA: Harvard University Press, 1963).

10. For a discussion of Satan as the central figure in an "Odyssean narrative pattern," and his first foray into Eden as a romance sequence, see Lewalski, *Rhetoric of Literary Forms*, 65–71 and 176–77.

11. See Ludovico Ariosto, *Orlando Furioso* 15.18–46; and Torquato Tasso, *Gerusalemme Liberata* 15.7–41. For a discussion of the connections between Satan's journey to earth in book 2 and Tasso's "boat of romance," see Quint, *Epic and Empire*, 253–56.

12. See Lewalski, *Rhetoric of Literary Forms*, 220–21 for a discussion of the breakdown between the tragic (books 9 and 10) and the Christian heroic (books 11 and 12).

13. The invocation of the phrase "tinsel trappings" may be read as equivocal: it appears twice in *The Faerie Queene*, used to describe the horses of both Duessa and Florimell (1.2.13, 3.1.15), leaving the attentive reader to wonder whether the repetition suggests the precision of Duessa's disguise or calls Florimell's chastity more forcefully into question.

with his consideration of the future: "Should God create another Eve, and I / Another rib afford, yet loss of thee / Would never from my heart; no no" (9.911–13).[14] His use of the conditional conjures an imagined future blighted by the act of looking back, and the prospect of retrospect overwhelms Adam as his passionate *epizeuxis* of negation—"no no"—attests.[15] It is striking that a prelapsarian Adam can even conceive of the proleptic burden of loss, and though he does not bite the "fair enticing fruit" for another eighty-three lines, his vision of a future moment consumed with mourning for the past suggests an equivalence between deciding to fall and falling.[16]

Adam's decision gives rise to the poem's most pronounced interstitial space: the first couple lingers, though fallen, in Eden.[17] When God devises their expulsion, his rationale seems markedly in keeping with Milton's depictions of delay: "Lest therefore his now bolder hand / Reach also of the tree of life, and eat, / And live for ever, dream at least to live / For ever, to remove him I decree" (11.93–96). Disobedience may well be a slippery slope, but God seems less concerned that Adam's "now bolder hand" will sin again than he is worried about the consequences: gaining immortality, or even the "dream" of it, occasions preemptive expulsion.[18] God does not elaborate on the dangers of eternal life, taking for granted the perils of merely desiring a time that finds "no end."

Michael's directive that Adam and Eve must leave the garden is met with genuine surprise, and an eavesdropping Eve admits that she "had hope to spend, / Quiet though sad, the respite of that day / That must be mortal to us both" (11.271–73). Adam, by contrast, draws an elaborate picture of a postlapsarian Paradise:

> This most afflicts me, that departing hence,
> As from his face I shall be hid, deprived

---

14. Lewalski puts this internal monologue in the category of the poem's "tragic lyrics" (*Rhetoric of Literary Forms*, 247). For a reading of this scene in terms of Adam's sympathy that defines *Paradise Lost*'s particular brand of romance, see Burrow, *Epic Romance*, 284.

15. In *Is Milton Better than Shakespeare?* (Cambridge, MA: Harvard University Press, 2008), Nigel Smith points out the lack of verb that signals Adam's sense of loss and argues that Adam and Eve deal with a bond built of "material coextension" (54–56).

16. Adam's statement also expresses the peculiar ripple effect of Eve's transgression: if her Fall brings death into the world, those consequences reach even the potential unfallen Adam who will experience grief. Parker places the moment when the Fall is "already a foregone conclusion" a bit earlier (*Inescapable Romance*, 134).

17. For a discussion of interval, see Leslie Brisman, *Milton's Poetry of Choice and Its Romantic Heirs* (Ithaca, NY: Cornell University Press, 1973). See also Parker, *Inescapable Romance*, 128.

18. Smith points out that Milton adds God's mention of the "dream" of immortality to the moment from Genesis, even though that dream "seems to repeat how things were before the Fall anyway" (*Is Milton Better*, 139).

> His blessèd count'nance; here I could frequent,
> With worship, place by place where he vouchsafed
> Presence divine, and to my sons relate;
> On this mount he appeared, under this tree
> Stood visible, among these pines his voice
> I heard, here with him at this fountain talked:
> So many grateful altars I would rear
> Of grassy turf, and pile up every stone
> Of lustre from the brook, in memory,
> Or monument to ages, and thereon
> Offer sweet-smelling gums and fruits and flowers:
> In yonder nether world where shall I seek
> His bright appearances, or footstep trace? (11.315–29)

What begins as a lament over a lack of communion with God quickly devolves into an obsessive vision of melancholic loss. Adam's most obvious blunder comes from his assumption that "Presence divine" is materially linked to Eden. Michael corrects his impulse to "frequent . . . place by place" by assuring him that God is not subject to such geographical limitations: "[S]urmise not then / His presence to these narrow bounds confined / Of Paradise or Eden" (11.340–42). Though Michael's correction aptly addresses Adam's spatial emphasis on "here," it does not answer every facet of Adam's long question. Rather, the speech contains an undercurrent—a particular mode of expressing sorrow—that vindicates the epic's discomfort with wandering and stagnation. At first glance, his sad soliloquy seems to engage in a poignant anticipatory nostalgia. He imagines the stories he would "to [his] sons relate" of his precious encounters with God in a prelapsarian Eden. Yet, Adam's proleptic wistfulness does not inspire action in the present moment. Rather, his proposed future narrative stagnates; Adam's is a vision of future memory gone horribly wrong: looking forward to looking back has been stripped of both its pleasure and its inspiration. He laments a lost opportunity to ruminate on a past that is already irrecoverable. In the literature of Renaissance England, anticipatory nostalgia marks a mode of considering temporality that gains purchase because of a surprising, if not counterintuitive, sympathetic identification between now and later: the future is characterized not by radical difference, but by the underlying premise that the present and future will maintain a set of common values and assumptions. Adam's vision pushes such a conception a step too far—his conditional future imagines days ahead filled with precisely the same longing for the past that he experiences as he speaks.[19] We will eventually reach a vantage point from which, as Patricia Parker puts it, the Fall is "revealed retrospectively to have been 'fortunate,'" but in the interstitial garden, Adam's present and future wander toward a paralyzing fixation on the past.[20] Despite the mention of future sons and future narratives, his speech presents a dream of stagnation, a desire to dwell forever in a single collection of memories set in a prelapsarian past that can never be recuperated.

Adam's vision uncannily fulfills God's prediction that if he remained in the garden, his heart would become "variable and vain / Self-left" (11.92–93). His "place by place" inventory of Eden ostensibly catalogues God's appearances, but in short space he crowds the memory of these divine cameos by supplying himself a share of the spotlight in his own intended stories: "his voice / I heard"; "with him ... talked." He also emphasizes his own role in the construction of Edenic altars—"So many grateful altars I would rear"—without hesitating to consider the consequences: his plans would physically change Paradise, tearing up tufts of grass, and "pil[ing] up every stone / Of lustre" in the course of construction.

The imagined altars of an impossible future are shrines to Adam's memories and personal experience.[21] Not only are they inappropriate in Paradise, but they also ironically change Eden despite their primary objective of memorializing Adam's unfallen encounters with God. Beyond taking insistently material memories so far that they physically reshape the garden, Adam's memories of Paradise *in* Paradise fail to recapture the experience of the prelapsarian world. Moreover, his account of what he would have done itself resides in an interstitial space—his imagined future is not the substance of an Edenic future perfect, but of an infected Eden. These proposed memorial activities are hard matter for the future perfect not only because they are expressed in the conditional, but also because they can exist only in the temporary intermediary state between Fall and expulsion.[22] Adam's

---

19. Tellingly, Adam's speech picks up Satan's love of the counterfactual, as at 4.58–60. He echoes with striking precision Satan's conditional account of Eden at 9.114–23: "With what delight could I have walked ...," though Satan's vision of himself in Eden is both not as troubling as Adam's, and, as Catherine Belsey points out in *John Milton: Language, Gender, Power* (Oxford: Basil Blackwell, 1988), 87, a "romance landscape."

20. Parker, *Inescapable Romance*, 141.

21. See Parker for a discussion of books 5–8 as the poem's true "space for reflection" (*Inescapable Romance*, 143).

22. A prelapsarian "will have done" seems plausible, but a "would have done" is considerably harder to imagine. On the other hand, critics have pointed out that Milton's Eden even before the Fall boasts characteristics not entirely expected. Thomas Greene has called it "a little enervating," and A. Bartlett Giamatti has noted a "lack of vitality," using words like "slow," "aimless," "drooping," and "sluggish" in his description of the garden. See Thomas Greene, *The Descent from Heaven: A*

reverie—his absorption in what he "would have done"—is fundamentally fallen, both for its grammar and because he catalogues activities he would never have done—would never even have *thought* of doing—in a prelapsarian state.[23] As with the moments that precede his fall, it is striking that Adam can articulate this imagined, if impossible, Edenic future within the garden. His lament forces Eden itself to share the burden of the weight of the Fall, at least temporarily, as notions like nostalgia and loss indicate and create a tainted, postlapsarian Paradise.

On the brink of Michael's lengthy prophecy of the often painful days ahead, the gravest threat in Adam's soliloquy is not to Eden, but to the future. There is something grotesquely out of joint about those "grateful altars," not just because of their destructive manner of memorialization, but also because they bespeak a future consumed by meditation on the past. Adam projects a future devoid of possibility that boasts looking back as its principal activity. His claim that he will build these shrines "in memory, / Or monument to ages" evinces two separate, temporally distinct options: though both "memory" and "monument" invoke the relationship between past, present, and future, Adam's syntax aligns "memory" with what has come before, while the "monument to ages" imagines new construction for use by afterlivers in aftertimes. The "grateful altars" reared "in memory" form a completed thought, one that is only reopened at the start of the next line when the alternate option—"Or monument to ages"—is introduced. Both the conjunction "Or" and the future-oriented modifier "to ages" stress the difference between the recursive aspect of memory and the forward-looking aspect of memorialization. But Adam, despite his syntax, has it wrong. The work that goes into differentiating between "memory" and "monument" is futile: his versions of the past, whether now or later, are identical. Far from being a hinge between distinct temporalities, the imagined altar collapses the two temporal registers; no matter *when* he is, Adam is always looking back on the same prelapsarian past. As a result, looking forward to looking back provides no change, no pleasure of an imagined nostalgia, but rather a dead-end

---

Study in Epic Continuity (New Haven, CT: Yale UP, 1963), 402; and A. Bartlett Giamatti, *The Earthly Paradise and the Renaissance Epic* (Princeton, NJ: Princeton University Press, 1966), 303. Giamatti also argues that "within the garden, the potentiality for evil exists by the very presence of the forbidden fruit" (307). See also "Reforming the Garden: The Experimentalist Eden and *Paradise Lost*," *ELH* 72 (2005): 23–78, in which Joanna Picciotto argues that prelapsarian Paradise is clearly unperfected and characterized by labor. For a discussion of work in the garden and early modern gardening as recapturing Eden, see William Poole, *Milton and the Idea of the Fall* (Cambridge: Cambridge University Press, 2005), 11–12.

23. See, for example, Fowler's notes on the inappropriateness of fire and burned sacrifices in Eden (Milton, *Paradise Lost*, 614n327).

future still concentrated on recapturing the same loss, even if it includes a few new physical structures. He laments the lost opportunity for a future that is not only impossible, but also evacuated of possibility.[24]

Among the various strands of stagnation, wandering, and wasted time in *Paradise Lost*, it is the future stripped of potential that merits expulsion. Adam may long to spend eternity moping, but neither God nor Milton will support the endeavor. The poet's glance at a future compromised and corrupted by an obsession with the past, heightened by the inclusion of the word "monument," portrays a postlapsarian garden that bears a suspicious resemblance to Rome. Milton's disavowal of a fixation on an idealized, ineffable past in a landscape filled with memories and ruins—and a future engaged in the manufacture of *spolia*—adumbrates the dangers of the Renaissance interest in antiquity. In Adam's soliloquy, Milton articulates a threat inherent in a future spent looking back, in a future without possibility.

The prophetic history with which Michael responds might suggest another version of the same thing—an apocalyptic, if ultimately redemptive, future course already laid. It may look forward more earnestly, but it similarly curbs possibility. Adam certainly draws this lesson, voicing a pointed aversion: "Better had I / Lived ignorant of future" (11.763–64). The narration of this history takes up most of the poem's final two books, and it has long been a source of controversy for Milton's readers, offering what C. S. Lewis notoriously called an "untransmuted lump of futurity."[25] These books have been viewed as a departure from the poem on stylistic and aesthetic terms— Lewis also called them "inartistic."[26] For a crude version of this charge, we might compare Michael to Raphael, who throws into high relief the former's harsh lack of lyricism. Sent by God to "reveal / To Adam what shall come in future days" (11.113–14), Michael repeats this directive almost verbatim: "I am sent / To show thee what shall come in future days" (11.356–57). His narration of history delivers the future in two lumps. In the first, he silently interprets God's instruction to "reveal" as an invitation to "show." The series of visions that follow is recorded through an interchange between Michael's

---

24. Burrow makes a compelling case for the "election of the Son" as a positive, though complicated, treatment of the future predicated on the proleptic assurance of his "extraordinary future merit" (*Epic Romance*, 261).

25. C. S. Lewis, *A Preface to Paradise Lost* (London: Oxford University Press, 1942), 125.

26. As is well known, Joseph Addison writes in 1712 in the *Spectator* that the final two books are "not generally reckoned among the most shining Books of the poem," diagnosing that here "the Author has been so attentive to his Divinity, that he has neglected his Poetry" (as qtd. in Fish, *Doing What Comes Naturally: Change, Rhetoric, and the Practice of Theory in Literary and Legal Studies* [Durham, NC: Duke University Press, 1989], 251–52). Fish brilliantly recounts the fate of these books of the poem in the service of a history of literary criticism (*Doing*, 247–93).

repeated imperatives—"prepare" and "behold"—and the narrator's past tense verbs. When Michael eventually "perceive[s] / [Adam's] mortal sight to fail," he changes tack, declaring that "[h]enceforth what is to come I will relate" (12.8–11). The second lump relates biblical history in the future tense with the word "shall" in particularly heavy rotation.

By turns, Michael's prophecy misleads, alarms, chastens, and soothes Adam, but what accounts for the distinctive tenor of these lines? *Paradise Lost* elsewhere recounts and innovates familiar history without being accused of diminished quality. The two-part structure of Michael's narration could even testify to an experimental aspect of the straightforward content—the archangel revises his strategy in a manner reflected in Michael's grammar. Barbara Kiefer Lewalski has argued that "the prophecy is a highly complex aesthetic structure, organized so as to project the great themes of the poem on the epic screen of all human history, and at the same time, by means of this projection, to promote Adam's own development as a dramatic character."[27] However, this account of the prophecy's aesthetic does not say much about its details. As Stanley Fish has claimed, such a perspective reflects the logic underlying the rising fortune of the poem's final two books in twentieth-century criticism. In his view, they register "a change from the celebration of infinite variety (regarded by earlier critics as one of Milton's glories) to a celebration of a single monolithic vision."[28]

There is certainly ample evidence that the poem throws up resistance to any such unity. But what do we gain by returning our attention to that "infinite variety"? Despite troubled glances at a straightforward future, Milton does not settle on this version of aftertimes. Rather, the poem ends with the vocabulary of romance, and, in so doing, continues a long string of vacillations about time and its circles. For example, Sin's offspring—"yelling monsters" that "surround" her—are "hourly conceived / And hourly born" (2.795–97), providing what John Rumrich has termed a "chronological index of an unremitting process of terror and sorrow."[29] By contrast, in narrating the war in heaven, Raphael casually mentions that heaven too has "evening" and "morn," though in this context cyclical time is decorative: "We ours for change delectable, not need" (5.628–29). Sin pointedly recalls Spenser's Error and that monster's "endless train" in a manner that reactivates

---

27. Barbara Kiefer Lewalski, "Structure and the Symbolism of Vision in Michael's Prophecy, *Paradise Lost*, Books XI–XII," *Philological Quarterly* 42 (1963): 25.

28. Fish, *Doing*, 273.

29. John Rumrich, "Things of Darkness: Sin, Death, Chaos," in *The Cambridge Companion to Paradise Lost*, ed. Louis Schwartz (New York: Cambridge University Press, 2014), 33.

the earlier allegory and its foregrounded link to wandering. But this also means that Milton adapts a theological category into a romance trope. In this way, Sin, like Satan circling the Earth, is importantly neutralized, if not rendered benign.[30]

Milton's invocation at the start of book 7 seeks Urania's assistance to avoid poetic wandering ("Lest from this flying steed unreined . . . / on the Aleian field I fall / Erroneous, there to wander and forlorn" [7.17–20]). Yet, Milton's closing lines contain none of the disdain for romance and wasted time that the poem earlier expressed. Instead, wandering is recuperated as a mode of possibility. The prophecy allows Adam to relinquish his insupportable plans for looking back. To be sure, Adam and Eve remain aware of, and painfully influenced by, an irrecoverable past, but they exit the poem possessed of possibility "with wandering steps and slow" (12.648).[31] The fallen angels with which I began "found no end, in wandering mazes lost"—a description that the poem's close recalls. Those fruitless contemplations repeated and reversed their subject matter, but providence silently fell out of the equation between one line and the next. Milton's ending echo restores this omission:"The world was all before them, where to choose / Their place of rest, and providence their guide" (12.646–47). If providence and wandering are implicitly at odds, which prevails at the poem's end? The circles to which I have drawn attention have previously been marshaled as evidence for the poem's endorsement of providence. Edward Tayler privileges "the pattern of providential time" to argue that the "cycle of loss and restoration" signals "the circular movement from Eden to Eden."[32] The circles of romance might merely restore us to this deterministic ending.[33] However, the ubiquity of wandering suggests that it is

---

30. See Rumrich for a reading that traces this episode to show how Milton's God carefully *plots* disobedience, as well as the implications of Sin and Death for Milton's theodicy ("Things of Darkness," esp. 34–37).

31. Parker argues in favor of a deconstructive open-endedness in the poem, especially at its close, citing the activity of "standing" as an especially poignant articulation of "possibilities held open" (*Inescapable Romance*, 157–58). I would add that part of this sense of possibility and potential grows out of a conclusion of the wallowing in the past of which the poem seems incredibly wary; the ending, as a result, moves freely forward as the poem has accommodated and appropriately ordered the obstacles associated with both contemplating the past and facing a prewritten future.

32. Edward W. Tayler, *Milton's Poetry: Its Development in Time* (Pittsburgh: Duquesne University Press, 1979), 71, 63.

33. Fish's account is especially right in this regard. For example, J. Martin Evans's account of the "Miltonic moment" is alluring because he draws attention to Milton's "powerful sense of *intermediacy*," claiming that "nothing is more characteristic of [Milton's] works than their open-endedness" (*The Miltonic Moment* [Lexington: University Press of Kentucky, 1998], 4–5). However, what he actually means to recapture in Milton is a sense of transition, and that transition has a clear teleology that progresses from humanism to Christianity. Gordon Teskey has recently and provocatively asked, "Why is it that when writing about *Paradise Lost* we end up writing about modernity?" (*Delirious*

importantly difficult to pull a totalizing account out of *Paradise Lost*. Even if the mention of providence may preemptively sanction the first couple's errant motion, it does not erase it. Milton's poem bumps along to "wandering" and lands on singularity: "Through Eden took their solitary way" (12.648–49). The poem opens up its emphasis to include potential and possibility, the uncharted, boundless space that literature creates.[34]

I want to be careful to register this option without merely substituting one totalizing vision for another. Adam and Eve's "wandering steps and slow" might merit comparison to Sidney's "dulled" pen, but they are not identical to it. The writing destined to fade or blot in the *Old Arcadia* does not convey the same message about materiality as Spenser's either-or material mystery at the end of Arthur's treasured book.[35] Shakespeare's reclamation of artistic originality and authority from both the past and Italy may resemble Spenser's creation of the British past or Milton's aversion to *spolia*, but each operates independently even if they are powerful in aggregate. In the course of this book, I have discovered a persistent dynamic in which loss functions more readily as an equalizer than a barrier. The transit, through real or imagined art objects, between loss and memory surprisingly urges a replacement of the familiar story of rupture and ruin that privileges melancholy. That replacement, however, does not trumpet progress as the engine and destiny of the future. Rather, I have attempted to recover less freighted perspectives, ones less weighed down by the burden of anxious influence and less precious as tender buds in the garden of enlightenment. In Renaissance England,

---

Milton: The Fate of the Poet in Modernity [Cambridge, MA: Harvard University Press, 2006], 62). The answer he provides is harsh: "The modernist interpreter, lacking any secure ground on which to set up a monument to the modernist interpreter, is able to open a modern world in the reflection of texts and to see it, for the first time, as home" (62). Another kind of answer lies in the reception history of books 11 and 12 that Fish traces. He points, for example, to Geoffrey Hartman's classic essay "Milton's Counterplot" *ELH* 25, no. 1 (1958): 1–12, which makes "imperturbable Providence" the hero of the poem. Ironically, when celebrated by critics, providence is celebrated as a narrative of progress. According to this line of thinking, Michael's prophecy is skillfully crafted to shape and educate a better Adam, which is the defense offered to rehabilitate the maligned books. See Fish, *Doing*, 271–73.

34. My sense of Milton's project dovetails with Burrow's claim that Milton's "goal that flees him as he pursues, is the desirable and unattainable fact of becoming a poet writing a romance which is not quite a romance" (*Epic Romance*, 250). However, Burrow provides an alternative account of the effects on Milton's writing and future in terms of his literary debts and interest in the past at 284–89. For an alternative account of these closing lines as "ominous," see Parker, *Inescapable Romance*, 142.

35. The afterlives of these texts and their editions, whether altered or incomplete like *The Faerie Queene* and the *Arcadia*, lost and possibly damaged like *Titus Andronicus*, frustratingly singular like *Antony and Cleopatra* or *Cymbeline*, or carefully reordered like *Paradise Lost*, offer intriguing analogies to some of the dynamics charted here, but do not supplant them. For a compelling reflection on the implications of material study and its editorial practice, see Leah S. Marcus, *Unediting the Renaissance: Shakespeare, Marlowe, Milton* (London and New York: Routledge, 1996).

modernity was not only not inevitable, but also importantly not imaginable in our terms or even with that word. This is, in part, a technicality—"modern" was already actively in use in the period's vocabulary and in the way that sixteenth- and seventeenth-century subjects viewed themselves.[36] But it offers an important reminder that we must reconsider any assumption that the writers under examination represent an embryonic form of our concept of the modern. In *Untold Futures* I have attempted to recover a discursive space that dislodges the future from view if we attempt to approach it from either of the outer poles, the "never been or ever been." The ending of *Paradise Lost*, for example, furnishes an alternative to obstacles associated with contemplating the past on the one hand and facing a prewritten future on the other. These texts demand that we open the field to a new focus. Looking to the future urges us to rethink our approaches to and assumptions about the past. It also asks us to articulate both what we think we are looking for in the archive and in what sense literary texts furnish that archive.

In drawing attention to questions that have most profoundly shaped our practice by underpinning our conceptions of periodization, the readings I have offered speak to a more urgent methodological concern. These chapters recover an array of futures by foregrounding and seeking out the knowledge that literature produces. In so doing, I have attempted to show that we must reconsider our tendency to suppose that only other explanatory frameworks, whether historical, theological, or theoretical, can supply that knowledge. To the extent that this suggestion amplifies the place of the aesthetic, I also hasten to add that this does not mean that literature is a space of retreat from politics. By the same token, however, imaginative literature is not merely valuable when rendered legible (usually via paraphrase) as an allegory for or commentary upon history or politics. As Simon Jarvis has powerfully suggested, poems should not be "invited to display only those ideas that a philosopher or theorist could have made earlier," but rather to "operate across a deep unlikeness of kind."[37]

Milton's Adam and Eve do not give Eden up lightly. Michael has to hurry "[o]ur lingering parents" along; no sooner does he disappear than they look back (12.637–41). But eventually, they look forward, and as they do so, they evince an author attuned to the temporal signatures employed by

---

36. For a useful discussion of the term, see Margreta de Grazia, Hamlet *without Hamlet* (Cambridge: Cambridge University Press, 2007).

37. Simon Jarvis, "For a Poetics of Verse," *PMLA* 125, no. 4 (2010): 931. I take Teskey to be saying something similar when he writes that "poetics addresses itself to questions concerning how works are made, how they function according to the principles on which they are made, and what the differences are that make a difference between them" (*Delirious Milton*, 55).

his immediate literary forebears. Like those earlier writings, his verse registers an awareness of time and its own place in time. In Milton's poem, and especially in its ending, we catch glimpses of the archive of formulations and literary strategies I have traced in *Untold Futures*: the confrontation between a present and future self that calls into question subjective fantasies of stasis; the power *poiesis* has to unsettle the future; the danger of relying uncritically on the classical past; the grammatical determination of anticipatory nostalgia and the possible futures it brings to light; the manner in which artistic production both manages access to the past and provides access even to modest futures. The future anticipated by *Paradise Lost* advances that same desire for a continuous productive retrospection that is not trapped by its indebtedness to the models of the past, but rather embraces and exhibits the purpose and potential of literature, and carries it forward. In this regard, Milton's poem does not settle the questions at stake in these artistic experiments. Rather, it provokes their renovation and the continued investigation of how, alongside competing models of and resources for certainty, artistic production privileges, enables, and offers unique access to a future that is always untold.

Bibliography

Adelman, Janet. *The Common Liar: An Essay on* Antony and Cleopatra. New Haven, CT: Yale University Press, 1973.
Alpers, Paul. *What Is Pastoral?* Chicago: University of Chicago Press, 1996.
Anderton, Lawrence. *The English Nunne.* London, 1642.
Antoninus, Marcus Aurelius. *The Meditations of Marcus Aurelius Antoninus.* Edited by R. B. Rutherford. Translated by A. S. L. Farquharson. Oxford: Oxford University Press, 1989.
Ariosto, Ludovico. *Orlando Furioso.* Translated by Guido Waldman. Oxford: Oxford University Press, 1974.
Arnold, Oliver. *The Third Citizen: Shakespeare's Theater and the Early Modern House of Commons.* Baltimore: Johns Hopkins University Press, 2007.
Arnovick, Leslie K. *The Development of Future Constructions in English: The Pragmatics of Modal and Temporal* Will *and* Shall *in Middle English.* New York: Peter Lang Publishing, 1990.
Astell, Ann W. "Sidney's Didactic Method in the *Old Arcadia.*" *Studies in English Literature* 24, no. 1 (1984): 39–51.
Astington, John H., ed. *The Development of Shakespeare's Theater.* New York: AMS Press, 1992.
Attridge, Derek. *Peculiar Language: Literature as Difference from the Renaissance to James Joyce.* London: Methuen, 1988.
Augustine, Saint. *Confessions.* Translated by Henry Chadwick. Oxford: Oxford University Press, 1991.
———. *On Christian Teaching.* Translated by R. P. H. Green. Oxford: Oxford University Press, 1997.
Austin, J. L. *How to Do Things with Words.* Oxford: Clarendon Press, 1962.
Bacon, Francis. "Of Parents and Children" In *The Major Works*, edited by Brian Vickers, 351–52. Oxford: Oxford University Press, 1996.
Baker, David J. *Between Nations: Shakespeare, Spenser, Marvell, and the Question of Britain.* Stanford, CA: Stanford University Press, 1997.
Baker, J. H. *An Introduction to English Legal History.* 4th ed. London: Butterworths & Co, 2002.
———. "New Light on *Slade's Case*: Part I—The Manuscript Reports." *Cambridge Law Journal* 29, no. 1 (1971): 51–67.
———. "New Light on *Slade's Case*: Part II." *Cambridge Law Journal* 29, no. 2 (1971): 213–36.
Bakhtin, M. M. *The Dialogic Imagination: Four Essays.* Translated by Caryl Emerson and Michael Holquist. Austin: University of Texas Press, 1981.

Baldwin, T. W. *William Shakspere's Small Latine & Lesse Greeke.* 2 vols. Urbana: University of Illinois Press, 1944.
Balmford, James. *A Short and Plaine Dialogve Concerning the vnlawfulnes of playing at Cards or Tables, or any other game consisting in chance.* London, 1593.
Barish, Jonas. "Shakespearean Violence: A Preliminary Survey." In *Violence in Drama*, edited by James Redmond, 101–21. Cambridge: Cambridge University Press, 1991.
Barkan, Leonard. *The Gods Made Flesh: Metamorphosis & the Pursuit of Paganism.* New Haven, CT: Yale University Press, 1986.
———. "Making Pictures Speak: Renaissance Art, Elizabethan Literature, Modern Scholarship." *Renaissance Quarterly* 48, no. 2 (1995): 326–51.
———. *Unearthing the Past: Archaeology and Aesthetics in the Making of Renaissance Culture.* New Haven, CT: Yale University Press, 1999.
Barker, Francis. "Treasures of Culture: *Titus Andronicus* and Death by Hanging." In *The Production of English Renaissance Culture*, edited by David Lee Miller, Sharon O'Dair, and Harold Weber, 226–61. Ithaca, NY: Cornell University Press, 1994.
Barret, J. K. "The Crowd in Imogen's Bedroom: Allusion and Ethics in *Cymbeline*." *Shakespeare Quarterly* 66, no. 4 (2015): 440–62.
Barton, J. L. "The Early History of Consideration." *Law Quarterly Review* 85 (1969): 372–91.
Bate, Jonathan. *Shakespeare and Ovid.* Oxford: Clarendon Press, 1993.
Beard, Mary. *The Roman Triumph.* Cambridge, MA: Belknap Press of Harvard University Press, 2007.
Belsey, Catherine. "Cleopatra's Seduction." In *Alternative Shakespeares*, edited by Terence Hawkes, 2:38–62. London: Routledge, 1996.
———. *John Milton: Language, Gender, Power.* Oxford: Basil Blackwell, 1988.
Benjamin, Walter. "Theses on the Philosophy of History." In *Illuminations*, edited by Hannah Arendt and translated by Harry Zohn, 253–64. New York: Schocken Books, 1968.
Benkov, Edith Joyce. "*Philomena*: Chrétien de Troyes' Reinterpretation of the Ovidian Myth." *Classical and Modern Literature* 3, no. 4 (1983): 201–9.
Berger, Harry, Jr. *The Allegorical Temper: Vision and Reality in Book II of Spenser's* Faerie Queene. New Haven, CT: Yale University Press, 1957.
———. *Imaginary Audition: Shakespeare on Stage and Page.* Berkeley: University of California Press, 1989.
———. *Revisionary Play: Studies in the Spenserian Dynamics.* Berkeley: University of California Press, 1988.
Bernstein, Peter L. *Against the Gods: The Remarkable Story of Risk.* New York: John Wiley & Sons, 1996.
Black, Henry Campbell. *Black's Law Dictionary.* 6th ed. St. Paul: West Publishing, 1990.
Blackburn, William. "Merlin." In *The Spenser Encyclopedia*, edited by A. C. Hamilton, Donald Cheney, W. F. Blissett, David A. Richardson, and William W. Barker, 470–71. Toronto: University of Toronto Press, 1990.
Blake, N. F. *A Grammar of Shakespeare's Language.* New York: Palgrave, 2002.
Blank, Paula. *Broken English: Dialects and the Politics of Language in Renaissance Writings.* London and New York: Routledge, 1996.

Bloom, Harold. *The Anxiety of Influence: A Theory of Poetry*. New York: Oxford University Press, 1973.
Blumenberg, Hans. *The Legitimacy of the Modern Age*. Translated by Robert M. Wallace. Cambridge, MA: MIT Press, 1983.
Blumenfeld-Kosinski, Renate. *Reading Myth: Classical Mythology and Its Interpretations in Medieval French Literature*. Stanford, CA: Stanford University Press, 1997.
Boccaccio, Giovanni. *The Decameron Containing An hundred pleasant Nouels*. Translated by John Florio. London: Isaac Jaggard, 1620.
Bolton, Joseph S. G. "The Authentic Text of *Titus Andronicus*." *PMLA* 44, no. 3 (1929): 765–88.
Bowden, Caroline. "Sister Joan Seller, English Nun's Oath of Obedience (1631)." In *Reading Early Modern Women: An Anthology of Texts in Manuscript and Print, 1550–1700*, edited by Helen Ostovich and Elizabeth Sauer, 145–47. New York: Routledge, 2004.
Braden, Gordon. "Shakespeare's Roman Tragedies." In *A Companion to Shakespeare's Works: The Tragedies*, edited by Richard Dutton and Jean E. Howard, 1: 199–218. Oxford: Blackwell Publishing, 2003.
Brathwaite, Richard. *A Strappado for the Diuell*. London, 1615.
Brewer, David A. *The Afterlife of Character, 1726–1825*. Philadelphia: University of Pennsylvania Press, 2005.
Brinsley, John. *Ouids Metamorphosis Translated Grammatically, and also according to the propriety of our English tongue, so farre as Grammar and the verse will well beare*. London, 1618.
Brisman, Leslie. *Milton's Poetry of Choice and Its Romantic Heirs*. Ithaca, NY: Cornell University Press, 1973.
Brooks, Peter. *Reading for the Plot: Design and Intention in Narrative*. Cambridge, MA: Harvard University Press, 1984.
Bullokar, William. *A Bref Grammar for English*. 1586.
Burckhardt, Jacob. *The Civilization of the Renaissance in Italy*. Translated by S. G. C. Middlemore. New York: The Modern Library, 2002.
Burrow, Colin. *Edmund Spenser*. Plymouth: Northcote House Publishers, 1996.
———. *Epic Romance: Homer to Milton*. Oxford: Clarendon Press, 1993.
Bush, Douglas. *The Renaissance and English Humanism*. Toronto: University of Toronto Press, 1939.
Campion, Thomas. "Observations in the Art of English Poesy (1602)." In *Sidney's "The Defence of Poesy" and Selected Renaissance Literary Criticism*, edited by Gavin Alexander, 281–88. London: Penguin, 2004.
Cave, Terence. *The Cornucopian Text: Problems of Writing in the French Renaissance*. Oxford: Clarendon Press, 1979.
Charnes, Linda. "Anticipating Nostalgia: Finding Temporal Logic in a Textual Anomaly." *Textual Cultures* 4, no. 1 (2009): 72–83.
———. *Notorious Identity: Materializing the Subject in Shakespeare*. Cambridge, MA: Harvard University Press, 1993.
Cheney, Patrick. *Shakespeare's Literary Authorship*. Cambridge: Cambridge University Press, 2008.
Cipolla, Carlo M. *Clocks and Culture, 1300–1700*. New York: W. W. Norton & Company, 1967.

Cohen, Jeffrey J. *Medieval Identity Machines*. Minneapolis: University of Minnesota Press, 2003.
Colby, Alice M. *The Portrait in Twelfth-Century French Literature: An Example of the Stylistic Originality of Chrétien de Troyes*. Geneva: Librairie Droz, 1965.
Colie, Rosalie L. *Shakespeare's Living Art*. Princeton, NJ: Princeton University Press, 1974.
Copeland, Rita. *Rhetoric, Hermeneutics, and Translation in the Middle Ages: Academic Traditions and Vernacular Texts*. Cambridge: Cambridge University Press, 1991.
Copley, Anthony. *A Fig for Fortune*. London, 1596.
Cormack, Bradin. *A Power to Do Justice: Jurisdiction, English Literature, and the Rise of Common Law, 1509–1625*. Chicago: University of Chicago Press, 2007.
Cormier, Raymond, ed. and trans., *Three Ovidian Tales of Love (*Piramus et Tisbé, Narcisus et Dané, *and* Philomena et Procné*)*. New York and London: Garland Publishing, 1986.
Coulson, Frank T. *The "Vulgate" Commentary on Ovid's* Metamorphoses: *The Creation of Myth and the Story of Orpheus*. Toronto: Pontifical Institute of Mediaeval Studies, 1991.
Cowell, John. *The Interpreter*. Cambridge, 1607.
Crane, Mary Thomas. *Framing Authority: Sayings, Self, and Society in Sixteenth-Century England*. Princeton, NJ: Princeton University Press, 1993.
Culler, Jonathan. "Why Lyric?" *PMLA* 123, no. 1 (2008): 201–6.
Cummins, Juliet, ed. *Milton and the Ends of Time*. Cambridge: Cambridge University Press, 2003.
Cummings, Brian. *The Literary Culture of the Reformation: Grammar and Grace*. Oxford: Oxford University Press, 2002.
———. *Mortal Thoughts: Religion, Secularity & Identity in Shakespeare and Early Modern Culture*. Oxford: Oxford University Press, 2013.
Cunningham, Merrilee. "The Interpolated Tale in Spenser's *The Faerie Queene*, Book I." *South Central Bulletin* 43, no. 4 (1983): 99–104.
Curran, Brian A. "Love, Triumph, Tragedy: Cleopatra and Egypt in High Renaissance Rome." In *Cleopatra: A Sphinx Revisited*, edited by Margaret M. Miles, 96–131. Berkeley: University of California Press, 2011.
Dana, Margaret E. "The Providential Plot of the *Old Arcadia*." *Studies in English Literature* 17, no. 1 (1977): 39–57.
Daniel, Samuel. *A Defence of Ryme*. London, 1603.
———. "Musophilus: Containing a General Defence of Learning (1599)." In *Sidney's "The Defence of Poesy" and Selected Renaissance Literary Criticism*, edited by Gavin Alexander, 279–80. London: Penguin, 2004.
Danson, Lawrence. *Tragic Alphabet: Shakespeare's Drama of Language*. New Haven, CT: Yale University Press, 1974.
Davis, Kathleen. "The Sense of an Epoch: Periodization, Sovereignty, and the Limits of Secularization." In *The Legitimacy of the Middle Ages: On the Unwritten History of Theory*, edited by Andrew Cole and D. Vance Smith, 39–69. Durham, NC: Duke University Press, 2010.
Day, John, William Rowley, and George Wilkins. *The Travels of the Three English Brothers*. In *Three Renaissance Travel Plays*, edited by Anthony Parr, 55–134. Manchester: Manchester University Press, 1995.

de Certeau, Michel. *The Writing of History*. Translated by Tom Conley. New York: Columbia University Press, 1988.
de Grazia, Margreta. *Hamlet without Hamlet*. Cambridge: Cambridge University Press, 2007.
———. "Lost Potential in Grammar and Nature: Sidney's *Astrophil and Stella*." *Studies in English Literature* 21, no. 1 (1981): 21–35.
———. "The Modern Divide: From Either Side." *Journal of Medieval and Early Modern Studies* 37, no. 3 (2007): 453–67.
Dickson, Vernon Guy. "'A Pattern, Precedent, and Lively Warrant': Emulation, Rhetoric, and Cruel Propriety in *Titus Andronicus*." *Renaissance Quarterly* 62, no. 2 (2009): 376–409.
DiPasquale, Theresa M. "From Here to Aeviternity: Donne's Atemporal Clocks." *Modern Philology* 110, no. 2 (2012): 226–52.
Dipple, Elizabeth. "'Unjust Justice' in the *Old Arcadia*." *Studies in English Literature* 10, no. 1 (1970): 83–101.
Dolven, Jeff. *Scenes of Instruction in Renaissance Romance*. Chicago: University of Chicago Press, 2007.
Dubrow, Heather. "The Arraignment of Paridell: Tudor Historiography in *The Faerie Queene*, III.ix." *Studies in Philology* 87, no. 3 (1990): 312–27.
———. "'I Would I Were at Home': Representations of Dwelling Places and Havens in *Cymbeline*." In *Shakespeare and Historical Formalism*, edited by Stephen Cohen, 69–93. Aldershot, UK: Ashgate, 2007.
Dusinberre, Juliet. "Squeaking Cleopatras: Gender and Performance in *Antony and Cleopatra*." In *Shakespeare, Theory, and Performance*, edited by James C. Bulman, 46–67. London: Routledge, 1996.
Elyot, Thomas. *The Boke Named the Gouernour*. London: Thomas Bertheleti, 1531.
Enterline, Lynn. *The Rhetoric of the Body from Ovid to Shakespeare*. Cambridge: Cambridge University Press, 2000.
———. *Shakespeare's Schoolroom: Rhetoric, Discipline, Emotion*. Philadelphia: University of Pennsylvania Press, 2012.
Escobedo, Andrew. "From Britannia to England: *Cymbeline* and the Beginning of Nations." *Shakespeare Quarterly* 59, no. 1 (2008): 60–87.
———. *Nationalism and Historical Loss in Renaissance England: Foxe, Dee, Spenser, Milton*. Ithaca, NY: Cornell University Press, 2004.
Evans, J. Martin. *The Miltonic Moment*. Lexington: University Press of Kentucky, 1998.
Ewbank, Inga-Stina. "The Triumph of Time." In *The Winter's Tale*: A Casebook, edited by Kenneth Muir, 98–115. London: Macmillan, 1968.
Felperin, Howard. *Shakespearean Romance*. Princeton, NJ: Princeton University Press, 1972.
Felski, Rita. "'Context Stinks!'" *New Literary History* 42, no. 4 (2011): 573–91.
Ferguson, Arthur B. *Clio Unbound: Perception of the Social and Cultural Past in Renaissance England*. Durham, NC: Duke University Press, 1979.
Ferry, Anne Davidson. *Milton's Epic Voice: The Narrator in* Paradise Lost. Cambridge, MA: Harvard University Press, 1963.
Fish, Stanley. *Doing What Comes Naturally: Change, Rhetoric, and the Practice of Theory in Literary and Legal Studies*. Durham, NC: Duke University Press, 1989.

———. "The Law Wishes to Have a Formal Existence." In *The Fate of Law*, edited by Austin Sarat and Thomas R. Kearns, 159–208. Ann Arbor: University of Michigan Press, 1991.

———. *Surprised by Sin: The Reader in* Paradise Lost. 1967. Reprint, Berkeley: University of California Press, 1971.

Fletcher, Angus. *The Prophetic Moment: An Essay on Spenser*. Chicago: University of Chicago Press, 1971.

———. *Time, Space, and Motion in the Age of Shakespeare*. Cambridge, MA: Harvard University Press, 2007.

Fried, Debra. "Spenser's Caesura." *English Literary Renaissance* 11, no. 3 (1981): 261–80.

Füger, Wilhelm. "Ignaro." In *The Spenser Encyclopedia*, edited by A. C. Hamilton, Donald Cheney, W. F. Blissett, David A. Richardson, and William W. Barker, 388. Toronto: University of Toronto Press, 1990.

Fussell, Paul, Jr. *Poetic Meter and Poetic Form*. New York: Random House, 1965.

Fussner, F. Smith. *The Historical Revolution: English Historical Writing and Thought, 1580–1640*. New York: Columbia University Press, 1962.

Gallop, Jane. *Reading Lacan*. Ithaca, NY: Cornell University Press, 1985.

Gascoigne, George. "Certain Notes of Instruction (1575)." In *Sidney's "The Defence of Poesy" and Selected Renaissance Literary Criticism*, edited by Gavin Alexander, 237–47. London: Penguin, 2004.

Genette, Gérard. *Narrative Discourse: An Essay in Method*. Translated by Jane E. Lewin. Ithaca, NY: Cornell University Press, 1980.

Giamatti, A. Bartlett. *The Earthly Paradise and the Renaissance Epic*. Princeton, NJ: Princeton University Press, 1966.

Goldberg, Jonathan. "Dating Milton." In *Soliciting Interpretation: Literary Theory and Seventeenth-Century English Poetry*, edited by Elizabeth D. Harvey and Katharine Eisaman Maus, 199–220. Chicago: University of Chicago Press, 1990.

———. *Endlesse Worke: Spenser and the Structures of Discourse*. Baltimore: Johns Hopkins University Press, 1981.

———. *Voice Terminal Echo: Postmodernism and English Renaissance Texts*. New York: Methuen, 1986.

Goodman, Kevis. "Romantic Poetry and the Science of Thought." In *The Cambridge Companion to British Romantic Poetry*, edited by James Chandler and Maureen N. McLane, 195–216. Cambridge: Cambridge University Press, 2008.

Gosson, Stephen. *The School of Abuse*. London: Thomas Woodcocke, 1579.

Green, Douglas E. "Interpreting 'Her Martyr'd Signs': Gender and Tragedy in *Titus Andronicus*." *Shakespeare Quarterly* 40, no. 3 (1989): 317–26.

Greenblatt, Stephen J. *Learning to Curse: Essays in Early Modern Culture*. New York: Routledge, 1990.

———. "Sidney's *Arcadia* and the Mixed Mode." *Studies in Philology* 70, no. 3 (1973): 269–78.

Greene, Robert. *A Groats-worth of witte, bought with a million of Repentance*. London, 1592.

Greene, Thomas. *The Descent from Heaven: A Study in Epic Continuity*. New Haven, CT: Yale University Press, 1963.

———. *The Light in Troy: Imitation and Discovery in Renaissance Poetry*. New Haven, CT: Yale University Press, 1982.

Gross, Kenneth. *Spenserian Poetics: Idolatry, Iconoclasm, and Magic.* Ithaca, NY: Cornell University Press, 1985.

Guibbory, Achsah. *The Map of Time: Seventeenth-Century English Literature and Ideas of Pattern in History.* Urbana-Champaign: University of Illinois Press, 1986.

Guillory, John. *Poetic Authority: Spenser, Milton, and Literary History.* New York: Columbia University Press, 1983.

Gurr, Andrew. *Playgoing in Shakespeare's London.* Cambridge: Cambridge University Press, 1987.

Hacking, Ian. *The Emergence of Probability.* 2nd ed. Cambridge: Cambridge University Press, 2006.

Hadfield, Andrew. "Has Historicism Gone Too Far: Or, Should We Return to Form?" In *Rethinking Historicism from Shakespeare to Milton,* edited by Ann Baynes Coiro and Thomas Fulton, 23–39. Cambridge: Cambridge University Press, 2012.

Hagstrum, Jean H. *The Sister Arts: the Tradition of Literary Pictorialism and English Poetry from Dryden to Gray.* Chicago: University of Chicago Press, 1958.

Halpern, Richard. *The Poetics of Primitive Accumulation: English Renaissance Culture and the Genealogy of Capital.* Ithaca, NY: Cornell University Press, 1991.

Hardin, Richard F. "Ovid in Seventeenth-Century England." *Comparative Literature* 24, no. 1 (1972): 44–62.

Harper, Carrie Anna. *The Sources of the British Chronicle History in Spenser's "Faerie Queene."* Bryn Mawr, PA: Bryn Mawr College Monographs, 1910.

Harris, Jonathan Gil. *Untimely Matter in the Time of Shakespeare.* Philadelphia: University of Pennsylvania Press, 2009.

Hartman, Geoffrey. "Milton's Counterplot." *ELH* 25, no. 1 (1958): 1–12.

Harvey, Gabriel. *Fovre Letters, and Certain Sonnets.* London, 1592.

Harvey, Gabriel, and Edmund Spenser. *Three proper, and wittie, familiar Letters: lately passed betweene two Vniuersitie men: touching the Earthquake in Aprill last, and our English refourmed Versifying.* London, 1580.

Haydn, Hiram. *The Counter-Renaissance.* New York: Harcourt, Brace & World, 1950.

Hexter, Ralph J. *Ovid and Medieval Schooling.* Munich: Arbeo-Gesellschaft, 1986.

Heywood, Thomas. *The Fair Maid of the Exchange.* Edited by Barron Field. London: Shakespeare Society, 1846.

Hiltner, Ken. *What Else Is Pastoral? Renaissance Literature and the Environment.* Ithaca, NY: Cornell University Press, 2011.

Hinds, Stephen. *Allusion and Intertext: Dynamics of Appropriation in Roman Poetry.* Cambridge: Cambridge University Press, 1998.

Holmes, Eric Mills. "Stature and Status of a Promise under Seal as a Legal Formality." *Willamette Law Review* 29, no. 4 (1993): 617–68.

Horace. *Odes and Epodes.* Edited and Translated by Niall Rudd. Loeb Classical Library. Cambridge, MA: Harvard University Press, 2004.

Hulse, S. Clark. "Wresting the Alphabet: Oratory and Action in 'Titus Andronicus.'" *Criticism* 21, no. 2 (1979): 106–18.

Hunt, Maurice. "Compelling Art in *Titus Andronicus.*" *Studies in English Literature* 28, no. 2 (1988): 197–218.

Hutson, Lorna. *The Invention of Suspicion: Law and Mimesis in Shakespeare and Renaissance Drama.* Oxford: Oxford University Press, 2007.

Ibbetson, David. "Sixteenth Century Contract Law: *Slade's Case* in Context." *Oxford Journal of Legal Studies* 4, no. 3 (1984): 295–317.
Ingham, Patricia Clare. *Sovereign Fantasies: Arthurian Romance and the Making of Britain*. Philadelphia: University of Pennsylvania Press, 2001.
Jackson, Russell. "The Triumphs of *Antony and Cleopatra*." *SJH*, 1984, 128–48.
James, Heather. *Shakespeare's Troy: Drama, Politics, and the Translation of Empire*. Cambridge: Cambridge University Press, 1997.
Jameson, Fredric. "Magical Narratives: Romance as Genre." *New Literary History* 7, no. 1 (1975): 135–63.
Jarvis, Simon. "For a Poetics of Verse." *PMLA* 125, no. 4 (2010): 931–35.
Javitch, Daniel, "Rescuing Ovid from the Allegorizers." *Comparative Literature* 30, no. 2 (1978): 97–107.
Jones, Richard Foster. *Triumph of the English Language: A Survey of Opinions Concerning the Vernacular from the Introduction of Printing to the Restoration*. Reprint. Stanford, CA: Stanford University Press, 1953.
Kahn, Victoria. "'The Duty to Love': Passion and Obligation in Early Modern Political Theory." In *Rhetoric and Law in Early Modern Europe*, edited by Victoria Kahn and Lorna Hutson, 243–68. New Haven, CT: Yale University Press, 2001.
———. Introduction to "Early Modern Secularism." Special issue, *Representations* 105, no. 1 (2009): 1–11.
———. "Margaret Cavendish and the Romance of Contract." *Renaissance Quarterly* 50, no. 2 (1997): 526–66.
Kahn, Victoria, and Lorna Hutson, eds. *Rhetoric and Law in Early Modern Europe*. New Haven, CT: Yale University Press, 2001.
Kastan, David Scott. "'His Semblable Is His Mirror': *Hamlet* and the Imitation of Revenge." *Shakespeare Studies* 19 (1987): 111–24.
———. *Shakespeare after Theory*. New York: Routledge, 1999.
Keilen, Sean. *Vulgar Eloquence: On the Renaissance Invention of English Literature*. New Haven, CT: Yale University Press, 2006.
Kendall, Gillian Murray. "'Lend Me Thy Hand': Metaphor and Mayhem in *Titus Andronicus*." *Shakespeare Quarterly* 40, no. 3 (1989): 299–316.
Kermode, Frank. *The Sense of an Ending: Studies in the Theory of Fiction*. Oxford: Oxford University Press, 1966.
Kerrigan, John. "Coriolanus Fidiussed." *Essays in Criticism* 62, no. 4 (2012): 319–53.
———. *Revenge Tragedy: Aeschylus to Armageddon*. Oxford: Clarendon Press, 1996.
———. "Shakespeare, Oaths and Vows." *Proceedings of the British Academy* 167 (2010): 61–89.
Kerrigan, William. *Shakespeare's Promises*. Baltimore: Johns Hopkins University Press, 1999.
Kewes, Paulina. "'A Fit Memorial For the Times to Come . . .': Admonition and Topical Application in Mary Sidney's *Antonius* and Samuel Daniel's *Cleopatra*." *RES* 63, no. 259 (2011): 243–64.
King, Andrew. *The Faerie Queene and Middle English Romance: The Matter of Just Memory*. Oxford: Clarendon Press, 2000.
Koselleck, Reinhart. *Futures Past: On the Semantics of Historical Time*. Translated by Keith Tribe. New York: Columbia University Press, 2004.

Krueger, Roberta L. "*Philomena*: Brutal Transitions and Courtly Transformations in Chrétien's Old French Translation." In *A Companion to Chrétien de Troyes*, edited by Norris J. Lacy and Joan Tasker Grimbert, 87–102. Cambridge: D.S. Brewer, 2005.
Kunin, Aaron. "Poetry as Artifact." In *The Princeton Encyclopedia of Poetry and Poetics*, edited by Roland Greene, Stephen Cushman, Clare Cavanagh, Jahan Ramazani, and Paul Rouzer, 87–89. 4th ed. Princeton, NJ: Princeton University Press, 2012.
Lacan, Jacques. *Écrits*. Translated by Bruce Fink. New York: W.W. Norton, 2006.
Le Goff, Jacques. *The Medieval Imagination*. Translated by Arthur Goldhammer. Chicago: University of Chicago Press, 1988.
Levy, F. J. *Tudor Historical Thought*. San Marino, CA: Huntington Library, 1967.
Lewalski, Barbara Kiefer. *"Paradise Lost" and the Rhetoric of Literary Forms*. Princeton, NJ: Princeton University Press, 1985.
———. "Structure and the Symbolism of Vision in Michael's Prophecy, *Paradise Lost*, Books XI–XII." *Philological Quarterly* 42, no. 1 (1963): 25–35.
Lewis, C. S. *A Preface to Paradise Lost*. London: Oxford University Press, 1942.
Liebler, Naomi Conn. "Getting It All Right: *Titus Andronicus* and Roman History." *Shakespeare Quarterly* 45, no. 3 (1994): 263–78.
Lloyd, Richard. *A Briefe Discourse of the Most Renowned Acts and Right Valiant Conquests of those puisant Princes called the Nine Worthies*. 1584.
Lockey, Brian C. *Law and Empire in English Renaissance Literature*. Cambridge: Cambridge University Press, 2006.
Löwith, Karl. *Meaning in History: The Theological Implications of the Philosophy of History*. Chicago: University of Chicago Press, 1949.
Lyne, Raphael. *Ovid's Changing Worlds: English Metamorphoses, 1567–1632*. Oxford: Oxford University Press, 2001.
Maittaire, Michael. *The English Grammar: or, an Essay on the Art of Grammar, Applied to and Exemplified in the English Tongue*. London, 1712.
Mann, Jenny C. *Outlaw Rhetoric*. Ithaca, NY: Cornell University Press, 2012.
Marcus, Leah S. "Renaissance/Early Modern Studies." In *Redrawing the Boundaries: The Transformation of English and American Literary Studies*, edited by Stephen Greenblatt and Giles Gunn, 41–63. New York: Modern Language Association of America, 1992.
———. *Unediting the Renaissance: Shakespeare, Marlowe, Milton*. London and New York: Routledge, 1996.
Martindale, Charles. "Introduction." In *Ovid Renewed: Ovidian Influences on Literature and Art from the Middle Ages to the Twentieth Century*, edited by Charles Martindale, 1–20. Cambridge: Cambridge University Press, 1988.
———. *Redeeming the Text: Latin Poetry and the Hermeneutics of Reception*. Cambridge: Cambridge University Press, 1993.
Maslen, R. W. "Myths Exploited: The Metamorphoses of Ovid in Early Elizabethan England." In *Shakespeare's Ovid: The Metamorphoses in the Plays and Poems*, edited by A. B. Taylor, 15–30. Cambridge: Cambridge University Press, 2000.
Maus, Katharine Eisaman. *Inwardness and Theater in the English Renaissance*. Chicago: University of Chicago Press, 1995.

———. "Titus Andronicus." In *The Norton Shakespeare*. Edited by Stephen Greenblatt, Walter Cohen, Jean E. Howard, and Katharine Eisaman Maus, 371–77. New York: W.W. Norton & Company, 1997.

Mazzio, Carla. *The Inarticulate Renaissance: Language Trouble in an Age of Eloquence.* Philadelphia: University of Pennsylvania Press, 2009.

McCabe, Richard A. *The Pillars of Eternity: Time and Providence in* The Faerie Queene. Blackrock, Ireland: Irish Academic Press, 1989.

McCanles, Michael. "Oracular Prediction and the Fore-Conceit of Sidney's *Arcadia*." *ELH* 50, no. 2 (1983): 233–44.

McCoy, Richard C. *Sir Philip Sidney: Rebellion in Arcadia.* New Brunswick, NJ: Rutgers University Press, 1979.

McKisack, May. *Medieval History in the Tudor Age.* Oxford: Clarendon Press, 1971.

Metz, G. Harold. *Shakespeare's Earliest Tragedy: Studies in* Titus Andronicus. Cranbury, NJ: Associated University Presses, 1996.

Miège, Guy. *The English Grammar; or, the Grounds and Genius of the English Tongue.* London, 1688.

Miller, Anthony. *Roman Triumphs and Early Modern English Culture.* New York: Palgrave, 2001.

Miller, David Lee. *The Poem's Two Bodies: The Poetics of the 1590* Faerie Queene. Princeton, NJ: Princeton University Press, 1988.

Milton, John. *Paradise Lost.* Edited by Alastair Fowler. 2nd ed. London: Longman Group, 1998.

Minnis, A. J. *Chaucer and Pagan Antiquity.* Cambridge: D.S. Brewer; Totowa, NJ: Rowman & Littlefield, 1982.

Miola, Robert S. "*Cymbeline*: Shakespeare's Valediction to Rome." In *Roman Images: Selected Papers from the English Institute, 1982,* edited by Annabel Patterson, 51–62. Baltimore: Johns Hopkins University Press, 1984.

———. "Reading the Classics." In *A Companion to Shakespeare*, edited by David Scott Kastan, 172–85. Oxford: Blackwell Publishers, 1999.

———. *Shakespeare's Rome.* Cambridge: Cambridge University Press, 1983.

Moschovakis, Nicholas R. "'Irreligious Piety' and Christian History: Persecution as Pagan Anachronism in *Titus Andronicus*." *Shakespeare Quarterly* 53, no. 4 (2002): 460–86.

———. "Topicality and Conceptual Blending: *Titus Andronicus* and the Case of William Hacket." *College Literature* 33, no. 1 (2006): 127–50.

Moss, Ann. *Ovid in Renaissance France: A Survey of Latin Editions of Ovid and Commentaries Printed in France Before 1600.* London: Warburg Institute Surveys, 1982.

Mowat, Barbara A. "Lavinia's Message: Shakespeare and Myth." *Renaissance Papers*, 1981, 55–69.

Muldrew, Craig. *The Economy of Obligation: The Culture of Credit and Social Relations in Early Modern England.* New York: St. Martin's Press, 1998.

Mulryne, J. R. "Cleopatra's Barge and Antony's Body: Italian Sources and English Theatre." In *Shakespeare, Italy, and Intertextuality*, edited by Michele Marrapodi, 197–215. Manchester: Manchester University Press, 2004.

Nebeker, Eric. "Broadside Ballads, Miscellanies, and the Lyric in Print." *ELH* 76, no. 4 (2009): 989–1013.

Nevo, Ruth. *Tragic Form in Shakespeare*. Princeton, NJ: Princeton University Press, 1972.
Nicholson, Catherine. *Uncommon Tongues: Eloquence and Eccentricity in the English Renaissance*. Philadelphia: University of Pennsylvania Press, 2014.
Olson, Rebecca. *Arras Hanging: The Textile That Determined Early Modern Literature and Drama*. Newark: University of Delaware Press, 2013.
Otter, Monika. *Inventiones: Fiction and Referentiality in Twelfth-Century English Historical Writing*. Chapel Hill: University of North Carolina Press, 1996.
Ovid. *Metamorphoses*. Translated by George Sandys. Oxford, 1632.
———. *Ovid's Metamorphoses: The Arthur Golding Translation, 1567*. Translated by Arthur Golding. Edited by John Frederick Nims. Philadelphia: Paul Dry Books, 2000.
Panofsky, Erwin. *Renaissance and Renascences in Western Art*. Stockholm: Almqvist & Wiksell, 1960.
Parker, Patricia. "Cymbeline: Arithmetic, Double-Entry Bookkeeping, Counts, and Accounts." *Sederi* 23 (2013): 100.
———. *Inescapable Romance: Studies in the Poetics of a Mode*. Princeton, NJ: Princeton University Press, 1979.
———. "Romance and Empire: Anachronistic *Cymbeline*." In *Unfolded Tales: Essays on Renaissance Romance*, edited by George M. Logan and Gordon Teskey, 189–207. Ithaca, NY: Cornell University Press, 1989.
Patey, Douglas Lane. *Probability and Literary Form: Philosophic Theory and Literary Practice in the Augustan Age*. Cambridge: Cambridge University Press, 1984.
Peacham, Henry. *Thalia's Banquet*. London, 1620.
Peend, Thomas. *The Pleasant Fable of Hermaphroditus and Salmacis*. London, 1565.
Peraso, Alessandro, and John Sparrow, eds. *Renaissance Latin Verse*. Chapel Hill: University of North Carolina Press, 1979.
Petowe, Henry. *Philochasander and Elanira*. London, 1599.
Phelan, Peggy. "Introduction: The Ends of Performance." In *The Ends of Performance*, edited by Peggy Phelan and Jill Lane, 1–19. New York: New York University Press, 1998.
Picciotto, Joanna. "Reforming the Garden: The Experimentalist Eden and *Paradise Lost*." *ELH* 72 (2005): 23–78.
Pigman, G. W., III. "Versions of Imitation in the Renaissance." *Renaissance Quarterly* 33, no. 1 (1980): 1–32.
Pincombe, Mike. "Gascoigne's *Phylomene*: A Late Medieval Paraphrase of Ovid's *Metamorphoses*." In *Elizabethan Literature and Transformation*, edited by Sabine Coelsch-Foisner, 71–81. Tübingen: Stauffenburg-Verlag, 1999.
Plutarch. "The Life of Marcus Antonius." In *The Lives of the Noble Grecians and Romanes, compared together by that graue learned Philosopher and Historiographer, Plutarke of Chæronea: Translated out of Greeke into French by James Amyot . . . and out of French into English by Thomas North*, MMMM7v–QQQQ1v. London, 1579.
Poggioli, Renato. *The Oaten Flute: Essays on Pastoral Poetry and the Pastoral Ideal*. Cambridge, MA: Harvard University Press, 1975.
Politi, Jina. "'The Gibbet-Maker.'" *Notes and Queries* 236 (1991): 54–55.

Poole, William. *Milton and the Idea of the Fall.* Cambridge: Cambridge University Press, 2005.

Poulet, Georges. *The Interior Distance.* Translated by Elliott Coleman. Reprint, Ann Arbor: University of Michigan Press, 1964.

Puttenham, George. *The Art of English Poesy.* Edited by Frank Whigham and Wayne A. Rebhorn. Ithaca, NY: Cornell University Press, 2007.

Quinones, Ricardo J. *The Renaissance Discovery of Time.* Cambridge, MA: Harvard University Press, 1972.

Quint, David. *Epic and Empire: Politics and Generic Form from Virgil to Milton.* Princeton, NJ: Princeton University Press, 1993.

Rackin, Phyllis. "Shakespeare's Boy Cleopatra, the Decorum of Nature, and the Golden World of Poetry." *PMLA* 87, no. 2 (1972): 201–12.

———. *Stages of History: Shakespeare's English Chronicles.* Ithaca, NY: Cornell University Press, 1990.

Read, David. *Temperate Conquests: Spenser and the Spanish New World.* Detroit: Wayne State University Press, 2000.

Rees, Joan. "Justice, Mercy and a Shipwreck in *Arcadia.*" *Studies in Philology* 87, no. 1 (1990): 75–82.

Reynolds, William Donald. "The *Ovidius Moralizatus* of Petrus Berchorius: An Introduction and Translation." PhD diss., University of Illinois at Urbana-Champaign, 1971.

Richardson, Brian. "Beyond Story and Discourse: Narrative Time in Postmodern and Nonmimetic Fiction." In *Narrative Dynamics: Essays on Time, Plot, Closure, and Frames,* edited by Brian Richardson, 47–63. Columbus: Ohio State University Press, 2002.

Ricœur, Paul. *Time and Narrative.* Translated by Kathleeen McLaughlin and David Pellauer. 3 vols. Chicago: University of Chicago Press, 1984–88.

Roach, Joseph. "Kinship, Intelligence, and Memory as Improvisation: Culture and Performance in New Orleans." In *Performance and Cultural Politics,* edited by Elin Diamond, 217–36. London: Routledge, 1996.

Ross, David O., Jr. *Backgrounds to Augustan Poetry: Gallus, Elegy and Rome.* Cambridge: Cambridge University Press, 1975.

Rumrich, John P. *Milton Unbound: Controversy and Reinterpretation.* Cambridge: Cambridge University Press, 1996.

———. "Things of Darkness: Sin, Death, Chaos." In *The Cambridge Companion to Paradise Lost,* edited by Louis Schwartz, 29–41. New York: Cambridge University Press, 2014.

Sacks, David Harris. "The Promise and the Contract in Early Modern England: Slade's Case in Perspective." In *Rhetoric and Law in Early Modern Europe,* edited by Victoria Kahn and Lorna Hutson, 28–53. New Haven, CT: Yale University Press, 2001.

St. German, Christopher. *Doctor and Student.* Edited by T. F. T. Plucknett and J. L. Barton. London: Selden Society, 1974.

Schmitt, Carl. *Political Theology: Four Chapters on the Concept of Sovereignty.* Translated by George Schwab. Cambridge, MA: MIT Press, 1985.

Searle, John R. *Speech Acts: An Essay in the Philosophy of Language.* Cambridge: Cambridge University Press, 1969.

Seznec, Jean. *The Survival of the Pagan Gods: The Mythological Tradition and Its Place in Renaissance Humanism and Art.* Translated by Barbara F. Sessions. Princeton, NJ: Princeton University Press, 1972.

Shaheen, Naseeb. *Biblical References in Shakespeare's Tragedies.* Cranbury, NJ: Associated University Presses, 1987.

Shakespeare, William. *Antony and Cleopatra.* Edited by John Wilders, 3rd ser. London: The Arden Shakespeare, 1995.

———. *Coriolanus.* Edited by Philip Brockbank, 2nd ser. 1976. Reprint, London: The Arden Shakespeare, 2001.

———. *Cymbeline.* Edited by J. M. Nosworthy, 2nd ser. 1955. Reprint, London: The Arden Shakespeare, 2000.

———. *Hamlet.* Edited by Ann Thompson and Neil Taylor, 3rd ser. London: The Arden Shakespeare, 2006.

———. *King Henry V.* Edited by T. W. Craik, 3rd ser. London: The Arden Shakespeare, 1995.

———. *Macbeth.* Edited by Kenneth Muir, 2nd ser. London: The Arden Shakespeare, 1997.

———. *A Midsummer Night's Dream.* Edited by Russ McDonald. 1968. Reprint, New York: Penguin, 2000.

———. *Othello.* Edited by E. A. J. Honigmann, 3rd ser. London: The Arden Shakespeare, 1997.

———. "The Rape of Lucrece." In *The Complete Sonnets and Poems*, edited by Colin Burrow, 237–338. Oxford: Oxford University Press, 2002.

———. *Shakespeare's Sonnets.* Edited by Stephen Booth. New Haven, CT: Yale University Press, 1977.

———. *Titus Andronicus.* Edited by Jonathan Bate, 3rd ser. London: The Arden Shakespeare, 2002.

———. *The Winter's Tale.* Edited by J. H. P. Pafford, 3rd ser. 1963. Reprint, London: The Arden Shakespeare, 1996.

Sherman, Anita Gilman. *Skepticism and Memory in Shakespeare and Donne.* New York: Palgrave Macmillan, 2007.

Sidney, Sir Philip. *The Countess of Pembroke's Arcadia.* Edited by Maurice Evans. 1977. Reprint, London: Penguin, 1987.

———. "The Defence of Poesy." In *Sir Philip Sidney: A Selection of His Finest Poems*, edited by Katherine Duncan-Jones, 101–42. Oxford: Oxford University Press, 1994.

———. *The Countess of Pembroke's Arcadia (The Old Arcadia).* Edited by Katherine Duncan-Jones. 1985. Reprint, Oxford: Oxford University Press, 1999.

Simpson, A. W. B. *A History of the Common Law of Contract: The Rise of the Action of Assumpsit.* Oxford: Clarendon Press, 1975.

———. "The Place of Slade's Case in the History of Contract." *Law Quarterly Review* 74 (1958): 381–96.

Smith, Bruce R. *Ancient Scripts & Modern Experience on the English Stage, 1500–1700.* Princeton, NJ: Princeton University Press, 1988.

Smith, Molly Easo. "Spectacles of Torment in *Titus Andronicus*." *Studies in English Literature* 36, no. 2 (1996): 315–31.

Smith, Nigel. *Is Milton Better than Shakespeare?* Cambridge, MA: Harvard University Press, 2008.

Smith, Sir William, and Sir John Lockwood. *Chambers Murray Latin-English Dictionary*. 1933. Reprint, Edinburgh: Chambers, 1995.
Spenser, Edmund. *The Faerie Queene*. Edited by A. C. Hamilton. 2nd ed. New York: Longman, 2001.
Stern, Tiffany. *Rehearsal from Shakespeare to Sheridan*. Oxford: Clarendon Press, 2000.
Stewart, Alan. *Philip Sidney: A Double Life*. London: Chatto & Windus, 2000.
Stewart, Susan. *On Longing: Narratives of the Miniature, the Gigantic, the Souvenir, the Collection*. Baltimore: Johns Hopkins University Press, 1984.
St. Hilaire, Danielle A. "Allusion and Sacrifice in *Titus Andronicus*." *SEL* 49, no. 2 (2009): 311–31.
Sullivan, Garrett A., Jr. *Memory and Forgetting in English Renaissance Drama: Shakespeare, Marlowe, Webster*. Cambridge: Cambridge University Press, 2005.
Summit, Jennifer. "Monuments and Ruins: Spenser and the Problem of the English Library." *ELH* 70 (2003): 1–34.
Tassi, Marguerite A. "O'erpicturing Apelles: Shakespeare's *Paragone* with Painting in *Antony and Cleopatra*." In *Antony and Cleopatra: New Critical Essays*, edited by Sara Munson Deats, 291–307. New York and London: Routledge, 2005.
Tasso, Torquato. *Gerusalemme Liberata*. Edited by Lanfranco Caretti. Torino: Einaudi, 1971.
———. *Jerusalem Delivered*. Translated by Ralph Nash. Detroit: Wayne State University Press, 1987.
Tayler, Edward W. *Milton's Poetry: Its Development in Time*. Pittsburgh: Duquesne University Press, 1979.
Taylor, Anthony Brian. "The Clown Episode in *Titus Andronicus*, the Bible, and Cambises." *Notes and Queries* 46, no. 2 (1999): 210–11.
———. "Golding's 'Metamorphoses' and 'Titus Andronicus'." *Notes and Queries* 223 (1978): 117–20.
———. "Introduction." In *Shakespeare's Ovid: The* Metamorphoses *in the Plays and Poems*, edited by A. B. Taylor, 1–12. Cambridge: Cambridge University Press, 2000.
Teskey, Gordon. *Delirious Milton: The Fate of the Poet in Modernity*. Cambridge, MA: Harvard University Press, 2006.
Tilley, Morris Palmer. *A Dictionary of the Proverbs in England in the Sixteenth and Seventeenth Centuries*. Ann Arbor: University of Michigan Press, 1950.
Tillyard, E. M. W. *The Elizabethan World Picture*. London: Chatto & Windus, 1943.
Tricomi, Albert H. "The Aesthetics of Mutilation in 'Titus Andronicus.'" *Shakespeare Survey* 27 (1974): 11–19.
Turner, Frederick. *Shakespeare and the Nature of Time: Moral and Philosophical Themes in Some Plays and Poems by William Shakespeare*. Oxford: Oxford University Press, 1971.
Turner, William. *A Short Grammar for the English Tongue*. London, 1710.
van Es, Bart. *Spenser's Forms of History*. Oxford: Oxford University Press, 2002.
Verstegan, Richard. *Odes in Imitation of the Seaven Penitential Psalmes*. Antwerp, 1601.
Vickers, Brian. *Shakespeare, Co-Author: A Historical Study of Five Collaborative Plays*. Oxford: Oxford University Press, 2002.
Vorlat, Emma. *The Development of English Grammatical Theory, 1586–1737*. Leuven: Leuven University Press, 1975.

Waith, Eugene M. "The Metamorphosis of Violence in *Titus Andronicus*." In *Shakespeare Survey*, 10:39–49. Cambridge: Cambridge University Press, 1957.
Wall-Randell, Sarah. *The Immaterial Book: Reading and Romance in Early Modern England*. Ann Arbor: University of Michigan Press, 2013.
Waller, G. F. *The Strong Necessity of Time: The Philosophy of Time in Shakespeare and Elizabethan Literature*. The Hague: Mouton, 1976.
Walsh, Brian. *Shakespeare, The Queen's Men, and the Elizabethan Performance of History*. Cambridge: Cambridge University Press, 2009.
Watt, Tessa. *Cheap Print and Popular Piety, 1550–1640*. Cambridge: Cambridge University Press, 1991.
Wayne, Valerie. "Romancing the Wager: *Cymbeline*'s Intertexts." In *Staging Early Modern Romance: Prose, Fiction, Dramatic Resource, and Shakespeare*, edited by Mary Ellen Lamb and Valerie Wayne, 163–87. New York: Routledge, 2009.
Webbe, William. *A Discourse of English Poetrie*. Edited by Edward Arber. London: English Reprints, 1870.
Weimann, Robert. *Shakespeare and the Popular Tradition in the Theater: Studies in the Social Dimension of Dramatic Form and Function*. Edited by Robert Schwartz. Baltimore: Johns Hopkins University Press, 1978.
Werlin, Julianne. "Providence and Perspective in Philip Sidney's *Old Arcadia*." *Studies in English Literature* 54, no. 1 (2014): 25–40.
West, Grace Starry. "Going by the Book: Classical Allusions in Shakespeare's *Titus Andronicus*." *Studies in Philology* 79, no. 1 (1982): 62–77.
Wheatley, Chloe. "Abridging the *Antiquitee of Faery lond*: New Paths through Old Matter in *The Faerie Queene*." *Renaissance Quarterly* 58, no. 3 (2005): 857–80.
Whetstone, George. *Promos and Cassandra*. London, 1578.
Widmer, Kingsley. "The Iconography of Renunciation: The Miltonic Simile." *ELH* 25, no. 4 (1958): 258–69.
Wiles, David. *Shakespeare's Clown: Actor and Text in the Elizabethan Playhouse*. Cambridge: Cambridge University Press, 1987.
Wilkins, John. *An Essay Towards a Real Character and a Philosophical Language*. London, 1668.
Wilson, Luke. "Drama and Marine Insurance in Shakespeare's London." In *The Law in Shakespeare*, edited by Constance Jordan and Karen Cunningham, 127–42. Basingstoke, UK: Palgrave Macmillan, 2007.
——. *Theaters of Intention: Drama and the Law in Early Modern England*. Stanford, CA: Stanford University Press, 2000.
Wofford, Susanne L. "Epics and the Politics of the Origin Tale: Virgil, Ovid, Spenser, and Native American Aetiology." In *Epic Traditions in the Contemporary World: The Poetics of Community*, edited by Margaret Beissinger, Jane Tylus, and Susanne Wofford, 239–69. Berkeley: University of California Press, 1999.
Wood, Michael. *The Road to Delphi: The Life and Afterlife of Oracles*. New York: Farrar, Straus and Giroux, 2003.
Woodbridge, Linda. "'He Beats Thee 'Gainst The Odds': Gambling, Risk Management, and *Antony and Cleopatra*." In *Antony and Cleopatra: New Critical Essays*, edited by Sara Munson Deats, 193–211. New York and London: Routledge, 2005.

Woolf, D. R. "Erudition and the Idea of History in Renaissance England." *Renaissance Quarterly* 40, no. 1 (1987): 11–48.
——. *Reading History in Early Modern England*. Cambridge: Cambridge University Press, 2000.
——. "The Shapes of History." In *A Companion to Shakespeare*, edited by David Scott Kastan, 186–205. Oxford: Blackwell Publishers, 1999.
Zurcher, Andrew. *Spenser's Legal Language: Law and Poetry in Early Modern England*. Cambridge, NY: D.S. Brewer, 2007.

Index

Achilles, 212–13
Adam (biblical), 39, 122. See also *Paradise Lost* (Milton)
Adelman, Janet, 178n3
Aeneas, 96–97
The Aeneid (Virgil), 89
aesthetic capacity, 4, 11, 222
afterlife, 14, 20, 112, 158, 169, 173, 179, 182–83, 202, 208
allegory, 63–64, 66, 69, 82–84, 93, 99–100, 112–13, 115, 123, 153–54, 171, 220, 222
allusion, 20, 102, 105n2, 106–10, 112, 117, 128, 130–41, 144–45, 155, 176
ambition, 14, 15, 18, 167, 169–70, 172
amplificatio, 108, 112, 131, 137, 141, 144, 145
Anderton, Lawrence, *The English Nunne*, 37n
Anglica historia (Polydore Vergil), 67
anteriority, 90–91, 117
anticipation, 2, 15, 16, 44, 59, 62, 88–89, 108, 167, 169, 182–85, 206, 223. See also expectation
anticipatory nostalgia, 20–22, 152, 161, 166–75, 177, 215, 217, 222–23
antiquarianism, 67n4, 76, 81n31, 82, 93
antiquity, 6, 13, 18–21, 51, 67, 105–7, 128, 177, 178, 180, 181, 194, 196, 198, 205, 208, 212, 218
Antony, Mark (historical), 179n4, 180, 200–202. See also *Antony and Cleopatra* (Shakespeare)
Antony and Cleopatra (Shakespeare), 20–22, 177–85, 190–99, 201–3, 221n35
—CHARACTERS: Cleopatra, 20–21, 177–86, 190–98, 200–206; Enobarbus, 201–4; Iras, 182, 184; Mark Antony, 178–79, 181–85, 195–96, 201; Octavia, 182; Octavius Caesar, 177, 178n3, 179n4, 180–84, 193, 196–97, 199–200, 208
Apelles, 202n78
apocalypse, 4–5, 7–8, 13, 178n3, 218
Apollo, 30n, 112, 120

aposiopesis, 87
Arachne, 111
Arcadia (Sidney). See *New Arcadia*; *Old Arcadia*
archive, 4, 11, 16–17, 21–22, 222–23
Ariosto, Ludovico, 86n44, 123n65; *Orlando Furioso*, 66n3, 71n12, 71n14, 213
Arnold, Oliver, 131n80, 139–40
Arnovick, Leslie K., 25n4, 33n14
Arthur (historical), 90–92, 95, 96n62. See also *The Faerie Queene* (Spenser)
artistic production, 5, 11, 19–20, 22, 25, 31, 35, 49, 80–81, 104, 107, 152, 176, 177, 200, 206–8, 221, 223
Art of English Poesy (Puttenham), 79, 189, 192
assumpsit, 40–42, 45
Astell, Ann W., 49n60, 56n71
Augustine, 126, 165–66, 194
Augustus. See Octavius Caesar

backstory, 91–92, 99–100, 124
Bacon, Francis, 38, 41, 169
bad verse, 174, 190–92, 195, 206
Baker, David J., 74n18, 80
Bakhtin, Mikhail, 171
Baldi, Bernardino, 198n69
ballads, 190–93, 195
Balmford, James, 150n9
Barkan, Leonard, 108, 123n63, 131n82, 198nn67–68, 199, 207
Barker, Francis, 137
Bate, Jonathan, 106n6, 113n26, 116–17, 118n45, 121n, 129–30, 145n104
Beard, Mary, 180n7, 181n10
Belsey, Catherine, 183, 216n19
Benjamin, Walter, 175n
Berger, Harry, Jr., 72, 87n45, 88
Bernstein, Peter L., 150n10
Bersuire, Pierre (Petrus Berchorius), *Ovidius moralizatus*, 113n25, 120

INDEX

Bible, 87n47, 88, 97–98, 122, 126, 133, 137, 138n91, 140–42, 143n101, 144, 158, 219
Blumenberg, Hans, 8n10
Blumenfeld-Kosinski, Renate, 115n37, 123n62, 132n83
Boccaccio, *Decameron*, 149
The Boke Named the Governor (Elyot), 119
Bolton, Joseph S. G., 145n104
boredom, 20, 161, 166, 168, 175
boundless temporal possibility. *See* open-endedness
Bowden, Caroline, 37n
Braden, Gordon, 106
Brathwaite, Richard, 34n17
Brinsley, John, 120–21
broadsides, 193, 195
Brooks, Peter, 23n2, 53n66, 168, 172
Brutus legend, 65, 67, 80
Bullokar, William, 159–60, 164
Burckhardt, Jacob, 6n7
Burrow, Colin, 89n52, 210nn3–4, 212n7, 214n14, 218n24, 221n34

caesura, 75n20, 77–79, 88
Campion, Thomas, *Observations in the Art of English Poesy*, 189
cancellandum, 102n71
Cassius, Dio, 181n10, 198
Castiglione, Baldassare, 198–200, 208
Caxton, William, 116n37
Certain Notes of Instruction (Gascoigne), 34n17, 158n28, 188–89, 191, 195
certainty, 10, 15, 22–24, 26–27, 33, 53, 84–85, 148n3, 149–51, 159–61, 163–65, 169, 176, 192–94, 223
Charnes, Linda, 168, 179n4, 183n15, 185n19, 196n62
Chaucer, Geoffrey, 75n20, 116n37, 124n65; *Squire's Tale*, 75n20, 99n67
Cheney, Patrick, 105n2, 185
Chrétien de Troyes, *Philomena*, 113–16
chronicle, 65, 68–81, 84–88, 90–91, 93–95, 97, 99, 179
classical literature. *See* antiquity; Horace; literary history; Ovid; Seneca; Virgil
classicism, 179, 212
Cleopatra (historical), 179n4, 180–81, 196, 198–201
Cleopatra statue, 198–200, 208
Cleopatra tapestry, 21, 179, 200–205, 207–8
clowns, 134–45, 186–87
codex. *See* material text
Cohen, Jeffrey J., 17n

Coke, Edward, 38, 41n40, 45
Colby, Alice M., 114
Colet, John, 162
Colie, Rosalie L., 153, 155n20
comedians, 185, 190, 192
common law courts, 19, 24, 37–40
Common Pleas, 40–41
compurgation, 39–40, 45
conditional constructions, 51, 159–61, 163–64, 175, 214–16
conscience, 38, 45–47, 48n59
consideration, 42, 46–48
constancy, 29, 31, 35–36, 47–50, 148
contingency, 19, 22, 65–66, 92, 99–101, 194
contract, 19, 24, 36–48, 51, 54, 56–60
Copeland, Rita, 123, 133n
Cormack, Bradin, 169
counterfactual statements, 159–61, 163, 166, 168, 175, 216n19
couplets, 114, 158, 186, 190–92, 194, 197, 206
Cowell, John, *The Interpreter*, 46n54
Crane, Mary Thomas, 118–20
credibility, 19, 50, 67, 69, 86, 90–91, 93, 95–96
credit disputes, 39–40. *See also* debt
Culler, Jonathan, 14–15
Cummings, Brian, 8nn11–12, 148n3, 150n10, 151n12, 159n32, 160n36, 162
Cymbeline (Shakespeare), 15, 20–21, 147–61, 166–77, 179, 190, 200–205, 207–8, 221n35; Cleopatra tapestry in, 21, 179, 200–205, 207–8
—CHARACTERS: Arviragus, 20, 152–53, 156–57, 161, 166–75; Belarius, 148, 152–61, 166, 168, 170–74; Cloten, 155, 156, 160, 166, 175; Cymbeline, 147–48, 152–54, 159, 160, 175; Fidele, 155–56, 158–59, 166; Guiderius, 20, 152–53, 156–57, 160–61, 166–75; Iachimo, 149, 151, 176, 200, 202–8; Imogen, 147–49, 155, 175–76, 200, 206–8; Philario, 148, 152; Posthumus, 147–49, 151, 173–76, 190, 200, 206

Dana, Margaret E., 58
Daniel, Samuel: *Defence of Ryme*, 191–92, 197; *Musophilus*, 13
Daphne, 30n, 112, 115, 120, 122, 125
Davis, Kathleen, 7n10, 8n11, 9n13
dead-end futures, 142, 159–60, 168, 175, 177, 217–18
debt, 17, 19, 24, 33, 37–42, 46. *See also* obligation
Decameron (Boccaccio), 149

de' Capodiferro, Evangelista Maddalena (Fausto Romano), 199
deceit, 41n42, 45–47
Defence of Poesy (Sidney), 2, 14, 39, 49n, 69n9, 189n35, 192
Defence of Ryme (Daniel), 191–92, 197
deferral, 59, 79, 87, 97, 101, 108, 165
de Grazia, Margreta, 6nn6–7, 159, 222n36
determinism, 9, 11, 117, 133, 145, 150n10, 153–54, 158, 176, 220, 223; literary, 117, 133, 158
deus ex machina, 59–60, 150, 176
Diana and Actaeon, 110–11
Dickson, Vernon Guy, 106n6, 119n48
Dido, 96–97
Dipple, Elizabeth, 53n64
A Discourse of English Poetrie (Webbe), 187–89
display. *See* spectacle
divination, 2, 133, 151
Dolven, Jeff, 54, 57n73
Doubtful future, 160n36, 164
Dout-ful-preter, 159–60
Dubrow, Heather, 95, 98, 154
Dusinberre, Juliet, 184

early modern, 6–9, 22
Echo, 1, 111
Eden, 21, 212–17, 220–22
Egypt, 179n5, 193
ekphrasis, 27–29, 200–205, 207–8
elegy, 156–58
Elizabeth I, 65, 72, 81, 87, 91n58, 97n63, 197
Elyot, Thomas, *The Boke Named the Governor*, 119
empire, 13n21, 82–83, 97, 131, 213
enargeia, 94, 203–4
England, 12–13, 19, 21, 65, 207–8. *See also* national history
English language, future of, 12–15. *See also* grammar; vernacular
The English Nunne (Anderton), 37n
Enterline, Lynn, 116, 117n41
entrelacement, 85, 98
ephemerality, 2n3, 13–14, 47–50, 58, 60, 179, 185, 193–94, 200, 202, 205, 208
epic, 66, 88, 89, 95, 97, 210–13, 215, 219
epitome, 81–83, 85
epizeuxis, 97, 214
Escobedo, Andrew, 69, 71n14, 72, 152
eternal future, 177–78, 181, 183, 184, 193, 195, 197

etiology, 107, 111–12, 117, 124, 133, 137, 143, 148
Evans, J. Martin, 220n33
exemplarity, 12, 51–54, 59, 92, 109n16
expectation, 3, 7, 9, 15–18, 22, 25, 29, 33, 48, 54, 57–60, 66, 67, 80, 98, 109, 117, 136, 140–42, 156, 173, 183, 194. *See also* anticipation
experience, 19, 24–25, 104, 148, 193, 216; first-hand, 169, 171, 177, 216; imagined, 179–84; as potential narrative, 173; worthy, 174–75
experimentation, artistic, 3, 5, 12, 17, 18, 22, 78, 223
extemporal. *See* extemporaneity
extemporaneity, 20, 178, 183–96, 200. *See also* improvisation

Faerieland, 62, 81–83
The Faerie Queene (Spenser), 15, 19, 42n44, 62–104, 144, 213n13, 221; 1590 edition, 69, 75, 77, 78, 101–2; 1596 edition, 70n, 78, 101, 102n71; 1609 edition, 77, 79; Alma's Castle, 66, 83, 88, 102; *Antiquitee of Faery lond*, 65, 66, 68, 81–84; book 1 canto 9 (1.9), 62, 66; book 2 canto 3 (2.3), 72; book 2 canto 9 (2.9), 65–70, 76, 83–84, 88, 89, 102; book 2 canto 10 (2.10), 68–72, 74–75, 79–82, 84–85, 90–91, 95, 97–99; book 3 canto 2 (3.2), 92–93; book 3 canto 3 (3.3), 85, 87, 91; book 3 canto 9 (3.9), 65, 95–96; book 3 canto 11 (3.11), 62, 100; book 3 canto 12 (3.12), 101; book 4 canto 9 (4.9), 98, 101; book 4 canto 10 (4.10), 63, 91, 99–102; *Briton moniments*, 65, 66–81, 85, 87–88, 91, 97, 144; Temple of Venus, 63, 99, 101n
—CHARACTERS: Alma, 66, 68, 83, 102; Amoret, 63, 98, 100–102; Artegall, 89, 94–95; Arthur, 63–92, 94–95, 97–98, 221; Belphoebe, 72, 75; Britomart, 62, 65, 85–88, 92–98; Busirane, 100; Duessa, 213n13; Eumnestes, 65–69, 71, 75–76, 83, 87–90, 93, 102; Florimell, 62–64, 213n13; Glauce, 86; Gloriana, 82; Guyon, 65, 66, 68, 81–84, 88–89, 95, 98; Hellenore, 95, 97; Ignaro, 63, 99n69; Merlin, 65, 84–90, 92–95, 97–98, 102; Paridell, 65, 95–98; Phantastes, 83–84, 102; Redcrosse Knight, 93–94, 98; Scudamour, 63, 91, 98–102; Una, 66

The Fair Maid of the Exchange (Heywood), 187–88; Cripple, 187–88

INDEX

Fasti (Ovid), 119
fate, 23, 117, 128, 133, 137, 139–40, 142–43, 202, 210, 212–13
Favoriti, Agostino, 198n69
Ferry, Anne, 213n9
Fish, Stanley, 108n11, 212n8, 218n26, 219, 220n33
fixity, 19, 24, 38, 48–51, 61, 104, 165. *See also* permanence; stagnation; stasis
Fletcher, Angus, 164–65, 168
foreknowledge, 86, 150n10, 209–10
foreshadowing, 110, 114–17, 139
foresight, 24, 99n69, 100
foretelling. *See* divination; future prediction; prophecy
form, 2, 11, 12n20, 15–20, 27, 36–37, 47n57, 56, 60n82, 65, 81–83, 87, 145–46, 158, 162, 174, 177, 185–86, 191–95, 206, 207
Fowler, Alastair, 211
Freud, Sigmund, 164n54
future. *See* dead-end futures; eternal future; futures; imminent future; impossible future; modest future; visceral future
future history, 4–5, 9–10, 91–92, 103
future memory, 103, 166, 170–72, 215. *See also* anticipatory nostalgia
future perfect. *See* second future
future prediction, 1–2, 19–20, 23–24, 26, 28, 29, 33, 52, 64, 88, 92, 108, 133, 158, 183, 185, 191–94, 197, 207, 216–20
futures (alternative, flexible, possible, potential, unexpected, unknown, unpredictable, unscripted, would-be), 2–4, 6, 9, 12, 14, 17–22, 68, 223; in *Antony and Cleopatra*, 177–78, 180, 194–95, 205–8; in *Cymbeline*, 148, 152, 154, 158–59, 161, 163–64, 169, 176; in *The Faerie Queene*, 66, 92; in *Old Arcadia*, 25–27, 44, 59; in *Paradise Lost*, 211, 213–15, 217–18, 220–22; in *Titus Andronicus*, 107, 117, 142

Gascoigne, George, 116n37; *Certain Notes of Instruction*, 34n17, 188–89, 191, 195
Genette, Gérard, 161n
genre (macrostructures), 15–16, 18, 57–59, 61, 137, 154, 211–12
Geoffrey of Monmouth, 69, 75n20, 86, 95; *Historia Regum Brittaniae*, 67–68
Gerusalemme Liberata (Torquato Tasso), 213
Giamatti, A. Bartlett, 216n22
Goldberg, Jonathan, 5n5, 98, 99nn67–68, 101, 102n72, 111

Golding, Arthur, 110n18, 111, 112n23, 118nn44–46, 121–22, 124, 126
grace, 139–42, 144–45
grammar, 5, 16, 17, 20, 22, 33, 36, 50, 61, 120, 146, 148, 151–52, 158, 160–61, 165, 175–76, 217, 219, 223; English grammar books, 151, 159–64
grammar-school education, 118–21, 131n81, 161–62
Greenblatt, Stephen J., 13n21, 54n67, 58–59
Greene, Robert, *Groats-worth of witte*, 191
Greene, Thomas M., 7n8, 216n22; *The Light in Troy*, 6
Groats-worth of witte (Greene), 191
Guarini, Giambattista, 58

Hacking, Ian, 150n8, 150n10
Hadfield, Andrew, 10
half line, 72, 75, 77, 96
Halpern, Richard, 119, 121n
Hamilton, A. C., 86–89, 90n56, 97, 102
Hamlet (Shakespeare), 14–15, 109n14, 148n3
Harris, Jonathan Gil, 16n
Hartman, Geoffrey, 221n33
Harvey, Gabriel, 12–13, 33
Helen, 51, 95
Henry V (Shakespeare), 171
hermeneutics, 17, 19, 54, 105, 107, 111, 113, 116, 118, 120–44, 146, 148, 201n74
Heroides (Ovid), 95, 133n
Heywood, Thomas, *The Fair Maid of the Exchange*, 187, 189
Hiltner, Ken, 153
Hinds, Stephen, 85
Historia Regum Brittaniae (Geoffrey of Monmouth), 67–68
historical imagination, 64–66, 71, 72, 78, 83–84, 92, 94–95, 102–4
historiography, 17, 68–69, 82, 88
history, 7–8, 10, 17, 19, 21, 63–103, 105, 151, 175, 179, 194, 205, 207, 218–19, 222; of the future, 4–5, 9–10, 83, 91–92, 103, 218; historical time, 7, 10; writing/making (*see* historical imagination)
Holinshed, Raphael, 68, 95
Holmes, Eric Mills, 47n57
Homer, 12; *Iliad*, 211
Horace, 5, 13, 106, 129–34, 172, 181n9, 196

Iliad (Homer), 211
imitation, 6, 27, 106, 108, 109n14
immediacy, 20, 39, 179–82, 184

INDEX

imminent future, 20, 178, 180, 184, 186, 191, 193–97, 200, 205–8
immortality topos, 4, 7–8, 13–15, 20, 37, 65–66, 129–30, 178, 180–81, 183–84, 196, 199, 200–202, 205–6, 214
impossible future, 216–18
improvisation, 20, 22, 185–95, 197. *See also* extemporaneity
inaccessible past, 19, 62, 66, 102, 205
indeterminacy. *See* uncertainty
indicative mood, 159, 164
inevitability, 4, 9–11, 15, 19, 21, 22, 26, 33, 83, 92, 107, 108, 111, 117, 124, 148, 153, 157–59, 161, 166, 168, 210–11, 213, 220, 222
Ingham, Patricia, 83n38, 89n50, 90, 91n57
intention, 19, 24, 27, 33, 38–39, 44–48, 51, 60, 75
interiority, 24, 27–29, 31, 34–35, 43, 45–48
interpretation, 43n48, 88, 102, 107, 111, 118, 122–44, 192, 196–97. *See also* hermeneutics
The Interpreter (Cowell), 46n54
interstitial space, 21, 213–14, 216
Io, 129

Jackson, Russell, 180
James, Heather, 106n5, 116, 120n53, 131n80, 179n4, 185n19, 186n23
Jameson, Fredric, 57
Janus, 99–101
Jarvis, Simon, 11, 151n12, 222
Javitch, Daniel, 113n25, 123n65
judgment, 19, 24, 26–29, 31–32, 34, 42–44, 51–61, 102, 212
Julius II, 198–99
Jupiter, 123n63, 135–37, 142, 150, 176
justice, 25, 52–54, 56n71, 57–58, 60, 120, 135, 144–45, 154, 158

Kastan, David Scott, 11n17, 109n14
Kemp, Will, 187
Kendall, Gillian Murray, 127
Kermode, Frank, 59n80
Kerr, Walter, 184
Kerrigan, John, 26, 33n14, 52n, 109
Kerrigan, William, 33n17
King, Andrew, 79n26, 81n31, 91n58
King's Bench, 41
Koselleck, Reinhart, 6n7, 7, 150n10, 165n
Krueger, Roberta L., 113n30, 114n32, 115n35, 123n62

Lacan, Jacques, 167–68
Lady Macbeth, 15

language-level choices, 4–5, 11, 14, 16–17, 19, 26. *See also* grammar
Latin grammars, 162
law, 17, 19, 23–25, 27, 31–32, 37–39, 42, 45–47, 51–61, 102
legacy, 4, 15, 18, 20–21, 53, 125, 177–78, 180–81, 183, 199, 202
Le Goff, Jacques, 78
Leo X, 200
Lewalski, Barbara Kiefer, 211n5, 213n10, 213n12, 214n14, 219
Lewis, C. S., 218
The Light in Troy (Greene), 6
Lily, William, *A Shorte Introduction of Grammar*, 159n32, 162
Linacre, Thomas, *Rudimenta Grammatices*, 159, 162
linguistic structures. *See* grammar; language-level choices
literalization, 59, 64, 78, 80–81, 100, 108, 116, 120, 123–28, 134–37, 143, 198n67
literary agency, 10, 14, 18, 50, 177, 199, 206–7, 221
literary convention, 12, 23, 29, 58, 66, 71, 90, 108–10, 148, 154, 158, 204
literary history/culture, 5n5, 10, 20–22, 51, 106–7, 117, 176, 179
Lives (Plutarch), 106, 180, 181n10, 198, 201–2
Livy, 106, 181n9
Lloyd, Richard, 92
looking forward, looking back, 4, 9, 14, 18–19, 22, 23–24, 29, 53, 59, 62–65, 72, 89, 91, 92, 96, 99, 100, 102–3, 145–46, 148, 151, 165–67, 214–15, 217–18, 220, 222–23
Love's Labour's Lost (Shakespeare): Don Adriano de Armado, 189
Löwith, Karl, 7n10
Lucrece (historical), 149, 176, 208. See also *The Rape of Lucrece* (Shakespeare)
Luis de Molina, 159n33
Lyne, Raphael, 112n24, 118n44
lyric, 14, 38, 214n14, 218

macrostructures. *See* genre
Maittaire, Michael, 162–64
Marcus, Leah S., 6n7, 221n35
Marcus Aurelius, 205–6
marriage, 2, 3, 5, 14, 37n20, 42n47, 52, 56, 90n52, 175
Martindale, Charles, 110n18
material metrics, 74–80

INDEX

material text, 5, 18, 31, 36, 43, 47–50, 55, 60–61, 65, 67, 69–70, 75–81, 84, 97, 102, 107, 127, 129–32, 138, 144–45, 172, 221
Matthew, Gospel of, 88
McCoy, Richard, 35n, 55n, 56n
McKisack, May, 67n
memorialization, 131n81, 182, 216, 217
memorization, 131n81, 186–88
memory, 30, 43, 45, 47, 49n, 53n64, 55, 60, 66, 67, 69, 83, 84, 89, 93, 98, 103, 156, 166, 170–72, 186–89, 193, 201, 204, 205, 207, 215–18, 221
mercy, 57, 141, 144–45
metaphor, 34–35, 75n20, 112, 116, 123, 124–28, 134, 136–37, 191, 199, 210n3
meter, 12–13, 17, 65, 74–80, 87–88, 197
microstructures, 11, 16, 22
A Midsummer Night's Dream (Shakespeare): Peter Quince, 186–87; Snug, 186
Miège, Guy, 160, 163, 164
Milton, John, 5nn4–5, 212n7, 220n33. See also *Paradise Lost*
Minnis, A. J., 118n44, 124n65
Miola, Robert S., 105n3, 201n76
mockery. *See* parody
modernity, 6–9, 165n55, 220n33, 222
modest future, 5, 15, 22, 167, 171–72, 176, 223
monument, 8, 68n6, 129–30, 181, 182, 215, 217–18, 220–21
moralizatio (moral commentaries), 19, 107, 112–27, 132–34, 136, 141–42
Moschovakis, Nicholas R., 136n87, 137n88, 140n94, 142n, 144n102
Mowat, Barbara A., 109n15
Muldrew, Craig, 24, 39
Muses: Calliope, 71; Clio, 71; Urania, 220
Musophilus (Daniel), 13

Narcissus, 1, 111
narrative, 4, 10, 11, 14–15, 17; in *Cymbeline*, 20, 148, 151–54, 161, 166–76; in *The Faerie Queene*, 64–66, 71–72, 84–92, 94, 97, 99, 100, 102–3; in *Metamorphoses*, 111; in *Old Arcadia*, 24, 25, 29, 54, 55, 58–60; in *Paradise Lost*, 211–12, 215–19; in *Titus Andronicus*, 105, 111, 117, 125, 127, 133, 137, 142–43
narrative time, 62, 66, 72, 74, 85, 90–91, 102
national history, 13, 19, 21, 63–69, 72, 75n20, 80–85, 86n44, 87–91, 93–95, 97–98, 106n5, 151, 207, 221
national identity, 21, 149, 152, 172, 206–7

natural law, 56–58
"never been or ever been," 3–4, 11, 22, 222
Nevo, Ruth, 182nn12–13, 193, 195
New Arcadia (Sidney), 2n3, 53n64, 59n79, 60–61; Cecropia, 59n79; Pyrocles, 2n3
New World, 82–83, 213
Noah, 138
North, Thomas, 201n76
nostalgia, 21, 167, 169, 217. *See also* anticipatory nostalgia
Nosworthy, J. M., 155
novitiate vows, 37n

obligation, 18–19, 24, 27, 33, 35, 37–40, 46–48, 60, 208. *See also* debt
Observations in the Art of English Poesy (Campion), 189
Octavius Caesar (historical), 179n4, 180, 198–99, 208. See also *Antony and Cleopatra* (Shakespeare)
Oedipus Rex, 23, 29n
Old Arcadia (Sidney), 1–4, 15, 19, 23–38, 43–62, 104, 221
—CHARACTERS: Basilius, 23, 26, 28, 52–54, 60; Cleophila, 1–3, 13, 21, 29–30, 51; Euarchus, 52, 55–60; Gynecia, 52–54, 57n72, 60; Kalodoulus, 58; Miso, 48n58; Musidorus, 27, 30n, 52, 55, 57, 59n79; Pamela, 26, 55; Philanax, 52–53, 55–56; Philoclea, 2–5, 14, 18, 26–39, 42, 43–58, 60; Pyrocles, 1–3, 5, 14, 27–31, 51–57
open-endedness, 5, 7–9, 12–13, 21, 25, 205, 207, 221; in *Cymbeline*, 148, 161, 167; in *The Faerie Queene*, 80, 103; in *Old Arcadia*, 54, 59–61; in *Paradise Lost*, 220n31
oracle, 23, 29, 60, 105
origins, 65, 67, 69, 89, 90–92, 94–97, 100, 101, 103, 109, 111, 112, 118, 168
Orlando Furioso (Ariosto), 66n3, 71n12, 71n14, 123n65, 213; Bradamante, 86n44
Orpheus and Eurydice, 102
Othello (Shakespeare), 14–15
Ovid: *Fasti*, 119; *Heroides*, 95, 133n; *Metamorphoses*, 30n, 110n18, 111, 120n53, 124, 143, 155; moralization, 113, 117–28; in Shakespeare, 19, 105n2, 106–13, 115–18, 123–35, 137–38, 141–44, 155, 208
Ovide moralisé, 113, 115, 116n37, 122–23, 127, 132–33

palimpsest, 16n, 31, 48, 51, 55
Panofsky, Erwin, 6n6

Paradise Lost (Milton), 5n5, 15, 21, 25n6, 209–23; book one (1), 212; book two (2), 209–10, 219; book four (4), 216n19; book five (5), 219; book seven (7), 219, 220; book nine (9), 211–14, 216n19; book eleven (11), 214–18; book twelve (12), 219–22
—CHARACTERS: Adam, 5n5, 21, 39, 213–22; Eve, 213–14, 220–22; Michael, 214–15, 217–19, 221n33, 222; Raphael, 218, 219; Satan, 212–13, 216n19, 220; Sin, 219–20
paragone, 204–5, 207, 208
Paris, 95–96
Parker, Patricia, 174n, 210n4, 214n16, 216, 220n31, 221n34
parody, 53, 95–97, 190, 193, 195, 206. *See also* travesty
pastoral, 27, 153–58, 166, 172, 211n5
Patey, Douglas, 150n8
Peacham, Henry, *Thalia's Banquet*, 186
pedagogy, 54, 118–21, 131n81
Peele, George, 105n2
performance, 183–84, 190, 205; ephemerality of, 13–14; extemporal, 178, 185, 192–95
periodization, 6–9, 222
permanence, 19, 24, 33, 36, 37, 39, 44–45, 47–48, 50–51, 53, 55, 85, 177, 179, 194, 208, 215. *See also* fixity; stagnation; stasis
Petowe, Henry, 34n17
Petrarchism, 72, 114–16, 118
Phelan, Peggy, 193
Philomela, 108, 109n15, 111–15, 117, 122n60, 125, 131–33, 143, 176
Philomena (Chrétien de Troyes), 113–16
Picciotto, Joanna, 217n22
piety, 141–42, 145
Pincombe, Mike, 116n37
pity, 57, 141–42, 144–45, 156n25
pleasure, 5, 29, 68, 70, 79–81, 88, 94, 98, 101, 102, 118n44, 125, 167, 170, 172–73, 175, 176, 204, 215, 217
Plutarch, *Lives*, 106, 180, 181n10, 198, 201–2
poiesis, 31, 50, 66, 78, 81, 95, 223
possibility, 3, 13, 17, 22, 25, 27, 33, 48, 51, 54, 58–61, 64, 75, 81–82, 97, 107, 111, 144, 148, 149, 159, 163, 164, 173, 189, 211, 217–21. *See also* open-endedness
posterity, 104, 148, 169–70, 199
postlapsarian Eden, 21, 214, 217–18
potential mood, 159, 164
Poulet, Georges, 178, 194
predictability, 4, 25, 109, 193–95

prediction. *See* future prediction; prophecy
prelapsarian Eden, 214–17
present-tense immediacy, 20, 179, 181–82, 184
probability, 150, 151n11, 176
Procne, 108–9, 122n60, 143
progress, 4–5, 7, 10, 165n, 210, 213, 220n33, 221
prolepsis, 20–21, 28, 37, 44, 148, 166, 214–15, 218n24
Prometheus, 81, 82, 91
promise, 2–3, 5, 14, 16, 19, 22, 24–26, 29–30, 32–48, 50–53, 56, 59
"promise is debt," 33, 37, 45
promissory poetry, 33–38, 45
prophecy, 2, 8, 19; in *The Faerie Queene*, 65, 84–90, 94; in *Old Arcadia*, 23–29, 33, 57, 59–60; in *Paradise Lost*, 217–21; in *Titus Andronicus*, 133, 143. *See also* future prediction
prosody. *See* meter
proverbs, 33–34, 37, 45, 114, 129
providence, 8, 25n6, 59n80, 60, 88, 91, 102n74, 117, 133, 150, 159, 168, 209–10, 220–21
psychoanalysis, 164n54, 167–68
Puttenham, George, *Art of English Poesy*, 79, 189, 192
Pyramus and Thisbe, 33n17, 110

Quint, David, 211n6, 213n11
Quintilian, 188n32, 189, 191n42

Ramus, Petrus, 162
The Rape of Lucrece (Shakespeare), 149, 156n25, 206; Lucrece, 206; Tarquin, 206
Read, David, 82–83
reading, 55, 56, 60, 66, 68, 80–81, 84, 94, 97–98, 106, 124–27, 143. *See also* hermeneutics
recognition scene, 58–60
redemption, 117, 121, 123, 127, 134, 141–43, 145, 218
reenactment, 20, 107, 112, 170, 185, 190
reflection, 1, 3, 9, 10, 15, 48, 54, 64, 88, 94, 101, 111, 119, 167, 204, 216n21
Renaissance, 6–8, 20, 22, 208, 218, 221–22
repetition, 1–2, 20, 31, 35, 50, 64–65, 79, 80, 85, 89, 94–95, 97, 108, 133, 144, 154, 210, 212, 213n13. *See also* rhyme
retelling, 20, 53–56, 92, 97, 98, 167, 207

retrospection, 5, 14, 19, 23–27, 29, 53, 59, 62–63, 88, 99–100, 161, 164–65, 168, 170–71, 214, 216, 223
revenge, 55–56, 104–5, 107–9, 127, 129–30, 132, 134, 141–42, 144–45, 148, 154
revision, 18, 47, 48, 60, 62, 65, 92, 168
rhyme, 16–17, 20, 22, 207; in *Antony and Cleopatra*, 185–92, 195, 197, 200; in *Cymbeline*, 158, 174; in *Titus Andronicus*, 145
risk, 150, 151n11, 152, 161
Roach, Joseph, 193
romance, 16, 18, 19, 58, 60–61, 65, 66, 68, 83n38, 85, 90, 97–98, 105, 210n4, 211–13, 214n14, 216n19, 219–20, 221n34
Roman plays, 105, 146
Rome, 105–7, 124, 131, 179n5, 207, 208, 218
Ross, David O., 85
Rudimenta Grammatices (Linacre), 159, 162
ruins, 13, 21, 59, 97, 207, 208, 217–18, 221
Rumrich, John, 5n5, 219, 220n30
rupture, 6, 44, 76–78, 80–81, 89, 92, 96, 115, 221

Sabinus, Georgius, 124
Sacks, David Harris, 46
Sandys, George, 118n46
Savile, Sir Henry, 67n
saying grace, 139–40
Schmitt, Carl, 7n10
scientia media, 159n33
second future (future perfect), 20, 22, 151, 161, 163–73, 175, 216
secularization, 7–8
Seneca, 106, 143n101
sequence, 15, 17, 117, 127, 147, 153, 213n10
Seznec, Jean, 118n44
Shaheen, Naseeb, 143n101
Shakespeare, William, 4, 14, 19–21, 207–8, 221; *Coriolanus*, 163n48; *Hamlet*, 14–15, 109n14, 148n3; *Henry V*, 171; *Love's Labour's Lost*, 189; *Macbeth*, 15; *A Midsummer Night's Dream*, 186–87; *Othello*, 14–15; *The Rape of Lucrece*, 149, 206; *The Winter's Tale*, 163n48. See also *Antony and Cleopatra*; *Cymbeline*; *Titus Andronicus*
Sherman, Anita Gilman, 156
A Shorte Introduction of Grammar (Lily), 159n32, 162
Sidney, Sir Philip: *Defence of Poesy*, 2, 14, 39, 49n, 69n9, 189n35, 192. See also *New Arcadia*; *Old Arcadia*

simultaneity, 42, 46, 64, 66, 74, 78, 84, 87–88, 91, 98, 99, 103, 111, 178, 204
Slade's Case, 24, 37–38, 41–42, 47n56
Smith, Molly Easo, 137
Smith, Nigel, 214n15, 214n18
song, 156–59, 187, 189, 190n39, 191
spectacle, 87, 182, 184–85, 195n59, 196n62, 198–200, 203–5, 208
Spenser, Edmund, 12. See also *The Faerie Queene*
spolia, 218, 221
Squire's Tale (Chaucer), 75n20, 99n67
stagnation, 215–16, 218. See also fixity; permanence; stasis
Stanyhurst, Richard, 190–92
stasis, 15, 29, 31, 44, 51, 57n73, 85, 97, 132, 154, 172, 223. See also fixity; permanence; stagnation
Stern, Tiffany, 186n24, 186n27
St. German, Christopher, *Doctor and Student*, 45
stock character, 134–35, 137–39, 143
Stoicism, 153, 155n20, 162n44, 179n5, 205–6
subjectivity, 11, 27, 29, 44, 168, 222, 223. See also interiority
subjunctive mood, 159, 164, 175
succession, 74, 77, 87, 106, 147–49, 159, 175
Summit, Jennifer, 68n6, 69n7, 75, 90n53
suspicion, 15, 27–28, 30–33, 35, 43, 45, 153
Swinburne, Henry, 42n47
syntax, 17, 35, 65, 67, 94, 100, 173, 217

tangible metrics, 74–80
tapestry, 21, 108, 111, 114, 122n60, 131, 179, 200–205, 208
Tarlton, Richard, 186–87, 191
Tarltonizing, 186n24, 191. See also extemporaneity; improvisation
Tayler, Edward, 220
Taylor, Anthony Brian, 111n19, 119n48
teleology, 15, 21, 97, 104, 107, 109, 116, 124, 143, 148, 153, 158, 210, 212n8, 213, 220n33
temporal consciousness, 3, 6–10, 14, 17–19, 21–22, 29, 32, 63, 89–90, 166, 196, 205, 223
tentativeness, 5, 30–31, 79, 86
Tereus, 108, 112, 114–15, 122n60, 132, 143
Teskey, Gordon, 220n33, 222n37
testimony, 30–33, 36, 40, 43, 45, 50, 55, 59
Thalia's Banquet (Peacham), 186
theater. See paragone; spectacle

Tilley, M. P., 129
time, 3, 6, 9–11, 16–18, 22, 29, 32, 101–2; end of, 4–5, 8; historical, 7, 10 (*see also* history); linear, 4, 11, 85; mechanics of, 16; multidirectional, 63–66; overlap in, 151, 179. *See also* temporal consciousness; wasted time
timelessness, 10, 36, 44, 106, 179n5, 210
Titus Andronicus (Shakespeare), 19, 104–13, 115–17, 123–48, 221n35; hermeneutics, 134–43, 146; interpretive paradigms, 128–34, 144–46; and moralizing Ovidian commentary, 116–28, 132–37, 142; Roman setting, 105–7
—CHARACTERS: Aaron, 108, 125, 131, 133–34, 137; Alarbus, 109, 141; Bassianus, 108, 110, 133; Chiron, 108, 109, 112, 130, 131, 133; Demetrius, 108, 109, 130, 131, 133; Lavinia, 104, 108–9, 112, 115–17, 125, 129–33, 143; Lucius, 125, 137, 143–45; Marcus, 108, 110n18, 112, 115–16, 125, 128–29, 132; Martius, 110; Quintus, 110; Saturninus, 134, 136–37, 139; Tamora, 108, 110, 111n19, 117, 125, 132, 139, 141, 143–45; Titus, 104–9, 128–42
tragedy, 58–60, 105, 109, 110n18, 135, 148, 211–13
transitory, art as, 177, 208. *See also* ephemerality
The Travels of the Three English Brothers (Day, Rowley, and Wilkins), 187
travesty, 185–86. *See also* parody
trial, 23–24, 26, 52–60
Tricomi, Albert H., 127n
triumph, 20, 177–78, 180–84, 186n23, 194–99, 204n86, 208
Troy, 67, 87, 96–97, 211, 212
Troynovant, 65, 97
typography, 69, 72, 75, 77, 78n22, 79, 96, 102n71, 120

uncertainty, 3–5, 9, 12–14, 22–26, 47, 50, 53, 54, 58, 59, 61, 62, 65, 79, 85, 148n3, 151n11, 152, 153, 159, 168–69, 204

Uther Pendragon, 66, 72, 74, 79n26, 87, 90–91

van Es, Bart, 68n6, 71n13, 81n31, 89n49, 97n63
Vegius, Mapheus, 89n52
ventriloquism, 157, 159, 199, 208
Venus, 201–2
Vergil, Polydore, *Anglica historia*, 67
vernacular, 12–13, 37n, 113, 115n37, 162. *See also* grammar
Vickers, Brian, 105n2, 145n104
Virgil, 106, 133, 156, 179n4, 186n23, 190; *The Aeneid*, 89
visceral future, 182, 184
visuality, 204–5
vow, 26, 32–33, 35–36, 37n, 44, 48, 130. *See also* promise

Wales, 152–55, 158, 159, 161, 166, 168, 171, 176, 190
Wall-Randell, Sarah, 74n17, 79n27
Walsh, Brian, 7n8, 194
wandering, 209–11, 213, 215, 216, 218, 220–21
wasted time, 210, 212, 213, 218, 220
Wayne, Valerie, 148n4
Webbe, William, *A Discourse of English Poetrie*, 187–89
Weimann, Robert, 137
West, Grace Starry, 106n7, 131n81
Westminster. *See* common law courts; Common Pleas; King's Bench
Wheatley, Chloe, 81–83
Whetstone, George, 33n17
Widmer, Kingsley, 25n6
Wilkins, John, 164
Wilson, Luke, 41–42, 45n50, 150n8, 151n11
The Winter's Tale (Shakespeare), 163n48
Wofford, Susanne, 86n44, 89, 91
Woodbridge, Linda, 150n8
Woolf, D. R., 67n, 69n9

Zurcher, Andrew, 42n44

www.ingramcontent.com/pod-product-compliance
Lightning Source LLC
Chambersburg PA
CBHW032036300426
44117CB00009B/1075